Contemporary Wales

Volume 18

CONTEMPORARY WALES

Volume 18

Editors

Paul Chaney (Cardiff University)
Jonathan Scourfield (Cardiff University)
Andrew Thompson (University of Glamorgan)

Published on behalf of the Board of Celtic Studies
of the University of Wales

Cardiff
University of Wales Press
2006

www.wales.ac.uk/press

British Library Cataloguing in Publication Data
A catalogue record for this book is available from the British Library.

ISBN-10 0-7083-1992-0
ISBN-13 978-0-7083-1992-5
ISSN 0951-4937

Original cover design by Marian Delyth
Cover photograph: © Top Foto/ProSport
Printed in Great Britain by Cambridge Printing, Cambridge

CONTENTS

ARTS AND MEDIA

OTHER ARTICLES

Investigating Language Attitudes: Social Meanings of Dialect, Ethnicity and Performance by Peter Garret, Nikolas Coupland and Angie Williams (reviewed by *Wynford Bellin*)

Guidelines for contributors to *Contemporary Wales*   305

CONTRIBUTORS

David M. Barlow, School of Humanities, Law and Social Sciences, University of Glamorgan.

Wynford Bellin, Cardiff School of Social Sciences, Cardiff University.

Hywel Bishop, Centre for Language and Communication, Cardiff University.

David Brooksbank, Business School, University of Glamorgan.

Nickie Charles, Department of Sociology, University of Warwick.

Nikolas Coupland, Centre for Language and Communication, Cardiff University.

Charlotte Aull Davies, Department of Sociology and Anthropology, University of Wales Swansea.

Rebecca Davies was formerly lecturer in the Department of International Relations, University of Wales, Aberystwyth. She is presently an official in the Department of Constitutional Affairs, Whitehall.

Bella Dicks, Cardiff School of Social Sciences, Cardiff University.

Andrew Edwards, School of History, University of Wales, Bangor.

Nigel Exell, Department of Sociology and Anthropology, University of Wales Swansea.

Peter Garrett, Centre for Language and Communication, Cardiff University.

Chris Harris, Department of Sociology and Anthropology, University of Wales Swansea.

Lesley Hodgson, Centre for Lifelong Learning, University of Glamorgan.

William Housley, Cardiff School of Social Sciences, Cardiff University.

Panagiotis Kompotis recently completed a Masters degree in the School of Journalism, Media and Cultural Studies of Cardiff University.

R. Ross Mackay is an economist and an Honorary Fellow at the Welsh Institute for Social and Cultural Affairs.

Lynn Mainwaring, Department of Law, University of Wales Swansea.

Philip Mitchell, School of Humanities, Law and Social Sciences, University of Glamorgan.

Nigel J. Moore, Department of Law, University of Wales Swansea.

Tom O'Malley, Department of Theatre, Film and Television Studies, University of Wales, Aberystwyth.

Jeremy Segrott is a research officer in the School of Health Science, University of Wales Swansea.

Duncan Tanner, School of History, University of Wales, Bangor.

Kevin Williams, Department of Media and Communication Studies, University of Wales Swansea.

1. ONE WALES? REASSESSING DIVERSITY IN WELSH ETHNOLINGUISTIC IDENTIFICATION

Nikolas Coupland, Hywel Bishop and Peter Garrett

ABSTRACT

A new survey of 777 informants, widely distributed in Wales, allows us to reassess conventional understandings of ethnolinguistic diversity in Wales, particularly as regards subjective variables to do with ethnic identity and belonging. Our findings are set against Denis Balsom's widely cited 'three-Wales model', and against geographical data relating to Welsh-language competence from the 2001 census. The new data challenge the validity of the 'three-Wales' concept. They also qualify the wider assumption that Welsh-language competence and affiliative Welshness are necessarily closely related factors – the idea that speaking Welsh affords stronger Welsh identity. The overarching finding of the survey is that Welsh people across almost all geographical regions of Wales express very high levels of affiliation to Wales – that Welsh identity in many respects is buoyant and widespread. However, informant age, lived history and variable levels of support for the Welsh language are also statistically implicated.

APPROACHES TO WELSH CULTURAL PLURALITY

Commentaries on the cultural constitution of Wales have suggested that alternative types of 'Welshness' exist, that Welsh ethnic or national identity is experienced differently by people who are, as far as this is ever possible, uncontroversially Welsh. Different underlying social factors have been considered, although speculations about the effects of variable levels of Welsh-language competence and comments about varying intensities of 'Welsh identity' have been common. Different category systems of difference have been claimed, although geographical/

regional models have been most influential. The core questions have been 'How many Wales[es] are there?' and 'Where can we find them?'.

This tendency of debate has had important and in some ways unedifying implications, although we cannot consider them in detail here. 'How many Wales?' has focused debate on 'internal' cultural structures and processes, tending to downplay wider ethnic/racial differences and inequalities within Wales (but see C. Williams, 2003, for a powerful redressive analysis). Exploring Welsh cultural diversity has sometimes been framed as a cultural quest for 'the real Wales' and a nostalgic agonizing over the potential loss of an authentic cultural heartland. This is, of course, a recurrent ethno-nationalist narrative of Wales that mobilizes many academic agendas as well as policy initiatives. But it tends to view diversity as problematic, rather than orienting to the benefits of cultural pluralism. Sociolinguistic analysis within the 'how many Wales?' debate tends to reduce the Welsh language to a single organic entity, rather than accept its multiple varieties and ownerships. In fact, there is an acute need for a more rounded and open sociolinguistic account of contemporary Wales, going beyond the simplistic assumption that Welsh defines the cultural core of Wales.

On the other hand, it is obviously true that historical patterns of political, linguistic and socio-economic change in Wales have created a legacy of structural diversity which, in empirical terms, is there to be analysed. Complex social and sociolinguistic configurations can be detected, and they are shifting rapidly. Our main ambition in this article is to provide a more nuanced assessment of how Welshness is socially and geographically distributed in Wales than has been previously provided. We do this on the basis of data from an extensive new survey, mainly addressing subjective factors relating to ethnic identity and belonging. The value of the data, we suggest, is firstly to update existing findings. In particular, Denis Balsom's influential 'three-Wales model' (Balsom, 1985) derives from data collected some thirty years ago in radically different social circumstances and different climates of opinion. But, secondly, our own data cast substantial doubt over the adequacy of any simple regional account of distributed Welshness. Although regional factors are relevant, we need a far more complex account of interrelationships between geographical and other social and sociopsychological factors. Thirdly, the new data complement recently analysed Welsh census data, by relating known patterns of Welsh-language competence (deriving from the 2001 census) to patterns of subjective affiliation to Wales and to Welsh in our survey.

What have been the main approaches to Welsh cultural plurality to date? Within cultural studies there has been ample recognition of what Raymond Williams (2004) dubbed the 'two truths' about Wales. He had in mind, on the one hand, the more rurally framed, Celtic, Cymric, nationalist discourse of Wales, associated with an ancient language and a historically continuous culture. On the other hand, Williams recognized (and tended to prioritize) a more socialist, industrial, radical, anglophone discourse associated with the mining valleys of south Wales – think of Aneurin Bevan, Gwyn Alf Williams (1985) and Dai Smith (1984). This broad distinction is endorsed and discussed in several influential sociological studies of Wales (see, for example, Fevre and Thompson, 1999; Dicks, 2000), and also in some critical contemporary research on tourism (Morgan and Pritchard, 2003). Some aspects of our own earlier research have oriented to this same distinction. For example, we have traced shifts in both the linguistic and the visual (photographic) representations of Wales over the period 1850 to 2000 in an influential Welsh-American newspaper (Coupland, Bishop and Garrett, 2003; Garrett, Coupland and Bishop, 2005). American representations of Wales seem to have always prioritized Cymric, folk Wales, but to have increasingly commodified both the Welsh language and Welsh heritage since around 1960.

On the whole, contemporary sociological studies take a constructivist stance, allied to the social theory of Benedict Anderson (1983) and Hobsbawm and Ranger (1983). They stress the mythological construction of social identities and cultural traditions. Wales is therefore taken to be plural by being imagined differently at different times and in different contexts. No simple structural model of Welsh ethnic or ethnolinguistic diversity is defended, because constructivist theorizing is hostile to reifications of social categories. On the other hand, it is clear that particular mythic constellations of Welshness have dominated social life, and they are still being played out (and played to) in Welsh political debates. Other mythic constructions of Welshness presumably need to be added to Raymond Williams's two Welsh truths: perhaps 'Welsh-speaking elite Wales' and 'European waterfront Wales', and indeed the myth of 'one Wales' as ideologized in the Welsh Assembly Government's *Iaith Pawb* ('Everyone's Language') policy and programme of support for the Welsh language.

Constructivist approaches to 'Welshnesses' usefully capture the relative indeterminacy and the sheer complexity of Welsh cultural formations, although they are difficult to pursue through empirical designs. A far more literal and realist conception of Welsh cultural pluralism is conventional in some influential treatments of Welsh bilingualism. Aitchison and Carter (2004) provide a detailed analysis of the distribution of self-reported Welsh-language use from the 2001 census, where data for 2,805,701 people in Wales aged three and over were collected on 29 April 2001. This analysis has an essentially geographical basis, and Wales is therefore mapped in terms of where the largest numbers of Welsh speakers are to be found, and where their concentrations are most dense. Cultural pluralism in Aitchison and Carter's treatment is documented in terms of bilingual zones with varying degrees of vitality, with the 'most vital' zones (in terms of the density of Welsh usage among the population) to be found mainly but not exclusively in north-west and south-west Wales, distinguished from an otherwise predominantly monolingual linguistic landscape. Aitchison and Carter map the distribution of (bilingual) Welsh speakers at various levels of delicacy, but they show through cluster analysis techniques that a two-factor statistical solution organizes Wales into two zones – a western (or 'inner Wales') zone versus an eastern ('outer Wales') zone (see figure 1.1).

**Figure 1.1   A two-cluster model of 'inner' and 'outer' Wales,
after Aitchison and Carter (2004).**

☐ Cluster 1
▤ Cluster 2

Source: Aitchison, J. and Carter, H. (2004).

Some of our own earlier research has also developed a zonal account of cultural diversity in Wales, but based around the perceived distribution of accent/dialect zones of *English* within Wales. We found that six dialect regions of Wales are commonly identified, for example by school teachers, and associated with relatively distinctive social stereotypes (Garrett, Coupland and Williams, 2003). But by far the most influential treatment of Welsh cultural diversity to date is

Figure 1.2 The 'three-Wales model', after Balsom (1985).

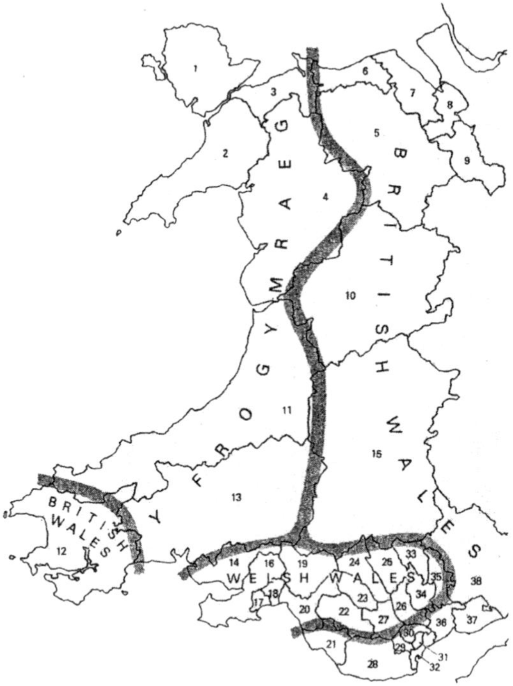

The Constituencies in 1983

	10 Montgomery	19 Neath	29 Cardiff West
1 Ynys Môn	11 Ceredigion and Pembroke	20 Aberavon	30 Cardiff North
2 Caernarfon	North	21 Bridgend	31 Cardiff Central
3 Conway	12 Pembroke	22 Ogmore	32 Cardiff South and Penarth
4 Meirionnydd Nant Conwy	13 Carmarthen	23 Rhondda	33 Blaenau Gwent
5 Clwyd South-West	14 Llanelli	24 Cynon Valley	34 Islwyn
6 Clwyd North-West	15 Brecon and Radnor	25 Merthyr Tydfil and Rhymney	35 Torfaen
7 Delyn	16 Gower	26 Caerphilly	36 Newport West
8 Alyn and Deeside	17 Swansea West	27 Pontypridd	37 Newport East
9 Wrexham	18 Swansea East	28 Vale of Glamorgan	38 Monmouth

Source: Balsom, D. (1985).

Denis Balsom's 'three-Wales model' (see above; also Balsom, Madgwick and Van Mechelen, 1983; 1984; see figure 1.2). It is based on a weakly justified combination of two different sorts of data collected in 1979, which Balsom calls 'a relatively low point in Welsh self-assertion' (1985, p. 3). The data were gathered by Gallop Poll under the guidance of Balsom and colleagues; 858 participants were interviewed, based on a two-stage random sample. The two empirical measures used to construct the 'three-Wales model' were self-attributed ethnic labels (respondents preferring to present themselves as, for example, 'Welsh' versus 'British'), which Balsom took as an index expressing Welsh national identity, and degrees of Welsh-language competence.

By combining the available data Balsom (1985) identified three Welsh zones which he labelled 'Y Fro Gymraeg', 'Welsh Wales' and 'British Wales'. 'Y Fro Gymraeg' was 'Welsh-identifying, Welsh-speaking Wales'; 'Welsh Wales' was 'Welsh-identifying, non-Welsh-speaking Wales'; 'British Wales' was 'British-identifying and non-Welsh-speaking Wales'. By means of the model Balsom and colleagues commented on trends in political voting in Wales and gave their personal assessment of the durability of a distinctive sense of Welsh identity. In the 1985 chapter Balsom concludes, pessimistically, that 'the sense of Welsh identity which is not anchored by the Welsh language [that is, outside 'Y Fro Gymraeg'] will be the principal casualty' (1985, p. 16). He sketches a depressing paradox – that the only socio-economically successful part of Wales will be that part – 'British Wales' – which is 'part of Southern Britain' and has little 'unique Welshness'.

In addition to the time-lag between Balsom's original research and the present, there are substantial methodological weaknesses in Balsom's analysis. In par-ticular, information on people's preferred, self-ascribed ethnic labels is a crude and undifferentiated measure of social identity. (It is one of the measures in our own survey, where it is complemented by many other measures – see below.) The summation of data on Welsh-language competence/use and ethnic self-labelling does not allow for potentially complex relationships between variables of this sort. Again, Balsom's geographical zones (in figure 1.2) are informally sketched, with boundaries necessarily cutting through some culturally complex and shifting communities. Above all, the model prioritizes geographical zoning, without adequate consideration of whether other social factors may explain different intensities of Welsh identification better or more richly. Even if a geographical model can predict Welsh identity, there is no reason to assume that it will be based on contiguous zones of the sort shown in figures 1.1 and 1.2.

The 'three-Wales model' has continued to be cited because it lends a measure of empirical support for cultural categories which are, we think, still quite widely imagined in Wales and which reach into many areas of social life, present and past. For example, Gwynedd and Anglesey have strong iconic status as a north-west Wales 'heartland', just as Ceredigion has in the south-west. Pembrokeshire has often been referred to as 'little England beyond Wales' and is picked out as part of 'British Wales' by Balsom. This is despite the also well-known cultural and linguistic phenomenon of the Landsker, a putative isogloss splitting more Welsh-speaking Pembrokeshire to the north from a more resolutely anglicized southern part. Balsom's 'Welsh Wales' is a rough demarcation of the south Wales Valleys, with their highly resonant socio-economic and political distinctiveness, echoing Raymond Williams's second 'truth'.

To what extent, then, should we and need we persist with a 'multi-model' of contemporary Wales? Do more robust and differentiated data than Balsom's support the 'three-Wales' conception, and to what extent? How well do Aitchison and Carter's two Welsh-language competence clusters fit with patterns of ethno-linguistic identification? The data most relevant here, we would argue, need to be geographically, socially and subjectively nuanced – able to capture a wide range of self-identity beliefs and sentiments, across smaller communities and against richer social profiles of informants.

THE NEW SURVEY SAMPLE AND DATA

We collected information from 777 adult informants distributed across Wales over the period September 2002 to January 2004. Informants completed a written questionnaire, in either English or Welsh, in five sections: (i) What you know about Wales (diverse factual questions about Wales); (ii) What you feel about Wales (questions about Welsh identity and affiliation to Wales); (iii) What you think about the Welsh language (questions about beliefs, feelings and orientations to the Welsh language); (iv) Welsh things that you do (questions about respondents' engagement with events and practices that culturally linked to Wales); and (v) Some information about yourself (questions about respondents' demographic backgrounds and self-assessed proficiency in Welsh). For this article we draw mainly on data from section (ii), one question each from sections (iii) and (iv), and the demographic data in section (v).

Informants were a convenience sample drawn from face-to-face street surveying and some personal network contacts. For example, we approached workers in different types of shops, offices and other workplaces in many town and city centres, where localities were selected partly to ensure good geographical coverage of Wales. A good range of occupational and non-working

Table 1.1
Demographic characteristics of the fourteen regions*

	Gwynedd and Anglesey n=56	Conwy n=58	Denbighshire and Flintshire n=38	North Pembs n=36	Wrexham n=34	Powys n=67	Ceredigion n=51
Mean Age	44.7	45.5	43.6	47.3	41.7	41.1	41.9
Male	15 (26.8%)	24 (41.4%)	8 (21.1%)	12 (33.3%)	11 (32.4%)	26 (38.8%)	25 (49.0%)
Female	40 (71.4%)	34 (58.6%)	29 (76.3%)	24 (66.7%)	23 (67.6%)	41 (61.2%)	26 (51.0%)
Born in Wales	37 (66.1%)	37 (63.8%)	28 (73.7%)	28 (77.8%)	25 (73.5%)	48 (71.6%)	40 (80.0%)
Born outside Wales	19 (33.9%)	17 (29.3%)	8 (21.1%)	8 (22.2%)	9 (26.5%)	18 (28.4%)	10 (20.0%)
Born in Wales and lived there all or most of my life	35 (62.5%)	33 (56.9%)	26 (68.4%)	27 (75.0%)	22 (64.7%)	38 (56.7%)	38 (74.5%)
Born in Wales but lived a lot of my life in another country	2 (3.6%)	4 (6.9%)	3 (7.9%)	1 (2.8%)	1 (2.9%)	6 (9.0%)	2 (3.9%)
Born outside of Wales but lived most of my life in Wales	12 (21.4%)	9 (15.5%)	7 (18.4%)	5 (13.9%)	9 (26.5%)	17 (25.4%)	6 (11.8%)
Born outside of Wales and lived all or most of my life outside of Wales	7 (12.5%)	12 (20.7%)	2 (5.3%)	3 (8.3%)	2 (5.9%)	6 (9.0%)	5 (9.8%)
L1 speakers of Welsh	34 (60.7%)	17 (29.3%)	4 (10.5%)	17 (47.2%)	6 (17.6%)	2 (3.0%)	29 (56.9%)
L2 speakers of Welsh	10 (17.9%)	14 (24.1%)	16 (42.1%)	8 (22.2%)	11 (32.4%)	22 (32.8%)	9 (17.9%)
Little ability in Welsh	8 (14.3%)	19 (32.8%)	14 (36.8%)	11 (30.6%)	14 (41.2%)	32 (47.8%)	12 (23.5%)
No ability in Welsh	4 (5.4%)	7 (12.1%)	4 (10.5%)	–	3 (8.8%)	11 (16.4%)	1 (2.0%)
Learning Welsh at moment	5 (8.9%)	2 (3.4%)	1 (2.6%)	2 (5.6%)	–	4 (6.0%)	5 (9.8%)
Not learning Welsh at moment	45 (80.4%)	53 (91.4%)	35 (94.7%)	33 (91.7%)	34 (100%)	63 (94.0%)	42 (82.4%)
Number of participants filling questionnaire out in Welsh	17 (30.4%)	8 (13.8%)	1 (2.6%)	1 (2.8%)	2 (5.9%)	–	27 (52.9%)
Number of participants filling questionnaire out in English	39 (69.6%)	50 (86.2%)	37 (97.4%)	35 (97.2%)	32 (94.1%)	67 (100%)	24 (47.1%)

	South and mid Pembs n=42	Swansea and Neath/Port Talbot n=50	Carms n=60	Valleys n=64	Newport and Mon n=46	Cardiff n=137	Vale and Bridgend n=38	All Wales N=777
Mean Age	43.7	40.6	43.5	36.8	36.7	35.4	46.9	41.7
Male	16 (38.1%)	24 (48.0%)	23 (38.3%)	25 (39.1%)	20 (43.5%)	57 (41.6%)	17 (44.7%)	312 (40.2%)
Female	26 (61.9%)	26 (52.0%)	37 (61.7%)	39 (61.9%)	26 (56.5%)	78 (56.9%)	21 (55.3%)	461 (59.3%)
Born in Wales	27 (64.3%)	37 (74.0%)	52 (86.7%)	55 (85.9%)	40 (87.0%)	101 (73.7%)	31 (81.6%)	581 (74.8%)
Born outside Wales	15 (35.7%)	11 (22.0%)	8 (13.3%)	9 (14.1%)	6 (13.0%)	36 (22.3%)	8 (19.4%)	193 (24.8%)
Born in Wales and lived there all or most of my life	24 (57.1%)	37 (74.0%)	50 (83.3%)	55 (85.9%)	38 (82.6%)	94 (68.6%)	29 (76.5%)	546 (70.3%)
Born in Wales but lived a lot of my life in another country	3 (7.1%)	–	2 (3.3%)	–	2 (4.3%)	7 (5.1%)	2 (5.3%)	35 (4.5%)
Born outside of Wales but lived most of my life in Wales	11 (26.2%)	10 (20.0%)	6 (10.0%)	6 (9.4%)	3 (6.5%)	23 (16.8%)	1 (2.6%)	125 (16.1%)
Born outside of Wales and lived all or most of my life outside of Wales	4 (9.5%)	2 (4.0%)	2 (3.3%)	3 (4.7%)	2 (4.3%)	12 (8.8%)	6 (15.8%)	68 (8.8%)
L1 speakers of Welsh	3 (7.1%)	8 (16.0%)	29 (48.0%)	6 (9.4%)	2 (4.3%)	23 (16.8%)	6 (15.8%)	186 (23.9%)
L2 speakers of Welsh	7 (16.7%)	12 (24.0%)	13 (21.7%)	23 (35.9%)	11 (23.9%)	46 (33.3%)	15 (39.5%)	217 (27.9%)
Little ability in Welsh	21 (50.0%)	19 (38.0%)	17 (28.3%)	29 (45.3%)	23 (50.0%)	53 (38.7%)	11 (28.9%)	283 (36.4%)
No ability in Welsh	11 (26.2%)	11 (22.0%)	1 (1.7%)	5 (7.8%)	10 (21.7%)	13 (9.5%)	6 (15.8%)	86 (11.1%)
Learning Welsh at moment	4 (9.5%)	3 (6.0%)	6 (10.0%)	9 (14.1%)	6 (13.0%)	10 (7.3%)	2 (5.3%)	59 (7.6%)
Not learning Welsh at moment	37 (88.1%)	45 (90.0%)	51 (85.0%)	54 (84.4%)	40 (87.0%)	126 (92.0%)	36 (94.7%)	694 (89.3%)
Number of participants filling questionnaire out in Welsh	1 (2.4%)	1 (2.0%)	9 (15.0%)	2 (3.1%)	–	13 (9.5%)	2 (5.3%)	85 (10.9%)
Number of participants filling questionnaire out in English	41 (97.6%)	49 (98.0%)	51 (85.0%)	62 (96.1%)	46 (100%)	124 (90.5%)	36 (94.7%)	692 (89.1%)

* Where percentages for a particular variable (for example, sex) do not add up to a hundred per cent this is due to participants not filling in this part of the questionnaire.

groups are represented in the sample, for example including retired people working in charity shops, bank managers, shop assistants, garage workers, butchers, civil servants and self-employed business people. Our approach to street surveying produced slight unevenness in the sample, for example in there being a preponderance of females over males. Table 1.1 sets out the sample characteristics in detail.

Responses were entered into an SPSS database and initially coded in line with the twenty-two current unitary authorities of Wales. However, in some cases we did not have enough participants from a particular authority. In these cases two or more authorities were combined to produce fourteen regions (see table 1.1). So, Gwynedd and Anglesey were combined, as were Denbighshire with Flintshire, Swansea with Neath/Port Talbot, Newport with Monmouthshire, and the Vale of Glamorgan with Bridgend. The region labelled Valleys in table 1.1 comprises a composite of the five unitary authorities of Rhondda Cynon Taff, Merthyr Tydfil, Blaenau Gwent, Caerphilly and Torfaen. On the other hand, we split the Pembrokeshire authority into northern and southern/mid regions, to reflect the widely recognized sociolinguistic differences between these zones (as discussed earlier).

In summary, the 777 participants were aged between 19 and 92 with a mean age of 41.7. Of these, 461 (59.3 per cent) were female and 312 (40.2 per cent) male, with 4 not specifying their sex on the questionnaire. In terms of country of birth, 581 (74.8 per cent) of participants stated that they were born in Wales, 145 (18.7 per cent) in England and 23 (3.0 per cent) 'in the UK'. The remaining 25 who specified their place of birth came from a diversity of countries such as Germany (4), Canada (3), Scotland (3), as well as others from New Zealand, Pakistan, Somalia, Sweden and Zimbabwe. 546 (70.3 per cent) participants stated that they were 'Born in Wales and had lived there all or most of [their] life'; 35 (4.5 per cent) stated that they were 'Born in Wales but had lived a lot of [their] life in another country'; 125 (16.1 per cent) said that they had been 'Born outside Wales but lived most of [their] life in Wales'; and 68 (8.8 per cent) stated that they had been 'Born outside Wales and lived all or most of [their] life outside Wales'. 59 (7.6 per cent) respondents said they were currently learning Welsh, while 694 (89.3 per cent) were not. Eighty-five (10.9 per cent) chose to fill out the questionnaire in Welsh.[1]

Values of identity and affiliation across fourteen Welsh regions
The survey gives us a range of data on informants' perceptions of their own Welshness and feelings about Wales. Section (ii) of the questionnaire asked informants to mark their responses to the following question and statements: 'How Welsh do you feel?', 'I feel Wales is my real home' and 'I feel very proud

to be Welsh'. Section (iv) included the question: 'How important is it to you to let other people know you are Welsh?' Notwithstanding the starkness of these items, perhaps particularly the first, and the inherent limitations of a written questionnaire format, they do give us some empirical purchase on the difficult ideas of 'Welshness' and 'Welsh identity', which we saw foregrounded in 'how many Wales?' debates. More particularly, the data allow us to assess the general *strength* of informants' affiliative responses, and the extent and distribution of *variation* in these responses across the different social and geographical dimensions of the sample. The individual questions and statements allow informants potentially to discriminate among subtly different ethnic subjectivities – a general sense of their own Welsh identity, a sense of cultural belonging to Wales and a sense of ethnic pride – and a more practice-oriented consideration of whether it matters to them to display their Welshness. All these responses were marked on seven-point Likert scales, where 1 represents the lowest possible value and 7 the highest possible value. The data can therefore be reported most simply as mean values across groups of informants, but then (later in the article) as results from more sophisticated statistical analysis of the relationships between these perceptions and other social and linguistic data.

It is worth emphasizing that the concept of 'Welsh identity' lies at the heart of the multi-model debate. We saw that Balsom's 'three-Wales' categories were derived partly from a coding of how his informants said they typically identified themselves through the ethnic labels 'Welsh' and 'British'. It is also interesting that Aitchison and Carter's concluding position in their 2004 analysis is that the future of Welsh lies largely in the process (which they advocate very directly) of fusing Welsh identity and Welsh-language competence:

the crucial problem is the need to create an association between being Welsh and speaking Welsh, for only with that firmly established is there real hope for the emergence of a truly bilingual Wales to replace the old polarized split between a Welsh-Wales and an Anglo-Wales. (2004, p. 140)

These are a priori assumptions, rather than conclusions from the authors' demographic research. The quotation also forecloses on the notion of 'being Welsh'. In a situation where highly influential researchers are making such claims, it becomes particularly important to deconstruct the notion of 'Welsh identity' and to test out relationships between articulations of Welshness and, among other things, the sociolinguistics of knowing and using Welsh. We do not claim that questionnaire responses of the sort we deal with here can comprehensively or fully adequately

Table 1.2

Mean scores for four subjective variables for fourteen different
Welsh regions embedded within Balsom's 'three-Wales model'

	'Y Fro Gymraeg'					'Welsh Wales'					'British Wales'				Overall Mean
	Gwynedd and Anglesey	Conwy	North Pembs	Cer	Carms	Swansea and Neath/Port Talbot	Valleys	Powys	Wrexham	South and mid Pembs	Denbigh and Flintshire	Cardiff	Vale and Bridgend	Newport Mon	
	n=56	n=58	n=36	n=51	n=60	n=50	n=64	n=67	n=34	n=42	n=38	n=137	n=38	n=46	N=777
How Welsh do you feel	5.51	5.05	5.47	5.67	6.03	5.28	5.20	4.46	4.71	5.05	4.84	5.04	4.74	5.65	5.19
Feel Wales is real home	6.04	5.96	6.33	6.14	6.60	6.06	6.08	5.85	5.76	6.02	5.61	5.81	5.53	6.11	5.99
Proud to be Welsh	5.58	5.67	6.19	6.04	6.48	5.84	5.91	5.66	5.50	5.95	5.69	5.49	5.51	6.17	5.81
Important to let other people know you're Welsh	5.37	5.35	5.49	5.69	5.92	4.77	5.25	4.03	5.29	4.88	4.89	4.64	4.68	5.52	5.07

Table 1.3
Mean values for four subjective variables across Balsom's 'three-Wales' categories

	'Y Fro Gymraeg' (n=235)	'Welsh Wales' (n=135)	'British Wales' (n=407)	All Wales (N=777)
How Welsh do you feel	5.52	5.43	4.91	5.19
Feel Wales is real home	6.23	6.13	5.81	5.99
Feel proud to be Welsh	5.94	6.02	5.66	5.81
Important to let other people know you're Welsh	5.54	5.32	4.73	5.07

model Welsh identity. But they do at least provide more extensive and differentiated data than has previously been available.

As a first step in testing the adequacy of Balsom's tripartite conception of Wales, we sorted our fourteen regions into the three zones of the 'three-Wales model'. We were then able to examine mean values for respondents' scalar responses to each of the four questions about Welshness and Welsh affiliation for each of the regions. Table 1.2 gives these descriptive statistics for each region, and table 1.3 gives aggregated means for each of Balsom's three zones.

Mean values across the fourteen regions ranged between 4.46 and 6.03 for the 'How Welsh do you feel?' responses; between 5.53 and 6.60 for the 'I feel Wales is my real home' responses; between 5.49 and 6.48 for the 'I am proud to be Welsh' responses; and between 4.03 and 5.92 for the 'It is important to let people know I am Welsh' responses. Since in each case 4.0 indicates the mid-point of the available scale (1.0 to 7.0), it is striking that not one mean score for any of the four questions for any of the fourteen regions falls below the mid-point. (The final column of table 1.2 shows that the overall mean values for each of the four questions ranged between 5.07 and 5.99.) We can already see that the survey shows overwhelmingly positive subjective orientations to Wales and Welshness by informants throughout Wales. These regions can be distinguished only in terms of *relative degrees of positivity*. Also, this pattern extends across the different dimensions of ethnic subjectivity. 'Feeling Welsh' and 'wanting to let others know I am Welsh' are expressed positively (at around 5.0 on the seven-point scale) by all informant groups. The strongest subjective orientations, remarkably approaching overall levels of 6.0, are expressed in relation to ethnic/national pride and a sense of being at home in Wales. The positivity of the overall responses is all the more remarkable when we recall the demographic diversity of the sample, and not least that substantial numbers of informants were born outside Wales (see table 1.1).

Reassessing existing multi-models

Table 1.2 does indeed show some tendency for the higher mean levels of positive orientation to Wales and Welshness to occur in the zone Balsom refers to as 'Y Fro Gymraeg'. Carmarthenshire produces clearly the highest values of all fourteen regions on all four questions. All four of the lowest mean values occur in the zone Balsom refers to as 'British Wales': Powys informants score lowest on 'How Welsh do you feel?' and 'How important is it to you to let other people know you are Welsh?', Cardiff informants score lowest on 'I am very proud to be Welsh' and the Vale and Bridgend region scores lowest on 'I feel Wales is my real home'. But we should again emphasize that these lowest values are in all cases above the scalar mid-point, and considerably so on dimensions of ethnic pride and Wales as real home. Mean responses for the regions that fall in Balsom's 'Welsh Wales' are generally not particularly high-ranked or low-ranked among the four mean values for each question.

Table 1.3 confirms, however, that the variance across Balsom's zones is small and that the zones are not always ranked in the order that Balsom's model predicts. For three of the four questions, the ranking of zones is in line with Balsom's claims – with 'Y Fro Gymraeg' exceeding so-called 'Welsh Wales', which in turn exceeds so-called 'British Wales' in values of reported Welsh affiliation – but the 'proud to be Welsh' responses position 'Welsh Wales' ahead of the other two zones. The general point is surely that the subjective data call into question both the zone labels coined by Balsom (see below) and the 'three-Wales model' itself as being an adequate representation of contemporary Wales. The descriptive numerical tendencies from our survey of self-reported Welsh affiliation in support of the Balsom model are slight, and they are swamped by the tide of positive affiliation reported by informants across the whole of Wales. On the basis of reported levels of affiliation to Wales, *all* of Wales is thoroughly 'Welsh' (as opposed to 'British') and there is little support for the idea of a Welsh 'heartland', 'Y Fro Gymraeg', as a zone of distinctively high Welsh affiliation.

Very similar conclusions can be reached when we reconfigure our affiliation data to respect the two zones of so-called 'inner' and 'outer' Wales that were generated in Aitchison and Carter's cluster analysis of Welsh-language competence from the census data (see figure 1.2). Given that the boundary of this two-cluster model cuts through both our Conwy and Swansea and Neath/Port Talbot regions, participants in these regions had to be split and recoded based on the town or city where they said they lived, in order to reflect the precise boundaries shown in figure 1.2. Thus, for our Conwy region, participants who lived in, for instance, Llandudno were coded into Aitchison and Carter's 'outer

Wales' zone, while those living in Conwy town itself were coded into the 'inner Wales' zone. Similarly, for the Swansea and Neath/Port Talbot region, participants who lived in Swansea were coded into the 'outer Wales' zone, while participants who lived in Llanelli, Glynneath or Pontarddulais were coded into the 'inner Wales' zone. Once again, mean values for affiliative Welshness differ only slightly between the two Aitchison and Carter sociolinguistic zones (see table 1.4) and not to an extent that would justify a 'heartland' versus 'non-heartland' distinction.

Table 1.4
Mean values for four subjective variables Aitchison and Carter's
two zones of Welsh-language use

	'Inner Wales' (n=257)	'Outer Wales' (n=520)	All Wales (N=777)
How Welsh do you feel	5.58	5.00	5.19
Feel Wales is real home	6.23	5.87	5.99
Feel proud to be Welsh	5.99	5.72	5.81
Important to let other people know you're Welsh	5.54	4.84	5.07

Complex regional patterns of Welsh ethnolinguistic identity
To simplify the analysis for the remainder of the study, we calculated statistical reliabilities among responses to the four affiliation questions, for the whole sample and for each region separately, to assess the degree of congruence between responses. Very high reliabilities were obtained, showing that, although responses to different questions spanned somewhat different ranges, informants responded with very similar tendencies to each of the four questions.[2] We therefore decided to enter a single value for each community under a statistically derived factor that we labelled 'affiliative Welshness' ('Welshness' for short reference). In later phases of the study it then becomes possible statistically to assess degrees of association between subjective Welshness and other social and contextual factors more efficiently.

Before turning to that analysis it is useful to continue to look informally at patterns in our data relating to the composite Welshness variable, levels of linguistic competence in Welsh and self-ascribed ethnic labelling. Table 1.5 shows mean values for the first two of these variables, across our original fourteen source regions.

Table 1.5
Ranking of fourteen regions by integrated index of 'Welshness' and by self-assessed
competence in Welsh

Regions	Welshness	Self-assessed competence
All participants (N=777)	5.6052	3.56
Carmarthenshire (n=60)	6.2583	4.78 (3)
North Pembs (n=36)	5.9571	4.33 (4)
Ceredigion (n=51)	5.9031	4.92 (2)
Newport and Monmouthshire (n=46)	5.8641	2.70 (12)
Gwynedd and Anglesey (n=56)	5.8529	5.45 (1)
Conwy (n=58)	5.7157	3.74 (5)
Valleys (n=64)	5.6587	3.19 (9)
Swansea and Neath/Port Talbot (n=50)	5.5691	2.86 (11)
South and mid Pembs (n=42)	5.5688	2.31 (14)
Denbighshire and Flintshire (n=38)	5.3929	3.26 (8)
Wrexham (n=34)	5.3790	3.47 (6)
Cardiff (n=137)	5.3288	3.28 (7)
Vale and Bridgend (n=38)	5.1622	2.92 (10)
Powys (n=67)	5.1017	2.68 (13)

This table once again confirms the inappropriateness of a simple geographical model of Welsh identity, according to the composite Welshness measure. The overall variance, as we have already mentioned, is small (this time ranging between about 6.3 and about 5.1 on the seven-point scale). If we did attempt to infer 'zones' based on degrees of affiliative Welshness, they would not be geographically contiguous. For example, Carmarthenshire stands out as a potential high-affiliation 'zone' on its own, but then we come (in rank order) to a cluster of next-highest affiliating regions – north Pembrokeshire, Ceredigion, Newport and Monmouthshire, Gwynedd and Anglesey. At the foot of the ranking, Vale and Bridgend pattern with Powys as a putative 'zone', just below Cardiff, Wrexham and Denbighshire and Flintshire.

If we look at how values of self-assessed competence in Welsh (deriving from the seven-point scale self-reports in our own questionnaire) sit alongside Welsh affiliation values, it is clear from the descriptive statistics alone that competence is not associated in any simple way with affiliative Welshness. We find regional groups of people with low declared Welsh-language competence affiliating very strongly with Wales – Newport and Monmouthshire, Valleys, Swansea and Neath/Port Talbot, south and mid Pembrokeshire. It remains true that, if we examine the means for three different Welsh-language competence groups across Wales as a whole, which we label *high competence* (people who assessed themselves as 6 or

7 on the Likert scale), *mid-level competence* (people who assessed themselves as 4 or 5) and *low competence* (people who assessed themselves as 1, 2 or 3 on the scale), a trend of association is apparent between language competence and Welshness. The details are: high competence (n=193, Mean=6.62); mid-level competence (n=141, Mean=5.77); low competence (n=399, Mean=5.05). It is clear that the strength of this association needs to be tested in a more robust statistical manner. (We do this through a regression analysis, see below.)

Finally, how does self-ascribed ethnic labelling – which was Balsom's indicator of ethnic identity and therefore a defining element of his 'three-Wales' categorization – pattern across the data? Aitchison and Carter express regret that the 2001 census in Wales generated data that were 'completely compromised' (2004, p. 140) in the absence of a tick box on the census form which would have provided the option 'Welsh' as an ethnic designation.[3] Data from our survey to an extent compensate for this absence. We asked informants to note down their preferred way of identifying themselves through an ethnic label. Table 1.6 shows percentages of self-ascription across all fourteen Welsh regions, coded into six sub-categories. (*Welsh + X* and *X + Welsh* refer to compound designations such as *Welsh-European* and *European-Welsh* respectively, since this was a free-response category in the questionnaire.)

Use of the simple label 'Welsh' is the only very frequently used category, accounting for 65.9 per cent of all self-ascriptions from the 755 respondents in the overall sample of 777 who answered this question. Table 1.6 ranks the fourteen regions by the proportions of respondents in a region who identified themselves simply as Welsh, high to low. Different n-values within the regional cells mean that caution is needed in making cross-region comparisons, and, since the responses are not hierarchical, we cannot use the table 1.6 data in later statistical comparisons. All the same, it is interesting to note that very high proportions of Welsh-self-labelling informants are recorded in some regions – in north Pembrokeshire, Carmarthenshire and Newport and Monmouthshire; also that almost all regions of Wales have clear majorities of Welsh-self-labelling informants (mainly in the range 60–80 per cent), except for Denbighshire and Flintshire. The overall pattern again suggests that no division into the categories of 'Welsh-identifying' and 'British-identifying' (the two 'identity' categories used by Balsom) is tenable. Only in Denbighshire and Flintshire, according to the new survey data, is the designation 'British' chosen by marginally more informants than the designation 'Welsh'. 'British' is the preferred label for less than 18 per cent of the overall sample.

Table 1.6
Patterns of self-ascribed ethnic labelling across fourteen Welsh regions

How do you describe yourself?	Welsh	Welsh + X	X + Welsh	British	English	Other
All participants N=755	512 (65.9%)	24 (3.1%)	20 (2.6%)	138 (17.8%)	27 (3.5%)	34 (4.4%)
North Pembs n=36	31 (86.1%)	–	1 (2.8%)	4 (11.1%)	–	–
Carmarthenshire n=57	50 (83.3%)	1 (1.7%)	–	5 (8.3%)	1 (1.7%)	–
Newport and Monmouthshire n=44	36 (78.3%)	–	–	7 (15.2%)	1 (2.2%)	–
Ceredigion n=51	37 (72.5%)	2 (3.9%)	1 (2.0%)	6 (11.8%)	1 (2.0%)	4 (7.9%)
Valleys n=62	44 (68.8%)	3 (4.7%)	1 (1.6%)	8 (12.5%)	1 (1.6%)	5 (7.9%)
Swansea and Neath/Port Talbot n=47	34 (68.0%)	3 (6.0%)	1 (2.0%)	6 (12.0%)	1 (2.0%)	2 (4.0%)
Vale and Bridgend n=38	25 (65.8%)	1 (2.6%)	1 (2.6%)	6 (15.8%)	4 (10.5%)	1 (2.6%)
Gwynedd and Anglesey n=56	36 (64.3%)	1 (1.8%)	2 (3.6%)	14 (25.0%)	2 (3.6%)	1 (1.8%)
South and mid Pembs n=42	27 (64.3%)	1 (2.4%)	3 (7.1%)	9 (21.4%)	–	2 (4.8%)
Cardiff n=135	86 (62.8%)	5 (3.6%)	3 (2.2%)	26 (19.0%)	6 (4.4%)	9 (6.6%)
Wrexham n=32	21 (61.8%)	–	2 (5.9%)	6 (17.6%)	3 (8.8%)	–
Powys n=66	40 (59.7%)	1 (1.5%)	2 (3.0%)	16 (23.9%)	3 (4.5%)	4 (6.0%)
Conwy n=54	32 (55.2%)	4 (6.9%)	1 (1.7%)	11 (19.0%)	2 (3.4%)	4 (6.9%)
Denbighshire and Flintshire n=38	13 (34.2%)	2 (5.3%)	2 (5.3%)	14 (36.8%)	2 (5.3%)	2 (5.3%)

Predicting Welshness: a multiple regression analysis

So far we have persisted with a basically regional perspective on Welsh identification in order to demonstrate the *limitations* of this perspective. That is, it has already become clear that a *purely* or *principally* regional/zonal model of Welshness is not able to account well for variance in our data. Firstly, that variance is not great, with strong and consistent levels of affiliation to Wales being reported in virtually all the demographic categories of our data. Then, where variance does exist, the descriptive statistics do not give confidence that regionality in fact provides the main or even a relevant model to explain it. We have seen that such 'zones' as might have (limited) explanatory potential for Welsh identification are in any case not geographically contiguous. It is therefore necessary to assess the relative predictive potentials of different social variables, through which we can finally establish whether regional factors are in fact statistically significant among the wider field of social factors potentially predicting affiliative Welshness in our data.

We did this through a multiple regression analysis. The Welshness composite variable was set as the dependent variable and the following eight items were established as independent variables:

• informants' commitment to supporting the Welsh language;
• informants' sex;
• informants' age;
• informants' socio-economic class;
• informants' country of birth;
• informants' overall competence in using and understand Welsh;
• Aitchison and Carter's 'two-Wales model' of language competence;
• Balsom's 'three-Wales model'.

The first six independent variables were values deriving from the questionnaire itself. The commitment data were from another scalar item included in the questionnaire in section (iii). Age was entered in actual years (rather than in grouped categories). Socio-economic class was made up of four hierarchically ordered categories, namely (i) professional/managerial, (ii) intermediate (for example, clerical, administration), (iii) upper working class (skilled occupations) and (iv) lower working class (unskilled and semi-skilled occupations), based on a recoding of informants' listing of their occupational titles. Country of birth was a recoding of informants' responses into two simple categories: born in Wales or born outside Wales.[4]

In the regression analysis the full model was significant, but the best significant predictors of affiliative Welshness were a linear combination of commitment to supporting the Welsh language, country of birth and age (R = 0.77, R^2 = 0.59, F = 60.04, p < 0.001). Beta weights and T values are presented in table 1.7. Overall, then, higher levels of affiliative Welshness are positively and very significantly related to only three variables: (i) higher levels of reported commitment to the Welsh language; (ii) informants being born in Wales rather than outside Wales; and (iii) age, with older age predicting stronger Welsh affiliative Welshness. We discuss each of these relationships in the final section of the article.

Table 1.7
Regression analysis predicting feelings of 'Welshness'

Variable	Beta	T
Commitment to supporting the Welsh language	0.31	8.56**
Country of birth	0.60	18.54**
Age	0.16	3.77**

** $p<0.001$

In many ways, however, it is some of the negative (non-significantly associated, non-predictive) results that are most notable. We had no particular reason to anticipate that Welshness would be predicted by the sex or social class of informants, even though Balsom reported that in his data from the 1970s women were 'the predominant carriers of Welsh identity' (1985, p. 6). These variables were not significant in the regression, showing that sex and class do not predict Welshness. Much more surprisingly, higher/lower levels of Welshness were also *not* significantly predicted by informants' ability to use or understand Welsh. This finding undermines the assumptions made by Balsom and by Aitchison and Carter, as we discussed them earlier. It is clearly *not* the case in our data that judging oneself to have limited competence in the Welsh language is a constraint on experiencing a strong Welsh identity. Welshness was also *not* significantly predicted (relative to the other variables) by informants living in the geographical areas contained within *either* Balsom's *or* Aitichison and Carter's geographical models.

DISCUSSION

The most robust finding we have reported here is that, simply put, where you live in Wales, in terms of conventionalized ethnolinguistic models, does not significantly predict a level of felt Welshness. Negative findings from our survey, and particularly the non-significant factors in the regression analysis, conclusively show the inadequacy of mapping Welshness in terms of simple geographical criteria. They point up the risk of over-determining the role of place in the production of subjective feelings towards the imagined social category 'Wales'. This is what we would expect in the complex, evolving socio-spatial circumstances of contemporary Wales. Welsh social institutions (relating to the arts, sport, tourism and so on) do seem to be moving towards greater inclusivity. A devolved Welsh Assembly Government is of course committed to reducing regional inequalities in Wales and to an inclusive, all-Wales framing of social policy generally. Without at all minimizing the extent of the political and economic challenges implied in this, we find it in many ways reassuring that virtually the whole of Wales is, our data suggest, already very well-disposed to the project of Wales, with which they affiliate strongly.

There is little to support the hoary old category of 'Y Fro Gymraeg' in our data, if we take the concept to imply a distinctively strong and 'heartfelt' sense of Welsh identity among the people who populate it. Aitchison and Carter fully recognize the social changes that have worked to undermine a Welsh ethnolinguistic 'heartland'. They write that 'there is now no way in which the old Welsh-speaking communities can be recreated, for the whole economic system and its social bases have been profoundly transformed and reconstituted' (2004, p. 17). 'The linguistic centre of gravity in Wales', they show, 'is slowly shifting' (2004, p. 65), although they comment that 'there still exists a core or heartland of predominantly Welsh speech'. But it is 'greatly attenuated in geographical extent and impaired in its internal structure . . . a relict area of a once much larger *Bro Gymraeg*' (ibid.). They mourn the lapsing of 'a core reserve' (2004, p. 134), 'a [regional] base into which the penetration of a more powerful language [English] is restricted' (2004, p.135), and they begin to articulate a cultural value system that approves of isolation and disapproves of immigration and what they refer to as the 'political correctness' of 'multiculturalism'.

These remarks seem to us to be based in far too narrow a conception of sociolinguistic processes, and indeed to stray into myopic and illiberal nationalist arenas. Like Balsom's earlier predictions, they may also be too gloomy. Our data suggest that, when we add a subjective profile of Welsh identification to the numerical profiling of the Welsh language at the 2001 census, there is a great deal to celebrate about the contemporary ethnolinguistic vitality of Wales and Welsh. Not only are the absolute numbers of Welsh speakers higher than those recorded in 1971 (at 542,425), but we can now also see that there is a groundswell of affiliative Welshness that will surely be fertile ground in which Welsh-language promotional initiatives can thrive. As regards the expression of Welsh identity in our data, all of Wales can plausibly be described as 'Y Fro Gymraeg', which might be to say that 'all of Wales is the real Wales'.[5] We have some empirical evidence that this is so, although grading the 'reality' of 'real Wales' is a dangerous business. In any event, there is simply no evidence of the 'reduced . . . integrity of identity' that Aitchison and Carter believe characterizes the linguistic-ally fractured *Bro Gymraeg* (2004, p. 130).

The Welsh language, however, remains a potent but complex consideration in relation to Welsh identity. Contrary to Balsom et al.'s (1983, 1984, 1985) findings that Welsh identification and Welsh-language competence were intim-ately linked, and undermining Aitchison and Carter's suggested policy of promoting the Welsh language as the sole meaningfully distinct fulcrum of Welsh identity, our regression analysis results show that levels of self-reported competence in Welsh do not predict subjective Welshness. This is *not* to say, however, that there is *no* association between these factors, as we saw from the mean scores for the three competence groups, above. Rather, that association is not sufficiently strong or consistent for the regression to have found it to be a significant predictor.

At the same time, informants' level of *support for* the Welsh language *is* a significant predictive factor (whether or not they report themselves as being actually proficient in Welsh). This finding could be taken to support a line of reasoning, which is commonly advanced informally, to the effect that the future of Welsh in large measure depends on the 'good will' of non-Welsh speakers, as much as on high levels of Welsh-language competence and use. Once again, the implications of our findings seem fairly reassuring. The mean value for expressed support for Welsh for the overall sample is reasonably positive, lying above the scalar mid-point at 4.73, and over 70 per cent of the sample answered 4 or above on this question. Further analysis of means shows that levels of com-mitment hardly differ at all by age (age group 19–35 = 4.74; 36–55 = 4.73; 56+ = 4.79). However, there is some difference in commitment levels with respect to informants' country of birth. Those who were born in Wales have a mean score of 4.96 while those born outside Wales have a mean of 4.04.

It is in many ways unsurprising that the country of birth variable significantly predicts degrees of affiliative Welshness (the composite variable). Feeling Welsh, feeling Wales is one's home, ethnic Welsh pride and particularly letting others know one is Welsh will be less readily endorsed by people born outside of Wales. On the other hand it would be wrong on the basis of our data to infer that an 'outsiders/insiders' category distinction polarizes Welshness subjectivities into 'very low Welshness' versus 'very high Welshness'. Informants born in Wales (N=577) show a mean score of 6.15, while those born outside Wales (N=158) show a mean of 3.66. If we split the category 'born outside Wales' into two, into those who have lived in Wales for most of their lives and those who have lived most of their lives outside Wales, we find a contrast between (n=106, Mean = 4.00) for the first subgroup and (n=52, Mean = 2.96) for the second. This shows that non-Welsh-born people who have lived in Wales for a considerable period do tend to assume moderate levels of Welsh cultural identification and affiliation.

Finally, age proves to be a significant factor in our data. Language planners are acutely aware of the implications of shifting age-profiles among speakers of Welsh. Aitchison and Carter comment that in 2001 under-16s accounted for more than half the speakers of Welsh in many south-east Wales local authorities, while in the rural 'heartland' these percentages were generally less than 25 per cent (2004, p. 86). Our survey adds the finding that, among younger adults, there is a significant tendency to record a somewhat *less strong* sense of affiliative Welshness. For example, when we recode our 777 adult informants into three broad age-bands, we find the following mean values for Welshness: age group 56+ years (n = 138) = 5.91; age group 36–55 (n = 293) = 5.52; age group 19–35 (n = 298) = 5.57. Our earlier research involving four groups of secondary school students in Wales (Coupland et al., 2005) showed that students in the age-band 16–18 (n = 222) reported a Welshness mean of 4.82. Although the overall age-pattern is not fully linear (and the regression statistics are of course based on far more intensive scrutiny of individuals in the adult sample), these numbers show a clear decline in felt Welshness across the age groups, older to younger.

Perspective is again crucial, as even the youngest group we have surveyed reports rather high levels of Welshness, well above the scalar mid-point overall. Even so, the mean for the age-group disguises rather large disparities between groups attending different schools in Wales, which include values for Welshness variables that are far lower than we find in the adult sample. This only serves to emphasize the fact that sociolinguistic and socio-psychological research involving late-teenagers remains a priority concern, to document their key role in the evolving story of ethnolinguistic identity and vitality in Wales.

Our core question has been 'How many Wales?', and in some senses we find the question unanswerable. Sociolinguists are acculturated to seeing diversity as the normal condition for communities, and indeed to presupposing that communities of practice – however we operationalize them empirically – will be what we might call 'units of structured diversity'. On this occasion we have focused on statistical patterns of subjective alignment with Wales, and a degree of significant measurable diversity has become apparent. But the concept of identity points us just as much to what is held in common across a community as to what is held as difference within it. As we have stressed, our most interesting findings in this research so far seem to us to be negative ones. Affiliative Welshness is not significantly structured on a regional basis in Wales, nor is it in any simple way predicted by Welsh-language competence. These negative findings, we suggest, require a rather radical overhaul of conventionalized models. If forced to give a particular answer to 'How many Wales?', we would have to say 'one', again on the understanding that we are dealing on this occasion with perceptions of ethnic identity and affiliation to Wales. There are very few corners of our data – regional or age-related – where the general pattern of a robust, vibrantly positive sense of Welshness breaks down.

However, it is also pertinent to think of why the 'How many Wales?' question has come to be asked (and for that matter, why so many influential studies of Welsh history and society are titled as questions; see Coupland, 2005). In the two sources with which we have mainly engaged critically here, the main rationale has been to establish qualitatively different categories of Welshness, mainly on regional bases. Concepts like Balsom's 'Y Fro Gymraeg', 'Welsh Wales' and 'British Wales', but also 'inner Wales' and 'outer Wales', posit a hierarchy of Welsh experience that is too easily readable in terms of cultural authenticity, and perhaps even in terms of intrinsic value, greater to lesser.

We find it gratifying that the first of these classificatory systems is shown to be wrong, in the sense of being empirically inconsistent with our data. Whether it was interpretively appropriate at the time of its conception we also doubt, because it has always seemed to imply that some formations of Welshness, and even some parts of Wales itself, are less legitimate than others. In a Wales where language policy (in what must be Rhodri Morgan's words) needs to encompass 'Monmouth as well as Maentwrog' (*Iaith Pawb*), and where performed identity spans the music of the Goldie Lookin Chain as well as Dafydd Iwan, it is unwise to be this restrictive.

We have discussed the second classificatory system in relation to Aitchison and Carter's bipartite cluster-model of Welsh-language competence, even though, in fairness, it is not a model that they particularly prioritize. Our data do, however, show that the demographic clustering of Welsh usage in Wales is not matched by clustering in terms of affiliative Welshness, precisely because affiliation is ubiquitous in Wales. This calls into question Aitchison and Carter's interpretive speculations about the need to boost what they call 'Welsh identity', and to forge stronger links between language and identity, as a mechanism for promoting the Welsh language.

Wales's most productive future must surely result from a self-consciously inclusive definition of Welshness, and not from privileging one sociolinguistic sector over another. Our own view is that widespread positive subjectivity in Wales in favour of Welshness – so evident in our data – is already providing a strong infrastructure for Welsh-language maintenance and growth. That growth is being achieved in diverse regions of Wales and by diverse social groups, but especially younger people. Not all of the new Welsh speakers can be expected to have the Welsh language at the heart of their ethnicity, although some certainly will. In fact, we need to know far more about the extent to which and the ways in which Welsh-speakers construe Welsh as an identity resource, and of what sort. But it seems to be time to set aside 'heartland' ideologies of ethnolinguistic purity and continuity and to welcome a new 'unity in diversity' in Wales. That would consist of a more open slate of ways of speaking in Wales – including, incidentally, support for the use of *more* than two languages, and more intralinguistic diversity too – and a more open slate of ways of being enthusiastically and progressively Welsh.

ACKNOWLEDGEMENTS

The research for this article was supported by funding from the Leverhulme Trust (Grant No. F/00407/D) to the Centre for Language and Communication Research, Cardiff University, for a larger project on Language and Global Communication. See *www.cardiff.ac.uk/encap/global/*. Betsy Evans and Angie Williams contributed significantly to the design and implementation of the present research, for which we are particularly grateful. We are also grateful to Richard Bowen, Julia Bullough, Rachel Coupland, Lowri Griffith, Dorothy Holloway, Dylan Jones, Manon Jones and Paul Tench, and many others, for their assistance with data collection.

NOTES

[1] Data from other populations are still becoming available to the survey. We are collecting information from diasporic Welsh groups outside Wales and Britain, including North America and Patagonia, and from ethnic Italians in south Wales. We have also collected and analysed a sample of school students from four secondary schools in Wales (see Coupland et al., 2005), although these data are not included in the present analysis.

2   The overall Cronbach's alpha reliability for the sample as a whole was very high =
     0.9100. Reliabilities across the fourteen regions were also high: Gwynedd and
     Anglesey = 0.9384, Conwy = 0.9257, Denbighshire and Flintshire = 0.9049, north
     Pembs = 0.8575, Wrexham = 0.9357, Powys = 0.9084, Ceredigion = 0.8896, south
     and mid Pembs = 0.9199, Swansea and Neath/Port Talbot = 0.9332, Carmarthenshire
     = 0.8223, Valleys = 0.8803, Newport and Monmouthshire = 0.9205, Cardiff = 0.9055
     and the Vale and Bridgend = 0.9075.

3   In the event the census analysis did record frequencies of the response 'Welsh'
     entered in the slot 'Any other White background'. Aitchison and Carter show that
     local authority areas did differ to some extent in the frequencies with which 'Welsh'
     was marked, even though the results are not valid. They were in the range between
     5.8 per cent (Flintshire) and 26.8 per cent (Gwynedd), with an overall frequency of 14
     per cent. Other relatively high areas were Carmarthenshire (23.4 per cent), Ceredigion
     (21.8 per cent) and Anglesey (19.4 per cent). Other low areas were Monmouthshire
     (6.9 per cent), Wrexham (9.4 per cent) and Torfaen (9.8 per cent).

4   When conducting linear multiple regression analyses using nominal data, such as place
     of birth, place of residence or socio-economic class, these variables must be recoded
     into binary 'dummy' variables (the sex variable satisfies this condition; see Norušis,
     1990). When attempting to use variables such as the Balsom categories and social class
     variables that consist of more than two (that is, non-binary variables), this is slightly more
     problematic. The general rule of thumb here is that $k - 1$ dummy variables are con-
     structed for a qualitative variable with k categories (where k stands for the overall number
     of categories, see Hardy, 1993; Lewis-Beck, 1993b). One of the categories for these
     variables is then used as a 'reference category', the choice of which Hardy points out
     is statistically arbitrary, which the other categories in a given variable are then
     measured against. For the Balsom variable, 'Y Fro Gymraeg' was used as the reference
     category, while for class the reference category chosen was professional/managerial.

5   In the light of our most recent analyses of Welsh identification in the North American
     diaspora, we can add that 'the real Wales' can plausibly be said to have vitality well
     beyond Wales too.

REFERENCES

Aitchison, J. and Carter, H. (2004). *Spreading the Word: The Welsh Language 2001*,
     Talybont: Y Lolfa.
Anderson, B. (1983). *Imagined Communities: Reflections on the Origins and Spread of
     Nationalism*, London: Verso.
Balsom, D. (1985). 'The three-Wales model', in J. Osmond (ed.), *The National Question
     Again: Political Identity in the 1980s*, Llandysul: Gomer Press.
Balsom, D., Madgwick, P. and Van Mechelen, D. (1983). 'The red and the green: patterns
     of partisan choice in Wales', *British Journal of Political Science*, 13, 299–325.
Balsom, D., Madgwick, P. and Van Mechelen, D. (1984). 'The political consequences of
     Welsh identity', *Ethnic and Racial Studies*, 7, 1, 160–81.

Coupland, N., (2005). Reviews of R. Williams (2003), *Who Speaks for Wales?*, Cardiff: University of Wales Press, and C. Williams et al. (eds) (2003), *A Tolerant Nation?*, Cardiff: University of Wales Press, *Journal of Multilingual and Multicultural Development*, 26, 1, 80–3.

Coupland, N., Bishop, H. and Garrett, P. (2003). 'Home truths: globalisation and the iconising of Welsh in a Welsh-American newspaper', *Journal of Multilingual and Multicultural Development*, 24, 3, 153–77.

Coupland, N., Bishop, H., Williams, A., Evans, B. and Garrett, P. (2005). 'Affiliation, engagement, language use and vitality: secondary school students' subjective orientations to Welsh and Welshness', *Journal of Bilingualism and Bilingual Education*, 8, 1, 1–24.

Dicks, B. (2000). *Heritage, Place and Community*, Cardiff: University of Wales Press.

Fevre, R. and Thompson, A. (eds) (1999). *Nation, Identity and Social Theory: Perspectives from Wales*, Cardiff: University of Wales Press.

Garrett, P., Coupland, N. and Bishop, H. (2005). 'Globalisation and the visualisation of Wales and Welsh America: *Y Drych*, 1948–2001', *Ethnicities*, 5, 4.

Garrett, P., Coupland, N. and Williams, A. (2003). *Investigating Language Attitudes: Social Meanings of Dialect, Ethnicity and Performance*, Cardiff: University of Wales Press.

Hardy, M. A. (1993). 'Regression with dummy variables', in M. S. Lewis-Beck (ed.), *Regression Analysis*, London: Sage.

Hobsbawm, E. and Ranger, T. (eds) (1983). *The Invention of Tradition*, Cambridge: Cambridge University Press.

Lewis-Beck, M. S. (ed.) (1993a). *Regression Analysis*, London: Sage.

Lewis-Beck, M. S. (1993b). 'Applied regression: an introduction', in M. S. Lewis-Beck (ed.), *Regression Analysis*, London: Sage.

Morgan, N. and Pritchard, A. (2003). 'Visualising mythic dreamlands: exploring contemporary postcard representations of Wales', *Journal of Tourism and Cultural Change*, 1, 2, 111–30.

Norušis, M. J. (1990). *SPSS Advanced Statistics Student Guide*, Chicago: SPSS Inc.

Smith, D. (1984). *Wales? Wales!* London: Allen and Unwin.

Williams, C. (ed.) (2003). *A Tolerant Nation? Exploring Ethnic Diversity in Wales*, Cardiff: University of Wales Press.

Williams, G. A. (1985). *When was Wales?* London: Penguin.

Williams, R. (2004). *Who Speaks for Wales?* Cardiff: University of Wales Press.

2. WELSH IDENTITY AND LANGUAGE IN SWANSEA, 1960–2002

Charlotte Aull Davies, Nickie Charles and Chris Harris

ABSTRACT

This article is based on a study of family and social change in Swansea using data from survey and ethnographic research carried out in 2002–3. The research was designed as a re-study of the classic study The Family and Social Change: A Study of Family and Kinship in a South Wales Town *(Rosser and Harris, 1965) carried out in Swansea in the early 1960s. We focus on changes in Welsh identity and language over the intervening four decades. The two collectivities 'Welsh' and 'non-Welsh' originally defined by Rosser and Harris on the basis of language are located in the 2002 survey and compared with the 1960 findings on a range of indicators. Changes in the position of the Welsh language – the increas in percentage of Welsh speakers among younger age groups, but its decline as a household language – are discussed, along with ethnographic data on perceptions about the language and its relationship to Welsh identity. The altered theoretical approach to ethnic and cultural identity since the 1960s is noted, and we use both our survey and ethnographic data from three contrasting areas, including one with a comparatively high ethnic minority population, to examine ideas about Welsh identity in contemporary Swansea. We conclude with observations about the policy implications of some of our findings.*

INTRODUCTION

The classic study *The Family and Social Change: A Study of Family and Kinship in a South Wales Town* (Rosser and Harris, 1965) was based on a survey of 2000 individuals and ethnographic research carried out in Swansea in the early 1960s. The study was concerned primarily with the nature and role of extended families in urban Britain under changing social conditions, especially increasing social and geographic mobility, and it was particularly intended as a comparison with the study that had been carried out in Bethnal Green in London by Young and Wilmott (1957). While addressing this broad comparative task, Rosser and Harris also managed to engage effectively with the specificity of their research site as a Welsh town and in the process provided an invaluable insight into Welsh culture and identity in the Swansea of the early 1960s. Beginning in 2001 we have conducted a re-study that reproduced the 1960 survey and, in addition, we have carried out extensive ethnographic research into the family in Swansea at the start of the twenty-first century. In this article we are primarily concerned with changes and continuities in Welsh culture and identity over the forty-year period between the two studies. We discuss the construction of the survey and choice of areas for ethnographic studies, before considering the measure of Welshness devised by Rosser and Harris to identify culturally Welsh individuals and comparing their findings about this collectivity with those drawn from the 2002 survey. In the next section, we focus more explicitly on the Welsh language in Swansea and changes in its position over these four decades. Finally, we discuss the shift in understanding of ethnicity since the original study and, using the broader definition of Welsh identity, based on self-assessment, that we developed for the 2002 survey, we look at its characteristics in the survey population and consider how it can be better understood with reference to our ethnographic data.

THE STUDY

The survey on which this article draws was administered between May and September 2002 and was a replication of the original survey conducted in 1960. The 2002 survey covers the electoral wards that correspond to the area included in the original survey and which, at that time, comprised the then County Borough of Swansea. The sample for the 1960 survey was a systematic random sample of the electoral register, constructed by taking every fiftieth name. The survey consisted of 1962 completed interviews, an achieved sample of 87 per cent (Rosser and Harris, 1965, p. 37). The 2002 survey tried to remain as close as possible to the original survey, while making necessary adjustments as required by changes in both social and theoretical environments (Davies and Charles, 2002). Those changes that were most significant for the subject matter of this article had to do with changes in cultural indicators of social status and changes in theoretical approaches to ethnic and cultural identities. Both are discussed later in this article. The 2002 survey sample was also constructed from the electoral register using systematic random sampling. The survey consisted of 1,000 completed interviews which represented an achieved sample of 43 per cent. The difference in the two percentages for achieved samples in 1960 and 2002 is a stark indication of the changes in the climate for social research over the past four decades.

The core of the interview schedule asked for detailed information about respondents' household composition, frequency and nature of contact with a broad range of relatives, patterns of residence since birth, and any marriage or marriage-like relationships. We also asked about employment, social class, religion, and ethnic and cultural identities. Here we are concerned with findings related to Welsh identity and language.[1]

The data from the 1960 survey were supplemented by detailed case histories of individuals taken from their random sample, as well as by participant observation – the two researchers 'lived in Swansea throughout the period of the study' (1965, p. 35) – and the study included ethnographic data from two localities, namely, Morriston and Sketty. We were able to incorporate more systematic and extensive ethnographic research in the re-study. We carried out semi-structured interviewing and six months' participant-observation in each of three areas of Swansea, selected for their distinctive characteristics. Interviews were conducted with 102 women and 57 men between the ages of 18 and 92 and were evenly distributed across these three areas. Participant observation took place in a variety of settings, including schools, local societies, religious organizations, carol services, St David's Day celebrations and community centres. The interviews mainly took place in people's homes and lasted between one and three hours. Of the three selected areas, the first, Fairview, was affluent, the second, Pen-cwm, was an area of deprivation, and the third, Parklands, was an inner-city area with a relatively high minority ethnic population.[2] All but one of our minority ethnic interviewees lived in this third area.

Fairview is an affluent suburban area centred on an old fishing village, with mainly terraced housing, surrounded by areas of more recent mainly detached houses with larger gardens. It is relatively homogeneous in terms of ethnicity and occupation, with 98.7 per cent describing themselves as 'white' in the 2001 census and almost two-thirds in professional and managerial occupations, compared with 16 per cent in manual occupations. The percentage able to speak, read and/or write Welsh is 10.8 per cent.[3]

Pen-cwm is one of the most deprived council estates in Swansea and one of the two or three areas with the worst reputation for crime and vandalism. It is in the top three within the City and County of Swansea for entitlement to free school meals and among the first 15 of 865 divisions in Wales on the index of multiple deprivation. Most housing (70 per cent) is a mix of older council houses and new housing association houses, with only very few (21 per cent) privately owned houses. This area too is relatively homogeneous in terms of ethnicity (99.5 per cent described themselves as 'white' in the 2001 census) and occupation (over half are in manual occupations, only 14 per cent in professional or managerial occupations). The percentage able to speak, read and/or write Welsh is 7.6 per cent.

In contrast to the social and cultural homogeneity of these two areas, Parklands is much more heterogeneous. It is ethnically mixed with 8.3 per cent of its population being 'non-white', most Bangladeshi (4.3 per cent). Housing is a mixture of large and small terraced houses, 56.5 per cent of which are owner occupied. The rest is either socially (13 per cent) or privately (30.5 per cent) rented. Occupationally it is also heterogeneous with the population fairly evenly spread between professional and managerial, secretarial and clerical, and manual work. The percentage of the population able to speak, read and/or write Welsh is 9.2 per cent.

Thus our findings in this article are based on: a random sample of 1,000 individuals drawn using the electoral register to ensure geographic spread over the city as a whole (although based, for comparative purposes, on the old county borough boundaries, rather than on the current City and County of Swansea); and ethnographic research in three areas of the city with contrasting social profiles intended to provide greater depth to the statistical findings.

'VERY WELSH' IN 1960 AND 2002

In their study of the extended family in Swansea in the early 1960s, Rosser and Harris looked at how it might be affected by the horizontal divisions of social class. They also considered a vertical division of the population based on cultural difference between the 'Welsh' on the one hand and the 'non-Welsh' on the other and compared these two collectivities on a wide range of factors relevant for understanding the nature of family and kinship relations. In order to examine the behavioural attributes of these divisions of class and culture, they first had to define them, so as to be able to assign individual respondents to a social class and a cultural collectivity ('Welsh' or 'non-Welsh'). To determine social class, they developed a complex and innovative procedure using three dimensions: the occupation of their respondent (or husband's occupation in the case of married women); the occupation of the respondent's father; and the respondent's self-assessment as to which class they belonged (1965, pp. 99–105). To determine the cultural division, they used a procedure based on two dimensions: Welsh-speaking ability of the respondent; and Welsh-speaking ability of the respondent's parents. They did not include the dimension of self-assessment, remarking that they were 'not here concerned with Welsh as a nationality . . . but with Welsh as a distinctive regional culture within Britain' (1965, p. 118). Thus respondents were deemed culturally 'Welsh' if either they or at least one parent were Welsh speaking, fluently or partly. This produced a 'Welsh' category of 896 persons (46 per cent of the sample) and a 'non-Welsh' category of 1061 persons (54 per cent). When we applied Rosser and Harris's definitions of 'Welsh' and 'non-Welsh' to the 2002 survey of 1,000 individuals, we found a 'Welsh' category of 331 persons (33 per cent) and a 'non-Welsh' category of 658 persons (66 per cent).

In the 'Welsh' category of the 1960 survey, 100 persons (5.1 per cent of the sample) were themselves Welsh speaking but did not have Welsh-speaking parents – 'probably having learnt it compulsorily at school, or possibly through marrying a Welsh-speaking spouse' (1965, p. 121). In the 2002 survey, there were 37 individuals in this category (3.7 per cent). Two of these had attended Welsh-medium schools and another seven had Welsh-speaking spouses or partners. We can only speculate as to where the other 28 acquired their Welsh, although the growth in Welsh classes for adults offers another possible explanation. In the next section we look at some of the motivations for learning Welsh among adults.

In examining the characteristics of their 'Welsh' and 'non-Welsh' collectivities, Rosser and Harris noted that the 'Welsh' group was older, with a mean age of 50.5, whereas the mean age of the 'non-Welsh' group was 46.2. This age discrepancy between the two groups increased slightly in the 2002 survey, and the survey population as a whole was older than in 1960. Thus in 2002 the 'Welsh' group had a mean age of 57.3 as compared to a mean age of 49.2 for the 'non-Welsh' group.

Rosser and Harris also noted that this variable measuring cultural Welshness had an identifiable spatial expression in the geography of Swansea. Basically they found that the north-eastern part of Swansea (the area they identified as the Tawe Valley, encompassing districts such as Morriston, Llansamlet and Bonymaen) had the highest proportion of residents – approximately two-thirds – who were culturally 'Welsh' on their measure. The town centre was the least 'Welsh', with approximately one-third of its residents being 'Welsh' on this measure. The coastal areas of west Swansea, such as Sketty and the Uplands, were intermediate on this measure, having about 40 per cent 'Welsh' (1965, p. 141). In the 2002 survey this basic pattern is unaltered with the highest proportion of 'Welsh' respondents remaining in the districts of the north-east and the lowest in the town centre. However, the Tawe Valley districts also registered the greatest decline (of just over 50 per cent), whereas some of the intermediate localities in 1960 actually recorded a percentage increase in 'Welsh' respondents in 2002 (see table 2.1).

Table 2.1
'Welsh'/'Non-Welsh' composition of selected localities in 1960 and 2002

	Locality					
	Morriston Glais	Morriston Llansamlet[2]	Sketty Uplands	Sketty Uplands	Mumbles Langland Killay West Cross	Newton Oystermouth Killay West Cross
	(1960)[1]	(2002)	(1960)	(2002)	(1960)	(2002)
'Welsh'	84%	41%	41%	27%	25%	33%
'Non-Welsh'	16%	59%	59%	73%	75%	67%
Total %	100%	100%	100%	100%	100%	100%
Total number	176	199	180	203	174	104

[1] 1960 figures from Rosser and Harris (1965, p. 141).
[2] Names and boundaries of some electoral districts have changed; localities in 2002 are approximations of those of 1960.

As they did with social class, Rosser and Harris looked at a number of cultural indicators to see if the categories they had constructed tended to show a systematic difference in relation to these indicators. In the case of the 'Welsh'/'non-Welsh' division, they looked for differences in indicators such as attitude to teaching Welsh to all in Swansea schools, Sunday opening of pubs, religious denomination and attendance at religious services. The role of such cultural indicators in the conduct of a re-study is quite problematic given the likely changes in their cultural significance during the intervening period of over four decades (see Davies and Charles, 2002 for a fuller discussion of these issues). For example, Rosser and Harris found the 'Welsh' group to be significantly more opposed to Sunday opening of pubs (58 per cent to 41 per cent). Clearly an indicator such as this has little relevance in the Wales of 2002 and we had no equivalent question on the 2002 survey. However, we have tried to compare the two groups on these cultural indicators where it seemed reasonable and meaningful to do so, and these findings are shown in table 2.2.

Table 2.2
'Welsh'/'Non-Welsh' cultural differences in 1960 and 2002 – all values are percentages

Topic	Replies	1960[1] 'Welsh'	'Non-Welsh'	Total	Topic	Replies	2002 'Welsh'	'Non-Welsh'	Total
Where brought up	In Wales	97	79	88	Where brought up	In Wales	94	73	80
	Outside Wales	3	21	12		Outside Wales	6	27	20
House ownership	Owners	56	41	48	Do you own this house/flat?	Yes	76	71	73
	Corporation tenants	22	35	29		No	24	29	27
	Tenants of other landlords	22	24	23					
Should Welsh be taught to all in Swansea's schools?	Yes	82	64	72	Agree with existing policy that all children be taught Welsh?	Yes	72	59	64
	No	13	26	20		No	28	41	36
	Don't know	5	10	8					
Religious denomination	Welsh Nonconformist	30	2	15	Religious denomination (for those with some religious attachment, n=327)	Welsh Nonconformist	6	1	3
	English Nonconformist	26	23	24		English Nonconformist	27	17	21
	Anglican	38	61	51		Church in Wales/Anglican	39	43	41
	Roman Catholic	4	10	7		Roman Catholic	11	20	16
	Other	2	4	3		Other/no response	17	19	19
Parents belong to Welsh-speaking church or chapel?	Yes	57	3	28	One or both parents belong to Welsh-speaking church or chapel?	Yes	46	2	17
	No	43	97	72		No	54	98	83
Subject (or husband) follows:	Rugby	22	16	18	Subject (or spouse/partner) follows:	Rugby	33	21	25
	Soccer	27	36	32		Soccer	8	15	13
	Both	16	14	15		Both	28	27	27
	Neither	35	34	35		Neither/no response	31	37	35

[1] 1960 figures from Rosser and Harris (1965, pp. 122–3).

For some of the indicators there has been very little change in either collectivity over the past four decades, for example, in where the respondent was brought up. In the matter of home ownership, any significant difference between 'Welsh' and 'non-Welsh' collectivities has disappeared with large increases in the percentage of home owners across both categories. Rosser and Harris found the 'Welsh' group to be more strongly in favour of teaching Welsh compulsorily to all children (82 per cent to 64 per cent). In the 2002 survey we asked a different, but comparable question about the existing education policy that all children be taught Welsh in schools and found that the two groups had moved closer together on this issue, with 72 per cent of the 'Welsh' group and 59 per cent of the 'non-Welsh' group in favour of this policy, but overall there had been a decline in those favouring 'compulsory' Welsh in schools. This may be an artefact of changes in the social context, in particular the much stronger interpretation of 'compulsory' Welsh in 2002, which requires it to be taught up to age sixteen in all Welsh schools, compared to 1960, when it was not compulsory at examination level.

Our main finding with respect to religious indicators was that these were no longer particularly relevant. In the 1960 survey, respondents were asked 'Which denomination do you belong to?' and 98 per cent responded by giving their denomination. In 2002 we asked a much weaker question, namely 'Do you feel any sense of belonging to or connection with any religious group or organization?' and only one-third of our respondents said yes. However, when we examine this subset of 327 respondents who claim some religious affiliation for differences between 'Welsh' and 'non-Welsh' categories, there is only one significant change since the 1960 survey which is the collapse of membership in Welsh Nonconformist denominations. This has fallen from 30 per cent of the 'Welsh' category in 1960 to 6 per cent of those in the 'Welsh' category who said they had some religious attachment in 2002. This collapse has occurred in spite of the fact that the percentage of the 'Welsh' category with one or both parents who had belonged to a Welsh-speaking church or chapel showed a decrease of only 11 points, from 57 to 46 per cent.

Interestingly for those who see national sports teams as significant for national identity, the percentage among the 'Welsh' category who follow rugby has increased from 22 to 33 per cent. This will be discussed more fully in the section on Welsh identity.

Rosser and Harris also looked at differences between the 'Welsh' and 'non-Welsh' regarding questions of household composition and family size. They noted in particular that a greater proportion of the 'Welsh' were in households of 'married couple alone' and a smaller proportion were in households of 'parents and unmarried children'. These differences are also apparent in the data from the 2002 survey as shown in table 2.3.

Table 2.3
Household composition for 'Welsh'/'Non-Welsh' in 1960 and 2002
– all values are percentages

Household type	1960[1]			2002		
	'Welsh'	'Non-Welsh'	Total	'Welsh'	'Non-Welsh'	Total
Person living alone	5	5	5	23	18	20
Married (or cohabiting, 2002) couples alone	22	17	19	35	30	32
Parent(s) and unmarried children	44	54	49	39	46	43
Others	29	24	27	3	6	5

[1] 1960 figures from Rosser and Harris (1965, p. 158).

A major reason for these differences in the 1960 data was that the 'Welsh' collectivity was on average older than the 'non-Welsh', which meant that a higher proportion were likely to be in a later phase of the family cycle, with children having moved out of the natal household, consequently leaving their parents on their own again. Nevertheless, Rosser and Harris argued that this explanation of the difference was partial and that 'the Welsh tend to have smaller families on the average than their non-Welsh counterparts, and they appear to have a larger proportion of childless couples' (1965, p. 160). They deduced this from two pieces of evidence. First, looking at the 297 married respondents without children, they noted that 64 per cent were 'Welsh' and only 36 per cent were 'non-Welsh', and, given that only 46 per cent of the sample were 'Welsh', this clearly suggested a greater likelihood of 'Welsh' couples being childless. When we looked at the group of married or cohabiting respondents in the 2002 survey, however, we found that this disproportionate level of childlessness among 'Welsh' couples no longer pertains. In fact, we found only 34 per cent of these childless couples to be 'Welsh', a figure that is virtually the same as the proportion of 'Welsh' respondents in our sample. The second piece of evidence that Rosser and Harris put forward to support their assertion was a consideration of the number of children born to married women aged over forty in the sample, arguing that this could be taken as their completed family size, with only a very few exceptions. They noted a strong tendency for smaller family sizes among the 'Welsh' collectivity and this was even more apparent when they looked just at the Welsh speakers from this group. When we repeated this analysis with the

2002 survey data, we found a similar pattern (see table 2.4). Thus 'Welsh' women were slightly more likely to have no children and more likely to have one or two children than 'non-Welsh' women, but less likely to have more than two children. When we looked at Welsh speakers only, this overall trend was intensified, with the percentage having no children increasing dramatically. These figures for Welsh-speaking women must be treated with caution due to the small size of this subset (n=32), but they do support the general conclusion that the 'Welsh' still tend to have smaller family sizes than the 'non-Welsh'.

Table 2.4
Family size of married women over forty for 'Welsh'/'Non-Welsh' in 1960 and 2002
– all values are percentages

Number of children born	1960[1] 'Welsh'	'Non-Welsh'	Welsh speakers n=203	Total N=595	2002 'Welsh'	'Non-Welsh'	Welsh speakers n=32	Total N=213
None	19	14	21	16	7	7	19	7
1 or 2	52	43	57	48	67	59	56	62
3 to 5	22	30	16	26	26	33	25	30
6 or more	7	13	6	10	0	1	0	1

[1] 1960 figures from Rosser and Harris (1965, p. 179).

This finding is linked to the well-known relationship between declining birth rates and increasing social class and educational levels. Although there were no significant differences between 'Welsh' and 'non-Welsh' on these latter two measures, when we compared Welsh speakers with non-Welsh speakers, we found 43.1 per cent of Welsh speakers in professional and managerial classes compared to 32.4 per cent of non-Welsh speakers. When we looked at educational levels, 38.1 per cent of Welsh speakers stayed in full-time education to age eighteen or over compared to 26.0 per cent of non-Welsh speakers.

Rosser and Harris also looked at the frequency of occurrence, among both Welsh speakers and non-Welsh speakers, of what they termed 'cross-cultural marriages', that is, marriages with one partner Welsh speaking and the other not. They were able to show that the frequency of such marriages was significantly greater for Welsh speakers than for non-Welsh speakers and furthermore that this frequency increased among those Welsh speakers who were more recently married while remaining virtually unchanged for non-Welsh speakers. When we introduced data from the 2002 survey, it was clear that this trend had continued to accelerate over the past forty years (see table 2.5).[4] Thus in our sample of 25

Welsh-speaking men in a relationship (marriage or cohabitation) that had begun since 1960, 17 (68 per cent) were in 'cross-cultural' marriages; out of 24 Welsh-speaking married or cohabiting women in a relationship that had begun since 1960, 18 (75 per cent) were in 'cross-cultural' marriages. The comparable percentages for non-Welsh-speaking men and women were 10.4 per cent and 6.8 per cent respectively.

Table 2.5
Changing proportion of cross-language marriages

Date of marriage	1914–39[1]		1940–60		1961–2002	
Language	Welsh-speaking (fluent or part)	Non-Welsh-speaking	Welsh-speaking (fluent or part)	Non-Welsh-speaking	Welsh-speaking (fluent or part)	Non-Welsh-speaking
Of men	26%	12%	43%	15%	68%	10%
Of women	23%	15%	48%	13%	75%	7%
Total number	231	382	202	523	49	390

[1] 1914–1939 and 1940–1960 figures from Rosser and Harris (1965, p. 246).

Important as these variables of social class and culture were for their characterization of society in Swansea, Rosser and Harris did not find them useful indicators of the retention or importance of kinship ties. 'The differences in the organization of the extended family by social class in Swansea, or by the Welsh/non-Welsh distinction, are slight, and only barely discernible' (1965, p. 290). Nor have the results of the 2002 survey altered this finding. However, ethnographic data reveal a widely held perception that 'very Welsh' families, often interpreted as those having Welsh-language links if not necessarily being Welsh-speaking households, place greater importance on extended family ties.

One woman in her fifties described how her extended family had been centred on her grandmother:

It was a matriarchal, I think that's probably a Welsh way actually, the mother probably does rule. But it certainly was in our house, and we were all very close to my grandmother. She was the nucleus, and we all, we were all very close to her. My mother, my sister, and my cousins, all girls, all women, very close to my grandmother. And she was the centre, she was the nucleus, yes. And she lived until she was 96, so yes, and her mother before her had been the same, and she'd lived until she was 95, so it is that sort of family unit. Yes. And they were all based in Swansea.

This extended family had been entirely Welsh speaking – including the grand-father who had come to Wales from Ireland – until the respondent's generation: 'My grandparents, both my grandparents, both sides of grandparents and my parents and all the aunts, they all spoke Welsh. We can understand it, but don't speak it very well. No. Which is a shame.'

Another interviewee felt that such close extended families, which she linked to Welshness, were disappearing in her part of west Swansea, but could still be found in other nearby areas:

I think all that Welshness has gone. You know, you go and there'd be, everything would be out for you, you know, they'd be baking, and you'd have these big family teas, you know . . . I think you'll find this part of Swansea totally different to some parts of Swansea, where it's still, even parts of Mayhill I would think and Townhill, they are far more family orientated there, they have big families there, and they all, you know, intermingle and intermarry, and that's more like this part of Swansea was years ago. You know, and Neath is another place . . . if you go to parts of Neath, that is like Swansea was years ago. And, you know, they, I go there quite a lot and I find that they are still very Welsh. In their family life, family outlook. (Female, sixties)

Two other interviewees contrasted the importance of families in Welsh culture with what they perceived to be their lesser role in English culture. One, referring to his experience of attending a funeral of a family member in England, noted, 'So all their family with wives came. Actually in much more, smaller numbers than our family. Because English people, I don't think on the whole the English members of the family have quite the same kind of family attachment as the Welsh do' (male, fifties). The second said that the importance of family may remain in some parts of England, 'but in the bigger conurbations, you know, Manchester, the Midlands and London, where I have had friends and met them, and spent time with them, I didn't feel that they had the same sort of attitude towards their family connections that I had towards mine' (female, seventies).

Thus many of our interviewees believed that large extended families that retained fairly close ties, for example, by coming together for important ceremonial occasions – such as funerals, which were mentioned more than once, along with weddings, an eighty-fifth birthday celebration and a music recital – were a defining feature of Welsh culture. For many this type of family is archetypically Welsh and may include an association with the Welsh language. Several felt that this type of family was less characteristic of present-day Welsh culture, or at least that it was to be found in other nearby communities rather than their own neighbourhood; and a few contrasted this aspect of Welshness with English culture.

THE WELSH LANGUAGE IN SWANSEA

In the 1960 survey, 28.5 per cent of respondents said that they could speak Welsh, 16 per cent fluently and 12.5 per cent partly. When we repeated this question in 2002, we found 15.5 per cent to be Welsh speaking, 7.5 per cent fluently and 8.0 per cent partly. The 2001 census reported 13.4 per cent Welsh speaking in the City and County of Swansea and 22.5 per cent having 'one or more Welsh language skills' which include 'understands spoken Welsh' in addition to speaking, reading and writing Welsh. However, whereas Rosser and Harris reported a steady decline in the percentage of Welsh speakers across the generations (1965, p. 118–19), we found an increase of 4 per cent in the number of fluent Welsh speakers in the youngest generation in our survey (born 1965–84) over the previous generation (born 1950–64), as is seen in table 2.6. The 2001 census suggests this increase will continue as it reported 21.8 per cent of people aged three to fifteen in Swansea to be Welsh speaking. This increase in the proportion of the population who can speak Welsh and its concentrations in the younger generation over the past four decades has been attributed primarily to the growth of Welsh-medium education, and our findings bear this out. Whereas in the sample as a whole 40 per cent of fluent Welsh speakers had attended Welsh-medium schools, among those in our youngest generation (born 1965–84), 71 per cent had attended Welsh-medium schools.

Table 2.6
Welsh speakers by generation in 2002

Welsh speaking?	Born before 1934	Born 1934–49	Born 1950–64	Born 1965–84
Fluent	14.3%	7.2%	2.3%	6.3%
Part	14.3%	8.3%	4.6%	4.9%
Not	71.3%	84.5%	93.1%	88.8%
Total number	230	277	217	268

Although our survey did not provide any data on other means by which people become Welsh speakers, our ethnographic interviews revealed a variety of motivations for adults learning Welsh. One eighty-five-year-old woman reported that her sister had learnt Welsh as a consequence of marrying into a Welsh-speaking family farther up the Swansea Valley:

And they are all Welsh up there you see, and of course she is all Welsh now, she brought the family up Welsh, because she married a Welsh man. I mean my father was Welsh, but as I said before my mother was English, we spoke English at home . . . But when Eileen got married, she got into all the Welsh, and she speaks Welsh now fluently, you see. And she brought the children up in Welsh. And they have brought their children up in Welsh you see. And their grandchildren are all Welsh, when you speak to them they are all Welsh, you see. (Female, eighties)

Another reported that her daughter's motivations were of a more instrumental nature:

[My eldest daughter] was eight when she came here [from England]. She did not consider herself Welsh at all . . . [My other daughter] was three, and does consider herself Welsh . . . And she took Welsh right through school, took A-level Welsh. Because she said 'I want to stay in Wales, if I want a good job in Wales I need to have Welsh.' And she went to Aberystwyth you see, very much a Welsh college. And she didn't carry on with her Welsh at Aberystwyth . . . but since she has come back to Cardiff, she has spent time brushing up her Welsh, and of course, if she hadn't had the Welsh she wouldn't have got the job in Cardiff University. So her ideas as a teenager turned out to be wise. If she wanted a job in Wales she would have to have the Welsh. (Female, sixties)

As the above example suggests, decisions to learn Welsh are often linked *inter alia* to issues of personal identity, with some interviewees learning the language as a further expression of their Welsh identity:

So I'm Welsh from my upbringing, even though it was, although I heard a lot of Welsh, but the immediate family, we spoke mostly English. Although there were words, we did speak some Welsh. And then it's partly a matter of choice, I've chosen to learn Welsh. And I've chosen to send my children to a Welsh school. So it's partly a matter, I suppose, of defining your own identity. You know you can say you are Welsh, but in what way, so I've chosen to learn the language and bring my children up. And it's a sort of gut thing as well, it's what you feel, you know. It's how you feel when you are away, and all that sort of stuff. I just am Welsh, and that's where my heart is, you know. (Female, forties)

Another interviewee, whose family had moved to Wales from England when she was a child, described a process of becoming Welsh in which learning the language had played a central role. In explaining her choice of a Welsh national identity as 'totally subjective', she emphasized:

the experience of learning a second language, and to the extent that I don't want that to be my second language, I want it to be part of me and how I see myself and being my kind of world I suppose. But the main thing is just that this is where I feel at home and this is where I understand myself and what I feel, giving me who I am. And it's not in an exclusive way, it's not that I want to be acknowledged as Welsh and not English, I don't mean it in that sense . . . But then there are relationships which I formed with people which I know purely only from speaking through the medium of Welsh. And a lot of cultural issues which are close to me are completely tied up with the Welsh language. A lot of experiences I've gone through just from the very experience of learning a minority language. So it's very important in the way I've been shaped. (Female, twenties)

We consider the question of the links between the Welsh language and Welsh identity further in the next section.

These comparatively optimistic findings regarding the Welsh language in Swansea and the effectiveness of Welsh-medium education must be tempered when we look at evidence for the use of the language within households. Only 8 respondents in our sample of 1,000 reported that Welsh was the primary language of the household, with another 11 saying that both Welsh and English were normally spoken in the household. Thus, although 15.5 per cent of Swansea households in our survey contain at least one Welsh speaker, only 1.9 per cent used Welsh as a normal household language, either as the primary language or alongside English. Certainly in some instances our respondent was the only Welsh-speaking member of the household. However, when we looked only at Welsh-speaking respondents who lived in a household with at least one other Welsh speaker, we found that in only 11 out of 45 households (24.4 per cent) was Welsh either the primary language or one of the languages of the household. When we looked at households where both the respondent and their spouse/partner were Welsh speakers, this figure drops further to 17.8 per cent (5 households out of 28). Although the very low numbers in these subsets require caution in their interpretation, it is clear that, in spite of increasing numbers of Welsh speakers, Welsh as a language of communication *within* families and households is on the verge of disappearing in Swansea. Furthermore, although the increasing likeli-hood of 'cross-cultural' marriages among Welsh speakers, that was identified by Rosser and Harris and that we found to have continued, may provide part of the explanation, these results argue that this is only a partial answer and that even households with both partners Welsh speaking are not likely to use the language at home. Rosser and Harris recognized that this was likely to occur with the breakdown of the spatial concentration of Welsh speakers that resulted from the creation of the new housing estates in the 1950s and 1960s:

The Corporation in the allocation of its 14,000 Corporation houses took no account of Welsh-speaking in its selection of tenants . . . The net result from the point of view of the Welsh-speakers was a sort of random scattering over the fifteen estates, with the inevitable consequences of this dispersion from the point of view of the language. Had, say, one of the fifteen estates been designated primarily for Welsh-speaking tenants a social concentration could have been produced sufficient to ensure the preservation of the language as the natural and dominant means of communication. (1965, p. 133)

Certainly the figures from the 2002 survey giving the percentages of 'Welsh' people in different parts of Swansea bear out the continued dispersion of Welsh speakers across the area. Particularly telling is the collapse in percentages of Welsh speakers in the older industrial communities of the Swansea Valley, leading to a loss of Welsh as a community language, which cannot be compensated by the increasing percentages of Welsh speakers in areas such as Sketty and Mumbles.

Rosser and Harris were also prescient in their recognition that education alone was not sufficient to retain the language. 'No matter how much Welsh is taught to schoolchildren, there can be little hope of the language surviving as a living tongue if the opportunities, and indeed the necessity, of speaking it in the daily lives of adults are constantly disappearing' (1965, p. 133). Certainly the Welsh-medium school movement has been vital in halting the decline and indeed increasing the percentage of those who are able to speak Welsh. But, as has been found in other studies (Gruffudd, 2000; Williams and Morris, 2000), it appears that fluency in Welsh acquired through education does not automatically transfer into the use of Welsh in families and households, nor in public places, even when the opportunity exists. In Swansea this appears to be the next major challenge facing those who hope to reinstate Swansea's Welsh-language heritage.[5]

WELSH IDENTITY

As already noted, Rosser and Harris elected not to include any element of self-assessment in the determination of their 'Welsh' category. Given that 86 per cent of the population of Swansea in the 1961 census were born in Wales, any such inclusion would doubtless have increased the size of the category, probably to the point of its not providing any useful basis for comparison. Although they do sometimes refer to the 'non-Welsh' category as 'English', Rosser and Harris recognized that this large collectivity was 'a very mixed bag of English, Irish, and Scots immigrants (or their descendants) together with a substantial – and annually increasing – proportion of anglicized Welsh at least "twice removed" by the test of language from Welsh cultural traditions' (1965, p. 121).

Since the 1960s the theoretical treatment of ethnic and cultural difference has shifted from a focus on cultural indicators (such as language, religion, food practices etc) that might identify ethnic groups to an interest in how individuals understand, and indeed construct, their ethnic and cultural identities, which are assumed to be multiple, and how these identities affect social interaction. For this reason, in the 2002 survey we included questions designed to provide some insight into the self-assessment of respondents' identity in terms of their identification with Welshness and any alternative, or complementary, ethnic or cultural identities. These questions were as follows:

- Do you consider yourself to be Welsh?
- Do you consider that you have any other cultural, ethnic or national identity?
- If yes, what is this identity?

A large majority of our respondents, 78.8 per cent, identified as Welsh, and 81.6 per cent of these did not lay claim to any other 'cultural, ethnic or national identity'. That is, 64.3 per cent of the entire sample identified as Welsh only. Among the category that we constructed as culturally 'Welsh' following Rosser and Harris (that is, respondents who spoke Welsh or had a Welsh-speaking parent), a significantly higher percentage, 92.4 per cent, self-identified as Welsh. This was slightly higher again (94.7 per cent) among fluent Welsh speakers but slightly lower (91.0 per cent) among all Welsh speakers. Among the 314 respondents who did select another 'cultural, ethnic or national' identity – whether they identified as Welsh or not – the most frequent choice was 'British' (44.3 per cent), followed by 'English' (25.8 per cent) and 'Scottish, Irish or other European identity' (13.3 per cent).

Our ethnographic data have allowed us to look behind these statistics for a better understanding of the meanings people attach to these various identities as well as their reasons for selecting or rejecting them. Those interviewees who claimed a British identity often did so as a rejection of 'separatism' rather than a sense of Britishness as the basis for a cultural identity:

Yes I am Welsh, but I consider myself Welsh but British. To me it's a load of nonsense splitting up the country. We should be living in harmony as British people. Altogether, as a family. Not splitting up. To me it's more important, I think these nationalists coming, look what it's cost in this country, having signs in Welsh, you know, what have you. (Male, seventies)

Others simply saw British identity as a convenient label for what they regarded as mixed parentage:

> I'm Welsh-Scottish. Half and half blood, born in Wales, I'm Welsh. Yeah it's, you know, to fill in forms or anything, nationality, I usually, British. Yeah British I'd say first. I see all of us as British not just separate, but saying that, British, but if I go to Spain or somewhere, and usually you know they say, 'You're English', and I say, 'No, I'm not English, I'm Welsh'. Yeah. They just see everyone from Britain as English, but British really, yeah. (Female, forties)

Interviewees often responded to our questions about identity by reflecting on their ancestry, mainly their parents and grandparents, which is not surprising since they had been told the research was about 'the family'. However, quite a few did not view ancestry as determinative and instead spoke of becoming Welsh, some using the metaphor of adoption, others by virtue of length of residence:

> I'm English, but I feel more Welsh than English, do you know that? And I often think I'd like to be known as an English lady that became a Welsh lady. Because I'm more Welsh than English. How long have I been down here? For over sixty years. That's a long time, isn't it? (Female, eighties)

There were three prominent themes in the meanings that people attached to Welsh identity: the importance of the Welsh language for Welsh identity; the expression of Welsh identity through support for national sports teams, especially rugby; and opposition to English, or occasionally British, identity. Very many of our interviewees in claiming Welsh identity felt obliged to explain their relationship to the Welsh language, in terms of competence as well as their attitude towards it. One said, 'I am Welsh. And I feel ashamed of myself that I don't speak Welsh. Unfortunately I put that down to education. Education policy at school, there is no point starting teaching languages at eleven, and this is a very un-Welsh-speaking area' (female, thirties). Another, asked if he saw himself as Welsh, told us:

> Yes. Even though I sort of go into Welsh mother and toddlers and not being able to speak Welsh is embarrassing, I've always said, I feel I ought to speak Welsh if I call myself Welsh. And I've always said I'm going to learn, but I get nowhere. My wife has tried to teach me but doesn't know enough of the grammar . . . I would need to go to proper lessons, and did look into it a few years back, but they all

started up at six and I'm not going out of work till seven, so it just didn't come together. I tried teaching myself, but I haven't got a particular flair for languages and I struggled. But yeah, I still see myself as Welsh even though I can't necessarily speak Welsh. (Male, thirties)

Most of our interviewees regarded the Welsh language as a positive attribute of Welshness and included some reference to it in their expressions of Welsh identity, often an explanation of why they did not speak Welsh, sometimes just an expression of support for the language. They did not, however, maintain that inability to speak Welsh disqualified them from claiming a Welsh identity, in the way that interviewees frequently did regarding ancestral roots outside Wales. Most seemed to have a proprietary view of the language, regarding it as part of their identity, whether Welsh speaking or not. Two interviewees, both non-Welsh speakers, made specific reference to Welsh road signs as a symbol of home: 'When I come over the Severn Bridge and I see the signs in Welsh, I'm happy' (female, sixties); and:

I'm Welsh and I'm proud that I'm Welsh. When I go over to England, because I mean I do travel around the country, when I go across to England, I say uh, that's England, but as soon as I come to it, I say yes I'm home. As soon as you see that Welsh sign you're home. Yeah. Very important that I'm Welsh. I mean I don't speak Welsh. (Female, thirties)

The second prominent theme raised in our discussions of Welsh identity was sports, particularly rugby, with interviewees often using support for national teams as a kind of touchstone of identity (cf. Jones, 2003). One man said he was 'as Welsh as the hills', an identity he shared with his father 'because he is part of the culture, the rugby and stuff like that, and you know I've grown up in that as well' (male, thirties). In some families, different identities were expressed primarily through support for different national teams. One woman with three children said that she was English, but:

I look at these [the two younger children] as Welsh. And [my brother] sees himself as English as well, I must admit. And my other two see themselves as Welsh now, and it's hard, because they, with the rugby, it's me and [my brother] for England, and then there is three of them, well one English boy and two Welsh boys, and they are supporting Wales, you know, so it's quite comical at times I must admit. (Female, twenties)

Others used the medium of sports to elucidate personal identity: 'I'm a natural-ized Welshman. All four of my grandparents were born in England . . . essen-tially I'm British. I mean, if Wales are playing England, I support Wales. If England are playing Germany, I support England' (male, sixties). This theme tended to be gendered, with men more likely than women to use it to explain their own identity.

The third theme that emerged from the interviews was that of Welsh identity being defined in terms of opposition to English identity and, less frequently, to British identity. Several people spoke of having to correct assumptions that they were English when they travelled abroad (see above):

> I do regard myself as Welsh, certainly when I'm abroad, I tend to automatically say I am Welsh, because there are a lot of things about the English that I'm uncomfortable with. I don't identify that much with the English. So I suppose I feel Welsh. But it's just being a sort of London Welshman you know it's not that clear-cut. And I'm not a sort of beer and rugby type Welshman. (Male, forties)

Interestingly, a few interviewees who identified as English also reported a sensitivity to this distinction: 'When I go abroad I feel more British than when I'm here. Talking to Welsh people here, like my Welsh friends, then I feel English, compared to them' (male, twenties). Those who spoke of Welsh identity in oppos-ition to Britishness generally felt that British identity was in some way under-mining Welsh culture and identity. One spoke of Wales as 'a conquered nation' (male, sixties). A second provided yet another example of the role of sports in defining national identities: 'It annoys me, in things, the Commonwealth games now, any bloody sports as far as that goes, where a Welsh athlete will do well and he suddenly becomes a British athlete. Right? Where an English athlete always stays an English athlete' (male, forties).

In our survey there were only 18 respondents who identified themselves as black or as belonging to another ethnic minority group; of these, only 1 (a black African) also identified as Welsh. A higher proportion of the minority ethnic interviewees in our ethnographic study identified either as Welsh (2 out of 14) or Welsh Bangladeshi (1). Three others included Britishness in their identities: British Muslim; British Asian; and Pakistani British. The ethnographic data provide access to a much more nuanced understanding of the range of relationships to Welsh identity among ethnic minorities. Thus one young woman, born in Bangladesh but who came to Wales when she was three, still felt that her primary identity was Bangladeshi: 'Because although I'm living here, I can't speak Welsh, I don't look like a Welsh person [laughter], I can speak English but I would still say I'm a Bangladeshi Muslim' (female, twenties). A second Bengali woman, born in this country but taken to live in Bangladesh until she was ten, initially rejected any idea that she was Welsh but then reflected further: 'But if I live here, I mean, I should say I'm Welsh because I've stayed that long here. Then I should say I'm Welsh because I stay here. I'm not going to go anywhere!' (female, thirties). Another woman said: 'I would say I was a Welsh Bangladeshi person. I'd have to say that I'm, sort of, in the middle. I'm not complete, you know Asian person or I'm not a complete Welsh person. I'm sort of, I've got both cultures in me, you see.'

Several people talked about their children's identity. One woman who said she was Indian with a British passport added that 'my children don't think anything other than Welsh'. And a man who was clear that his own identity was Bangladeshi decided on reflection that his children were free to adopt a Welsh identity:

Interviewer: So, this is a question about ethnicity, because we are in Wales would you say . . .
Respondent: Bangladeshi is my ethnicity.
Interviewer: You wouldn't say you were Welsh then?
Respondent: No, me, no. Because I cannot. Even though, you know, I respect the people of Wales, I'm happy that I'm living in Wales. But my ethnicity always will be Bangladeshi.
Interviewer: Yes.
Respondent: Because that was my country of origin. Because there's a difference between ethnicity and nationality. My nationality can be British, I'm a British subject, I've got a British passport. Yes I may be British citizen, but my ethnicity and my children's ethnicity always will be Bangladeshi, because that's my country of origin.
Interviewer: And your culture as well?
Respondent: Yes, but saying that, if my children wanted to describe themselves as Welsh, I'd have no control to that. They are quite free to what you want to describe them as. This is a choice of individual. (Male, thirties)

As part of the ethnographic fieldwork in this locality we attended St David's Day celebrations at two primary schools, one with a high proportion of ethnic minority children, who mostly originate from the Sylhet region of Bangladesh and speak Sylheti at home. At this school, as at others, the children have to learn Welsh as well as English, but we were told the ethnic minority children find Welsh easier as it has more similarities with Sylheti than does English. The St David's Day celebrations at this school lasted a full week with different classes performing on different days. We attended the last day when it was the turn of the oldest children and the main event was the chairing of the bard. Welsh was the primary language in use during the hour-long celebrations, everyone was sporting a daffodil or leek and most of the staff and some of the children were wearing red, mainly Welsh rugby shirts or Welsh national costume. Most of the children were in school uniform. The head teacher opened the proceedings in Welsh, repeating what he had said in English, and the children sang 'Sosban fach'. He then announced the results of the poetry competition which had required the children to write poems about Wales. Before the winning poet was named, a group of five boys entered dressed in druidic robes. When they reached the bardic chair, the head teacher announced the winner. The 'archdruid' spoke in Welsh, then went to escort the winner to the chair, first putting a red cloak and crown on her. The winning poem was read (in English) followed by harp and piano music, singing (all in Welsh) and dancing by other groups of children. In contrast, at the other primary school – with a far less pronounced ethnic minority component – while all the children wore either Welsh rugby shirts or Welsh national costume for their celebrations, the medium of communication was English.

The importance of conveying Welsh cultural practices through the medium of Welsh was clearly recognized in the first school. However, their St David's Day celebrations contrasted with other school events such as the Christmas play where, although there was some Welsh in evidence, the main language was English. (See Exell, 2004, for a discussion of the role of school eisteddfodau in supporting Welsh identity.) Similarly, in the daily life of the school, English was the main language although the children spoke several different languages amongst themselves. These practices mark Welsh as the language of 'Welsh culture' rather than the language of daily life, even within the school, and mean that children, although learning Welsh, do not perceive it as a means of everyday communication.

CONCLUSIONS

This article has discussed continuities and changes in Welsh identity and language in Swansea over four decades. When we compared the culturally 'Welsh' to the 'non-Welsh', using a language-based distinction developed by Rosser and Harris (1965) in the 1960s, we found that these two collectivities had moved closer together on a number of indicators, for example, home ownership and a general decline in religious affiliation. In other ways, trends that had been identified in the 1960s continued to be apparent, in particular smaller family sizes for Welsh speakers and a higher proportion of 'cross-cultural' marriages.

In common with the 1960s study, we did not find significant differences in the role or importance of the extended family between 'Welsh' and 'non-Welsh' collectivities. However, our ethnographic data does reveal a widely held perception of 'very Welsh' families that characteristically have the mother at the centre and retain close ties through large family occasions. This cultural stereotype was sometimes linked as well with Welsh speaking, and often was presented as a phenomenon either located in the past or in another part of Swansea or its surrounding region.

The research also shows both the clear successes of the Welsh schools movement in the significant increases in Welsh speakers among younger age groups and the very serious decline, indeed the virtual disappearance, of the Welsh language as a family and community language in Swansea. These findings clearly have implications for the likely realization of the National Assembly's goal of a fully bilingual Welsh nation. In its strategy document for the Welsh language, *Iaith Pawb*, the National Assembly commits itself to achieving a number of key targets by 2011. One of these is to ensure that 'the decline in the number of communities where Welsh is spoken by over 70 per cent of the population is arrested' (Welsh Assembly Government, 2003, p. 11). Our research draws attention once again to the vital importance of considerations of spatial distribution and density of speakers in supporting a minority language, and our findings underline the necessity for the Welsh language to be a part of all planning decisions, particularly those relating to housing and employment, if the destruction of Welsh-speaking communities rooted in particular localities, such as has occurred in Swansea, is to be avoided. Another key target is to ensure that by 2011, 'the percentage of families where Welsh is the principal language of conversation/communication between adults and children at home has increased' (Welsh Assembly Government, 2003, p. 11). Further research is needed to improve understanding of how such a goal might be achieved. In particular we need to know more about the dynamics of language choice and use within families, from a variety of social and cultural backgrounds, and how these are affected by linguistic and educational patterns in the broader community. Our research cannot shed much light on these questions, but it does strongly suggest that Welsh-language competence, even of both partners in a relationship, does not of itself ensure use of the language within the household.

Our research also looked at Welsh identity in terms of self-ascription and found a widespread, generally positive and unselfconscious assumption of Welsh identity. When asked to elaborate on what this meant to them, people tended to refer to support for national sports teams and to contrast Welshness with English, sometimes British, identity. They also tended to explain their relationship to the Welsh language, clarifying why they could not speak it and expressing mostly positive, often quite proprietary attitudes about the language. Our ethnographic research with those from ethnic minorities has found a degree of openness regarding the possibility of becoming Welsh, through length of residence, along with an acceptance that their children learn Welsh in schools and were themselves free to choose a Welsh identity. Most of our ethnic minority interviewees, in common with the ethnic minority respondents to the survey, did not see themselves as Welsh. However, a significant minority did identify as Welsh, and a Welsh identity appeared to be no more problematic to ethnic minority interviewees than British identity.

This raises some important points about the way in which immigrants have been incorporated into the British state and how this process relates to ideas of both Britishness and Welshness. The policy response to immigration developed by the British state has been characterized as a pragmatic and particularistic approach that allows for cultural difference within a common concept of British citizenship. Britishness defined in this way does not privilege either full cultural assimilation or ancestry as determinative (Melotti, 1997; Pilkington, 2003). Thus the past decade has seen the emergence of 'Black British' as a viable identity, grounded in British citizenship, for some ethnic minorities. However, it has been suggested that ethnic minorities in devolved regions find cultural identities, such as Welsh and Scottish, more problematic.[6] Our research into Welshness suggests that this is not the case. Our interviewees, both 'white' and ethnic minority, talked about Welsh identity with reference to place of birth, residence, ancestry and language, but none of these seemed to be definitive. That is, in spite of the fact that Welsh citizenship has no clear legal meaning, there was considerable openness to different ways of being Welsh among nearly all of our interviewees which suggests that most of them were working implicitly with a citizenship model of Welshness that fits easily with the National Assembly's emphasis on inclusivity.

ACKNOWLEDGEMENT

The research on which this article is based is funded by the ESRC (R000238454) and is part of the project 'Social change, family formation and kin relationships'.

NOTES

1   For more detailed information on differences in the two samples regarding gender, age, ethnicity, stratification and a comparison of findings about household composition and extended families, see Charles, Davies and Harris (2003).
2   Fictitious names are used for these areas to protect the anonymity of our interviewees.
3   The census figures for these three areas were produced for us by the Performance and Strategic Planning Division of the City and County of Swansea, to whose Director and Strategic Planning Officer we are deeply indebted.
4   Clearly this trend of increasing 'cross-cultural' (i.e., cross-language) marriages is, to a large degree, an artefact of the decreasing proportion of Welsh speakers in the population. Our intent here is not to explain why this increase in 'cross-cultural' marriages has occurred but to note its continuance over the period 1914–2002 and its significance for the position of Welsh as a household language in Swansea.
5   The Welsh Language Board has recognized the importance for language maintenance of encouraging the use of the Welsh language within households. In particular the Twf project, set up in 2001 to run for three years, works through health professionals and other channels to persuade new and expecting parents to speak Welsh to their children.
6   See, for example, comments by Yasmin Alibhai-Brown at the 'Global Britons Forum in Wales' held in Cardiff, 11 February 2003.

REFERENCES

Charles, N., Davies, C. A. and Harris, C. (2003). 'Family formation and kin relationships: 40 years of social change', paper presented to the British Sociological Conference, University of York, 11–13 April 2003.

Davies, C. A. and Charles, N. (2002). 'The piano in the parlour: methodological issues in the conduct of a restudy', *Sociological Research Online*, 7, 2, *www.socresonline.org.uk/ 7/2/davies.html*

Exell, N. D. (2004). 'Expressions of Welsh identity in secondary schools in Wales', unpublished Ph.D. thesis, University of Wales.

Gruffudd, H. (2000). 'Planning for the use of Welsh by young people', in C. H. Williams (ed.), *Language Revitalization: Policy and Planning in Wales*, Cardiff: University of Wales Press.

Jones, S. (2003). 'Supporting the team, sustaining the community: gender and rugby in a former mining village', in C. A. Davies and S. Jones (eds), *Welsh Communities: New Ethnographic Perspectives*, Cardiff: University of Wales Press.

Melotti, U. (1997). 'International migration in Europe: social projects and political cultures', in T. Modood and P. Werbner (eds), *The Politics of Multiculturalism in the New Europe: Racism, Identity and Community*, London: Zed Books.

Pilkington, A. (2003). *Racial Disadvantage and Ethnic Diversity in Britain*, Basingstoke: Palgrave Macmillan.

Rosser, C. and Harris, C. (1965). *The Family and Social Change: A Study of Family and Kinship in a South Wales Town*, London: Routledge and Kegan Paul.

Welsh Assembly Government (2003). *Iaith Pawb: A National Action Plan for a Bilingual Wales*, Cardiff: Welsh Assembly Government.
Williams, G. and Morris, D. (2000). *Language Planning and Language Use: Welsh in a Global Age*, Cardiff: University of Wales Press.
Young, M. and Wilmott, P. (1957). *Family and Kinship in East London*, London: Routledge and Kegan Paul.

3. DEFINING OR DIVIDING THE NATION? OPINION POLLS, WELSH IDENTITY AND DEVOLUTION, 1966–1979

Andrew Edwards and Duncan Tanner

ABSTRACT

The overwhelming rejection of devolution by Welsh voters in 1979 was one of the most traumatic events in Welsh political history. Explanations of the causes of that rejection have assumed a mythical status over the past quarter of a century. On the one hand, the blame for the defeat of Labour's devolution proposals has been placed firmly on the backs of the anti-devolutionists who opposed the measure so vociferously and effectively in the late 1970s. On the other, the rejection of devolution has been portrayed as a crisis of Welsh identity, a spineless rejection of self-government by a nation lacking self-confidence and torn by geographical and linguistic differences.

Engaging with newer approaches to national identities this article questions whether the defeat of devolution in 1979 marked a crisis of identity or a crisis of political attempts to represent and construct that identity. Focusing on opinion poll data from the 1960s and 1970s the article shows how 'evidence' of support for devolution could be contradictory and often misleading. Building on the work of political scientists, the article draws on evidence from the archives of the political parties and the Royal Commission on the Constitution to show that opinion and identity was not fixed and could be moulded and manipulated by the nature and timing of pollsters' questions. The article thus shows how opinion poll evidence which has provided the basis of much existing work was not a value-free measure of opinion but part of the process through which opinion was constructed. Whilst polls were used to create the impression that a single and strong sense of national identity existed in the 1960s, the article argues that this could not be mobilized as a force for change because pro-devolutionists could not agree on the type of society that the Assembly should create. As a result, opponents of devolution were able to construct the terms of the debate, exploit existing divisions and help erode even further the already limited support for devolution.

INTRODUCTION

The twenty-fifth anniversary of the first Welsh devolution referendum campaign on 1 March 2004 marked one of the defining – and deflating – moments in modern Welsh political history. Yet, despite the fact that a quarter of a century has passed since that overwhelming rejection of devolution by the people of Wales, we have yet to understand fully the complexities behind the referendum campaign, or the battles for and against devolution in the years preceding it. In the aftermath of the 1979 result, few tried to confront, let alone objectively evaluate, one of the most painful events in Welsh history.[1] A collective depression – almost a form of political post-traumatic stress disorder – set in, manifest both in literature and in politics.[2] Instead, it became common to seek scapegoats and in particular to place the 'blame' for the 'betrayal' of Wales at the door of some notable contemporary opponents of devolution (most of whom emanated from with Labour's ranks). One aim of this article is to question the historical accuracy of these still-prevalent impressions.

Our analysis is part of a larger project on the history of Welsh devolution. Until recently, the only full academic analysis of popular attitudes to devolution was that conducted a little after the 1979 referendum by the political scientists Denis Balsom and Barry Jones (Balsom, 1979; Jones and Wilford, 1979; Foulkes, Jones and Wilford, 1983). Ken Morgan's account of Welsh history before 1980 and Vernon Bogdanor's summary of the devolution process in the UK as a whole were the only studies that put 1979 in a broader perspective (Morgan, 1981; Bogdanor, 1979). Balsom's work was perceptive, informed – but close to the events in every sense. Although he relied heavily on analysis of opinion polls, some of which he organized and conducted himself for the BBC, he was no mere number-cruncher. Balsom felt there was a connection between the limitations of a Welsh identity, the nature of political campaigning and the result in 1979. Nonetheless, two developments since 1979 mean that it is possible to see the referendum in a new light. The first is the development of new conceptions and approaches to national identity, derived from both sociology and political science – and applied to Wales in a series of original and significant studies (Wyn Jones, 2001; Evans and Trystan, 1999; Rebecca M. Jones, 2003). The second is the opening of political and governmental archives, allowing historians to develop new insights into the period before the referendum. By putting these two approaches together we substantially add to current understanding of the 1979 results, as the popular attitudes expressed in 1979 and described in existing studies were largely shaped during the preceding period. If this is something that historically focused political scientists have started to recognize (McLean and McMillan, 2003) our analysis gets behind the numbers to understand the way that numbers were structured and interpreted.

Across the last twenty-five years, research on national identity has developed in a far more sophisticated manner and through a variety of disciplinary perspectives. It has produced an awareness of the constructive 'imagining' of nations by intellectuals in the past, and of 'competing identities', 'contested identities' and 'multiple identities' (Smith, 1991). In particular, analysts of national identity now regularly draw a distinction between a sense of cultural, ethnic or linguistic identity on the one hand, and a sense of civic identity on the other (Smith, 1991). Political scientists who utilize opinion polls these days ask questions which try to unpick the complexities of peoples' sense of identity, rather than simply asking if they feel themselves to be 'Welsh' (Wyn Jones, 2001). Research on the construction of national identity within real political contexts shows that political rhetoric seldom focuses on a wholly 'ethnic' not wholly 'civic' conception of the nation, and helps to demonstrate the weakness of national appeals which are based largely on the former (Smith, 1998; Webber, 1999). Wales is no exception. There is certainly a proven relationship between the Welsh language, Welsh identification and support for devolution since 1979. Yet it is also clear that people who spoke Welsh and felt Welsh took very different views on political and constitutional issues in 1979 (Balsom, 1983; Evans and Trystan, 1999) – and that shifts in the views of Welsh-speaking Welsh identifiers are insufficient to explain changes between 1979 and 1997. Rather than accepting popular assumptions about a 'weak' sense of Welsh identity and its impact on the result of the 1979 referendum, we look at whether it was a crisis of identity in 1979 or a crisis of political attempts to represent and construct that identity in the preceding decades which created the apparent 'failure' of the Welsh nation.

In looking beyond the statistical evidence, and in seeking to explain it, we draw on archival evidence from a variety of sources not previously available to scholars. This includes material from the Labour, Conservative and Plaid Cymru archives and newly released material relating to the Kilbrandon Commission and its activities. We have also utilized a much wider range of contemporary opinion polls (including some conducted for the political parties) from the decade before the referendum. We use these to show that opinion and identity were not fixed and that 'hard' evidence on popular attitudes was in fact influenced by the nature and timing of the questions which pollsters asked. Opinion polls – the basis of much existing work – were not a value-free measure of opinion, but part of the process through which opinion was constructed.

INTERPRETING THE POLLS, 1966–70

A considerable amount of attention has been paid to extra-parliamentary Welsh-language campaigning as an influence on the development of a stronger sense of Welsh identity in the 1960s (Phillips, 1998). There was clearly an increased awareness of Wales as a potential national entity at this time, which was reflected in the opinion polls. Asked in 1966 how they would describe themselves, nearly two-thirds of the Welsh population described themselves as Welsh rather than British – and, given that a reasonable percentage of people in Wales were recent in-migrants from England, this is quite a substantial result (ORC, 1966). In the same survey, commissioned by Conservative Central Office, over 70 per cent felt it was important to preserve both the Welsh language and Welsh customs and traditions, and more than half the population wished to see Welsh used more in education. Thus it would appear that there was some sense of a cultural or ethnic identity, extending well beyond the Welsh-speaking areas of Wales. Polls also suggest that there were good prospects for constructing a sense of national identity focused around Wales as a mechanism for delivering better *civic* rule. A poll conducted for the Conservatives in 1968 asked if it would be better for Wales if fewer decisions about Welsh affairs were made in London; 78 per cent agreed. The same survey also showed that around half the population were unhappy about the level of government spending on Wales, about people having to leave Wales for jobs in England, and about the extent to which Wales was governed from London and by people with little awareness of Welsh affairs (ORC, 1968). This had some political ramifications. In November 1967, although support for Plaid Cymru stood at only 7 per cent, 24 per cent of those polled supported 'self-government for Wales' (NOP, 1967).[3]

Newspaper headlines and party enthusiasts for devolution claimed that polls showed there was considerable support for devolution as a means of delivering on national sentiments.[4] However, the true picture was more complicated because the questions asked were sometimes ambivalent. For example, the 1966 ORC poll asked people the rather leading question of whether they felt things would be better for Wales if it had its own parliament. Unsurprisingly, 42 per cent agreed (ORC, 1966). Further polls in 1967 and 1968 showed 60 per cent of the population supporting the idea of a Welsh Assembly (*Western Mail*, 1967; ORC, 1968). So why then did the 1979 referendum result in just a quarter of the

Welsh people voting for devolution? The campaign by dissident Labour MPs against devolution – which may have been influential in determining the *extent* of the No vote – has diverted attention away from some rather more significant influences.

In some respects, headline figures suggesting a strong sense of national identity and considerable enthusiasm for devolution in the 1960s masked the fact that this commitment was less than complete. Although the 1966 ORC poll, for example, suggested that there was support for the preservation of Welsh culture and language, it also showed that this was not a priority even for many Welsh speakers. Whilst 73 per cent thought it was either very or fairly important to preserve the Welsh language and 79 per cent thought it very or fairly important to preserve Welsh customs and traditions, asked whether it was more important to preserve the traditions and cultures of Wales or improve the standard of living, 91 per cent of Welsh voters – and 87 per cent of Welsh nationalist voters – said it was more important to improve the standard of living. Pollsters for the Conservative Party found that voters' priorities were essentially practical (their term) – with the preservation of full employment and the standard of living being mentioned by more than half. Nearly a third of the population mentioned lower taxes as a priority – something noted with interest by Conservative Party managers. Only 5 per cent mentioned a Welsh Parliament and 4 per cent complete independence. Neither did Welsh voters feel oppressed by English cultural imperialism, or by the 'invasion' of an alien 'Other' which they resented. Only 10 per cent of the sample agreed very strongly with the statement that 'the English have deliberately tried to destroy our national traditions and national character' (ORC, 1966). Neither did Welsh voters feel that Wales suffered unreasonably as part of the union. For example, 80 per cent (and 83 per cent of Welsh nationalists) believed that the standard of Welsh education was equal to or better than that offered in England. Only 4 per cent believed that Wales got a 'raw deal' from the existing system of UK governance. The deep-rooted sense of cultural and economic injustice that was the motor of nationalist movements in other countries was underdeveloped within Wales (Wright, 1999). This was not simply because the Welsh language was less pervasive and hence a less generalized source of resistance. It was also because a great many Welsh speakers themselves did not share the view of UK government developed by Plaid Cymru activists. The existence of a gap between nationalist activists and the Welsh people should not be wholly surprising. There was a similar gap between Labour activists and Labour voters (Tanner, 2000a). Opinion polls identified features of popular opinion that pro-devolutionists needed to address. They invariably failed to do so.

A further range of questions about popular priorities was put to voters by ORC in 1968. Asked whether more teachers, better buildings or the Welsh language should be a priority within education, only 15 per cent chose the Welsh language. When asked which language should be taught alongside English in Welsh classrooms, 42 per cent said Welsh, 57 per cent French or German. Even 38 per cent of Welsh speakers preferred their children to learn French or German rather than Welsh (ORC, 1968). Although many voters supported greater devolution, only a third of voters supported the idea of Wales having more control over its own affairs, if this meant people would be worse off financially. This was compared to half in the Scottish sample (ORC, 1968). Even amongst Welsh nationalists, only 52 per cent believed that Wales could or should run its own affairs. Just two years later, much of this was confirmed by a larger NOP sample. Nearly 60 per cent believed that too many decisions about Wales were made in London. Around 50 per cent were in favour of internal self-government for Wales, 'to deal just with Welsh affairs', rising to 63 per cent amongst young people. But the answers also showed resistance to the compulsory teaching of Welsh in education, and doubts about separatism, even amongst advocates of change. As the pollsters concluded, 'a good many Welsh Nationalists do not want complete independence and doubt the economic benefits' (NOP, Sept/Oct 1970).

The extra-parliamentary campaigning of the 1960s attracted attention and increased support for the introduction of bilingual road signs and other changes. However, it did not necessarily create permanent shifts in the public's views on how Wales should be governed, especially once people reflected on the issues. Restlessness on individual concerns did not necessarily spill over into support for national separatism. Plaid Cymru's proposed 'solution' for Wales's problems was rejected by all but 18 per cent of the population in 1967 and support was only 2 per cent higher in 1970. Thus, in trying to construct a sense of Welsh identity around cultural identities, or a rejection of England, or the idea of a separate Wales, Welsh nationalists were going against the tide of Welsh public opinion. It would need a very compelling form of public discourse to counteract rooted fears and doubts.

THE PARTIES AND PUBLIC OPINION

This was not easy to achieve. Plaid was an alliance of people with very different views. The party's campaign rhetoric often had little appeal to the type of public opinion identified in the polls. For example, T. Glynne Davies's reaction to Labour's proposals for a new town in Mid Wales was anti-English, rooted in traditional nationalist values and opposed to the emphasis on material prosperity which the polls showed was the primary concern even of Welsh speakers:

> This is an opportunity for Birmingham to share its smoke with Wales . . . it is not an attempt to put mid-Wales on its feet. Politically, spiritually and socially it can do no good from the Welsh perspective. At a time when people inside and outside the Labour party are attempting to make people discover the Welshness in their hearts, here is Welshness being drowned by a flow from England that couldn't care less about Welshness, and as figures count in a democracy, here is an eternal blow to Welshness. In one blow the percentage of Welsh speakers will decline dramatically. In one blow a county that is solidly religious will quite possibly turn into a materialistic mess, the 'werin' being swallowed up by the proletariat. (In A. C. Edwards, 2002, p. 301)

Despite the attempts of Dafydd Wigley, Phil Williams and other party modernizers in the 1960s and 1970s to expand Plaid's appeal, it was often difficult to escape the hold of the past.[5] In focusing their attack on the inadequacies of the Welsh Language Bill, and by developing an education policy that seemed to stress the language of delivery rather than anything else, Plaid's apparent prioritization of the Welsh language could easily alienate potential supporters. It has been suggested that even the most prominent 'cultural' nationalists within Plaid Cymru had also developed a 'civic' dimension to their nationalism (Wyn Jones, forthcoming). However, it was the popular perception of the nationalists' orientation that mattered. Political opponents and the press were able to stress the primacy of Plaid's cultural and linguistic concerns, aided by statements from some Plaid supporters and by the high-profile activities and priorities of some militant activists. The political dangers of emphasizing language became even more evident once the Kilbrandon report was published. Its research seemed to indicate that whilst there was a 'notable degree of sympathy amongst non-Welsh speakers for the idea of preserving and teaching the Welsh language, there is also a feeling that those who speak Welsh would be the ones to gain most from devolution' (Royal Commission on the Constitution, 1973). Labour opponents of devolution, notably Leo Abse, capitalized upon such fears during the referendum campaign. Plaid Cymru tried to address these concerns, but never really came to terms with the doubts of an often sceptical Welsh public, either in public or in private. Wrapped up in its own internal debates about how to approach devolution, and often focusing on opposition to Labour rather than the case for change, it struggled to nullify these concerns and win support for devolution. Gwynfor Evans wrote privately 'of the difficulty I am encountering in persuading my own people that the government is utterly determined to get the measure through the House'. Dafydd Wigley, on the other hand, blamed Plaid's indecision and insecurity on the lack of leadership within the party: 'At the dawn of one of the most important milestones in Welsh history, the nationalist movement is unsure of itself, is afraid and nervous. It is like a child preparing for an important exam, but refusing to acknowledge its importance in case he fails it.'[6]

These problems were not confined to Plaid Cymru. Poll findings also presented problems to the less studied advocates of devolution within the Labour Party. This element did not just consist of the 'good' Labour nationalists who had supported the Parliament for Wales campaign in the 1950s (J. G. Jones, 1992). From the late 1960s onwards, Labour's Cardiff head office was dominated by advocates of a national assembly with considerable powers.[7] These Labour supporters of devolution focused on the way in which devolution would place Welsh industry and Welsh public services under Welsh control. They argued that this was Wales's right as a nation, asserted that devolution was more democratic and that it would lead to better services and policies. However, there were a number of obstacles to the full development of this 'civic' case for a Welsh assembly. First, whilst Welsh Labour's headquarters in Cardiff was supportive, many in London opposed their ideas. They argued against the need for 'special' Welsh treatment, attempted to tone down the party's support for devolution in its evidence to the Kilbrandon Commission and tried to ensure that any new Assembly had limited powers. (Tanner, 2000b, p. 279–80). Many in London had felt that Wales should have a regional assembly, comparable to those being proposed for the English regions. Only the limited enthusiasm of those regions prevented this from being adopted as Labour policy (Tanner, forthcoming). Secondly, it was very difficult for Welsh Labour supporters of devolution to make the case for a devolved government, based on the limitations of a centralized British system to deliver the economic goods, when Labour had been in power for much of the 1960s and 1970s. The party's *Notes for Speakers* in the 1979 referendum based the case for change largely on the assumed economic advantages of devolution. At the same time, the party was also campaigning on what (Labour's) central government had done for Wales (Labour Party Wales, 1978). Finally, in the same way that Plaid contained a good deal of baggage from the past, so Labour was in no position to wrap itself in the Welsh flag or to pose as leaders of a new Welsh civic nationalism. The party contained high-profile opponents of devolution, like George Thomas, who ridiculed nationalism in his *Daily Post* column in the early 1970s (Edwards, 2002). Moreover, actions of Labour-dominated county councils in south Wales did not lend credibility to the idea that a Labour-dominated (civic) Welsh state would produce better, let alone more 'Welsh', governance. Writing to Richard Crossman in 1966, Gwilym Prys Davies highlighted the potential problems of a case couched in civic terms:

> Manned by too many opportunists and non-thinkers at local government level and parliamentary level the Labour Party appears to have been stripped of its radical idealism and to have transformed itself into a domineering caucus in local affairs and into a permanent alternative government in the set up of ins and outs. There is a very ancient Welsh attitude of not trusting such a party. In these circumstances we cannot afford the delusion that the Welsh people will continue to support Labour candidates where sermons are hollow . . . there are only a few thousand Welsh nationalists who accept no limitations on the demands nationalism makes on them, but they should not be dismissed too lightly. (In Edwards, 2002, p. 320)

By the late 1970s, a Labour-dominated devolved assembly was seen by many – especially in the north of Wales – not as the champion of a Welsh polity, but as the narrow defender of the economic interests and cultural values of south Wales. It was not that their 'Welshness' declined in salience – it was rather that the 'Welshness' of Labour was not the 'Welshness' of cultural nationalists, or of Plaid Cymru supporters who wanted effective (to them, non-Labour-dominated) civic governance for Wales. Although a civic nationalism was potentially more inclusive than Plaid's traditional cultural nationalism, it was too easily under-mined and fragmented by the limitations of Labour's notion of civic nationalism and by the partisan sentiments of a politicized community.

Of course, there were other potential influences on public opinion. In the 1960s popular organizations were emerging which challenged the traditional collectivism of the Labour Party and its claim to be the voice of working-class opinion (Shapely, 2004; Daunton and Hilton, 2001). The 1960s were not just the decade of language protests. Consumers, tenants, the peace movement and others challenged Labour's policies. However, contemporary opinion polls suggest that the impact of protest on conservative values has been overstated and hence that the size of this emerging civil culture was weak.[8] Moreover, Welsh organizations such as Welsh county and borough councils generally opposed the changes, which threatened to reduce their powers. There were few national institutions and symbols around which to rally, and no widespread success at constructing a non-partisan case for change. The cross-party Wales for the Assembly Campaign (WFAC) was no alternative, relying on parties to mobilize support and assuming to the last that success was simply a matter of mobilizing the vote, rather than winning the argument. Even in the final weeks of the referendum campaign, WFAC still believed that devolution could be won by 'concentrating on winning Labour dissident and Liberal party votes; attack(ing) Tories as anti-Welsh party; persuading Plaid Cymru to concentrate on north and west Wales' (WFAC, 1979). This presented no challenge to the No campaigners. Dissident Labour MPs towards the end of the devolution campaign did not undermine the case for devolution. It was potentially weak even when it appeared to be strong in the 1960s, because in Wales there were multiple identities, argued by people who were mutually suspicious of one another. There were two distinct Welsh campaigns for change in 1979 and at least two types of Welsh identity – as there had been for much of the century.

INFLUENCING THE PEOPLE: THE CIVIL SERVICE AND OPINION POLLS

If the case made for devolution was not well constructed, opponents of devolution reflected and at times developed the worries and concerns of a divided nation. On the Labour side, opponents of change – like Neil Kinnock – initially gauged opinion through nothing more scientific than their roots within coalfield communities and an awareness of what motivated Labour activists.[9] Their gut feelings were confirmed by the pollsters, not constructed by them. The Conservatives were more scientific, using polls to ascertain the potential for resisting change, although not necessarily developing an overwhelmingly strong campaign around the opportunities it created. Whilst the findings of polls in the 1960s were important in developing the case for devolution in the 1960s, later opinion polls also played an important part in setting the agenda for opponents of that process. When the Labour government set up the Kilbrandon Commission, it established its own polling team to measure the nature of public sentiment. The civil servants chose to use not one of the larger polling companies but a new organization, Social and Community Planning Research, or SCPR. Louis Moss of the Government Social Survey Department was the key person here. He felt that SCPR would be keen to 'make their mark' and that their project design would be 'capable of developing into the kind of job which the Commission wants done'.[10] Moss held a meeting at Nuffield College, Oxford to discuss the nature of the questions that pollsters would ask. The meeting was organized by D. N. Chester, in the absence of Lord Hunt. Writing up the results, Hunt concluded that the poll would have to be sophisticated: 'No useful survey of attitudes can be made by inviting people to summarise a complex state of mind in answer to a single all-embracing and perhaps misleading question (e.g. are you in favour of more Home Rule for Scotland?)' (Government Social Survey Department, 1970a).

Moss heartily agreed. He wanted to 'tease out' whether people *really* wanted more devolved governance or whether they simply wanted things to get better. Such questions would, he felt, provide a 'much better idea of the rather mixed nature of people's thinking on the issues'. In particular, he wanted to avoid poll findings that would give nationalists an opportunity to claim mass support. Describing the commission's pilot survey aims, he noted a desire to identify the view of people who had not been engaged in protests, and to 'induce people to consider and review their experience'. In this way, they would get 'a more considered response than if informants were simply confronted with a bald question inviting a sweeping generalized answer' (Government Social Survey Department, 1970b). Moss's response to the first pilot surveys was hardly neutral. He felt that support for change might well evaporate if only people were more informed, and knew what could and was being achieved within the existing system. The response of people in Wales to questions about the Welsh Office and what it did for them was 'one of ignorance'. Only 'about half' the respondents knew of the existence of the Scottish Office and the Welsh Office, although knowledge of the Welsh Office was 'slightly greater and more cohesive'. Moss believed this was largely due that the fact that the Welsh Office was constantly in the news (as a result of its problems with Welsh nationalists). Welsh voters were 'conditioned by the flow of information which reached them', and this information was inflating the support for change. As the report continued:

> The main drift of the survey was that people did not want more opportunities to share in the running of things, but that they did think those responsible for running things should be more conscious of their needs and feelings . . . This defect did not necessarily call for a constitutional remedy . . . It might well be possible to reduce their dissatisfaction without any change of machinery at all . . . It would be interesting to know whether those who wanted devolution had in mind devolution of policy, or the devolution of its execution and administration. (Government Social Survey Department, 1970c)

The Kilbrandon public opinion polls were thus designed to reveal *differences* of opinion over devolution, rather than provide support for the idea of change. Whilst the polls could have been a useful tool for governments trying to identify and match public demand, they instead reflected a predetermined view that support for devolution was limited. When poll findings were published, this emphasis was carefully reinforced by the civil servants. Statements to the contrary were repressed. Before publication of one document in 1971, they asked for several sections to be toned down. In its opening paragraph, the report noted 'widespread feeling of dissatisfaction' with the system of government. Civil servants asked for this to be removed as misleading. Thus far, they continued, the Royal Commission's impression was that whilst there was 'undoubtedly dissatisfaction in many parts of the country there is no evidence of seething discontent'.[11] Moss was not ill-disposed to such ideas. He had felt that the Kilbrandon survey had identified 'shallow feelings and sentiments about subjects of which the respondents knew little'. Many people in Wales, he noted, were happy with the idea of a regional authority for north or south Wales. They felt less different from the rest of the UK than people in the south-west of England or in Yorkshire. If it were not for ill feeling about poor roads, they would have found little dissatisfaction with the UK government. There was, he concluded, 'no evidence of a strong feeling for change'. On the contrary, the results were 'something of a triumph for the United Kingdom'.[12]

INTERPRETING THE POLLS, 1970–9

The Kilbrandon Commission opinion polls asked voters their views on various means by which Wales might be governed. They did not, as in the past, ask if people felt Welsh or ask questions that simply highlighted a desire for change. In a sense rightly, they felt the time for that had passed. The questions asked, and the responses given, are summarized in table 3.1. Option 3 reflected the government's interest in testing popular support for 'regionalism' all round. The nature of the response set the tone of debate for the rest of the 1970s. Subsequent polls, also noted in table 3.1, used similar questions. What the press noted as a result was not evidence of dissatisfaction with centralized governance, but evidence of limited support for any *one* of the proposed alternatives. Once the commission reported, the debate was set in these terms, and reported as such in the press, for the pollsters and the public now had a concrete resolution to consider.

As table 3.2 indicates, once the details of the Devolution Bill became known and direct questions were asked about their merits, support for devolution never rose above 34 per cent. All the divisions of opinion over devolution evident in the 1960s were reidentified and mobilized from the early 1970s. The arguments used against devolution certainly evolved, but there was little movement in opinion across this period, apart from a brief surge of support at the start of the referendum campaign and a decline from this peak in the last month of the campaign. It was far too easy to fear what an assembly would be like, to see it as neither a strong civic power nor a successful defender of a culture under threat. It was far too difficult for one assembly to be a proper representative of (at least) two identities. Polls that had probably been used to exaggerate the desire for devolution in the 1960s were now probably used to undermine and minimize the desire for some form of change.

Table 3.1
Constitutional preferences in Wales, 1970–1979

Kilbrandon survey 1970		BES, February 1974		WES, May 1979	
For running . . . (name region) as a whole, which of these five alternatives would you prefer overall? (%)		There has been a lot of discussion recently about giving more power to Wales. Which of the statements on this card come closest to what you yourself feel should be done? (%)		Ideal form of government for Wales should be? (%)	
Leave as they are	15.2	Keep the governing of Wales much as it is now	23.7	No change	71.4
Keep things much the same but more government understanding	27.1	Make sure the needs of Wales are better understood by the government in London	33.6	Proposed Assembly	7.1
Keep the present system but more regional decisions	21.1	Allow more decisions to be made in Wales	27.5	Stronger Assembly	11.7
Have a new system of government for the region	23.4	Wales should completely run its own affairs	9.9	Complete self-government	5.0
Let the region take over complete responsibility	12.9				
Don't know	0.3	Don't know	5.3	Don't know	4.8
N	*697*	*N*	*131*	*N*	*858*

Source: McLean and McMillan, 2003.

Limited support for devolution in 1979 was thus *not* the consequence of the Labour dissidents' campaign. Nor did it stem from Labour voters in south Wales turning away from devolution, or of non-Welsh speakers or voters in the border areas taking a 'British' as opposed to 'Welsh' line. Even many of those who *identified themselves as Welsh and who spoke Welsh* opposed devolution in 1979. Results from a BBC poll in 1979 showed just how successfully the opponents of change had built a case around the concerns expressed in the 1960s (BBC Wales, 1979). Those who voted against devolution saw the proposed assembly as an expensive additional layer of bureaucracy, which would encourage the break-up of the UK and threaten jobs. Labour's 'civic' case for devolution as a means of delivering better governance had floundered. A majority of Plaid's supporters voted for devolution, perhaps placing far more emphasis on it as Wales's right, or as a means of defending Welsh cultural and other interests – this had certainly been the emphasis of the party's Welsh-language campaign literature (McLean and McMillan, 2003). However, in 1979 – as in the 1960s – most Welsh speakers did not prioritize these concerns. Between 56 and 60 per cent of Welsh speakers wanted no change in the system of governing Wales (BBC Wales, 1979). Only 22 per cent of Welsh identifiers voted for devolution, with 42 per cent voting against and 36 per cent abstaining (Evans and Trystan, 1999). Mobilizing a sense of cultural identity had proved no more effective in persuading the public of the need for change than had Labour's very different emphasis. There were two cases being made, at least two conceptions of what 'Welshness' should mean for the form and aims of Welsh governance, and they were competitive in their expression and their reception rather than complimentary. There was not a single, linguistically defined, conception of Welsh identity (R. Merfyn Jones, 1992). As a result, it is no surprise that political scientists find that national identity is of limited significance in explaining 1979. Opponents of the proposed changes (like Neil Kinnock and the secretary of the Labour No campaign, Barry Moore) did not reject their Welsh identity, although what they meant by that was left unstated. They rejected devolution as a form of governance and nationalism as an ideology.[13] Thus 1979 was not a cultural crisis, a crisis within different Welsh identities. It was a political crisis, a reflection of the failure to weld together and construct a political case for a form of governance that could embrace and represent the complex mesh of sentiments that constituted 'Welshness'.

Table 3.2
Questions about devolution proposals for Wales

Fieldwork	For (%)	Against (%)	Don't know (%)	Number of interviews
12 December 1975 (Research and Marketing)	30	39	31	500
6 December 1976 (Research and Marketing)	27	40	33	1000
19 March 1977 (Research and Marketing)	27	53	21	1000
5 May 1978 (Abacus)	34	39	27	1000
15 September 1978 (Abacus)	31	44	25	1029
1 February 1979 (Abacus)	27	41	31	908

Source: Rose and McAllister, 1979.

CONCLUSION

In some respects our attempt to question the myths of 1979 parallels the conclusions of political scientists like Wyn Jones and Trystan (2000). It extends the work of more historically focused political scientists, who argue that the (mis)reading of opinion polls had been a significant influence on the progress of devolution (McLean and McMillan, 2003). However, as historians we go further – by looking at how the poll results were influenced both by the actions and inactions of politicians and through the wording of the questions. Although we focus on the period before 1974, arguing that the terms of debate were already laid down by this time, we could easily show (using further, hitherto unstudied, private opinion polls) that parties continued to use such polls to inform campaigning and to structure opinion in the run-up to 1979. Polls were used to create the idea that there was a single and strong sense of national identity in the 1960s. This could not be mobilized as a force for change because those who believed in a Welsh Assembly could not agree on the type of society that the assembly was meant to create. By contrast, those who opposed devolution in 1979 were able to construct the terms of the debate, to exploit divisions between people, many of whom saw themselves as 'Welsh', or to draw a line between 'Welshness' and 'devolution'. If this analysis is of obvious relevance to the historical analysis of Welsh devolution and to those concerned with the construction of identity, it also has a more contemporary relevance. Explanations of changes in opinion between 1979 and 1997 place a good deal of emphasis on national identity and use 1979 as their baseline and comparator. We provide a fuller understanding of the 1979 referendum results and the concepts used to analyse them – and demonstrate that we should treat opinion polls carefully and not simply as a source of empirical 'facts'. We have used them here to challenge some of the myths that surround the history of devolution. But we have also portrayed them as tools in the construction – and destruction – of the national ideal.

ACKNOWLEDGEMENT

This article was originally presented as a paper to the conference, 'Datblygu Hunaniaeth: Llenyddiaeth, Cymdeithas a Gwleidyddiaeth Cymreig, 1880–2003' held at the University of Wales, Bangor in November 2003 and jointly organized by the Economic and Social Research Council's Devolution and Constitutional Change Research Programme and Bangor's Welsh Institute for Social and Cultural Affairs (WISCA). We are grateful to Richard Wyn Jones for his comments on the paper. Research for the paper was carried out as part of ESRC grant number L219252120.

NOTES

1   A notable exception was John Osmond (1979, 1985).
2   See Erfyl (1979), Williams (1985) and Jones and Wilford (1979). For literature, see, for example, Aaron (2000) and Hunter (1998).
3   These results were extracted from within UK-wide samples, and were thus confined to no more than 100–200 voters. It was only in specific polls (as in the 1968 ORC poll) or when NOP over-polled in Wales and Scotland in September/October 1970 that the sample was acceptable by modern standards. NOP Bulletins used here are from the Harold Wilson papers at the Bodleian Library, Oxford.
4   See for example *Western Mail* (1967, 1968a, 1968b).
5   Wigley and Williams were highly influential in 'modernizing' Plaid's policies and its appeal in the 1960s and in drawing up the party's respected 'Economic Plan' in 1969. For more on this see Edwards (2002, p. 228–88).
6   Evans to Michael Foot, 1 January 1978, Plaid Cymru Papers, file L26, NLW, Dafydd Wigley, 'Datganoli – papur trafod: y dewis i'r Blaid', 18 May 1978, Plaid Cymru papers, File L26, NLW.
7   The most prominent of these figures was Emrys Jones, Labour's Welsh organizer during the 1970s.
8   For example, the Gallup Political Index Report no 141 reported that 66 per cent felt that students taking part in sit-ins should be prosecuted. In September 1966, NOP found that 82 per cent favoured the return of hanging. In May 1968, two-thirds of those questioned agreed with Enoch Powell's recent pronouncements on race relations.
9   This conclusion derives more from an examination of the Bedwellty Labour Party papers (Gwent County Record Office, esp. file D3784.19) than it does from the Kinnock papers.
10   These comments are in recently released files relating to the work of the Government Social Survey Department. Louis Moss to Witzenfeld, 25 February 1970, Public Records Office, RG 40/493.
11   J. Kingdom to L. Moss, 10 June 1971, PRO RG 40/493.
12   This report is described as 'Minutes of meetings of the Committee of the Constitution', and has notes on a discussion of the attitudes survey with Louis Moss. It is filed in PRO RG 40/493.
13   See the Labour No campaign document, *Facts Against Fantasies*, and Barry Moore's draft but unpublished contribution to the *National Question Again*, both in Bedwellty Labour Party papers, file D3784.117.1.

REFERENCES

Aaron, J. (2000). '"Glywi di 'nghuro i?"': agweddau ar waith Angharad Tomos, 1979–1997',
    in J. Rowlands (ed.), *Y Sêr yn eu Graddau: Golwg ar Ffurfafen y Nofel Gymraeg
    Ddiweddar*, Cardiff: University of Wales Press.
Balsom, D. (1979). 'The nature and distribution of support for Plaid Cymru', University
    of Strathclyde, Centre for the Study of Public Policy, Research Paper No. 36.
Balsom, D. (1983). 'Public opinion and Welsh devolution', in D. Foulkes, J. B. Jones and
    R. A. Wilford (eds), *The Welsh Veto: The Wales Act 1978 and the Referendum*, Cardiff:
    University of Wales Press.
BBC Wales (1979). BBC Wales poll. Pre-referendum 1979, in Labour Party Wales
    Archive, File 110, Aberystwyth: National Library of Wales.
Bogdanor, V. (1979). *Devolution*, Oxford: Oxford University Press.
Daunton, M. and Hilton, M. (2001). *The Politics of Consumption: Material Culture and
    Citizenship in Europe and America*, Oxford: Berg.
Edwards, A. C. (2002). 'Political change in north-west Wales, 1960–75: the decline of the
    Labour Party and the rise of Plaid Cymru', unpublished Ph.D. thesis, University of Wales.
Erfyl, G. (1979). 'Golygyddol', *Barn*, 194, March.
Evans, G. and Trystan, D. (1999). 'Why was 1999 different?' in B. Taylor and K. Thomson
    (eds), *Scotland and Wales: Nations Again?*, Cardiff: University of Wales Press.
Foulkes, D., Jones, J. B. and Wilford, R. A. (1983). *The Welsh Veto: The Wales Act 1978
    and the Referendum*, Cardiff: University of Wales Press.
Government Social Survey Department (1970a). 'Proposal for public opinion survey to
    measure the demand for participation and the ingredients and strengths of nationalism',
    Norman Hunt, second draft, n.d., File RG 40/493, Public Record Office, London.
Government Social Survey Department (1970b). 'Pilot survey to be carried out on behalf
    of Commission on the Constitution', Louis Moss, 24 July 1970, File RG 40/493, Public
    Record Office, London.
Government Social Survey Department (1970c). 'Discussion with Mr Louis Moss and
    Miss Jean Morton-Williams', n.d., File RG 40/493, Public Record Office, London.
Hunter, T. G. (1998). 'Poetry, 1969–1996' in D. Johnston (ed.), *A Guide to Welsh Literature
    c.1900–1996*, Cardiff: University of Wales Press.
Jones, J. B. and Wilford, R. A. (1979). *The Welsh Veto: The Politics of the Devolution
    Campaign in Wales*, Centre for the Study of Public Policy: University of Strathclyde.
Jones, J. G. (1992). 'The Parliament for Wales Campaign 1950–66', *Welsh History Review*,
    16, 207–36.
Jones, R. Merfyn. (1992). 'Beyond identity? The reconstruction of the Welsh', *Journal of
    British Studies*, 31, 330–57.
Jones, Rebecca M. (2003). 'From referendum to referendum: national identity and
    devolution in Wales, 1979–1997', unpublished Ph.D. thesis, University of Wales.
Labour Party Wales (1978). 'Speakers' notes: the record of the Labour government in Wales,
    1974–78', Labour Party Wales archive, File 116, Aberystwyth: National Library of Wales.
McLean, I. and McMillan, A. (2003). 'How we got there – the devolution debate in the
    1970s. Or why it is not a good idea to change government policy on the basis of one
    quota poll', paper presented to the CREST conference, Cardiff.
Morgan, K. O. (1981). *Rebirth of a Nation: Wales 1880–1980*, Oxford: Clarendon Press
    and Cardiff: University of Wales Press.

National Opinion Polls (NOP) (1967) *Bulletin*, November 1967.
National Opinion Polls (NOP) (1970) *Monthly Bulletin*, September/October 1970.
ORC (1966). Opinion poll for the Conservative Party. Conservative Party Archive, File CCO 180/29/1/1, Bodleian Library, Oxford.
ORC (1968). *The Scope for Conservative Advance in Wales*, Conservative Party Archive, CCO/180/32, Bodleian Library Oxford.
Osmond, J. (1979). 'Mr Morris and the elephant: the referendum, the election and the future of Welsh politics', *Planet*, 48, May 1979.
Osmond, J. (ed.) (1985). *The National Question Again: Welsh Political Identity in the 1980s*, Llandysul: Gomer.
Phillips, D. (1998). *Trwy Ddulliau Chwyldro? Hanes Cymdeithas yr Iaith Gymraeg, 1962–1992*, Llandysul: Gomer.
Rose, R. and McAllister, I. (1979). Extract from United Kingdom Politics: 'Basic Facts', in Labour Party Wales Archive, NLW, file 116.
Royal Commission on the Constitution 1969–1973 (Kilbrandon Report). (1973). *Royal Commission on the Constitution 1969–1973, Volume 1, Report*, London, HMSO, 110.
Shapely, P. (2004). 'Tenants arise! Consumerism, tenants and the challenge to council authority in Manchester, 1968–1978', paper submitted to *Urban History*.
Smith, A. D. (1991). *National Identity*, London: Penguin.
Smith, A. D. (1998). *Nationalism and Modernism*, London: Routledge.
Tanner, D. M. (2000a). 'Labour and its membership', in D. M. Tanner, P. Thane and N. Tiratsoo (eds), *Labour's First Century*, Cambridge: Cambridge University Press.
Tanner, D. M. (2000b). 'Facing the new challenge: Labour and politics, 1970–2000', in D. M. Tanner, C. Williams and D. Hopkin (eds), *The Labour Party in Wales 1900–2000*, Cardiff: University of Wales Press.
Tanner, D. M. (forthcoming). 'Labour and the challenge of separatism', in A. C. Edwards and D. M. Tanner (eds), *Four Nations: Labour, Socialism and the Challenge of Nationalism Since 1960*, London: Ashgate Press.
Webber, J. (1999). 'Just how civic is civic nationalism in Quebec?' in A. C. Cairns et al. (eds), *Citizenship, Diversity and Pluralism*, Montreal and Kingston: McGill-Queens University Press.
Western Mail (1967). 'Six out of ten voters in Wales want to see the nation have its own parliament', 22 November 1967.
Western Mail (1968a). 'We want our own parliament say 60 p.c. in Wales', 25 September 1968.
Western Mail (1968b). 'A nation split down the centre', 26 September 1968.
WFAC, Wales for the Assembly Campaign (1979). 'Strategy paper', Plaid Cymru archive, File L27, National Library of Wales, Aberystwyth.
Williams, G. A. (1985). *When Was Wales?*, London: Penguin.
Wright, S. (ed.) (1999). *Language, Democracy and Devolution in Catalonia*, Multilingual Matters: Clevedon.
Wyn Jones, R. (2001). 'On process, events and unintended consequences: national identity and the politics of Welsh devolution', *Scottish Affairs*, 37, 34–57.
Wyn Jones, R. (forthcoming). *Rhoi Cymru 'n Gyntaf*, Cardiff: University of Wales Press.
Wyn Jones, R. and Trystan, D. (2000). 'A "quiet earthquake": the first elections to the National Assembly for Wales', paper presented to the American Political Science Association annual conference, Washington.

4. OBSERVANCE OF ST DAVID'S DAY IN SECONDARY SCHOOLS IN WALES: A NATIONAL SURVEY, 2002

Nigel Exell

ABSTRACT

The inculcation of a sense of national belonging and citizenship has long been established as a function of state education in nation states. Recent political change has resulted in increasing opportunities for the creation of a uniquely Welsh cultural dimension to the schools curriculum in Wales. Key features of this dimension are Welsh-language teaching and the cross-curricular theme, the Curriculum Cymreig (Y Cwricwlwm Cymreig). In the school year 2001–2, ethnographic research was undertaken at three schools in south Wales, seeking to understand how these two initiatives were received at schools, and how they influenced school activities aimed at promoting a sense of Welsh awareness or identity among pupils. The research found that St David's Day celebrations were a key part of this dimension, although the significance of events varied both between schools and also among members of staff at each of the three schools. A national survey was undertaken to establish the extent to which such events were held in secondary schools across Wales, and the kinds of activities which characterized them. It was found that holding an event is very popular, and that the Urdd and National Eisteddfodau are cited as influential, but that there was considerable variation in the use of symbols of Wales, the language spoken or sung during activities, and the types of activities which comprised the event. This article presents data from the national survey describing both the kinds of events held and also discusses the influence of region or medium of instruction on this variation.

INTRODUCTION

National education systems can be understood as having two distinct aspects to what they teach. The school is a means of both inculcating a sense of national identity among its citizenry and teaching skills relevant to the national economy (for example, Durkheim, 1956; Gellner, 1983; Green, 1990). The development of a sense of group identity among pupils is particularly significant in circumstances where the survival of an ethnic or linguistic group is in need of support (Edwards, 1985, p. 118), or where a cultural identification with an emergent political institution is being developed, for example, in the contemporary European context (Shore, 1993, 2000; Shore and Black, 1994). Wales can be viewed as an example where both these aspects are relevant.

Changes to education policy in the United Kingdom since 1988, and the more recent devolution of education policy-making powers to the National Assembly for Wales, have created opportunities for the establishment of a strong Welsh cultural dimension in the schools' curriculum in Wales (Jones and Lewis, 1995; G. E. Jones, 1994). All pupils now take Welsh language lessons throughout the compulsory attendance years. Wales-specific teaching examples are largely incorporated into curriculum subjects (most notably in history (see Phillips et al., 1999), geography, art and Welsh), in accordance with the requirements of the statutory cross-curricular theme, the Curriculum Cymreig (ACCAC, 2001) which states that 'pupils should be given opportunities to develop and apply knowledge and understanding of the cultural, economic, environmental, historical and linguistic characteristics of Wales'. Clearly, within the age five to sixteen schools' curriculum in Wales there is now a cultural dimension firmly established in statutory requirements.

Beyond the formal curriculum, the use of patriotic images in classroom or corridor displays may help create a more constant Welsh ethos in the quotidian atmosphere. Primary schools often feature year-round classroom decorations on a Welsh theme, employing common stereotypes such as daffodils, dolls in Welsh costume and leeks (see Estyn, 2001), and these may be understood to contribute to a daily reminding or 'flagging' in Billig's (1995) sense, and of pupils identifying themselves and their classroom as 'Welsh' (see Scourfield, Davies and Holland, 2003, p. 93). The organization of teaching space in the secondary sector, however, where each curriculum subject tends to be taught in a room dedicated to that subject rather than all subjects being taught in one 'class' room as in primary schools, requires a commitment among a larger number of staff to ensure that the classroom material culture incorporates an effective Welsh dimension as well as enhancing teaching of individual subjects. In my research in three case study schools in south Wales, it was found that this dual pressure on secondary school teachers, combined with the tendency for 'things Welsh' to gravitate towards the Welsh department in the absence of a strong management lead in this area in the two English-medium schools studied, has the potential to undermine the development of a school-wide Welsh ethos (see Exell, 2004). The national patron saint's day would appear to offer a special opportunity for schools to overcome any such organizational barriers and encourage the participation of the whole school in a celebration of Welshness.

For about a century, a celebration of Welsh culture has been held on or close to St David's Day in schools in Wales, and has sought to invoke a sense of nationhood. During the First World War, St David's Day celebrations were encouraged through the publications of the Welsh Department of the Board of Education (Welsh Department Board of Education, 1916, p. 4) as an opportunity to recognize not only Welsh culture but also British patriotism, stressing Wales's place in the Empire. The celebration of St David's Day has continued through the twentieth century; G. E. Jones, writing on post-1944 education in Wales, comments that 'most primary and secondary schools observed St David's Day in some fashion' (1994, p. 7). An event on St David's Day is not compulsory, however, and there is no official requirement as to its form. The lack of any policy regarding celebration of national patron saints' days in schools may be a reflection of the circumstance that for most of the twentieth century education policy in Wales was determined by that of 'England and Wales' and that no equivalent event takes place in England, nor is there any British event which would apply to both. The nature of the event is determined at the local level, by staff in each school. Like the inclusion of a Welsh cultural dimension in the curriculum teaching in secondary schools more generally, the scope of the event can be expected to reflect both the school ethos and the attitudes of staff who get involved in its preparation, as well as reflecting the views of staff and pupils as to what kinds of activities are appropriate.

Furthermore, schools' autonomy in deciding what kinds of activities or decoration will be employed on St David's Day could be expected to result in variation in practice across the country, reflecting the plurality of expressions and meanings of Welshness which characterize the country (see Day, 2002). Identification of patterns in this variation would contribute to an understanding of the nature of this plurality. In addition, a survey of the material culture employed is also relevant to discussions of the way in which things become recognized as significant in this context (Kopytoff, 1986) and the ways in which groups which have limited access to particular symbols may seek alternatives to serve the same purpose (Miller, 1987, p. 163). Throughout this article references to expressions of Welsh culture in schools are made in consideration of this and do not assume that there is one common experience of Welsh culture or national identity. Given the geographic patterns of Welsh-language fluency and education through the medium of Welsh, which are to some extent reflected in differences between local education authority (LEA) policies, it is worth considering that celebrations of St David's Day may also vary across regions. Early analysis of the survey data presented here suggested that there were significant differences between the character of events held in the south Wales valleys particularly compared with schools in LEAs which form the area of 'Y Fro Gymraeg' in Balsom's 'three-Wales model' (Balsom, 1985). While a general model such as Balsom's cannot reveal the subtleties behind local expressions of Welshness (Day, 2002, p. 250), and Welsh identity clearly cannot be simplified to a 'one of three' model, Balsom's regions can still be seen to relate to regional Welsh-language patterns; there is a higher provision of Welsh-medium secondary education in 'Y Fro Gymraeg' (Welsh Office, 2001, p. 151) and a higher level of Welsh language ability (Ibid., p. 40) in this region than in the other two regions. Also, an analysis of the voting trends in the 1997 devolution referendum indicates that the percentage of 'Yes' votes, although showing a smaller range of values across the regions than in the 1979 referendum voting, shows 'Y Fro Gymraeg' as having a higher share of the 'Yes' vote (61.4 per cent) than 'Welsh Wales' (46.56 per cent) and 'British Wales' (41.9 per cent)[1] (see also Wyn Jones and Trystan, 1999, p. 83–4, for the relevance of Balsom's model for recent election results).

While a faithful examination of the way in which St David's Day school events may relate to the ethos and organization of the school could only be realized by a detailed study of St David's Day events in a number of schools across Wales, this article is able to present a comprehensive snapshot of what kinds of events were taking place in secondary schools in Wales on or around 1 March 2002.

RESEARCH DESIGN AND COLLECTED DATA SETS

The research aimed to find out if secondary schools in Wales held events to observe St David's Day 2002 and, if so, what kinds of activities were held. The data was collected in two ways. Firstly, events at three secondary schools in south Wales were observed and a number of staff were interviewed. These studies gave a good idea of the kinds of things schools did on or around the patron saint's day and this informed the design of the questionnaire employed in the second kind of data collected in a national survey. The national survey was conducted as a postal survey and asked secondary schools in Wales to complete and return a two-page questionnaire. The questionnaire was sent to all secondary schools in Wales in mid-March 2002, and asked for details of any events that were held to mark St David's Day that year. The questionnaire was prepared in both English and Welsh, and copies of each, together with a bilingual covering letter, were addressed to the head of Welsh/person responsible for Welsh. A stamped, addressed envelope was included for the return of the questionnaire. An understanding of the internal organization of the school gained from fieldwork visits gave the impression that the heads of Welsh departments would be most sympathetic to the research and most likely to find time to complete and return the questionnaire.

A total of 259 questionnaires were posted and 149 (57.5 per cent) were returned. Of these, 142 (95.3 per cent) cases had held an event. While this response was very good, it was suspected that the low number of returned questionnaires which indicated that no event had been held may be due to schools not holding an event also not responding. To improve the response rate 65 schools who had not responded by post were subsequently asked by e-mail if they had held an event. This follow-up exercise increased the response number by a further 32 cases, making the total number of responses 181 (69.9 per cent). Of these, 170 cases (93.9 per cent) stated that they had held an event. Hence the proportion of schools holding an event to mark St David's Day 2002 is very high for schools who responded to this survey, and this number of cases remains significant even when considered in relation to the total population of 259 secondary schools in Wales (see table 4.1). The survey found that *at least* 170 secondary schools (65.6 per cent of all secondary schools in Wales) held an event to mark the occasion in 2002. Furthermore, the large number of fully completed and returned questionnaires is a substantial database with which to explore the character of the events held.

As established above, many secondary schools in Wales hold an event to mark St David's Day. It is worth noting again here that the event is an entirely voluntary activity that, while wholly appropriate to the objectives of the Curriculum Cymreig, is not a required component of it or any other formal part of the curriculum. The popularity of the event was evident across regions and also in both Welsh-medium and English-medium schools. In many of the attributes of the event, however, there is significant variation both regionally and between Welsh- and English-medium schools as a whole in Wales. In the following section of the article these variations are presented.

Table 4.1
Postal/e-mail survey of secondary schools' observance of St David's Day 2002

	Sent	Returned (% of sent)	Cases holding an event (% of returned)	Cases not holding an event (% of returned)
Postal survey	259	149 (57.5)	142 (95.3)	7 (4.7)
E-mail follow-up	65	32 (49.2)	28 (87.5)	4 (12.5)
Total*	259	181 (69.9)	170 (93.9)	11 (6.1)

* This row includes the responses to the initial postal survey and responses to the follow-up e-mail survey of a number of cases who had not responded to the postal survey.

Scope of data: geographical spread and school type

All local education authorities (LEAs) are represented in the sample, as are independent schools. An important factor in some of the data analysis in this article is the medium of instruction: Welsh-medium and English-medium schools are represented in this sample (19.5 per cent and 80.5 per cent respectively) in similar proportion to their presence for the total population of secondary schools in Wales (20.1 per cent and 79.9 per cent respectively).

The kinds of events held

St David's Day is observed on 1 March, and although most schools mark the occasion by holding an event on the date itself this may not always be possible. The date may not fall on a school day (Monday to Friday) for example, or the school may find it necessary to organize events more directly related to curriculum teaching on that day, such as practice or 'mock' examinations. In the majority of the cases, however, the event was held on or near to 1 March (82.6 per cent), with a further 10.1 per cent holding an event in 'early/mid February'. Typically the event is held at the school (95.8 per cent) during normal school hours, and in one or more halls, depending on their size and the number of pupils in attendance, though in a few cases a local hall or theatre was used. The events last between ten minutes and two days. This huge variation is true for both Welsh-medium and English-medium schools, with the average duration in each sector being 212.8 minutes and 211.1 minutes respectively, that is around 3.5 hours in both. A large number of both English- and Welsh-medium schools hold events that last for one or two days (45.7 per cent and 51.8 per cent respectively).

The most common form of the event comprises a number of performance activities typically taking place on a stage before an audience of pupils. In many schools (78.3 per cent) the performances are competitive with pupils on stage competing on behalf of their house team, or their form class, in order to win points for that group. Pupils may be seated according to their house or class and in some cases wear an item of clothing in their 'house colour'. This obvious sense of group identity can generate fierce support for their representatives on stage.

Pupil participation
Not all schools hold an event that involves the whole school, although many do. This does not seem to be a function of the size of the school, and, even though there will be cases where it is impossible to accommodate all the school's pupils into one venue on the school premises, many will choose to run two events simultaneously at school or hold separate events for particular year groups at different times, while a few make use of large halls or theatres in the school locality. Where schools do not hold events that include all pupils, the choice of which pupils participate is biased towards the lower years, particularly those in the pre-GCSE (General Certificate of Secondary Education) course years of 7, 8 and 9 (see table 4.2). One possible explanation is that pupils in years 10 and 11 often have examination pressures at the very time that St David's Day occurs, and although a few schools celebrate the patron saint's day on an alternative date earlier or later in the year, many others simply choose to focus the event on younger pupils. Data from interviews in the three case-study schools indicates that in some schools this decision is also influenced by the decreasing willingness to participate in stage events as pupils get older. Younger pupils are 'more used to that sort of thing from primary' one teacher told me, adding that by year 10 pupils are difficult to motivate for any such events. Assembly singing also follows this trend, with some secondary teachers liaising with those in their feeder primary schools to ensure that some of the songs sung in year 7 assemblies are familiar to pupils from their primary school assemblies. It could be argued that, in the desire to hold an event that is positive and celebratory, teachers decide it is better to eliminate that older group of pupils who are perceived as likely to introduce a rather negative mood.

There does not appear to be any regional trend to levels of pupil participation: the four cases of Welsh-medium schools not holding an all-school event are from different LEAs and are distributed between north and south Wales.

Table 4.2
Pupil participation and medium of instruction

Pupil group	Teaching medium		Total (%)
	Welsh (%)	English (%)	
Whole school	22 (75.9)	44 (38.9)	66 (46.5)
From years 7, 8, 9 only	4 (13.8)	61 (54.0)	65 (45.8)
All but year 11 and/or year 13*	2 (6.9)	2 (1.8)	4 (2.8)
Other mix	1 (3.4)	6 (5.3)	7 (4.9)
Total	29 (100)	113 (100)	142 (100)

* Years in which external examinations are taken in May/June.

Exploring regional trends
The data set generated by the survey is representative of the total population at three principal levels: the sample is a significant proportion of the total number of secondary schools in Wales; both Welsh- and English-medium schools are represented in proportions corresponding to those of the total population; and there is distribution of cases across LEA regions. Hence the data provides a sound basis for exploration of trends between regions or language of instruction. However, whereas the number of cases in the grouping according to language of instruction is large enough to allow meaningful comparison, the numbers of cases in each of the twenty-two LEA regions are not. It is beyond the scope of this survey to develop a regional model from data; certainly the number of cases is not sufficient to do so reliably. To explore regional variation a pre-existing and appropriate means of grouping the cases into larger areas is desirable.

Balsom's 'three-Wales model' (1985) presents a viable means of examining regional trends in my own survey data. This regional model utilizes political, national and linguistic measures of personal identity obtained through surveys. These themes are germane to those of my own survey findings presented in this article and the relatively small number of regions makes comparative analysis statistically more viable than between LEA regions. Balsom's three regions are: Welsh-speaking, Welsh-identifying ('Y Fro Gymraeg'), Welsh-identifying, non-Welsh-speaking ('Welsh Wales'), and British-identifying, non-Welsh-speaking ('British Wales'). The geographical areas covered by these regions relate to the groupings of unitary authorities shown in table 4.3.[2]

Table 4.3
Groupings of unitary authorities corresponding with Balsom's 'three-Wales model'

Welsh Wales	Y Fro Gymraeg	British Wales	
Blaenau Gwent	Anglesey	Bridgend	Newport
Caerphilly	Carmarthenshire	Cardiff	Pembrokeshire
Merthyr Tydfil	Ceredigion	Denbighshire	Powys
Neath Port Talbot	Conwy	Flintshire	Vale of Glamorgan
Rhondda Cynon Taff	Gwynedd	Monmouthshire	Wrexham
Torfaen			
Swansea			

The use of national symbols

The use of symbols is a very effective and highly salient way of representing imagined communities and nations in particular. The role of national symbols in asserting a sense of a national culture in the classroom has been a key aspect of the curriculum debates, particularly concerning history teaching (for example, Phillips et al., 1999). Shore (2000) argues that the development and promotion of appropriate symbols is a key aspect of the development of a European citizenry, and Shore and Black indicate the importance of education in this context (1994, p. 295). Johnson (1980) highlights the role of material culture in asserting a dominant national culture over more local forms of cultural expression. Although schools in Wales are administered by the state, they are not required to observe St David's Day, nor to use any particular symbols in marking it. The choice is theirs, yet they are likely to draw on a repertoire of symbols from the wider society commonly understood as 'national'. The data presented here, therefore, gives an impression of what practitioners understand to be appropriate representations of Welsh culture on this occasion.

Decoration of the venue

In Wales national symbols such as the flag and the anthem are not as regularly employed in school life as they are in the USA or Thailand, for example, where they are used daily to affirm allegiance to a nation or monarch, but they are prevalent in celebrations of St David's Day in some secondary schools in Wales. On this occasion, the Welsh language, flags, songs and other symbols of Wales are employed in many schools to create an especially Welsh mood which may not be as intense at other times. The questionnaire included a list of images that might be used to decorate the venue for the event, and schools were asked to indicate which images they had used. Table 4.4 summarizes the responses according to teaching medium and also in groupings of LEAs influenced by Balsom's 'three-Wales model' discussed above.

Table 4.4
Decoration of the venue for St David's Day events

Item	Balsom's 'three-Wales' regions			Medium of instruction		Total (%)
	Welsh Wales (%)	Y Fro Gymraeg (%)	British Wales (%)	Welsh (%)	English (%)	
Daffodil	42 (80.8)	16 (72.7)	53 (77.9)	20 (69)	91 (80.5)	111 (78.2)
Welsh flag	40 (76.9)	14 (63.6)	52 (76.5)	14 (48.3)	92 (81.4)	106 (74.6)
Dragon	30 (57.7)	9 (40.9)	43 (63.2)	9 (31.0)	73 (64.6)	82 (57.7)
Leek	22 (42.3)	3 (13.6)	27 (39.7)	5 (17.2)	47 (41.6)	52 (36.6)
School badge	19 (36.5)	8 (36.4)	13 (19.1)	10 (34.5)	30 (26.5)	40 (28.2)
School name	16 (30.8)	4 (18.2)	14 (20.6)	6 (20.7)	28 (24.8)	34 (23.9)
Celtic art	8 (15.4)	1 (4.5)	12 (17.6)	1 (3.4)	20 (17.7)	21 (14.8)
House badges/names	8 (15.4)	3 (13.6)	6 (8.8)	5 (17.2)	12 (10.6)	17 (12.0)
St David	6 (11.5)	0 (0.0)	9 (13.2)	0 (0.0)	15 (13.3)	15 (10.6)
Castles	3 (5.8)	0 (0.0)	8 (11.8)	0 (0.0)	11 (8.8)	11 (7.7)
Welsh landscape	4 (7.7)	0 (0.0)	5 (7.4)	0 (0.0)	9 (8.0)	9 (6.3)
Mining	3 (6.7)	0 (0.0)	1 (1.5)	0 (0.0)	4 (3.6)	4 (2.8)
Sheep	1 (1.9)	0 (0.0)	2 (2.9)	0 (0.0)	3 (2.7)	3 (2.1)

Pupils' dress

These results indicate the widespread popularity of the daffodil, the Welsh flag and the dragon in decorating the venue for the event. These images are more often used in English-medium than in Welsh-medium schools, however. In fact, it appears from this data that images representing Wales the nation are more popular generally in English-medium schools. This is not the case for images that represent identification with the school, however. The percentages of schools displaying the school name or badge, or the badges or names of school houses, are more comparable between teaching medium groups. Notably, several images are not used in Welsh-medium schools in this sample: St David, castles, Welsh landscape, mining, sheep, with Celtic art being used in only one case in the Welsh-medium group. It is noticeable that for these images, there is a great similarity between the data for 'Y Fro Gymraeg' and that for Welsh-medium schools across Wales (including 'Y Fro Gymraeg'). This indicates that in the non-use of these images, English-medium schools in 'Y Fro Gymraeg' are more similar to Welsh-medium schools in that area (and elsewhere across Wales) than to other English-medium schools and supports the significance of Balsom's regions regarding these images. It is interesting to note that Estyn, Her Majesty's Inspectorate for Education and Training in Wales, on reviewing the development of a Welsh ethos in schools in Wales, reports that:

Displays in some schools give too much emphasis to stereotypical images of Wales. Dolls in Welsh costume, red dragon flags, daffodils, castles and sheep are all useful in conveying standard images of Wales and help to convey a sense of identity to younger pupils. However, there is a danger, that when used with older pupils, they convey an image of the country that gives a false impression of modern Wales. (Estyn, 2001, p. 20)

The data presented here argues that the view of Estyn (although here aimed more generally at school displays in corridors and classrooms) is more in accord with the practices of schools in 'Y Fro Gymraeg' than in other regions.

Pupil dress – leeks, daffodils and rugby shirts
St David's Day is a festival and its celebration in schools has been an occasion for activities that may create an altered atmosphere, a sense of fun or even carnival. The wearing of a uniform can indicate group membership, but this can be indicative of power relations and social control (Joseph and Alex, 1972). In particular, school uniforms are part of the control the school exercises over a pupil's corporal freedom (for example, Okely, 1996) and offer a site for pupil resistance (Gordon, Holland and Lahelma, 2000, pp. 167–72). Several questions on the survey asked whether any relaxation of school uniform was sanctioned for the event, or if leeks or daffodils were worn. Table 4.5 shows the trends for the whole sample of schools holding an event. Some trends were noticed when using Balsom's model. The wearing of leeks and daffodils is most popular in 'Welsh Wales' (71.2 per cent), but less common in 'British Wales' (59.7 per cent) and 'Y Fro Gymraeg' (57.1 per cent). A similar trend is evident in the wearing of a Wales rugby shirt: 'Welsh Wales', 44.2 per cent; 'British Wales', 23.9 per cent; and 'Y Fro Gymraeg', 20.0 per cent. There is an increase in the percentage of schools relaxing uniform rules if only cases where the event lasts one day or more are selected (53.1 per cent).

Influence of eisteddfodau
Eisteddfodau comprise cultural performances understood to be essentially Welsh. In staging an event intended to celebrate Welsh identity largely through performance, whether as stage performer or audience, the Urdd eisteddfodau and the Eisteddfod Genedlaethol Cymru (the National Eisteddfod) could be expected to provide examples of the kinds of activities that would be appropriate. The survey found that a large proportion of schools (82.4 per cent) incorporated elements in their St David's Day events that mirrored those of the Urdd eisteddfodau or Eisteddfodau Cenedlaethol. Performances at eisteddfodau are competitive, with the major

prizewinner being presented at a 'chairing ceremony'. The survey investigated the prevalence of these particular characteristics across the regions and in both English- and Welsh-medium schools and found that the influence of the eisteddfod is of similar strength: in the total sample of schools holding an event, 69.5 per cent replied that 'types of performances' were influenced by the eisteddfod, 55.3 per cent that 'competitions categories' (for example, solo instrument, choir, group drama) were organized in reflection of those of the Urdd or Eisteddfodau Cenedlaethol, and 47.5 per cent that a chairing ceremony was held. Clearly the Urdd eisteddfodau and the Eisteddfod Genedlaethol Cymru are significant references for types of performances put on in celebration of Welsh culture/identity for St David's Day in secondary schools across Wales.

Table 4.5
Pupil dress during the event

	Balsom's 'three-Wales' regions			Medium of instruction		Total (%)
	Welsh Wales (%)	*Y Fro Gymraeg* (%)	*British Wales* (%)	Welsh (%)	English (%)	
Uniform rules were relaxed during the event	30 (57.7)	7 (24.1)	21 (35.6)	12 (44.4)	46 (40.7)	58 (41.4)
At least some pupils wore leek or daffodil	37 (71.2)	16 (55.2)	36 (61.0)	19 (65.5)	70 (63.1)	89 (3.6)
At least some pupils wore Wales rugby jersey	23 (44.2)	5 (17.9)	15 (25.4)	8 (28.6)	35 (31.5)	43 (30.9)
At least some pupils wore Wales soccer jersey	9 (17.3)	2 (7.1)	8 (13.6)	4 (14.3)	15 (13.5)	19 (13.7)
At least some pupils wore a top in their house colour	15 (28.8)	4 (14.3)	12 (20.3)	5 (17.9)	26 (23.4)	31 (22.3)

Language use
Welsh-medium schools surveyed here strongly favour the use of Welsh in performances, and with the exception of a small percentage of 'small group song' events, eschew the use of English alone in performances. In English-medium schools bilingual performances are more popular than in Welsh-medium schools and, taken together with the use of Welsh alone, demonstrate a high level of use of Welsh in this sector also, although most often combined with English. Clearly,

performances in the Welsh language are viewed as particularly appropriate to the event. There is a higher level of use of modern foreign languages (MFLs) in English-medium schools than in Welsh-medium schools with the notable exception of the 'pop song' category. This category has a higher level of English-only performances in English-medium schools, suggesting a differentiation between more 'traditional' Welsh activities of singing, poetry and to a lesser extent drama, and the pop song that represents the ultimate in contemporary performance. Whereas Welsh is used for the more traditional activities, English is the medium of popular culture. In Welsh-medium schools pop songs are performed mostly in Welsh and this probably reflects both the greater ease of access to Welsh-medium pop music for pupils and teachers in that sector and the greater resources for producing performances in translation (in one of the three case-study schools several pop songs originally recorded in English were performed in Welsh, having been translated by pupils).

There is considerable conformity to Balsom's regions of this variation in language usage patterns in stage items. In all five of these stage items the use of Welsh, including Welsh with a MFL, was most prevalent in 'Y Fro Gymraeg', and in four of the five 'Welsh Wales' had the next highest use and 'British Wales' the lowest. The exception here is 'small group song'. In all five items, however, the use of English, including English with a MFL, was highest in 'British Wales', then 'Welsh Wales', then 'Y Fro Gymraeg' – the reverse of the pattern for Welsh in four of the items.

Competition

As mentioned above, many schools said that their St David's Day event was influenced in some part by the competitive format of Urdd eisteddfodau and Eisteddfod Genedlaethol Cymru. Where events are competitive, pupils generally earn prizes for their team that may be organized by registration class or by school house or *llys* (literally 'court'). In schools where competitive events are held (78.3 per cent of those holding some event), an inter-house competition is the most popular way of organizing the event to reward pupil successes – a finding that is consistent for both English- and Welsh-medium schools and for all regions in the Balsom model. Earning points for one's registration class was less popular overall, but was more common in English-medium schools (20.2 per cent) than Welsh-medium schools (5.9 per cent), and in the 'British Wales' region (6 per cent). Typically, houses are named after Welsh historical heroes and have a 'house colour'.

The national anthem

As illustrated in table 4.6, the popularity of singing the national anthem at St David's Day events is, while generally popular across Wales, much more prevalent in 'Welsh Wales'. This finding, that would appear to fall in line with other data presented here suggesting that symbolic representations of nationhood are more popular in 'Welsh Wales', is nevertheless something of a surprising result, given that the singing of the national anthem might be expected to be quite a convenient means of invoking a sense of nation among a group of pupils. Although the questionnaire did not ask schools to specify in which language the anthem was sung, it was assumed that this would most likely be in Welsh. If this assumption is correct, then the greater popularity of the item in English-medium than Welsh-medium schools is also surprising and suggests that English-medium schools generally, and particularly those in 'Welsh Wales', are keen to employ symbols typically employed more widely in a international context. The international sporting context may be a significant influence here.

Table 4.6
Singing of the Welsh national anthem

	Balsom's 'three-Wales' regions			Medium of instruction		Total (%)
	Welsh Wales (%)	*Y Fro Gymraeg* (%)	*British Wales* (%)	Welsh (%)	English (%)	
National anthem was sung	47 (90.4)	20 (66.7)	40 (66.7)	17 (58.6)	90 (79.6)	107 (75.4)

CONCLUSION

This article has reported that St David's Day is recognized as an important occasion by the majority of secondary schools in Wales. The festival is typically observed during normal school hours on or near 1 March, and events range from special assemblies lasting ten or twenty minutes and involving only the younger year groups to whole school events taking place in school halls over one or two days. A large percentage of secondary schools in Wales hold an event which focuses on stage performances of music or drama items. The organization and style of these performances and their competitive nature are greatly influenced by those of eisteddfodau, and in the majority of schools holding competitive events pupils' successes are rewarded with points for their school house. Welsh-language performances are popular and a number of symbols of the Welsh nation are used in decorating venues in many schools. While there is no recommendation to schools by any authority to mark the event in any particular way, St David's Day is clearly understood by schools to be a time to celebrate Welshness and an opportunity to provide some Welsh cultural education to pupils in larger groups than the normal class size and in an atmosphere less structured by curriculum requirements.

While there is much in common between the events held in schools across the country, examination of the data presented here also reveals a number of significant variations between regions or medium of instruction. The involvement of the whole school in the event is almost twice as likely in Welsh-medium schools as in English-medium schools, where there is a much greater tendency to hold events restricted to the lower year groups. Undertaking an event which involves the whole school and which suspends normal teaching for a considerable period of time for both rehearsals and performances clearly involves a great deal of organizational effort as well as requiring the support of parents. Hence a commitment to involve the whole school in a celebration of *Welsh* culture perhaps reflects the strength of a general *Welsh* ethos in the school and the close relation of this particular cultural theme to a sense of a school community. The exclusive use of the Welsh language in performances at St David's Day events is, as might be predicted, higher in Welsh-medium schools than in English-medium schools, yet it also plays a significant part in performances in the latter. Many activities in English-medium schools are in Welsh and/or other modern foreign languages and, although there is a tendency for performances to be bilingual in English-medium schools, it is clear that the Welsh language is recognized as an important element in this celebration of Welsh culture.

The languages used in stage performances is one feature of the event which follows Balsom's regional pattern (which itself incorporates language fluency), with Welsh featuring strongly in both Welsh- and English-medium schools in 'Y Fro Gymraeg', and the use of Welsh without English (including Welsh with a MFL) being less frequent in 'Welsh Wales' and less again in 'British Wales'. This trend is reversed in the use of English without Welsh (including English with a MFL). That is, it is most common in 'British Wales', less in 'Welsh Wales' and less again in 'Y Fro Gymraeg'. Certain patterns in the use of material culture also relate to Balsom's model. The greater percentage of schools where pupils wear Welsh rugby jerseys on St David's Day in 'Welsh Wales' than in the other two regions is probably related to the greater density of top-flight rugby clubs in this area. Rugby remains a strong aspect of community identity in this area of Wales (see S. P. Jones, 1997). The popularity of singing the Welsh national anthem in 'Welsh Wales' on St David's Day provides food for thought, suggesting perhaps that the anthem is most often connected with Wales in the context of international sporting events. A native of south Wales myself, I can think of few other occasions when the anthem is heard. The popularity of wearing a national rugby team jersey indicates that this garment has become incorporated into the repertoire of things employed in symbolizing the nation, becoming of wider cultural significance than its initial purpose. In the south Wales valleys, where this has become most popular, the Wales rugby jersey also appears to be displacing the 'coalminer' and 'folk' costume worn by primary school-age boys on St David's Day. It is beyond the scope of this survey to speculate further on the ways in which these material things 'matter' to participants (both staff and pupils) in individual schools (Miller, 1998), and the way in which a commodity comes to be utilized in this way, but this area would be worthy of further investigation. Also, the applicability of Balsom's model to the variation in these expressions of Welshness in secondary schools on St David's Day across the country suggests that distinctive social histories and geographies of the regions may be an influence on the different ways of observing this national occasion.

Perhaps less predictable than the influence of rugby in south Wales is the greater use of material symbols of Wales in English-medium compared to Welsh-medium schools. While such symbols are far from absent in 'Y Fro Gymraeg', the percentages of schools employing the popular symbols are consistently lower than in the other two regions, and the range of symbols is considerably smaller. Taken as a whole, the data concerning material culture suggests that there is a greater emphasis on the use of national symbols in English-medium schools compared to Welsh-medium schools (and English-medium schools in 'Y Fro Gymraeg'). A possible explanation is that for schools where the Welsh language has greater prominence in everyday school life, this serves as a strong daily reminder of Welsh culture. This would be in accordance with Billig's 'flagging' effect referred to earlier. Hence, at the St David's Day event, there is less of a need to *create* a Welsh atmosphere as it is already a strong quotidian feature of the school. In schools where such 'flagging' is less pervasive, there would be a correspondingly greater need to employ some means of invoking a Welsh mood, and symbols such as flags, dragons and daffodils, as well as the Welsh language, are a popularly understood resource in this context. If symbols create a sense of ritual space, of time set apart, by creating a phase of separation or a liminal phase (Turner, 1969, pp. 94–5), then the extent to which groups utilize them can be taken as an indication of the character not only of the ritual event, but equally of routine life. That is, the less groups use symbols to create a difference between routine and festival, the closer is the everyday culture to that being celebrated at the festival. It is also a possibility that the lesser confidence in the use of the Welsh language in English-medium schools results in a strategy of employing a range of other symbols to assert a sense of Welshness and that this acts as an impetus for the incorporation of more contemporary material goods such as rugby jerseys, flags and inflatable plastic daffodils.

This article provides a unique survey of the kinds of events that are held. Despite the intensity of curriculum subject teaching duties, many secondary schools take time out to organize an event on St David's Day to celebrate Welsh culture. While there is a common understanding of the repertoire of material symbols and performances that are culturally Welsh, there is clearly significant variation in the ways in which they are employed.

ACKNOWLEDGEMENTS

The research presented in this article was a part of my Ph.D. studies at the University of Wales Swansea, undertaken with the support of a university studentship. I would like to express my appreciation to the university for this opportunity afforded me. I would also like to take this opportunity to thank all the schools that participated in this survey. I hope you find the results useful.

NOTES

[1]   These figures are based on Welsh Office statistics (Welsh Office, 2001, p. 34).

[2]   Although Balsom's model is highly appropriate to an analysis of my own research data, there are a number of issues to be addressed regarding boundaries. Balsom used parliamentary constituencies as his smallest discrete unit whereas schools are most conveniently grouped according to LEA. As LEA boundaries in 2001 are not entirely coincident with those of the parliamentary constituencies of 1983, the regrouping of LEAs into Balsom's regions presents some problems in organizing the cases. Firstly, Conwy LEA extends further east than the Conwy in Balsom's map, yet because of a greater congruence between my own data for the Conwy region and that for Gwynedd or Anglesey, Conwy LEA is included in 'Y Fro Gymraeg'. A second difference is that schools in the Llanelli area are now administered within the Carmarthenshire LEA – a part of 'Y Fro Gymraeg' – whereas in Balsom's model they are included in 'Welsh Wales'. In my data set schools in the Llanelli area have been included in 'Welsh Wales'. In Balsom's model, the Pembrokeshire constituency is smaller than the present LEA, which extends further up the west coast. All the valid cases from Pembrokeshire LEA are from within the constituency boundary of 1983, however, so no regrouping is necessary.

REFERENCES

ACCAC (Awdurdod Cymwysterau, Cwricwlwm ac Asesu Cymru) (2001). *Common Requirements Across the National Curriculum, www.accac.org.uk/uploads/documents/1378.doc*

Balsom, D. (1985). 'The three-Wales model' in Osmond, J. (ed.), *The National Question Again: Welsh Political Identity in the 1980s*, Llandysul: Gomer, pp. 1–17.

Billig, M. (1995). *Banal Nationalism*, London: Sage.

Day, G. (2002). *Making Sense of Wales: A Sociological Perspective*, Cardiff: University of Wales Press.

Durkheim, E. (1956). *Education and Sociology*, New York: The Free Press.

Edwards, J. (1985). *Language, Society and Identity*, London: Blackwell.

Estyn (2001). *Y Cwricwlwm Cymreig: The Welsh Dimension of the Curriculum in Wales: Good Practice in Teaching and Learning*, Cardiff: Estyn.

Exell, N. D. (2004). 'Expressions of Welsh identity in secondary schools in Wales', unpublished Ph.D. thesis, University of Wales.

Gellner, E. (1983). *Nations and Nationalism*, Oxford: Blackwell.

Gordon, T., Holland, J. and Lahelma, E. (2000). *Making Spaces: Citizenship and Difference in Schools*, Basingstoke: Macmillan.

Green, A. (1990). *Education and State Formation*, Basingstoke: Macmillan.

Johnson, N. B. (1980). 'The material culture of public school classrooms: the symbolic integration of local schools and national culture', *Anthropology and Education Quarterly*, 11, 3, 173–90.

Jones, B. and Lewis, I. (1995). 'A Curriculum Cymreig', *The Welsh Journal of Education*, 4, 2, 22–35.

Jones, G. E. (1994). 'Which nation's curriculum?: the case of Wales', *The Curriculum Journal*, 5, 1, 5–15.

Jones, S. P. (1997). 'Still a mining community: gender and change in the Upper Dulais Valley', unpublished Ph.D. thesis, University of Wales.

Joseph, N. and Alex, N. (1972). 'The uniform: a sociological perspective', *American Journal of Sociology*, 77, 4, 719–30.

Kopytoff, I. (1986). 'The cultural biography of things: commoditization as process', in A. Appadurai (ed.), *The Social Life of Things: Commodities in Cultural Perspective*, Cambridge: Cambridge University Press.

Miller, D. (1987). *Material Culture and Mass Consumption*, Oxford: Blackwell.

Miller, D. (1998). 'Why some things matter', in D. Miller (ed.), *Material Cultures: Why Some Things Matter*, London: UCL Press.

Okely, J. (1996). *Own or Other Culture*, London: Routledge.

Phillips, R., Goalen, P., McCully, A. and Woods, S. (1999). 'Four histories, one nation? History teaching, nationhood and a British identity', *Compare*, 29, 2, 153–69.

Scourfield, J., Davies, A. and Holland, S. (2003). 'Wales and Welshness in middle childhood', *Contemporary Wales*, 16, 83–100.

Shore, C. (1993). 'Inventing the "Peoples' Europe": critical approaches to European Community "cultural policy"', *Man (N.S.)* 28, 779–800.

Shore, C. (2000). *Building Europe: The Cultural Politics of European Integration*, London: Routledge.

Shore, C. and Black, A. (1994). 'Citizens' Europe and the construction of European identity', in V. A. Goddard, J. R. Llobera and C. Shore (eds), *The Anthropology of Europe: Identities and Boundaries in Conflict*, Oxford: Berg.

Turner, V. W. (1969). *The Ritual Process: Structure and Anti-Structure*, London: Routledge and Kegan Paul.

Welsh Department Board of Education (1916). *Patriotism: Suggestions to Local Education Authorities and Teachers in Wales Regarding the Teaching of Patriotism*, London: Welsh Department Board of Education.

Welsh Office (2001). *Digest of Welsh Local Area Statistics*, Cardiff: Welsh Office.

Wyn Jones, R. and Trystan, D. (1999). 'The 1997 Welsh referendum vote', in B. Taylor and K. Thomson (eds), *Scotland and Wales: Nations Again?*, Cardiff: University of Wales Press.

5. CITIZENSHIP, CIVIL SOCIETY AND COMMUNITY IN WALES

Lesley Hodgson

ABSTRACT

Central and regional governments are increasingly concerned with creating 'active' citizens through encouraging engagement in voluntary and community activities. This article examines the way that the three concepts, citizenship, civil society and community, have become increasingly intertwined both in political rhetoric and in reality. It examines moves to create active citizens in Wales and suggests that true citizenship requires a platform for dissent and criticism that may be absent in the current political climate of consensus. Concerns are raised about the funding of voluntary activity and the current drive toward the professionalization of voluntary and community groups. Questions are also raised about the extent to which involvement in volunteering is translated into political activity.

INTRODUCTION

The last two decades have seen an increased interest in three interrelated concepts: citizenship, community and civil society. The connection between the latter two has intensified as the former has been 'revived' through the idea of active citizenship. This article investigates the way in which these three concepts have become bound together in Wales, by examining the idea that active citizenship can be promoted through engagement in voluntary activity. The primary data is drawn from interviews with members of forty-eight civil society and community groups, including the coordinators of a Welsh Assembly Government programme, introduced in 2000 aimed at providing a community-centred approach to regeneration, called 'Communities First'.[1] Initial interviews took place in 2000 and were added to and updated in 2004. The interviews were based in south-east Wales and encompassed a range of what could be termed mainstream activities; although typical, they were as diverse as crochet clubs, housing associations, cycling 'clubs' and national charitable bodies.

The article is in three sections. First, some definition and clarification of terms is needed to outline what is meant by citizenship, community and civil society. At first glance these seem apparently straightforward and commonsensical terms; however, all are capable of being used differently by academics, commentators and policy-makers of differing political and ideological persuasions. This section includes, therefore, an overview of the political and ideological environment within which these concepts have developed. The article then takes a closer look at the development of civil society and community in contemporary Wales, before examining the ways in which the three concepts have become interlinked. The article concludes that whilst there are many new channels through which individuals can participate in voluntary activities, the Assembly Government is more concerned with producing 'responsible' citizens with whom it can liaise rather than active citizens in the true sense.

CITIZENSHIP, COMMUNITY AND CIVIL SOCIETY

Whether the recent growth in interest in the concept of citizenship can be attributed to concerns over globalization and migration, asylum issues, threats to welfare provision, political changes initiated by developments in central and eastern Europe in the late 1980s and early 1990s or some other development is a matter of debate. What is clear, however, is that this contested concept increasingly permeates the minds and rhetoric of policy-makers and others concerned with issues of governance. There can be little doubt that Roche was correct in his assumption that citizenship is a 'strategically important idea in [the] late twentieth century' (1992, p. 1). From the relatively new category of 'Citizens of the Union' set out in the Maastricht Treaty in 1992 to the introduction of 'citizenship classes' in UK schools, and from the increased importance of the citizen in UN Development Reports (for example, UN, 2002) to the calls for a 'Citizens' Constitution' from Charter 88, at all levels we have witnessed a plethora of initiatives targeted at the development of a 'citizen' culture. However, like many other terms within this debate, citizenship can mean different things to different people and can be utilized for seemingly diverse ends. There is, therefore, a need to consider the interconnected dimensions of the term 'citizenship'.

Lister (1997) proposes that at its very core citizenship has traditionally been concerned with the balance between individual rights and obligations; the extent to which one feels either rights or obligations should dominate often depends on your political persuasion or world-view. In his seminal work, T. H. Marshall extracts the key elements of citizenship: 'a status bestowed on those who are members of a community. All who possess the status are equal with respect to the rights and duties with which the status is endowed' (1950, pp. 28–9). This reading suggests that citizenship is concerned with our membership status; a membership bound together by a mixture of rights and obligations that implies equality and justice. Marshall was particularly concerned with the political, legal and social rights that underpin citizenship, what has been identified as citizenship as 'status'. Others favour the idea of citizenship as 'practice', viewing citizenship as an active rather than a passive condition; this view focuses on the attitudes and actions of individuals (see Oldfield, 1990). Whichever view we favour, what becomes clear is that citizenship is a dynamic identity (Faulks, 2000).

Roche (1992) points out that in Britain the citizenship debate has witnessed a shift away from a discussion of rights to a discussion increasingly focused on obligations. Indeed, this would seem to be a defining feature of the New Labour discourse on citizenship, wherein the emphasis has been laid on responsibilities, exemplified by the revamped Clause 4 statement 'where the rights we enjoy reflect the duties we owe'. One way that citizens can shoulder their duties or obligations is through becoming involved in a 'citizenship culture'. A 'citizenship culture' has been defined as a society where the inhabitants 'think it normal, right and even pleasurable to be concerned with and actively involved in public affairs' (Crick, 2001, p. 1). The idea of a citizen culture, therefore, favours 'citizenship as practice', a citizenship that is centred on participation and obligation, rather than the more traditional view of citizenship as a set of rights.

'Active' citizenship has been promoted from a variety of diverse standpoints. The Conservative Party of the 1980s, for example, used the term as part of its wider remit to 'roll back the state' through encouraging individuals to be more neighbourly, to provide care in the private sphere and to be involved in charitable ventures either through monetary donations or by volunteering. The Green movement uses the idea of active citizens to promote ideas of 'ecological citizenship' which not only encourages local activism but stretches the concept of citizenship to the limits of its global boundaries, producing a form of 'global citizenship' (Dadzie, 1999). Pahl's (1990) definition of citizenship is also concerned with participation: 'local people working together to improve the quality of their own life and to provide the conditions for others to enjoy the fruits of a more affluent society' (cited in Lister, 1998, p. 52). Here then is the link between citizenship, community and civil society. If citizenship is being redefined as obligations, responsibilities and duties ('citizenship as practice' before 'citizenship as status'), then one way that we can become active citizens is through engaging with civil society and/or our community. Crick states that our being 'involved in public affairs' is not confined to our relationship with the state, 'but also to all those institutions intermediate and mediating between the individual and the state which we call civil society' (2001, p. 1). Similarly, Lister invokes Jean Leca's definition that citizenship is located amongst the 'myriad of voluntary associations of civil society most particularly the kinds of campaigning organisations and community groups' (1997, p. 29).

Civil society, at its most basic level, refers to the sphere in which individuals can freely organize themselves into groups and associations and engage in 'uncoerced human association' or 'voluntary' activity (Walzer, 1995; Deakin, 2001). Whether that association is social, cultural or political, whether it is self-fulfilling or carried out for the benefit of others, its defining feature is that it is undertaken voluntarily, without pressure or interference from others. Academics debate the extent to which civil society, the state, market and private spheres overlap and influence each other. Indeed, the extent to which civil society influences democracy or facilitates a deeper political participation is often a matter of intense deliberation (see later discussion). For the purpose of this article, civil society refers to the plethora of voluntary associations of differing sizes, shades and hues that comprise a given society.

Community, 'an ostensibly straightforward term' (Adamson and Jones, 2004, p. 12), represents another multifaceted combination of ideas that defies simple explanation and often produces conflicting and contradictory outcomes (Delanty, 2003). Closely linked to civil society, it is, at least in government rhetoric, still located in 'place' and 'neighbourhood', a traditional view of 'community as Gemeinschaft' – a people bound by shared experiences and tradition. Commentators have noted, however, that community has increasingly become bound up in a larger 'moral' discourse centred on social responsibility, civic obligation and social regeneration (Fairclough, 2000). Thus we witness the current focus on values, family, education, neighbourhood and associations in contemporary political rhetoric (see also the work of Etzioni, 1996). Rose (1999) suggests that 'community' has become part of a quasi-governmental discourse that has provided us with a new language and indeed this would seem to be the case as we witness a growing range of words prefixed by the word community: regeneration; initiatives; experts; policing; development; safety.

Whilst those on the right of the political spectrum have a long-standing attraction to civil society, seeing it as a viable alternative to the state provision of welfare, recent years have seen those on the left develop a liking for the ideas of civil society and community. Lyndsay (2001) outlines a number of reasons for this, some pragmatic – civil society can play a role in fulfilling a need; some political – civil society is capable of mustering the support of the populace. An individual interested in current or public affairs, for example, may pursue this interest by becoming involved in a local action group, a lobbying/pressure group, through volunteering, fund-raising or other activity rather than in more 'formal politics'. The Labour government has been quick to see the value of utilizing these channels in developing active citizens.

An ideological dimension can also be added to New Labour's interest in civil society. Drawing on the work of Giddens (1998) and communitarian influences (for example, Etzioni, 1996), Blair has interwoven discussion about civil society and community into political discourse so that they have become integral to the 'third way'. Shortly after taking up the leadership of the Labour Party, Blair put forward his view of society: 'individuals cannot be divorced from the society to which they belong. (My view of society) contains a judgement that individuals owe *a duty to one another and to a broader society*' (Blair, 1994, p. 12, brackets and italics inserted). From this viewpoint community and civil society are well placed to facilitate an individual's connection to wider society, the forum within which they can 'do their duty'. In this regard, Giddens (1998) suggests that government has a role to play in creating a 'civic culture' through which active citizens can play a part. The idea here is that a well-developed civil society offers an alternative political arena in which governments can reach the people (Giddens, 2000). In this way, civil society and community can be seen as vital partners in creating a citizen culture.

Similarly, a recent policy statement from the Labour Party states that 'strong communities are the foundation of a vibrant political culture' and thus the Labour Party is committed to 'strengthening and renewing civil society . . . building up the commitment to community that underpins engagement in politics' (2003, p. 4). The suggestion is that, while traditional forms of politics are in decline, a 'new politics' is developing, centred around 'active citizens, partici-pating in their community and taking more of the decisions made in their name'. Thus, 'Community really matters' (2003, p. 5). These ideas have come to the fore in a raft of policy initiatives throughout the UK such as Urban Regeneration and Community Development (Northern Ireland), Social Justice (Scotland), New Deal for Communities (England) and Communities First (Wales).

There are critics of the 'citizen as participants' approach. Elrick (1999), for example, argues there is an inherent danger in active citizenship developments. He suggests that the promotion of active citizens may turn out to be little more than an exercise in expanding responsibilities and sacrificing rights. He argues that individual needs or interests become subsumed as consensus becomes the key focus of democracy, with the effect of hampering or suppressing debate. Tam warns that individuals will be 'reluctant to participate if they perceive institutions as being mere puppets of decision-making processes centralized in Whitehall' (2001, p. 125). He further remarks that the call for greater community involvement rings hollow when it is repeatedly contradicted by directives which override local preferences. Finally, concern has been voiced about the independence of the voluntary and community sectors as they increasingly find themselves caught up in a web of financial dependency, consultation overload and professional-ization. Hodgson (2004a, 2004b) suggests that civil society is at the very least being stifled and at worst manufactured by the state. Similarly, Lyndsay (2001) warns that, while the voluntary organizations are well placed to provide the space for citizens to participate, there is a danger that the sector could end up becoming virtual agents of the state. Some of these concerns are reiterated later in this article. First, however, the following section examines ideas of civil society and community in Wales.

COMMUNITY AND CIVIL SOCIETY IN WALES

There are a number of competing assessments of community and civil society in Wales. One asserts that Wales has a vibrant community spirit based on civil and civic participation, while the other maintains that civil society in Wales is weak and needs to be created. Hain (1999) asserts, for example, that Wales entertains a greater attachment to community and civic participation than other parts of the United Kingdom. He presents a view of Wales as a 'community of communities', filled with activists involved in multifarious forms of association, a Wales where people are culturally predisposed to participate in collaborative ventures. For Hain, although individualism, social stress and the disintegration of community threaten Wales, it still holds fast to ideas of civic and civil participation. Thus, he espouses the development of a new form of community politics and sees the National Assembly for Wales as a means of engendering a common citizenship.

Other commentators have suggested that Wales has a somewhat weaker civil society than other parts of the UK, most notably Scotland. This analysis suggests that civil society in Wales is underdeveloped and needs to become increasingly dynamic (Osmond, 1998). Once again, the Welsh Assembly is seen to be the body with the ability to re-energize civil society. The logical conclusion, therefore, is that while the 'fragile plant' that is 'civil society was not the precursor to devolution it may yet be among its progeny' (Paterson and Wyn Jones, 1999, p. 183). These views are based on assumptions about the nature of Welsh civil society, assumptions that also determine the development of public and social policy. Both views suffer from tunnel vision in that Wales, and indeed civil society, is seen in one particular way. Both, however, present the Assembly as the means of saving civil society and developing a new sense of citizenship (Hain, 1999; Jones and Osmond, 2002).

A more recent analysis of civil society undertaken by the Wales Council for Voluntary Action (WCVA, 2003), the representative body that promotes itself as the voice of the more formalized voluntary sector in Wales, suggests that civil society in Wales is of 'medium strength'. The WCVA took the lead from CIVICUS (the World Alliance for Citizen Participation) in defining civil society as the 'arena, outside of the family, the state, and the market where people associate to advance common interests' (CIVICUS, nd). This concept of civil society, however, which sees civil society as a sphere outside of the traditional political arena, a place where individuals collaborate to pursue agreed goals, is not unproblematic. The findings of the survey report that the WCVA authors encountered 'confusion as to the definition of civil society', which was cited as a reason for 'not replying to the survey at all' (only 23 per cent of recipients responded to the questionnaire, WCVA, 2003a, pp. 1 and 11). The subsequent WCVA Manifesto, *Civil Society, Civil Space*, outlines a number of ways civil society can be strengthened, including the need to ensure 'user-led policies' and 'increased participation and civil responsibility' (2003b, p. 3). Once again the Assembly is seen to be the catalyst within which civil society can flourish.

Whatever the truth of some of the above claims, the true extent of involvement in voluntary activity in Wales is largely unknown. The WCVA estimates (2003) that 48 per cent of the adult population (1.12 million people) and 89 per cent of young people (165,600 11–15 year-olds) volunteer in formal and informal activities. There are an estimated 30,000 formal organizations involved in community, voluntary or charitable work; the vast majority of these, 23,000, are local organizations (as distinct from national or regional). These organizations are operated by 22,900 paid employees, representing 1.8 per cent of the total paid workforce. It should be noted, however, that these figures are based on data from a variety of published sources and that the true extent of voluntary activity is unknown largely because involvement in informal activity (by its very nature) defies calculation. It can be argued, however, that to the extent these figures are reliable Wales would seem to have a healthy civil society, and thus a bedrock on which to build active citizens through voluntary or community activity.

ACTIVE CITIZENS AND THE WELSH ASSEMBLY

The National Assembly, in line with Westminster initiatives, promotes active citizenship through voluntary activity. The 'General Principles' of the Voluntary Sector Scheme (VSS), the document that outlines how the Assembly realizes its legal commitments to the voluntary sector, states that one of the aims of the National Assembly is to 'encourage . . . the idea that voluntary activity is an essential part of active citizenship', recognizing that 'volunteering is an important expression of citizenship and . . . an essential component of democracy' (NAfW, 2000, pp. 3–5). In fact, the VSS is littered with references to the 'promotion', 'development' and 'support' of voluntary organizations.

Volunteering in Wales is encouraged through a variety of diverse mechanisms, some concerned with funding, such as the Volunteering in Wales Fund and others concerned with the promotion of volunteering and community development, for example the 'volunteering Wales' website (*www.volunteeringwales.net/ www.gwirfoddolicymru.net*). Various schemes that encourage volunteering, such as the Active Communities Unit and Millennium Volunteers, have been set up. In addition, Communities First underpins much of the work undertaken by volunteers in the community context, encouraging the development of new volunteers and community groups within the most deprived areas of Wales. Part of the remit of Communities First, as emphasized in the *Community Vision Framework* (WAG, 1999), is the development of 'active' communities which will produce community members that can 'engage freely with the local and national democratic processes'.

The idea behind many of the schemes mentioned above is that volunteering is a means not only of giving back to the community but also of building the capacity of the individuals involved in volunteering 'to encourage them to take responsibility for their community, to develop the skills needed . . . transferable skills, that can be used elsewhere. To develop good citizens that can play an active part in the social regeneration of their community' (Communities First Co-ordinator). Indeed, the recent Independent Commission analysing the Voluntary Sector Scheme suggest, that 'Volunteering . . . promote(s) active citizenship, cohesive communities and positive attitudes . . . it improve[s] confidence, skills and employment prospects, [and makes] people more socially aware . . .' (2004, p. 107). Whilst acknowledging that volunteer activity in Wales has a better infrastructure than previously, the commission's findings suggest a number of issues that need to be addressed in relation to volunteering and community activity: the funding of training and levels of support given to voluntary activity; the emphasis on economic rather than social or environmental regeneration; and problems with the consultation processes. It will be interesting to see how the Assembly Government responds to these issues.

FORMING ACTIVE CITIZENS – SOME CONCERNS

There is little doubt that since devolution there has been an increase in the channels through which individuals can participate in voluntary activity. There are, however, specific tensions within the voluntary and community sectors that are likely to increase and that may have a direct impact on the development of active citizens. For example, we increasingly witness the use of voluntary organizations in the provision of services traditionally provided by the state. The idea here is that voluntary organizations are closer to the people and are more aware of their needs; they also use innovative modes of delivery and are generally more trusted than public service providers. The outcome of this is most likely to be that increasing numbers of voluntary organizations are going to be involved in service provision and thus dependent on contracts and funding emanating from the state. Indeed, more than a third of the organizations interviewed suggested that at some point they had needed to take on service provision in order to survive even though this had taken them away from the main core of their work.

One chief executive involved in an organization devoted to the needs of older people highlighted, for example, that 47 per cent of his funding was tied to service contracts and that, whilst this money would ensure the organization's survival for the forthcoming year, it meant that many of the paid and voluntary members would be working on projects that were not part of their core work. It also meant that the organization was caught up in competing for contracts against other voluntary organizations in what has become a constant chase for short-term contracts and project funding. This means, in practice, that groups need constantly to think up new and innovative projects so that their core work is secured. As one chief executive of an organization concerned with children's play suggested: 'You have to be one step ahead of everyone else, guard new ideas and think about ways of making projects seem new, even where they aren't, just to survive.'

In addition, as much of this funding comes through state bodies, voluntary and community groups are increasingly finding themselves in the vulnerable position of having to toe the line for fear of losing funding. As one respondent suggested: 'You can't rock the boat, or argue with the local authority when they are the ones giving you the money.' Thus, while the sector provides great opportunities for voluntary activity, and therefore the potential for the creation of active citizens, it may be the case that in the future organizations involved in the formal voluntary sector become little more than another set of employers without the independence and freedom afforded to the private sector because of funding constraints (Lyndsay, 2000). In this case the creation of active citizens could be said to be concerned with creating employees rather than developing freethinking individuals with the skills to enable community regeneration.

More worryingly, however, there is also evidence that both voluntary and community groups are becoming increasingly bureaucratized, sometimes to the extent of becoming top-heavy with administration staff as they employ the 'necessary' personnel involved in liaising with statutory agencies, writing funding bids and evaluation reports. This means that core work is increasingly being carried out by unpaid voluntary members rather than core staff and there is evidence to suggest that this is affecting the numbers of people willing to volunteer:

> It's one thing to ask people to lend a helping hand – we are now asking these people to take on real responsibilities and sometimes this is just too much to expect. It's beginning to affect the numbers of people that are willing to volunteer for us and I have the constant worry that I am frightening people off. In fact we need to take on more volunteers to offset the workloads.

In addition, the professionalization of voluntary activity is also having an impact on the nature of volunteering at a fundamental level. Volunteering, by its nature, is often transitory with fluctuations occurring in both the numbers of people involved and the time they devote to activities. The professionalization of volunteering, however, means that groups are continually looking for 'experts', those with the right type of skills, largely because groups of all sizes are increasingly required to produce business plans, performance records, strategy documents and the like when they apply for even moderate amounts of funding. In addition, fund-raising has become a much more complex phenomenon than in the past, with groups having to compete by using increasingly commercial mechanisms of promotion. One manager of a community group described how much of her time was spent in thinking up logos and advertising slogans to promote the group. She described this as an increasingly 'necessary part of her job' if they are to survive. This professionalization means either spending much needed resources on training and/or employing individuals, or if possible utilizing local individuals to act as volunteers and use their skills. There is evidence to suggest that grass-roots initiatives increasingly see the benefits to be had in sourcing a locally based 'expert' and often target new residents with much needed expertise, calling into question the role of voluntary agencies in building the capacity and skills of those within the community. As one respondent suggested: 'In truth, one retired expert, or one not retired would be even better, but one retired expert is worth more than five volunteers, if that expert can write up a funding bid and bring in more money.'

Communities First initiatives, in particular, pride themselves on building the capacity of local community members and many coordinators feel that this is being accomplished with individuals developing a range of skills (for example, committee skills) that facilitate community and voluntary involvement. Even here, however, there is a tendency to use local 'experts' as often as possible in the various partnership boards and forums. What this means in practice is that a select core of individuals serve on a range of committees and partnerships (arguably individuals with the necessary skills already in place). Thus, the extent to which grass-roots involvement is encouraged and grass-roots opinions are fed through is questionable. Indeed, one coordinator explained that their partnership meetings are dominated by the voices of local councillors who attend the meetings, whilst another suggested that 'experts' outweighed community members by four to one on the partnership board.

Moreover, many of the coordinators felt that consultation had taken place early on in the life of Communities First and that they had the 'best interests' of the community at heart. Not only does this call into question the extent to which 'new' active citizens are being created, it also threatens the bottom-up approach that Communities First is built upon. Indeed, one coordinator voiced concerns that as Communities First develops it is becoming 'increasingly bureaucratic and increasingly driven by us the coordinators and those above us'.

It would seem therefore that, whilst the opportunities for creating active citizens are plentiful and whilst much is being done to upgrade the capacity of all involved in voluntary activity, there is an ever present danger that much that is done in the name of a bottom-up approach may increasingly be directed by elite individuals targeted for their expertise rather than their local knowledge. What appears therefore to be 'grass-roots working' may in practice be a managerial approach which is in fact directed by the Assembly Government.

Another role of civil society is to pursue social change through acting as an opponent to government. This does not mean that all civil society groups are inherently unfavourable to government but rather that their role is to induce change through campaigning and lobbying. Although funding is a major issue here, the present dialogic climate in Wales, where consensus seems to be at the heart of the decision-making process, also produces tensions for organizations involved in these processes. Whilst the Welsh Assembly Government has provided the fora for debate and discussion (largely through the Voluntary Sector Partnership and consultation documents) some groups voiced concern about the lack of space given over for dissension. Indeed, one respondent suggested that whilst at times she wanted to argue with some of the policies being generated by the Assembly she instead found herself being 'a proof-reader for the Assembly'. This has raised questions as to what the Assembly Government means when it talks about creating active citizens. It would appear that, in the minds of some at least, this is little more than an exercise in getting people 'on side'. As one Communities First coordinator asked:

> Does the Assembly really want to create active citizens? I don't think they could handle it if we started churning out 'bolshie' people who would question their every move. Active citizenship is more about producing people who can do things for themselves, make their communities better and who have the capacity to liaise with various agencies that will help them do that.

It seems therefore as if Elrick's (1999) fears may be justified and that, for some, the idea of active citizenship is more concerned with 'responsibilizing' individuals than it is about political engagement. Indeed, it seems as though, while providing a forum for debate and discussion, the Assembly Government may be at the same time stifling debate in the name of liaison and consensus.

There is a further set of fundamental questions related to active citizenship which pertain to the idea of a link between voluntary/community involvement and political engagement. The academic literature about this suggests that belonging to civil society facilitates the building of certain 'democracy building functions' (Diamond, 1994). Diamond proposes that involvement with others in voluntary activity can engender feelings of political efficacy, civil obligation and the development of a sophisticated political outlook that can be translated into political activity. Almond and Verba's (1989) account acknowledges that certain skills can be developed, most notably amongst those who are involved in long-term voluntary activity, but suggests that while these may be 'transferred' to the political realm they can just as readily be transferred to the job market. Discussions involving voluntary members suggest that the latter is more likely. One project manager involved in environmental work suggested that there are problems surrounding the amount of time and money spent in building the capacity of individuals who then go off and use those skills in the market place. Whilst it was recognized that it 'goes with the territory' and was an 'age old' dichotomy, concerns were raised about the extent to which groups are increasingly being used in providing work-based skills rather than concentrating on their area of need. Similarly, a Communities First coordinator queried where active citizens were going to exercise their ability to 'engage with local and national democratic processes':

> We can develop their capacity, they can negotiate with the local authority (but many could do that anyway there just wasn't the forum in the past to engage like there is today), they can write up funding bids and chair a meeting, take minutes. So what? What do they do then – they go off and find a job. There is no forum for them to develop any political skills beyond what we provide. And I think that's what the government wants, people in jobs. I'm happy with that outcome, it's part of social regeneration.

Only time will tell whether the new initiatives put in place by the Welsh Assembly Government will creative active citizens involved in democratic processes. In Wales we now have the infrastructure for voluntary groups to be increasingly involved in decision-making and policy development; however, whether that involvement is translated to the individual has yet to be decided.

CONCLUSION

Voluntary organizations have a responsibility to represent the interests of large sections of society. They are also a vital aspect of democratic life. Yet in order to be able to carry out either of these roles they have to be trusted. To that end they constantly have to juggle when and how far they should become involved with political institutions. Many of those interviewed felt that the new mechanisms for dialogue with the Assembly and the input they have into policy development is better than before devolution. There are, however, rumblings of disquiet amongst those who feel that their ability to criticize the Assembly Government is being compromised by their reliance on the Assembly as a funding mechanism. In addition, it would seem for many that the government's active citizenship agenda is closely tied to fostering employability rather than fostering true community participation.

While voluntary and community organizations are well placed to provide the space for new ideas and the arena for participation and/or creation of active citizens, what we now need to ensure is that participation is not constrained by the funding, bureaucracy or professionalization of voluntary and community-based organizations. It needs to be realized that the creation of active citizens is not solely dependent on involving people or getting people 'on side', but it is vital that we allow citizens and the organizations they join to have the space to develop their own ideas and to have the freedom to dissent where needed.

NOTE

1   Although the National Assembly for Wales has a relatively short history, major changes have already taken place in the nature and functioning of the Assembly. Initially, the Assembly was to operate as a single corporate body; however, following a review in 2001 the National Assembly for Wales now operates on a largely parliamentary model with executive powers resting with the executive – the Welsh Assembly Government (WAG). It is in this context that Communities First is seen as a WAG initiative (see Patchett, 2003; Osmond, 2003; Chaney and Drakeford, 2004; for a further discussion).

REFERENCES

Adamson, D. and Jones, S. (2004). 'Continuity and change in the Valleys: residents' perceptions in 1995 and 2001', *Contemporary Wales*, 16, 1–23.

Almond, G. and Verba, S. (1989). *The Civic Culture Revisited*, London: Sage.

Blair, T. (1994). *Socialism*, London: Fabian Society.

Chaney, P. and Drakeford, M. (2004). 'The primacy of ideology: social policy and the first term of the National Assembly for Wales', *Social Policy Review*, 16, 121–42.

CIVICUS (n.d.). *Civil Society Index*, *www.civicus.org/new/media/CSIpercent20Methodology %20and%20Conceptual%20Framework.doc*

Crick, B. (ed.) (2001). *Citizens: Toward a Citizenship Culture*, Oxford: Blackwell.

Dadzie, S. (1999). *Making a Difference: A Resource Pack for People Who Want to Become More Active Citizens*, Leicester, NIACE.

Deakin, N. (2001). *In Search of Civil Society*, Basingstoke: Palgrave.

Delanty, G. (2003). *Community*, London: Routledge.

Diamond, L. (1994). 'Rethinking civil society: towards democratic consolidation', *Journal of Democracy*, 5, 3, 4–17.

Elrick, D. (1999). 'Debating the state: a growth in active citizenship, special issue on citizenship', *Concept*, 9, 2.

Etzioni, A. (1996). *The New Golden Rule: Community and Morality in a Democratic Society*, New York: Basic Books.

Fairclough, N. (2000). *New Labour, New Language?*, London: Routledge.

Faulks, K. (2000). *Citizenship*, London: Routledge.

Giddens, A. (1998). *The Third Way: the Renewal of Social Democracy*, Cambridge: Polity Press.

Giddens, A. (2000). *The Third Way and its Critics*, Cambridge: Polity Press.

Hain, P. (1999). *The Welsh Third Way?*, London: Tribune.

Hodgson, L. (2004a). 'Manufactured civil society: counting the cost', *Critical Social Policy*, 24, 2, 139–64.

Hodgson, L. (2004b). 'Civil society, consultation and the National Assembly for Wales', *Politics*, 24, 2, 88–95.

Independent Commission (2004). *Review of the Voluntary Sector Scheme*, www.wales. gov.uk/ themesvoluntarysector/content/annualreport/final/report-e.pdf

Jones, B. and Osmond, J. (eds) (2002). *Building a Civic Culture: Institutional Change, Policy Development and Political Dynamics in the National Assembly for Wales*, Cardiff: IWA and WGC.

Labour Party (2003). *Democracy, Political Engagement, Citizenship and Equalities*, www.labour.org.uk/crimejusticecitizenshipequalitiespolicy/

Lister, R. (1997). *Citizenship: Feminist Perspectives*, Basingstoke: Macmillan.

Lister, R. (1998). 'New conceptions of citizenship', in N. Ellison and C. Pierson (eds), *Developments in British Social Policy*, Basingstoke: Macmillan.

Lyndsay, I. (2000). 'The voluntary sector', in B. Crick (ed.), *Citizens: Toward a Citizenship Culture*, Oxford: Blackwells.

Marshall, T. H. (1950). *Citizenship and Social Class*, Cambridge: Cambridge University Press.

National Assembly for Wales (NAfW) (2000). *The Voluntary Sector Scheme*, Cardiff: NAfW.

Oldfield, A. (1990). *Citizenship and Community*, London: Routledge.

Osmond, J. (ed.) (1998). *The National Assembly Agenda*, Cardiff: Institute of Welsh Affairs.

Osmond, J. (2003). 'From corporate body to virtual parliament: the metamorphosis of the National Assembly for Wales', in R. Hazell (ed.), *The State of the Nations 2003: The Third Year of Devolution in the United Kingdom*, Exeter: Imprint Academic.

Pahl, R. (1990). 'Prophets, ethnographers and social glue: civil society and social order', paper presented to ESRC/CNRS Workshop on Citizenship, Social Order and Civilising Processes, Cumberland Lodge, September.

Patchett, K. (2003). 'The new constitutional architecture', in J. Osmond. and J. B. Jones (eds), *Birth of Welsh Democracy: The First Term of the National Assembly for Wales*, Cardiff: Institute of Welsh Affairs and Welsh Governance Centre.

Paterson, L. and Wyn Jones, R. (1999). 'Does civil society drive constitutional change?', in B. Taylor. and K. Thomson (eds), *Scotland and Wales: Nations Again?*, Cardiff: University of Wales Press.

Roche, M. (1992). *Rethinking Citizenship*, Cambridge: Polity Press.

Rose, N. (1999). *Powers of Freedom*, Cambridge: Cambridge University Press.

Tam, H. (2001). 'The community roots of citizenship', in B. Crick (ed.), *Citizens: Toward a Citizenship Culture*, Oxford: Blackwell.

United Nations (2002). 'Deepening democracy in a fragmented world', *Human Development Report*, UNDP, hdr.undp.org/reports/global/2002/en/

Volunteering in Wales, www.volunteeringwales.net/www.gwirfoddolicymru.net

Wales Council for Voluntary Action (WCVA) (2003a). *Wales Voluntary Sector Almanac 2003: a New Era?*, Cardiff: WCVA.

Wales Council for Voluntary Action (WCVA) (2003b). *Civil Society: Civil Space – a Manifesto*, Cardiff: WCVA.

Walzer, M. (1995). 'The civil society argument', in R. Beiner (ed.), *Theorising Citizenship*, Albany: State University of New York Press.

Welsh Assembly Government (WAG) (1999). *Community Vision Framework Annex D, Communities First: Guidance for Co-ordinators*, www.wales.gov.uk/ themessocialdeprivation/ content/guidance

6. BANAL BRITISHNESS AND RECONSTITUTED WELSHNESS: THE POLITICS OF NATIONAL IDENTITIES IN WALES

Rebecca Davies

ABSTRACT

Elected devolution and the creation of the National Assembly for Wales have increased the prominence of 'national identity' – and in particular Welsh national identity – in our political life. This article argues that these new constitutional arrangements for Wales only came about as a result of significant changes in the nature and meanings of national identities that have occurred since the 1979 Welsh devolution referendum. Drawing upon the work of Michael Billig and Tom Nairn, this article explores how and why the political consequences of national identities in Wales changed between 1979 and 1997. This discussion aims both to enhance understanding of the role of national identity in bringing about the pro-devolution shift, and to provide a sophisticated theoretical context for understanding the role of national identity in Wales – and the UK – in the post-devolution era.

INTRODUCTION

Wales has always been now. The Welsh as a people have lived by making and remaking themselves in generation after generation, usually against the odds, usually in a British context. (Williams, 1985, p. 304)

Since 1997, devolution has brought into sharp focus the whole question of the relationship between national identity and politics in the United Kingdom, both within the constituent parts and at the state level. While it is clear that Welsh national identity has acquired a different and 'far more prominent role' in Welsh political life, it has also been argued that there can scarcely be any UK government that has devoted quite so much time to the question of what it means to be British (Wyn Jones, 2001, p. 48). Indeed, one of the key features of the New Labour administration thus far has been the search for, and the questioning and redefinition of, Britishness (see, for example, Kearney, 2000; Parekh, 2000; Aughey, 2001).

While devolution precipitated the increased prominence of 'national identity' in our political life, this article argues that elected devolution itself only came about as a result of changes in the nature and meanings of national identities in the UK prior to 1997. Indeed, while the Welsh electorate voted in favour of devolution for Wales by a margin of only 6,721 votes in September 1997, the result represented a 30 per cent shift in favour of devolution amongst the Welsh electorate since the first devolution referendum, held eighteen years previously. This was greater than the 23 per cent pro-devolution shift that occurred in Scotland during the same time period.

Analysis of this remarkable change in attitudes towards devolution in Wales between 1979 and 1997 has dismissed some potential explanations, and em-phasized the importance of national identity in explaining the pro-devolution shift. For instance, devolution was not approved in 1997 simply because of a growth in the proportion of the Welsh population constituted by groups who were among those most likely to support devolution in 1979. There was only a small (4.1 per cent) increase in the percentage of Welsh national identifiers between 1979 and 1997.[1] Nor was there any other demographic shift (such as an increase in Plaid Cymru identifiers or Welsh speakers) sufficient to explain the scale of change in voter preferences that occurred. Turn-out was not a major explanatory factor of change: there was no significant change in the turn-out of Welsh identifiers, as they were the most likely to turn out and vote in both 1979 and 1997. Rather, the most important element to an explanation of why Wales decisively rejected devolution in 1979 but approved it in 1997, it has been argued, is that the political consequences of Welsh national identity changed between 1979 and 1997 (Jones, 2003; Evans and Trystan, 1999; Wyn Jones and Trystan, 1999).

The change in the political consequences of Welsh national identity between 1979 and 1997 has been described as the 'politicization' of Welsh national identity, evidence of which can be found in the pro-devolution swing amongst the Welsh and the working class,[2] and an increase in positive attitudes towards Plaid Cymru as identified in the Welsh Election Study 1979 and the Welsh Referendum Survey 1997 (Evans and Trystan, 1999). This infers that in 1997 Welsh national identity was politically salient, but that this had not been the case in 1979, and that this change determined the referendum vote.

This claim is problematic for two key reasons. First, Welsh national identity has always been political, whether it be historically manifest in support for Wales's role in the British Empire – therefore strengthening the union between Wales and the UK – or in the more distinct political traditions of Liberalism and then Labourism during the nineteenth and twentieth centuries (see Morgan, 1981; Balsom, Madgwick and Van Mechelen, 1983). Secondly, Welsh national identity was politically salient in 1979, although for the majority of Welsh identifiers there was little distinction between the political consequences of Welsh national identity and of British national identity. While those with a Welsh national identity were more likely to vote in favour of devolution in 1997 than they had been in 1979, this does not necessarily mean that Welsh national identity has become more politicized, as it is not the political nature of Welsh national identity but the nature of the political consequences of that identity that has changed. This is a subtle, but important distinction and the key question therefore becomes how and why the political consequences, or more specifically the impact of Welsh national identity on referendum voting behaviour, changed.

This critique is more than merely a dispute about terminology, as the concept of politicization infers a whole set of underlying assumptions about the meaning and political consequences of Welsh national identity, which need to be challenged. Snicker speaks of an 'identity transformation in Wales since 1979' (1998, p. 141) and, although it is undisputed that the Welsh became more pro-devolution, by labelling this process 'politicization' the key questions of how and why the relationship between national identity and politics changed are overlooked. Welsh national identity was political in 1997, no less than it had been eighteen years previously. However, shaped by the intervening period of socio-economic and political change, Welsh national identity carried some quite different political implications for many citizens by 1997.

This article will examine the question of how and why the political consequences of national identity changed between 1979 and 1997. The first part will draw insights from the work of two authors, Michael Billig and Tom Nairn. The second part will apply these insights to Wales post-1979. In doing so, the article will not only enhance understanding of the role of national identity in bringing about the pro-devolution shift, but also provide a more sophisticated, theoretical context for understanding the role of national identity in Wales and, more broadly, the UK post-devolution.

BANAL NATIONALISM: WELSHNESS AND BRITISHNESS

A brief overview of the work of Billig and Nairn identifies five key points, which not only challenge and question the assumptions behind the 'politicization' thesis but, when applied to Wales, transform our understanding of the politics of national identity. First, I argue that the political consequences of national identity cannot simply be equated with nationalism, the political ideology of campaigning 'nationalist' parties. Secondly, in the Welsh context, as already stated, the political consequences of Welsh national identity do not equal support for Plaid Cymru. Thirdly, both Welsh and British identity, and Welsh and British nationalism, exist in Wales, and fourthly, these identities are not fixed, but change according to changes in political, economic and social circumstances. Finally, given Wales's location within the UK state, political, economic and social change at the state level, as well as within Wales, impact upon the political consequences of national identities within Wales.

Billig argues that traditionally the term 'nationalism' has been used in a restricted way; that it has been equated with the outlook of nationalist movements, and subsequently, where no such movements exist, nationalism has not been regarded as an important issue (1995, p. 16). Taking the argument a step further, Billig coined the phrase 'banal nationalism', which he argues is a broadening of the concept of nationalism to cover the ways that established nation-states are routinely reproduced. He argues: 'this frequently involves a 'banal' nationalism, in contrast with the overt, articulated and often fiercely expressed nationalism of those who battle to form new nations' (1995, p. 16). In order to illustrate this, he cites the example of Flemish speakers and the Belgian state, arguing that nationalism is not merely the ideology which is impelling Flemish speakers to resist the Belgian state, but it is also the ideology which permits states, including the Belgian state, to exist. In the absence of an overt political challenge, like that mounted by the Flemish speakers, this ideology might appear banal, routine and almost invisible (1995, p. 15).

Billig argues that banal nationalism has its socio-historical location within the era of nation-states, as primarily a 'political principle, which holds that the political and the national unit should be congruent' (see Gellner, 1983, p. 1). In this context, the political principles of nation-state nationalism appear natural. Billig argues, therefore: 'In established nations, it seems "natural" to suppose that nationalism is an over-heated reaction, which typically is the property of others. The assumption enables "us" to forget "our" nationalism.' (1995, p. 37) In evaluating the political consequences of national identity, he goes on to say that 'what this means is that national identity is more than an inner psychological state, or an individual self-definition: it is a form of life, which is daily lived in the world of nation-states' (1995, p. 69). For Billig, there is no distinct difference between national identity and banal nationalism. He suggests, therefore, that the study of national identity should search for the common-sense assumptions and ways of talking about nationhood (1995, p. 61).

Billig's approach transforms our understanding of national identity and its relationship with nationalism, significantly broadening the traditional parameters of the debate. Indeed, Billig's approach focuses attention away from traditional 'nationalist' groups to look at the daily, subtle manifestations of nationhood. Billig's approach is especially useful in Wales, not least given Wales's position within the UK state, as it infers the existence of both a Welsh and British state identity within Wales. Nationalism in Wales cannot therefore be reduced to Welsh nationalism, competing against a non-nationalist alternative. Rather, if, as Billig argues, nationalism is a universal feature of modernity, then what we have in Wales are two nationalisms: Welsh and British. British nationalism, described by Nairn as 'a taken for granted belief system which informs state attitudes' (2002, p. 13), has been and continues to be rendered 'banal' by all kinds of state and society related practices, while Welsh nationalism is being underpinned by other factors and institutions. Billig's description of banal nationalism as a feature of daily life within the nation-state, rising out of a process of modernity, is therefore a useful tool in explaining British nationalism, and British national identity in Wales.

More recent conceptualizations of nationalism and national identity have described Wales as a 'sub-state nation', or a 'nation without a state' (Guibernau, 1999; Keating, 2001; McCrone, 1998, 1999, 2002). 'Nations without states' are defined as:

> Cultural communities sharing a common past, attached to clearly demarcated territory and wishing to decide upon their political future, with a lack of a state of their own . . . All these nations have ethnic origins that can be traced back to an era previous to the rise of the nation state. (Guibernau, 1999, pp. 1 and 9)

Although Billig does not specifically address this, Wales's status as a sub-state nation within the UK suggests that Welsh national identity, or nationalism, may be different in type and meaning as it is pre-modern and underpinned by different factors to the British state identity (see Nairn, 1981; McCrone, 1998; Guibernau, 1999). These (British and Welsh) identities could therefore be fused, shared or competing, and subsequently have a variety of political consequences.

THE BREAK-UP OF BRITAIN?

The central focus of Nairn's argument is that the growth of Welsh nationalism and the political consequences of Welsh national identity can only be explained in the greater context of the decline of the British nation-state. It is insufficient to judge what he calls Britain's 'new nationalisms' in terms of their own self-consciousness and ideology, as he argues that the key to understanding lies in the 'slow foundering of the British state, not in the Celtic bloodstream' (1981, p. 71).

According to Nairn's account, nationalism in Wales and Scotland is an attempt by the peripheral elite to counteract the impact of uneven development, and to protect or renew the traditional community identity, and that nationality is the only factor available to the peripheral elites for political mobilization against the economic dominance of the centralized state (1981, p. 341). The key point here is that the bourgeoisie use the symbols of nationality as a mobilization tool: 'Naturally, communities can fight for this philosophy best when they have a strong ethnic and linguistic basis. So the particular vehicles of nationality are seen as especially significant' (1981, p. 200), as they are distinct from the identity of the British state.

In this sense, he argues that Wales occupies an 'ambiguous midway position' in the context of Hobsbawm's distinction between historic and non-historic nations (1981, p. 202). Although there are several criteria employed by Hobsbawm in his distinction between historic and non-historic nations, Nairn focuses on the central problem of underdevelopment and overdevelopment. Nairn includes Corsica, Brittany and Galicia as examples of the underdeveloped regions, as they are characterized by 'depopulation, cultural impoverishment and a psychology of powerlessness' (1981, p. 203). On the other hand, Catalonia, the Basque Country and Scotland are cited as examples of overdeveloped regions, characterized by a more rapid and successful economic development than the territories that surround them. The motivation for their nationalism is different, and described as 'dynamic middle class enclaves in a more backward country, capitalist societies struggling to be free, as it were' (1981, p. 203). In this case, he argues:

> Wales shows many of the features of forced under-development: depopulation, cultural oppression, fragmentary and distorted development and so on. These features are strongly evident in the Welsh national movement too, insofar as it has been a battle for the defence and revival of rural-based community and traditional identity – an identity evoked overwhelmingly by literary and musical culture, and having as its mainspring in the language question. But of course in another key respect Wales is more akin to the relatively over-developed group: like them, it is a great secondary centre of the European industrial revolution. (1981, p. 208)

It is clear, then, that whilst Nairn locates the motivation for Welsh nationalism as a response to underdevelopment, it is argued that areas of Wales characterized by overdevelopment could have different characteristics of national identity, and subsequently different types of nationalism could emerge, potentially explaining the traditional association between Welsh national identity and the Labour or Liberal tradition, for example. Nairn thus suggests the possibility and indeed likelihood of heterogeneity in terms of types and meanings of national identity linked to different patterns of economic development. The political consequences of national identity in Wales could vary in these two distinct economic environments.

Nairn's central point is therefore that the relationship between material politics and cultural or national politics has been a varied project in Wales. Nairn clearly suggests that different economic circumstances could result in the mobilization of different aspects of national identity, as further changes in the economic fortunes of the United Kingdom and the subsequent change in social and political structures could have an impact on national identities within the UK. In this sense, Nairn's analysis of Wales's role in the context of the UK state, and the emphasis on the importance of the economic relationship between Wales and the UK, provides not only a means of understanding the underpinnings and meanings of Welsh and British national identity, but also a means of understanding *change* in the nature and meaning of those identities, of the relationship between them and the subsequent political consequences.

Nairn argues that the break-up of Britain was indeed under way throughout the 1980s and 1990s, and that 1979 marked the beginning of an acute period in the decline of Britishness. Although he suggests that there are 'different formulae being debated over the outcome;' for example, 'devolution', 'independence in Europe' an 'association of British states', 'and so on' (Nairn, 2000, p. 4), he argues that the decline in Britishness is terminal (Nairn, 2002, p. 14). This has direct implications for definitions and redefinitions of national identity and the politics of national identity, in particular the redefinition of the majority identity within the UK, that is, the British identity (Nairn, 2000, p. 15). This erosion of Britishness, a nationless identity, not only has implications for the English, but also for the other national identities within the UK (see Nairn, 2002, p. 16). Nairn's assertion is therefore that the altered conditions of the UK state at the end of the twentieth century have key implications for the redefinition of national identities in the UK, and subsequently the political consequences of those identities.

Secondly, Nairn argues that both Welsh and British identity in Wales are linked with the economic and political structures of the UK state. The decline of the UK state therefore has direct consequences for the meaning and (re)definition of these national identities. By examining the decline of Britain, Nairn therefore provides a means of explaining and examining a change in the meaning, and in the political impact of national identities in Wales. It could be argued that the structures of social meaning and attachment previously associated with banal Britishness may be loosening, with a subsequent impact both on national identity and referendum voting in 1979 and 1997.

This very brief overview of the key arguments of Billig and Nairn facilitates a more sophisticated understanding of the changing political consequences of national identities in Wales between 1979 and 1997, and the politics of national identity more broadly.

First, it is clear that national identity must be understood in a much broader sense than the traditional equation of national identity with campaigning nationalist groups. The political consequences of Welsh national identity are not confined to support for explicitly nationalist movements, but have also historically been associated with the Labour and Liberal traditions in Wales. Put in this way, the political consequences of Welsh national identity are also clearly related (in a negative way) with support for the Conservatives.[3]

Secondly, as Billig's exposition of 'banal nationalism' illustrates, when we understand that nationalism is not confined to support for explicitly nationalist movements, it becomes clear that there are two main versions of national identity at play in the Welsh context: Welsh and British. Both national identities have different meanings, social underpinnings and cultural indicators, which may result in different political attitudes and practices. Understanding the politics of national identity in Wales cannot be reduced to an analysis of Welsh nationalism and national identity, but must also include an analysis of British nationalism and identity. The most basic hypothesis rising from this is that we would expect the political practices of Welsh and British identifiers to be different from each other, with Welsh identifiers being more in favour of devolution for Wales, and British national identifiers being more in favour of the status quo. Indeed, the Welsh were more likely than the British to vote in favour of devolution in both 1979 and 1997 (Evans and Trystan, 1999; Jones, 2003).

However, thirdly, the implications of multiple identities in Wales are more far reaching than this in their political consequences. This is apparent when we address the third point, that national identities are not a given, fixed or static entity, but that they change according to political, cultural, social and economic circumstances. Consequently, not only did social and economic change in Wales impact upon national identities in Wales but, given Wales's location within the UK, changes at the latter level also impacted on national identities in Wales.

DEVOLUTION AND THE POLITICS OF NATIONAL IDENTITIES

The history of multiple identities in Wales is intertwined with the history of the development of the relationship between state and nation and Wales's place and role within the UK (Nairn, 1981; Morgan, 1991). Although it can be traced back much further, it is common to speak of an emerging Welsh political consciousness in Wales from the 1880s onwards (Morgan, 1981). Although it is argued that this rebirth was partly a result of intellectual trends throughout Europe during this period, Morgan suggests that it was a specific reaction to the unique circumstances of Wales, not least a response to its relationship with and its role within the United Kingdom.

Described as the awakening of cultural patriotism, the characteristics of this awakening were encapsulated in the Cymru Fydd movement. This grouping embraced the liberal ideal of home rule and other more distinctively 'Welsh' characteristics of temperance, Nonconformity, Welsh literature and the Welsh language. Although it was unsuccessful in its attempts for home rule, it is argued that the characteristics that defined the Cymru Fydd movement have since been identified as the key markers of Welsh national identity for most of the nineteenth and twentieth centuries (see Griffiths, 1995).

However, these were not the characteristics of a homogeneous or all-inclusive identity. At the same time, a different type of identity was flourishing in Wales, one whose pride lay in Wales's industrial contribution to the success and expansion of the British Empire, and Wales's exclusive role within the United Kingdom. It was Dr John Dee, a Welshman, who first coined the phrase 'British Empire'. Lloyd George, Britain's famous wartime prime minister, was a proud Welshman, and embodied the pride that many Welsh people felt in Britain and her institutions. As McCrone argues: 'Being British was not an alien imposition, but a complimentary identity to one's nationality, and, above all, one with strong imperial connotations in which people took pride and confidence' (2002, p. 182). In more recent times, pride in the institutions of Britain, most notably the welfare state system and the NHS, is characteristic of Britishness within Wales (see Osmond, 1998, p. 6). For much of the twentieth century, therefore, Welshness and Britishness have existed as two sides of the same coin. McCrone argues, in the context of the British Empire, that for both the Scots and the Welsh a set of nested identities existed as a set of concentric circles moving outward from the local to the national to the British to the imperial and so on (1998, p. 139). Furthermore, it is argued that it was possible for these plural identities to so exist side by side, and that the resolution of national identities had been relatively straightforward (1998, p. 139; 1999, p. 4). In this sense, McCrone's insightful remarks about the Scots in the imperial age can also be applied to Wales, as in the age of Empire: 'They were Scottish and British too. There was no inherent contradiction, especially when being British was such a fuzzy identity . . . like being a Roman, "civis Britannicus sum" conferred multiple opportunities rather than ambiguities and confusion' (1998, p. 4).

The first devolution referendum of 1979 brought to a head the issue of multiple identities in Wales. The question of whether or not Wales should have its own elected Assembly challenged the patterns of nested identities. Indeed, No campaigners argued that support for the constitutional status quo was not incompatible with having a Welsh national identity, and that Welsh identity was about hearts and minds, not institutions and the politics of nationhood: 'We do not need an Assembly to prove our nationality or our pride. That is a matter of hearts and minds, not bricks, committees and bureaucrats' (Labour 'No' Assembly Campaign, 1979, quoted in Osmond, 1999, p. 4). On the other hand, Yes campaigners saw the devolution referendum as an opportunity to assert their Welsh national identity, and to equate it with a distinctive political institution (Osmond, 1985).

For pro-devolution campaigners, defeat in the 1979 devolution referendum was regarded as a watershed in the development of Welsh political identity – any prospect for giving it a clear constitutional coherence seemed at an end. Pro-devolution campaigners argued that all previous assumptions about Welsh politics, and indeed Welsh identity itself, seemed fatally undermined. Gwyn Alf Williams summed this up when he said: 'They [the "Welsh"] rejected the political traditions to which the modern Welsh had committed themselves. They declared bankrupt the political creeds which the modern Welsh had embraced. They may in the process have warranted the death of Wales itself' (1985, p. 295). Interpretations of the relationship between Welsh national identity and referendum vote in 1979 have mostly focused on the strength, and indeed political salience, of British identity vis-à-vis a weak Welsh national identity, a sense of which, for the majority of Welsh national identifiers did not include the concept of Wales as a viable political unit. Balsom, Madgwick and Van Mechelen argue that referendum voting was 'overwhelmed by British factors' (1983, p. 312), whilst Osmond argued that 'the fact is that Welsh-ness, as a political identity, is crossed by conflicting loyalties: by the local community on the one hand, and by a wider sense of Britain on the other' (Osmond, 1985, p. xx).

Given the lack of data on multiple identities in 1979, these claims are difficult to assess. The limitations in the available data prevent us from assessing the prevalence of dual identities in Wales, or the balance between Welsh and British identity. Any claim about the nature of Britishness and the nature of Welshness, and their mutual impact on referendum vote in 1979, is thus difficult to quantify. Given that the pattern of exclusive identity remained reasonably consistent between 1979 and 1997, there is reason to believe that dual identity was equally, if not more, prevalent in 1979, although the balance between Welsh and British identity is impossible to measure (see Jones, 2003). However, the fact remains that the majority of Welsh national identifiers voted against devolution in 1979 and in favour in 1997. The question of why this change occurred remains to be addressed.

The answer to this question, I contend, lies in fundamental socio-economic and political changes that occurred at both the British-state and Welsh level between 1979 and 1997, which subsequently impacted on the meaning of both Welsh and British national identity in Wales. As Nairn suggests, 'British-ness' was in decline during this period, its 'banal' nature more easily exposed as a result. From 1979 this 'terminal', or 'last stage British-ness' entered an acute phase (Nairn, 2002, pp. 16 and 102; see also Davies, 1999). As McCrone argued:

> The old bargain which had sustained the British state such that national and state identities could co-exist was unravelling, and economic and cultural sinews which had kept this 'fuzzy' state together . . . The demise of Empire, the erosion of monarchy and the diminishing capacity of quintessentially British institutions like the BBC to manufacture and sustain a unified and homogenized British culture have helped to weaken the sense of Britain. (2002, p. 185)

This demise in Britishness has been largely attributed to a decline in the British Empire in the post-Second World War period. However, an acceleration of decline since 1979 has been attributed to eighteen years of Conservative government in the UK, and particularly the impact of Thatcherism (Leys, 1989; Evans, 1997; Nairn, 2002). Heath and Kellas identify an end to the economic consensus that had characterized economics and politics in the UK post-Second World War, under the Thatcher administration, and a subsequent polarization of the political spectrum between 1979 and 1997 (1998, p. 137). Both an erosion of the welfare state and the destabilization of the industrial structure were consequences of the Thatcher era (Evans, 1997, pp. 65 and 117–18).

The decline in these institutions, which were regarded as traditional features of Britishness had an impact not only on politics and society in the UK as a whole, and Wales in particular, but also on national identities. In a sense, therefore, eighteen years of Conservative rule helped to change what it meant to be British. Britishness was less and less a collectivist identity bound with a pride in the Empire and the values associated with the welfare state (Marr, 2000, p. 19). This change in British identity subsequently impacted on other national identities in the UK. Indeed, in Scotland McCrone argues that this fundamental change resulted in a

> re-definition in terms of what it means to be Scottish in terms of socio-political values. Thus, being collectivist, social democratic, liberal was conveniently juxtaposed from 1979 until the 1990s against a Thatcherite government which was seen to be none of these things, and – almost by default – somehow spoke for 'the English' because the Conservatives got elected on the back of English votes. (2002, p. 178)

A similar process has been identified in Wales during this period, in particular increasing hostility towards the Tories between 1979 and 1997, and a sense of anger that English voters decide who runs Wales (Wyn Jones, Scully and Trystan, 2002). Both these factors were associated with a Yes vote in the 1997 devolution referendum (Jones, 2003).

The starting point for the critique of the 'politicization' thesis outlined above was that the political consequences of Welsh national identity are more widespread than support for the nationalist party – Plaid Cymru (see Balsom, Madgwick and Van Mechelen, 1983). In 1979 there was a widespread sense of Welsh national identity amongst Labour Party identifiers as well as amongst Plaid Cymru identifiers. The Labour tradition was based on a working-class tradition associated with the dominance of heavy industry, particularly in the south Wales valleys. This was predominantly a socialist tradition, tied to the values of central economic planning and the welfare state. Trade unionism, a social practice associated with this tradition, was entrenched in the same values structure (see Pelling, 1992). The evidence suggests that, in 1979, devolution was regarded as a nationalist issue, while the values of the Welsh Labour tradition were associated with support for the constitutional status quo.

Widespread social and economic change fundamentally undermined this tradition. The decline of heavy industry disrupted traditional communities and their associated values and practices. High levels of unemployment, the erosion of the welfare state and the 'feminization' of the workforce had a crucial impact on the identities of men (Aaron et al., 1994). This change did not occur in a political vacuum, but was presided over by a series of Conservative governments. The influences of Conservativism had a crucial impact on the Labour Party and its members: not only in terms of a change in attitude to devolution policy (see also Aughey, 2001, p. 94–5), but also more fundamentally in provoking a critical reassessment of the values associated with the Labour Party in the UK, and the subsequent creation of New Labour (see Hughes and Wintour, 1990). Thus, the

Labour tradition associated with a Welsh identity that had been crucial in explaining referendum vote in 1979 had been fatally undermined by 1997. At the same time, the Tories were also instrumental in the development of 'civic' Wales. The expansion of Welsh-medium education, the creation of S4C, the expansion of the functions of the Welsh Office and the proliferation of Welsh public bodies arguably provided a framework for a new expression of a Welsh national identity, one not directly associated with Plaid Cymru (Osmond, 1999, p. 7).

Eighteen years of Conservativism thus had profound effects on economic, social and political life in Wales, and in particular in shaping the electoral fate of, and attitudes towards political parties. The change in attitudes was not only linked to the democratic deficit, but was also associated with a change in the meaning of Welsh national identity between 1979 and 1997, especially amongst Labour Party identifiers. This had an impact on referendum voting in two key ways. First, if the status quo was regarded by many as the protector of a socialist tradition in 1979, by 1997 devolution was seen by some as 'a way to protect Scotland and Wales from the Tories' (Mitchell, 1998, p. 486). Secondly, by 1997, the Conservatives were the only party arguing in favour of the status quo and opposing devolution. As Heath and Kellas suggest, in Scotland, 'Conservatives arguing for the Union are seen by nationalists as denying their Scottish identity' (1998, p. 137). Arguably, this sentiment was also prevalent in Wales in 1997, not just amongst Plaid Cymru identifiers, but also amongst Welsh national identifiers within the Labour Party.

By 1997, therefore, devolution was no longer regarded as merely a 'nationalist' issue, because Welsh identity had become increasingly associated with support for constitutional change. The change in the political mood of Wales between 1979 and 1997 was associated with changes in national identity. Wales became less British as the meaning of the former identity changed. However, there was also a fundamental change in Welsh national identity. The concept of the 'politicization' of Welsh national identity does not adequately address this; Welsh national identity was as political in 1979 as it was in 1997, but the nature of the political consequences of that identity changed fundamentally. This can only be explained in the context of political, social and economic change that occurred in both Wales and the UK between 1979 and 1997.

CONCLUSION

Rapid social, economic and political change during the 1980s and 1990s had profound implications for both Wales and the British state. On a broad level, the end of the Cold War and the decline of Empire led to an increased questioning of the role and continuing existence of the state (see Nairn, 2000, 2002; Marr, 2000; Aughey, 2001). Described by McCrone as state reformation, this process began to have implications for national identity (1996, p. 43), nowhere more so than in stateless or sub-state nations such as Wales, where plural and shifting identities are a common feature (McCrone, 1998, p. 138). The meaning of Welsh national identity was recast between 1979 and 1997. This change came about as a result of a redefinition of both Welsh and British identity that was inextricably linked to social, political and economic change between 1979 and 1997, not least: the dismantling of the traditional industrial infrastructure in Wales and other large-scale socio-economic changes; the impact of eighteen years in opposition for the Labour Party; and the growth in 'civic' Wales. The interaction between social, economic and political change and national identity in Wales was crucial in bringing about the pro-devolution shift, as the meaning of social, economic and political change vis-à-vis the meaning of national identity shaped and reshaped each other.

The current consistent questioning of 'who we are' is linked to the very basic political question of 'why we are' or 'why is Britain?' (Aughey, 2001, p. 101; see also Nairn, 2002). This question penetrates the core of government, not only in defining the social values and boundaries that may define the 'we', but also in questioning the role of the state in order to answer the 'why?' These questions, which are essentially about identity, lie at the heart of the daily (re)production of the British state and the way that it is governed. The answers to these seemingly theoretical questions are of practical political significance. Between 1979 and 1997 the answer to the question of who we are in Wales changed fundamentally, with clear political implications in terms of a transformation of attitudes towards devolution, and a fundamental change in how the Welsh chose to be governed.

NOTES

[1] The figures cited in this article are derived from the Welsh Election Study 1979 and the Welsh Referendum Survey 1997. The Welsh Referendum Survey 1997 (WRS) was undertaken by the Centre for Research into Elections and Social Trends (CREST) in collaboration with the Department of International Politics at Aberystwyth. Fieldwork was conducted by Social and Community Planning Research (SCPR). Between 19 September and 30 October 1997, 686 interviews and self-completion questionnaires were successfully completed, which represented a response rate of 72.8 per cent (for further technical detail see Taylor and Thomson, 1999). The Welsh Election Study (SSRC project HR 4732/1) commissioned Social Surveys (Gallup Poll) Ltd to conduct a two-stage random sample survey of the Welsh electorate as of 3 May 1979. Between May and September 1979, 858 interviews were successfully

completed, which represented a response rate of 70 per cent. Whilst this article does not focus on this data, many of the arguments are reinforced by statistical analysis based on this data (see Wyn Jones and Trystan, 1999; and Jones 2003).

2   In 1979, 21.7 per cent of Welsh identifiers voted 'Yes' in the devolution referendum. By 1997, this had increased to 39.3 per cent, a pro-devolution shift of 26.6 per cent. This was far greater than the 7.3 per cent shift in favour amongst English identifiers and 12.2 per cent shift amongst British identifiers in Wales. Similarly, 31.6 per cent of the working class (subjective, self-defined) voted 'Yes' in 1997, compared to only 15.7 per cent in 1979. This represents a pro-devolution shift of 26.8 per cent, greater than the 12.2 per cent shift amongst the middle class.

3   For detailed empirical evaluation about the relationship between Conservative Party identity and Welsh national identity in Wales, see Balsom, Madgwick and Van Mechelen, 1983; Jones, 2001; and Wyn Jones, Scully and Trystan, 2002.

REFERENCES

Aaron, J., Rees, T., Betts, S. and Vincentelli, M. (eds) (1994). *Our Sisters' Land: The Changing Identities of Women in Wales*, Cardiff: University of Wales Press.

Aughey, A. (2001). *Nationalism, Devolution, and the Challenge to the United Kingdom State*, London and Sterling, VA: Pluto Press.

Balsom, D., Madgwick, P. and Van Mechelen D. (1983). 'The red and the green: patterns of partisan choice in Wales', *British Journal of Political Science*, 13, 299–325.

Billig, M. (1995). *Banal Nationalism*, London: Sage.

Davies, N. (1999). *The British Isles: A History*, London: Macmillan.

Evans, E. J. (1997). *Thatcher and Thatcherism*, London: Routledge.

Evans, G. and Trystan, D. (1999). 'Why was 1997 different?', in B. Taylor and K. Thomson (eds), *Scotland and Wales: Nations Again*, Cardiff: University of Wales Press.

Gellner, E. (1983). *Nations and Nationalism*, Oxford: Blackwell.

Griffiths, D. (1995). *Thatcherism and Territorial Politics*, Aldershot: Avebury.

Guibernau, M. (1999). *Nations Without States: Political Communities in a Global Age*, Cambridge: Polity Press.

Heath, A. and Kellas, J. (1998). 'Nationalism and constitutional questions', special issue 'Understanding constitutional change', *Scottish Affairs*, 110–28.

Hughes, C. and Wintour, P. (1990). *Labour Rebuilt*, London: Fourth Estate.

Jones, R. (2001). 'Is Wales an anti-Conservative country?', paper presented to the Annual Conference of the Political Studies Association, Manchester, April.

Jones, R. (2003). 'From referendum to referendum: national identity and devolution in Wales 1979–1997', unpublished Ph.D. thesis, University of Wales.

Kearney, H. (2000). 'The importance of being British', *The Political Quarterly*, 71, 1, 15–25.

Keating, M. (2001). *Nations Against the State: The New Politics of Nationalism in Quebec, Catalonia and Scotland*, (2nd edn) Hampshire: Palgrave.

Leys, C. (1989). *Politics in Britain: From Labourism to Thatchersim*, London: Verso.

Marr, A. (2000). *The Day Britain Died*, London: Profile Books.

McCrone, D. (1996). 'Autonomy and national identity in stateless nations: Scotland, Catalonia and Quebec', *Scottish Affairs*, 17, 42–8.

McCrone, D. (1998). *The Sociology of Nationalism: Tomorrow's Ancestors*, London: Routledge.
McCrone, D. (1999). 'The local and the global: national identity in the new Scotland', paper presented at Colloque Annuel de Generation Quebec, 'Un Quebec Ouvert Sur le Monde', Montreal, Quebec, April.
McCrone, D. (2002). *Understanding Scotland: The Sociology of a Nation*, 2nd edn, London: Routledge.
Mitchell, J. (1998). 'From unitary state to union state: Labour's changing view of the UK and its implications', *Regional Studies*, 30, 6, 607–11.
Morgan, K. O. (1981). *Rebirth of a Nation: Wales 1880–1980*, Oxford: Clarendon Press.
Morgan, K. O. (1991). *Wales in British Politics 1868–1922*, 1st paperback edn, Cardiff: University of Wales Press.
Nairn, T. (1981). *The Break up of Britain: Crisis and Neo-Nationalism*, 2nd edn, London: New Left Books.
Nairn, T. (2000). *After Britain: New Labour and the Return of Scotland*, London: Granta.
Nairn, T. (2002). *Pariah*, London: Verso.
Osmond, J. (ed.) (1985). *The National Question Again: Welsh Political Identity in the 1980s*, Llandysul: Gomer.
Osmond, J. (1998). *New Politics in Wales*, London: Charter '88.
Osmond, J. (1999). *Welsh Politics in the New Millennium*, Cardiff: Institute of Welsh Affairs.
Parekh, B. (2000). 'Defining British national identity', *Political Quarterly*, 71, 1, 4–14.
Pelling, H. (1992). *A History of British Trade Unionism*, 5th edn, London: Macmillan.
Snicker, J. (1998). 'Strategies of autonomist agents in Wales', in H. Elcock and M. Keating (eds), *Remaking the Union: Devolution and British Politics in the 1990s*, London: Frank Cass.
Taylor, B. and Thomson, K. (eds) (1999). *Scotland and Wales: Nations Again?*, Cardiff: University of Wales Press.
Williams, G. A. (1985). *When was Wales?*, London: Penguin.
Wyn Jones, R. (2001). 'On process, events and unintended consequences: national identity and the politics of Welsh devolution', *Scottish Affairs*, 37, 34–57.
Wyn Jones, R., Scully, R. and Trystan, D. (2002). 'Why do the Conservatives always do (even) worse in Wales?', in L. Bennie, C. Rallings, J. Tonge and P. Webb (eds), *British Elections and Parties Review vol. 12: The 2001 General Election*, London: Frank Cass.
Wyn Jones, R. and Trystan, D. (1999). 'The Welsh referendum vote', in B. Taylor and K. Thomson (eds), *Scotland and Wales: Nations Again?*, Cardiff: University of Wales Press.

7. LESSONS IN NATIONALITY: CONSTRUCTING IDENTITIES AT YSGOL GYMRAEG LLUNDAIN

Jeremy Segrott

ABSTRACT

This article explores how Welsh identities are constructed at Ysgol Gymraeg Llundain (the Welsh School, London), and is divided into three sections. First, it discusses the experiences of parents and their involvement in the school, and traces the connections between language, education and identity in their narratives. The second section examines how attempts to establish an 'authentic' Welsh school in London have created a form of Welsh identity that 'recreates' life back home, but embodies subtle differences from similar schools in Wales itself. It is argued that the significant problems that Ysgol Gymraeg Llundain has encountered in accessing sustainable funding point to the ambiguity of the Welsh as a collective group in England. Thirdly, the article explores the bilingual practices of children at the school, and the ways in which they locate their identities through attachments to multiple spaces and places. National identity might be seen as highly problematic when viewed in terms of homogenous cultural groups located exclusively within a single bounded territory (Gilroy, 1993). The article argues that a diasporic conceptualization of Welsh identity has significant theoretical and political potential because it recognizes the possibility of forging self and national identities through multiple geographical attachments, and because it highlights the problems of drawing neat boundaries around supposedly discrete cultural groups.

INTRODUCTION

In this article I explore the construction of Welsh identities in London, drawing upon research undertaken at Ysgol Gymraeg Llundain (the Welsh School, London) as part of a wider project on Welsh life in the city (Segrott, 2001a, 2001b, 2001c, 2003). London occupies an important place in Welsh life, both as a major migration destination and as the fulcrum of British state politico-economic power (Jones, 2001). While the Welsh in London have developed networks and institutions to create a Welsh community away from home, they have also played a major role in the cultural and political life of Wales from outside its geographical border (Jones, 1981). Although my concern here is with contemporary Welsh life in London, it should nevertheless be noted that Welsh migration to the city and the construction of London Welsh identities have a long and rich history (see for instance Jones, 1981, 1985, 2001; Segrott, 2001a). In this article I argue that examining the construction of Welsh identities in London raises important questions about how we conceptualize self and national identity, particularly in relation to Wales.[1] As Fevre and Thompson (1999) suggest, scholarly work on Welsh nationality is increasingly concerned with the production, experiences and contestation of multiple Welsh identities, in which questions of inclusivity and diversity take on a heightened importance.

Three key themes are developed through an exploration of the stories of the children and parents at Ysgol Gymraeg Llundain. First, the complex links between language, education and identity that run through many of the parents' stories are considered. Secondly, I examine how the efforts of staff and parents to 'recreate' a Welsh school in London produce a form of Welsh identity that is both similar to and very different from life in Wales. Thirdly, the article suggests that the identities constructed within Ysgol Gymraeg Llundain highlight the problematic nature of national identity. In particular I am concerned with the tendency to view national identity in terms of a homogenous cultural group located exclusively within a single bounded territory (Gilroy, 1993; Coupland, Bishop and Garrett, 2003). The difficulties in obtaining funding for a Welsh school in England and the identity narratives of the children point to the problems of 'locating' national identity in this way, and highlight the ambiguous position of the Welsh as an ethnic group in England (Cohen, 1994). I examine the ways in which the children practise being bilingual in their everyday lives, and how their identities are located through multiple geographical attachments. I argue for a diasporic conceptualization of Welsh identity, which, drawing on ideas of migrancy and travel, recognizes that national and self identities can be constructed in multiple spaces and forged through de-centred attachments (Gilroy, 1993; Clifford, 1994; Cohen, 1997; Mac Éinrí, 2000). The potential of such a theoretical framework is further strengthened when one considers the Welsh in London as part of an international diaspora, drawing destinations such as England, Patagonia, Australia and the United States into complex social networks of Welsh identity and belonging

(Knowles, 1997; Langfield, 1998; Coupland, Bishop and Garrett, 2003). While the term 'diaspora' has traditionally been used to describe the migration of populations from their homeland to multiple destination countries, it has also been developed as a conceptual tool for thinking through identities more generally (Ní Laoire, 2003). It points to the problematic nature of attempting to equate cultural forms with a single national space, and of drawing absolute lines of difference around supposedly separate national groups (Gilroy, 1993).

BACKGROUND AND METHODS

Ysgol Gymraeg Llundain was founded in 1958 to offer children in London a Welsh-medium education, between the ages of four and eleven (E. Edwards, 1999; Roberts, 1971; see Segrott, 2001a, for a more detailed account of the school's history). An *ysgol feithrin* (nursery school) and *cylch chwarae* (playgroup) also cater for the needs of younger children.[2] In 1961 the school moved to the Sunday School rooms in Willesden Green Welsh chapel, a home that it occupied until 2000 when the chapel closed. Ysgol Gymraeg Llundain then found alternative accommodation, at Stonebridge Park School in Harlesden, north London. At the time that the research on which this article is based was carried out in 1999, the number of pupils had been increasing for some time and there were sixteen full-time students, and another sixteen who attended the school through a form of 'day release' from their local schools on Fridays. Questionnaires were distributed to parents to elicit information about their involvement with the school. Interviews were conducted with six parents, and members of teaching staff. In January 1999 I undertook participant observation at the school, and conducted two group interviews with seven of the older children, whose ages ranged between approximately seven and eleven. Further participant observation and three group interviews were conducted with children in September 1999. Although the fieldwork carried out at Ysgol Gymraeg Llundain did not focus primarily on issues of class, most (but not all) of the pupil and parent participants can be said to come from a broadly middle-class background, where relevant information was supplied. All of the children who took part in the study had been born in London. While some of the children came from families where both parents were Welsh and spoke Welsh, a common situation was where one parent had been born in and moved from Wales (usually the mother), whilst the other parent was English and had been born in London or another area of England (usually the father). These patterns point to interesting issues surrounding the gendering of parental choice (Reay, 2000), but they are beyond the scope of the present article.

IDENTITY, LANGUAGE AND EDUCATION – THE PARENTS' STORIES

Language and education are often entwined in the construction and contestation of identities at a variety of scales, taking on symbolic and strategic qualities. In Wales, language has often been at the heart of multiple definitions and contestations of nationality (Curtis, 1986; Gruffudd, 1995). Colin Williams (1991) has explored the relationship between large nation-states and minority languages such as Welsh (in Britain) and French (in Quebec), drawing out comparisons between these linguistic communities. He suggests that the formation of large nation-states in Europe involved nationalizing space, and the creation of uniformed, homogenous national cultures tied to bounded geographical territories (see also Anderson, 1991). The attempt to create unified nation-states placed great pressure upon minority cultures: 'Attempts by minorities to resist assimilation were deemed to be expressions of primordial sentiments and a spurning of the individual's opportunity to advance within the liberalizing framework of the new, open society, where rationalism displaced parochialism' (1991, p. 6). Williams describes 'the attempts of linguistic minorities to maintain control of their historic territories and so thereby guarantee some degree of success in reproducing their cultures, ideologies and interests in the face of enormous assimilatory pressures from majority cultures' (1991, p. 7).

As Heller (1999) has argued, nations have frequently sought to reproduce particular forms of national identity (including the linguistic) through the educational system. J. Edwards suggests that 'education has often been perceived as the central pillar in group-identity maintenance, providing an essential support for linguistic nationalism and ethnic revival' (1985, p. 118). The campaign to open Welsh-medium schools from around the 1930s highlights both how debates about nationality and language have been framed within the context of the educational system, and the way in which schools and children are endowed with a national, symbolic significance (Griffiths, 1997). As Griffiths suggests, the campaign to establish Welsh-medium schools was predicated upon a belief that the future survival of Welsh national culture was linked to the strength of the Welsh language, and the school was a key site through which this could be achieved. For Baker the 'development of bilingual education in Wales is not a purely educationally derived phenomenon . . . Rather, such growth is both an action and reaction in the general growth of consciousness about the virtues of preserving an indigenous language and culture' (1993, p. 9).

The questionnaire and in-depth interviews conducted at the school sought to explore such interconnections between language, education and identity, in terms of both the backgrounds of the parents and the meanings that Ysgol Gymraeg Llundain held for them. For nearly all of the parents, the chance for their children to learn or be educated in Welsh was the key reason for sending them to the school (see table 7.1).[3] However, a number of other qualities linked to the school were also put forward by the parents. For Manon, the Welsh-medium education that her children received gave them access to wider cultural traditions:

Mae'n rhaid i fi weud o'n i heb sylweddoli cyn hela'r plant, mor bwysig byddai cael y diwylliant Cymraeg o'r ysgol. Er enghraifft mae'r plant yn dysgu caneuon o'n i'n cofio dysgu yn yr ysgol; maen nhw'n dysgu darnau bach o'r Beibl Gymraeg a phethe fel 'ny a canu emynau Cymraeg, a jyst popeth i wneud â'r diwylliant. Bydden i ddim wedi meddwl oedd e'n mor bwysig . . . Wy'n gwerthfawrogi'r ochr 'ny'n fawr iawn achos wy'n teimlo bydd y plant yn teimlo'n fwy Cymraeg wedi cael y diwylliant yn ogystal â'r iaith.

(I have to say that I hadn't realized before I sent the children, how important the Welsh culture that comes from being at the school would be. For example, the children learn songs that I remember learning in school. They learn parts of the Welsh Bible and things like that, and sing Welsh hymns and just everything to do with the culture. I wouldn't have thought that it was so important . . . I value that side very much, because I feel that the children will feel more Welsh having had the culture as well as the language.) (Manon, thirties; moved to London in the 1970s)

Table 7.1
The importance of a Welsh-medium education at Ysgol Gymraeg Llundain

. . . eisiau i'r plant gwybod rhywfaint o'r iaith.
(. . . I wanted the children to have at least some grasp of the language.)

Babi yn dri mis oed – eisiau iddi ddysgu Cymraeg . . .
(My baby is three months old – I want her to learn Welsh . . .)

Dysgu Cymraeg.
(To learn Welsh.)

Bilingual education.

Iddyn nhw gael siarad a deall yr iaith ac i gyfathrebu gyda phlant eraill yn yr iaith.
(For them to be able to understand the language and to communicate with other children in the language.)

I roi cyfle iddo glywed yr iaith Gymraeg a chymdeithasu yn Gymraeg.
(To give him the opportunity to hear Welsh and socialize in Welsh.)

Other aspects of the school, which were less closely linked to its linguistic identity, were also put forward as being important in the decision-making processes. Dylan (an English father) described this sentiment clearly:

> the lengths that [parents] go to [to bring their children to the school across London] are not justified entirely by the language. Obviously the culture that surrounds it is important, but I think also the school itself has special qualities over and above the Welsh language. Although obviously that's the catalyst to it all, it has qualities over and above [the language] that it's developed over the years . . . all the things which stack up over and above the Welsh language itself.

One such 'special quality' was the school's high educational standards, including the positive impact of a bilingual education:

> Chi 'mod, mae safon yr addysg yn yr ysgol Gymraeg mor dda, chi 'mod? Mae'r plant byti dwy, tair blynedd ymlaen o ran eu cyfoedion, chi 'mod, mewn ysgolion lleol Saesneg . . . – yn hawdd, pan maen nhw'n darllen a sgwennu. Maen nhw'n wastad wneud yn dda yn y SATs a wy'n siwr bod e'n, wel rhan o'r rheswm, os nad yn gyfangwbl, oherwydd maen nhw'n medru dwy iaith.

> (You know, the standard of education in the Welsh school is so good, you know? The children are perhaps two, three years ahead of their peers, you know, in local English schools . . . – easily, in terms of reading and writing. They always do well in the SATs and I'm sure that it's well, perhaps part of the reason if not entirely, because they speak two languages.) (Louise, Welsh parent, forties; born in London)

Ysgol Gymraeg Llundain as an individual school was perceived as achieving high educational standards in comparison with other local schools. A number of parents suggested that they would not have sent their children to the school if they had found its educational standards wanting:

> . . . ar ôl gweld yr ysgol a'r awyrgylch a'r safon – mae'r safon addysg yn uchel iawn. Mae'n lot well na beth 'sai hi'n [ein merch] medru cael yn yr ysgolion lleol. So oedd hwnna wedi helpu ni i benderfynu cymaint â'r iaith *really*.

> (having seen the school and the atmosphere and the standard – the standard of the education is very high. It's a lot better than she [our daughter] would get in the local schools. So that helped us to decide as much as the language really.) (Jane, thirties; moved to London in the 1980s)

A number of reasons were put forward for the achievement of high educational standards, including the quality of the teaching and the size of the school. Children worked in small classes, allowing teachers to know each child as an individual. Dylan (a father) explained how he was 'convinced that my children are getting as good a Welsh-language education in London as they would in Wales – even in a Welsh-speaking part of Wales where they would be surrounded by Welsh to a greater extent outside school. They would no doubt be in a much larger class getting far less individual attention' (Dylan, thirties; born in London).

Clearly, then, the parents who participated in the study had made careful decisions about their children's schooling. As recent studies of parental education choices have shown, such decision-making may be mediated in complex ways by social class, gender, race and ethnicity (Reay and Lucey, 2000, 2003, 2004; Vincent, Ball and Kemp, 2004). A number of these studies are concerned with how some middle-class London parents' school selection practices can both reproduce social status and be potentially socially exclusive. While educational standards play an important role in parents' decision-making in relation to Ysgol Gymraeg Llundain, their narratives suggest a deeper engagement with the school as a social and cultural institution. Thus, in ways which contrast with the findings of Reay and Lucey (2004), middle-class parents who send their children to Ysgol Gymraeg Llundain are committed not only to their individual children's education but also to the creation of a community and 'local' school. Given its 'minority' status, uncertain financial situation and the presence of parents and pupils from different backgrounds, the school arguably occupies an unusual position in the current 'marketization' of education in London and other similar cities.

A QUESTION OF LOCATION

The small size and intimacy of the school has enabled the creation of a strong sense of community, encapsulated in the idea that Ysgol Gymraeg Llundain feels like a 'village school' in the heart of London. The fact that issues of language, educational standards and relationships between staff and pupils figure in the parents' stories in this way is not perhaps significant in itself. Indeed, the evocation by parents of Ysgol Gymraeg Llundain as a village school, where Welsh is the natural medium, suggests that rural Welsh culture has been authentically recreated in the heart of London. But, as Barkan and Shelton suggest, 'diasporic cultures evolve that are both unlike the home culture and inseparable from them' (1998, p. 3). There are a number of aspects of Ysgol

Gymraeg Llundain which are very different from comparable schools 'back home', even as it strives to emulate them, and these stem directly from its geographical location in London.

One of the most positive sentiments expressed by parents was the belief that the importance of being and speaking Welsh had become stronger since they had been living outside Wales, a kind of strengthening of identity to which many research participants referred (Segrott, 2001a). This indicated not only that parents' motivations for sending their children to Ysgol Gymraeg Llundain were caught up with their own senses of identity, but that such motivations were heightened through migrating to London. Because many families live long distances from Ysgol Gymraeg Llundain, transporting children to the school requires significant effort and commitment – justified by the meanings it holds for parents. Reflecting the characteristics of the London Welsh as a whole, Ysgol Gymraeg Llundain operates as a central institution for a highly dispersed ethnic group (Jones, 1985; Knowles, 1997) which has no single concentration in any particular area of London. Drawing upon notions of rurality, Manon suggested that the fact that different families were scattered across London, and that people had to travel long distances to reach the school, had to some extent reinforced a sense of community: 'Mae'n rhoi sens o cymuned mawr i rieni sy' 'ma – mae fel byw mewn pentre bach yng Nghymru. Ond wrth gwrs ni gyd wedi dosbarthu dros Lundain i gyd a ni'n dod man hyn er mwyn ffurfio pentre bach.' ('It gives parents a real sense of community – it's like living in a little village in Wales. But of course we are all spread out over London and we all come here in order to form a little village.') (Manon, thirties; moved to London in the 1970s)

The considerable distances that many parents travel each day is seen as worth the effort involved, therefore, and, in a rather circular fashion, as increasing the value and sense of community that they place upon the school. But it is ironic, perhaps, that the private status which has been forced upon the school by the reluctance of local and central government to fund it is the one of the most important factors in creating a strong sense of community. Parents make an annual contribution towards the cost of their children's education (though the school never bars children due to the inability of their parents to pay these fees), but this leaves a major shortfall, met to a large degree by intensive fund-raising efforts by parents and supporters, including the operation of a catering business and removals firm at various points in the school's history (E. Edwards, 1999). Many parents volunteer to supervise the children at lunchtimes, and clean the school each day, and therefore have daily contact with staff and pupils.

The reluctance of local and national government to pay for its operation highlights wider issues about how national identity (and particularly Welsh identity) is conceptualized. The Welsh Office and the National Assembly have been unable to provide permanent funding for the school (though some money has been made available, especially via the Welsh Language Board, and the Welsh Assembly recently made a grant to help fund the school for several years), primarily because of its location outside of Wales (the nation), and to some extent its private status. Yet bodies in London with responsibility for funding schools are also either unable or unwilling to cover its costs. The Department for Education in England cannot fund Ysgol Gymraeg Llundain because it does not follow the English National Curriculum at all age levels (and is therefore marked out as different). Meanwhile, Woodward (2000) suggests that the local council does not consider the Welsh to be an ethnic group, meaning that it is not eligible for funding available to ethnic minorities. The rejection of the status of the Welsh as an ethnic group in London by the education authorities was something that certain parents felt extremely strongly about:

Wy'n gobeithio y byddwn ni'n cael rhyw help o'r llywodraeth i achub yr ysgol, ceisio cael mwy o gynghorwyr Llundeinig i weld bod ni'n bodoli, bod ni yn gymuned ethnig . . . A felly ni'n ceisio dod â'r argyfwng ysgol Gymraeg i sylw Ken Livingstone a Paul Boateng. Wel maen nhw'n aelodau seneddol yn Brent, a chi 'mod, os maen nhw'n mor pybyr dros lleiafrifoedd eraill, allan nhw fod cystal pybyr dros y Gymraeg, a falle bydd hynny'n helpu.

(I hope that we will get some help from the government to save the school, to try and get more London councillors to see that we do exist, that we are an ethnic community . . . And so we're trying to bring the Welsh school's crisis to the attention of Ken Livingstone and Paul Boateng. Well, they're members of Parliament in Brent, and you know, if they're so concerned about other minorities, they can be just as concerned about the Welsh, and perhaps that will help.) (Louise, forties; born in London)

The school thus highlights the ambiguous position of the Welsh in England. On the one hand, it lies outside of the space of the nation (the frame through which national cultural life is viewed), and is therefore not viewed as a wholly constituent part of Welsh life. It problematizes the exclusive location of culture and language within the bounded territory of the national space called Wales (Clifford, 1997). As a Welsh school in England, Ysgol Gymraeg Llundain is denied access to mainstream education funding in part because it embodies difference (employing another national curriculum). On the other hand, the school lies simultaneously outside the (Welsh) nation, but inside the (British) nation-state. Whilst a Welsh school in London is somehow out of place (not in its proper place), its difference is not fully legitimized, for it is not viewed as an ethnic group. As Taylor (1992) suggests, demand for recognition by others is a key facet of nationalist movements, including minority groups. And as Skeggs (1999) has argued, the politics of identity recognition are often linked to issues of visibility and legitimacy in particular kinds of spaces, a point that Louise is clearly aware of in the quotation above. In this respect, the ambiguous, anomalous position of the Welsh in England shares many similarities with the experience of the Irish in London. According to Walter (1999, p. 319), 'Irish invisibility in Britain . . . reflects a paradox. On the one hand, Irish people are strongly identified as different, inferior, but on the other hand they are too much "the same" for their separate identity to be recognised.' Meanwhile Williams (1991) considers the way in which Welsh nationality has been both racialized and depicted as inferior within some discourses of 'British national collectivity' while at the same time, the experiences and identities of minority groups in Wales itself have suffered from a lack of recognition or conferred legitimacy.

GROWING UP IN LONDON – THE CHILDREN'S STORIES

The parents and staff therefore have well-defined ideas about what the school means to them, and how they wish its pupils to relate to the Welsh language and culture. But the children who are taught there are distinctive social actors who construct their own senses of identity (Heller, 1999; Norton, 2000; Prout and James, 1990; Zentella, 1997). The children interviewed at Ysgol Gymraeg Llundain generally viewed their identities as Welsh speaking and bilingual in very positive ways, and therefore conformed to the meanings that their parents had attached to the school. But pupils actively negotiated such meanings and could articulate subtle reasons for embracing bilingualism, rather than simply reproducing their parents' experiences and motivations (Heller, 1999; Holloway and Valentine, 2000). Dai, for instance, aligned himself with his parents' view of bilingualism, but his own identity as a bilingual speaker was derived partly through reference to his friends outside the school who came from other ethnic groups and the idea that speaking two languages was a common experience in a multilingual city. To some extent the children linked their embracing of being able to speak two languages to the practical advantages that it offered them in everyday life. Peter, for instance, valued the fact that he had access to two sets of vocabulary, which increased his linguistic powers. One language could be used to find out words in the other for instance. Elizabeth, who was one of the younger pupils in the class, had one Welsh-speaking and one monolingual English parent.

She explained that being able to speak two languages meant that secrets could be kept from her father, who did not speak Welsh.

Although the children found the ability to mix the two languages useful and empowering, they also felt that Welsh and English should be held apart because of the danger of diluting linguistic purity and creating a hybrid language. In relation to the mixing of individual English words into Welsh speech, Dai explained that 'Os ych chi'n deud e gormod chi fel yn dechre deud e fel gair Cymraeg so chi fel yn newid e mewn i gair Cymraeg' ('If you say it too much you, like, begin to say it as a Welsh word, so you, like, change it into a Welsh word'). The idea that English and Welsh should be kept apart was linked to the fact that the children connected the use of the languages to particular spaces of their day to day lives, and made sense of their bilingualism through this geography. Whereas English was all around them in London, speaking Welsh tended to occur within specific spaces in the city, particularly school and home. The understanding of the language as being located within specific, mostly institutional sites was also linked to the idea that the children used Welsh primarily with people that they knew. The use of Welsh and English within partially differentiated contexts was therefore a key way in which the children made sense of their ability to speak two languages in their everyday lives, to some extent defined for them by parents or teachers. But there was a clear sense in which they made active choices about their use of language. The children mix with Welsh-speaking friends at school, and some of them also meet in the evenings and at weekends. But because, on the whole, the pupils are scattered across a wide area of London, most of them have predominantly non-Welsh-speaking friends outside of school. The pupils knew that they had to speak Welsh in school, but outside of this space they could choose which language they used, even where their friends might be Welsh speakers: 'fel yn yr ysgol chi'n gorfod siarad Cymraeg – chi ddim yn cael siarad Saesneg. Ond os fel chi yn tŷ ffrind, chi'n gallu siarad Saesneg a Cymraeg, so mae'n iawn siarad Saesneg achos dyw e ddim yn drwg.' ('like in the school you have to speak Welsh – you're not allowed to speak English. But if you are, like, in a friend's house, you can speak English and Welsh, so it's OK to speak English because it's not naughty.')

While speaking Welsh is therefore encouraged (and in some ways prescribed) within the formal spaces of the classroom, the children have more freedom to choose their language during their break times in the playground. Heller's (1999) study of a French-medium school in an English-speaking area of Canada similarly found that children actively renegotiated and contested linguistic norms in the more private spaces of schools which were not closely supervised by adults. While one mother at Ysgol Gymraeg Llundain described her irritation at the fact that some children reverted to speaking English in the playground, another parent suggested that this was less so now than in the past, indicating that the school was succeeding in making Welsh something all-embracing and 'natural' in the minds of pupils. A number of parents described how the Welsh language should be something natural, which infused the school's activities, rather than something which was forced upon the children, highlighting the different ways in which linguistic norms and expectations operate.

GEOGRAPHY AND IDENTITY

The children therefore expressed a strong Welsh linguistic identity, mapped out through a geography in which certain spaces were associated with the language. Other notions of the geographical also threaded through their understandings of being Welsh, including the role of Wales as a symbolic space. All of the children interviewed as part of the research had grown up in London, and it was the primary place in which they located and made sense of their Welsh identities (a 'London Welsh' identity as opposed to a Welsh identity in London). Being and speaking Welsh was not always understood primarily in terms of referring back to Wales, therefore. Through the way in which pupils such as Dai and Jon located the Welsh language in London, they 'deterritorialized' an essentialized Welsh identity bounded within the national space of Wales (Brah, 1996).[4] They articulated an identity stretching beyond the borders of the nation, echoing what Clifford (1997, p. 251) has described as 'identification outside the national time/space'. Moreover they did not merely substitute one bounded identity (negotiated in London) for one based around Wales. Wales was one reference point in a series of multiple, lateral attachments (Cohen, 1994) that contributed towards the children's understanding of their own identities:

JS: Ych chi'n meddwl falle, ych chi ddim yn colli Cymru, achos bo' chi wastad trwy'r amser wedi byw yn Llunden?
Dai: Ie, achos wel ych chi dal yn gallu siarad Cymraeg yn Llundain hefyd.
Jon: Wel ych chi'n gallu siarad Cymraeg unrhywle chi eisiau – os ych chi'n Cymraeg chi'n gallu fel siarad Cymraeg unrhywle – Awstralia hyd yn oed . . .
JS: So mewn un synnwyr, mewn un sens yr iaith sy'n bwysig i chi . . .
Dai: Dim y lle.
JS: Reit.
Dai: Dim ble dych chi.

(JS: Do you think perhaps that you don't miss Wales because you've always lived
        in London?
Dai: Yes, because you can still speak Welsh in London.
Jon: Well you can speak Welsh anywhere you want to – if you're Welsh you can
        speak Welsh anywhere – even in Australia . . .
JS: So in one sense, in one sense it's the language that's important to you . . .
Dai: Not the place.
JS: Right.
Dai: Not where you are.)

The fact that the children's identities were negotiated primarily within London
did not mean, however, that Wales played no part in their lives. The group related
to Wales in two key ways: as a collective group of Welsh speakers, and as a
repository of particular landscapes. The rather ambivalent relationship that the
group expressed towards Welsh speakers in Wales, for instance, reaffirms the idea
that Wales as a territory is one relational attachment in their identities, rather than
their only point of reference. Returning to the issue of mixing languages, some
members of the group felt that children in the Principality (especially from urban
areas) were likely to make less effort in terms of keeping the two languages separate:

Child 1:   Fi'n meddwl bod ni yn siarad Cymraeg yn well achos o'n ni 'di mynd i'r
            lle 'ma a oedd plant Caerdydd yna a um, oedd nhw ddim, o'n nhw jyst yn
            deud 'ie' mewn pob brawddeg. Oedden nhw'n deud rhywbeth yn Saesneg
            neu'n siarad Cymraeg a Saesneg yn yr un brawddeg . . .
Child 2:   Dau gair yn Saesneg – o'n ni jyst yn deud fel tua un gair [Saesneg] mewn
            paragraff neu rywbeth.

(Child 1:   I think that we speak Welsh better, because we had been to this place and
            there were some children from Cardiff there, and they were just saying
            'yeah' in every sentence. They were saying something in English, or
            speaking Welsh and English in the same sentence . . .
Child 2:   Two words in English – we were just saying maybe one [English] word in
            each paragraph or something.)

The children suggested that they spoke better Welsh than some of their peers in
Wales who did not need to make an effort to speak the language because it was
all around them anyway. The children at Ysgol Gymraeg Llundain were much
more likely to use English because it dominated their lives outside the bounded
spaces where they tended to speak Welsh, but they felt that they made more of an
effort to use the language because of their position outside of Wales.

The way in which the group imagined Wales through a particular set of landscapes frequently operated through a set of binary oppositions with their daily lives in London. London as a cosmopolitan, dirty, modern city was sometimes juxtaposed with Wales as a rural, peaceful place filled with mountains and seashores. These comparisons were often value judgements that further emphasize that, although Wales was a place that they enjoyed visiting, London was the children's home. It also underlines the highly nuanced constructions of identity that the children articulated. The most positive sentiment expressed about life in London related to the range of leisure activities (including shopping), and the ease with which it was possible to travel around the city. Whilst the busy, urban atmosphere was one that the children bought into, it was often linked to certain socio-environmental problems, including rubbish, smoking and graffiti. The rurality that the children experienced in Wales was often described in positive terms, as it contrasted with the claustrophobic and polluted environment that they encountered at home: 'Dw i'n hoffi Cymru achos mae [hi] mor neis ac wy'n hoffi'r mynyddau a pethau . . . Yn Llundain mae 'na tŷ y tu ôl tŷ, ac yn Cymru mae 'na parciau tu ôl y tai a ceffylau a'r môr a pethe.' ('I like Wales because it's so nice, and I like the mountains and things . . . In London there is house behind house, and in Wales there are parks behind the houses and horses and the sea and things.') But the quiet, quaint character of much of Wales was also seen negatively, in that it offered a lack of activities compared with life in London: '[Mae] jyst cwpl o *post offices* yn rai llefydd a cwpl o tai . . . Yn Llundain mae lot o *museums*, uh, lot o pethe fel 'na.' ('There are just a couple of post offices in some places and a couple of houses . . . In London there are lots of museums, uh, a lot of things like that.') The children's attitude towards life in Wales was, however, highly contextualized. Each year they undertook an annual visit to Llangrannog (the Urdd's or Welsh Youth Association's residential centre) in rural mid Wales, an event to which they looked forward. Within this context they found the prospect of spending a week in the countryside highly appealing because of the range of outside and adventure activities they could undertake. It was also true that when the group was asked about life in the urban areas of Wales, they could foresee being happy living in a major city such as Cardiff. The perception of Wales as a space of rurality appeared to be underpinned by the context in which the children usually went there. Wales was a place that was 'visited' for holidays, where they stayed with grandparents, creating the dominant idea of Wales as a space of leisure.

CONCLUSION

In this article I have sought to explore the creativity and complexity of constructing Welsh identities outside of Wales. The stories of the parents and children (important in their own right) might also point to different ways of thinking about Welsh identity and the dynamics of the self and the nation more generally. The founding of Ysgol Gymraeg Llundain in the 1950s, and the enormous efforts to sustain its existence, point to the fact that the school is something more than a straightforward island of Welshness in the heart of London. The school derives its central meaning and distinctiveness through the Welsh language. But the linguistic identity of the school only makes sense when its interconnections with notions of education, community, rurality and ethnicity are considered. The attempt to construct an 'authentic' Welsh school in London produces something that is both faithful to cultural forms in Wales, and at the same time has a distinctive identity, derived from its specific geographical context. As Gilroy (1993) points out, as cultural forms track around the world they maintain their specificity, but their interactions with new sets of social and political relations can produce something different and distinct. Migration and the move away from Wales can act to strengthen feelings of identity, and, in the case of a number of parents at Ysgol Gymraeg Llundain, it infused the chance to educate their children through the medium of Welsh with a heightened meaning. To create a traditional Welsh-medium school with a strong sense of community in the heart of London has involved considerable investment of time and money by parents and others. Yet, in part, it is exactly the challenges that the school has faced which have helped forge a strong sense of community and cultural identity.

The meanings and identities articulated by adults in the school are not merely transmitted to and 'soaked up' by the children educated there. The children actively negotiate linguistic and cultural norms, using them as what Zentella (1997) describes as 'strategic resources'. The children employ language in the creation of their own senses of identity, creatively, mixing and holding Welsh and English apart. For the children taking part in the research, being Welsh and speaking Welsh were incredibly important. But their cultural and linguistic identities were located primarily in London, or through connections to multiple places with Wales acting as an important, yet de-centred, relational attachment.

The construction of the children's identities, together with the issue of who should fund their school, points to wider issues about national identity. It unsettles the dominant view of national identity and culture as being located exclusively within a single bounded space. The existence of a large Welsh population in London (within which multiple communities and networks exist), and the important role that they collectively played in the life of Wales, suggest the need for a more expansive view of Welsh identity, that stretches beyond national borders. Such a view would consider the Welsh in London (and the London Welsh) as a constituent part of Welsh identity.

The difficulties that Ysgol Gymraeg Llundain has encountered in obtaining long-term funding also point to the ambiguity of the Welsh as a collective group in London. They occupy shifting positions of sameness and difference, visibility and invisibility, and ethnicity and nativity in the British capital. The story of Ysgol Gymraeg Llundain offers a number of salutary lessons on the problems of national identity: of locating Welsh culture exclusively within the borders of Wales, the difficulties of drawing neat geographical borders around different cultural or ethnic groups, and the inherent instability of national identities. At the same time it highlights the commitment of Welsh people living beyond the borders of Wales to sustaining its linguistic and cultural traditions.

ACKNOWLEDGEMENTS

The article is based upon Ph.D. research which was funded by the University of Wales Swansea and the Economic and Social Research Council (award no. R00429834673), and I am grateful to both organizations for their support. My thanks are due to the staff, parents and pupils at Ysgol Gymraeg Llundain. Thanks are also due to Dr Pyrs Gruffudd for his help and advice, and to two referees for their helpful comments and suggestions.

NOTES

[1]   By 'self identity', I mean the construction of an individual or personal identity, which, might be negotiated through wider social ties (e.g. nationality, class, gender, sexuality). National identity here refers to the construction and envisioning of collective or group identities, to which individuals can align themselves, and in turn exclude or include others.

[2]   Ysgol Gymraeg Llundain's website can be accessed at *www.llundain.freeserve.co.uk/*

[3]   Pseudonyms have been used for the children taking part in the interviews as for all adult interviewees. However, due to the large number of pupils taking part in some of the interviews, it has not been possible to identify all interviewees.

[4]   This is not to say, however, that most or all Welsh identities constructed in Wales are inherently geographically bounded or essentialized in such a way, and cultural or linguistic practices need not necessarily be framed around a delimited space.

REFERENCES

Anderson, B. (1991). *Imagined Communities: Reflections on the Origins and Spread of Nationalism*, London: Verso.

Baker, C. (1993). 'Bilingual education in Wales', in H. Baetens Beardsmore (ed.), *European Models of Bilingual Education*, Avon: Multilingual Matters.

Barkan, E. and Shelton, M. (1998). Introduction to E. Barkan and M. Shelton (eds), *Borders, Exiles and Diasporas*, California: Stanford University Press.

Brah, A. (1996). *Cartographies of Diaspora: Contesting Identities*, London: Routledge.

Clifford, J. (1994). 'Diasporas', *Cultural Anthropology*, 9, 3, 302–38.

Clifford, J. (1997). *Routes: Travel and Translation in the late Twentieth Century*, London: Harvard University Press.

Cohen, R. (1994). *Frontiers of Identity: The British and Others*, London: Longman.

Cohen, R. (1997). *Global Diasporas: An Introduction*, London: UCL Press.

Coupland, N., Bishop, H. and Garrett, P. (2003). 'Home truths: globalisation and the iconising of Welsh in a Welsh-American newspaper', *Journal of Multilingual and Multicultural Development*, 24, 3, 153–77.

Curtis, T. (1986). Introduction to T. Curtis (ed.), *Wales: The Imagined Nation – Essays in Cultural and National Identity*, Bridgend: Poetry Wales Press.

Edwards, E. (1999). 'Welsh-medium education in London', transcript of lecture given to the Honourable Society of Cymmrodorion, February.

Edwards, J. (1985). *Language, Society and Identity*, Oxford: Blackwell.

Fevre, R. and Thompson, A. (1999). 'Social theory and Welsh identities', in R. Fevre and A. Thompson (eds), *Nation, Identity and Social Theory*, Cardiff: University of Wales Press.

Gilroy, P. (1993). *The Black Atlantic: Double Consciousness and Modernity*, Cambridge: Harvard University Press.

Griffiths, M. (1997). 'The growth of Welsh-medium schools', in M. Griffiths (ed.), *The Welsh Language in Education*, Cardiff: Welsh Joint Education Committee.

Gruffudd, P. (1995). 'Remaking Wales: nation building and the geographical imagination, 1925–50', *Political Geography*, 14, 3, 219–39.

Heller, M. (1999). *Linguistic Minorities and Modernity: A Sociolinguistic Ethnography*, London: Longman.

Holloway, S. and Valentine, G. (2000). 'Children's geographies and the new social studies of childhood', in S. Holloway and G. Valentine (eds), *Children's Geographies: Learning, Living, Playing*, London: Routledge.

Jones, E. (1981). 'The Welsh in London in the seventeenth and eighteenth centuries', *Welsh History Review*, 10, 4, 461–79.

Jones, E. (1985). 'The Welsh in London in the nineteenth century', *Cambria*, 12, 1, 149–69.

Jones, E. (ed.) (2001). *The Welsh in London 1500–2000*, Cardiff: University of Wales Press.

Knowles, A. (1997). *Calvinists Incorporated: Welsh Immigrants on Ohio's Industrial Frontier*, Chicago: University of Chicago Press.

Langfield, M. (1998). 'The Welsh Patagonian connection: a neglected chapter in Australian immigration history', *International Migration*, 36, 1, 67–91.

Mac Éinrí, P. (2000). Introduction, in A. Bielenberg (ed.), *The Irish Diaspora*, Harlow: Pearson Education.

Ní Laoire, C. (2003). 'Editorial introduction: locating geographies of diaspora', *International Journal of Population Geography*, 9, 275–80.

Norton, B. (2000). *Identity and Language Learning: Gender, Ethnicity and Educational Change*, Harlow: Pearson Education.

Prout, A. and James, A. (1990). 'A new paradigm for the sociology of childhood? Provenance, promise and problems', in A. James and A. Prout (eds), *Constructing and Reconstructing Childhood*, London: Falmer Press.

Reay, D. (2000). 'A useful extension of Bordieu's conceptual framework? Emotional capital as a way of understanding mothers' involvement in their children's education?', *The Sociological Review*, 48, 4, 568–85.

Reay, D. and Lucey, H. (2000). 'Children, school choice and social differences', *Educational Studies*, 26, 1, 83–100.

Reay, D. and Lucey, H. (2003). 'The limits of "choice": children and inner city schooling', *Sociology*, 37, 1, 121–42.

Reay, D. and Lucey, H. (2004). 'Stigmatised choices: social class, social exclusion and secondary school markets in the inner city', *Pedagogy, Culture and Society*, 12, 1, 35–51.

Roberts, J. (1971). 'Cipolwg ar hanes sefydlu Ysgol Gymraeg Llundain', unpublished pamphlet.

Segrott, J. (2001a). 'Identity and migration: an ethnography of the Welsh in London', unpublished Ph.D. thesis, University of Wales.

Segrott, J. (2001b). 'Today and tomorrow', in E. Jones (ed.), *The Welsh in London 1500–2000*, Cardiff: University of Wales Press.

Segrott, J. (2001c). 'Language, geography and identity: the case of the Welsh in London', *Social and Cultural Geography*, 2, 3, 281–96.

Segrott, J. (2003). 'Constructing communities away from home: Welsh identities in London', in C. Davies and S. Jones (eds), *Welsh Communities: New Ethnographic Perspectives*, Cardiff: University of Wales Press.

Skeggs, B. (1999). 'Matter out of place: visibility and sexualities in leisure spaces', *Leisure Studies*, 18, 3, 213–32.

Taylor, C. (1992). *Multiculturalism and the Politics of Recognition*, New Jersey: Princetown University Press.

Vincent, C., Ball, S. and Kemp, S. (2004). 'The social geography of childcare: making up a middle-class child', *British Journal of Sociology of Education*, 25, 2, 229–44.

Walter, B. (1999). 'Inside and outside the pale: diaspora experiences of Irish women', in P. Boyle and K. Halfacree (eds), *Migration and Gender in the Developed World*, London: Routledge.

Williams, C. (1991). 'Linguistic minorities: west European and Canadian perspectives', in C. H. Williams (ed.), *Linguistic Minorities: Society and Territory*, Clevedon: Multilingual Matters.

Woodward, W. (2000). 'Nobody's baby', *Guardian*, 25 July.

Zentella, A. (1997). *Growing Up Bilingual*, Oxford: Blackwell.

8. REASSESSING RADIO: ROLE, SCOPE AND ACCOUNTABILITY

David M. Barlow

ABSTRACT

Radio continues to be a popular and expanding medium in Wales. Although the emerging digital audio broadcasting (DAB) services command most media attention, analogue licences are still being issued and will be for some time. Listener behaviour has also changed with significant numbers now tuning in via the Internet, television and mobile phone. Furthermore, Wales's two-sector radio system has expanded with the recent addition of community radio, although the BBC and commercial operators remain the dominant players. However, despite radio's pervasive presence, an examination of public debate on Wales and its media lends weight to the idea of an 'invisible medium', with attention focused almost exclusively on television. Only recently have critical comments on the provision and quality of commercial radio services and concerns about the future of DAB in Wales entered public discourse. This article comprises three main sections. The first provides a brief historical context, addressing the development of BBC, commercial and community radio in Wales. The second illustrates how Wales's radio ecology has been shaped by a succession of regulatory regimes. The third illuminates the extent to which decisions that ultimately shape the provision of radio in Wales are made beyond its boundaries. The article suggests that these developments – and future decisions to be taken about radio services in Wales – have implications for an informed democracy and cultural expression.

INTRODUCTION

Radio's continuing popularity has been helped by a rapid expansion of analogue and digital audio broadcasting (DAB) services throughout the UK over the last decade or so.[1] Moreover, the ways in which listeners access radio is changing, with 12 per cent of adults doing so through the Internet, 15 per cent via television and 2 per cent by mobile phone (Ofcom Advisory Group, 2003, p. 32). There is, though, concern in Wales about the overall range and quality of radio services:

> The development of radio in Wales has not kept pace with that in England. Much of Mid Wales is still without satisfactory local radio coverage and the number and range of stations and formats in other areas is more limited than is ideal . . . [T]here is also a suspicion that Wales has been low on the priority list of entrepreneurs and regulators in the broadcasting industry. (National Assembly for Wales, 2002a, p. 50)[2]

Furthermore, there is also unease about the future of DAB services in Wales. A report commissioned by the National Assembly for Wales (NAfW) highlights the need to ensure that 'the development of digital radio does not fall behind the rest of the UK and does not place Wales's own national and local stations at a competitive disadvantage to UK radio networks' (Ofcom Advisory Group, 2003, p. 32).[3] Such disquiet is understandable given that radio, as an information and music medium, is inextricably linked with debates about national identity, democracy and cultural expression (see, for example, Allan and O'Malley, 1999; J. Davies, 1994; Mackay and Powell, 1997; Welsh Affairs Select Committee, 1999).

This article focuses on the role and scope of radio and, inevitably, matters of accountability.[4] It is organized into three sections; the first provides a brief historical context, the second illustrates how earlier developments have shaped the current radio ecology, and the third examines the extent to which citizens and their democratically elected representatives have a role in determining the provision of radio services in Wales.

SHAPING RADIO: CENTRE AND PERIPHERY

In their canonical text, Lewis and Booth (1989) outline three models of radio: public service, free-market (or commercial) and community. All three models are now evident in Wales, although the BBC and commercial operators remain the dominant players in what is still, essentially, a two-tier radio system.

Commencing in 1923, the first BBC radio broadcasts from within Wales were distinctly local. Transmitted from Cardiff, but with only a limited broadcast reach, the service included a variety of local presenters, personalities and musicians, although Welsh-language programmes barely featured (J. Davies, 1994, p. 392; Lucas, 1981, pp. 22 and 24–6).[5] Some commentators have described this period as an exemplary – but brief – demonstration of local radio (J. Davies, 1994, pp. 6–7; Scannell and Cardiff, 1991, p. 304). It was brief because the BBC decided to centralize power in London and introduce a regional and national broadcasting network, thereby extinguishing any sense of local autonomy (Crisell, 1997, p. 25).

As John Davies reminds us, there was a 'struggle between Cardiff and Head Office' from the earliest days of radio (cited in Morris, 1995, p. 6). Having been lumped in with the south-west of England to form the BBC Western Region, the corporation's arguments that Wales could not have separate 'regional' status ultimately proved to be spurious (Evans, 1944, p. 7).[6] The eventual emergence of a 'Welsh Region' in 1937, the creation of a Welsh Regional Advisory Committee (WRAC) in 1947 – later to become the Broadcasting Council for Wales (BCW) in 1953 – and the establishment of BBC Wales in 1964 are illustrative of a gradual and hard-fought battle to wrest some power back from London (see, for example, Briggs, 1965, p. 321; J. Davies, 1994, pp. 160–71; Lucas, 1981, p. 199).

The Sound Broadcasting Act 1972, introduced by Edward Heath's Conservative administration, signalled the end of the BBC radio monopoly. It paved the way for the introduction of commercial services, known initially as Independent Local Radio (ILR). The Independent Broadcasting Authority (IBA) assumed responsibility for the regulation of both radio and television.[7] Swansea Sound, Wales's first ILR station and the UK's first bilingual radio service, began operating in 1974 (Baron, 1975; Watkin, 1976). This was followed by the Cardiff Broadcasting Company in 1980 and, in Wrexham, Marcher Gold in 1983 and MFM 103.4 in 1989. Significantly, the Sound Broadcasting Act 1972 also outlawed the setting up of BBC local radio stations in any of the 'national regions'. As a result, BBC Wales was informed by HQ in London that 'local radio in Wales [would] be a station for the whole of Wales' (J. Davies, 1994, p. 308).

The Conservative government under Margaret Thatcher signalled the next step-change in radio policy, relaxing regulation and sparking a surge in radio developments. The Broadcasting Act 1990 dispensed with the IBA and established a Radio Authority (RA) solely responsible for radio. This marked the beginning of a 'light touch' regulatory regime that became even 'lighter' following the Broadcasting Act 1996 (Carter, 1998, pp. 9–10). A flurry of activity in Wales saw ILR stations introduced at Aberystwyth, Newtown, Colwyn Bay, Swansea, Ebbw Vale, Caernarfon, Bridgend, Narberth and Carmarthen (see figure 8.1). A regional licensee, Real Radio, was added in 2000. Based in Radyr, this station broadcasts to a potential audience of 1,409,000 across south and south-west Wales.

Figure 8.1 Local radio services in Wales showing year of licence award[8]

The next milestone for radio, and communications more generally, occurred during the New Labour administration of Tony Blair. In 2000, the government flagged its intentions to 'make the UK home to the most dynamic and competitive communications and media market in the world', stating that it would minimize regulation wherever possible (Department of Trade and Industry/ Department of Culture, Media and Sport, 2000, pp. 1.1.25, 1.2.1, 1.3.9). The Office of Communications (Ofcom), a new multi-sectoral regulator, was established to oversee implementation of the Communications Act 2003.

Anticipating further deregulation and a likely reorganization of the radio ecology, the RA had already begun preparing for a new third sector of radio (Stoller, cited in Everitt, 2003, p. 2).[9] Piloted as 'Access Radio', but later rebadged as 'Community Radio', this emergent third tier of broadcasting is non-profit and non-commercial, the intention being to encourage community participation and achieve 'social gain' (Ofcom, 2004a, p. 3).[10] GTFM 106.9, a joint operation by the Glyntaff Tenants' and Residents' Association and the University of Glamorgan, emerged as Wales's only pilot station and begun broadcasting to Pontypridd and surrounds in 2002.[11]

WALES'S RADIO ECOLOGY: FITTING, OR 'FITTED UP'?

As a result of the Sound Broadcasting Act 1972, the radio landscape in Wales differs markedly from that of England. Whereas the BBC operates local, or county-wide, radio services in England, in Wales it is the commercial operators that have the local brief, with Radio Wales and Radio Cymru operating as national services. The barring of local BBC radio in Wales shaped the broadcasting ecology in two ways. First, it removed a potentially competitive hurdle for commercial operators hoping to start local services.[12] Secondly, the creation of a competitive operating environment impacted on radio provision by BBC Wales.

The pressure to provide a more comprehensive radio service in both English and Welsh languages led to the BBC splitting the single service to create Radio Wales and Radio Cymru in 1977, the former relaunching in November 1978 and the latter in November 1979 (J. Davies, 1994, pp. 311, 347, 351; Lucas, 1981, p. 230). However, evidence of the London 'centre' remained ever present. In the period between their emergence and relaunching, Radio Wales and Radio Cymru operated as opt-outs from BBC Radio 4 and both assimilated aspects of the London station's persona (J. Davies, 1994, p. 347). Similarly, BBC Radio 2 was the sustaining service and 'on-air' model for Radio Wales after its relaunch (J. Davies, 1994, p. 386).

While the Broadcasting Council for Wales (BCW) was confident that Radio Cymru could rely for its audience on the 'unity of Welsh Wales', it was concerned about the prospects for Radio Wales, believing that 'English Wales' would have to be 'coaxed into unity through a constructive acknowledgement of its diversity' (J. Davies, 1994, p. 350). This led to the BBC introducing regional opt-outs from Radio Wales and experimenting with *Radio Bro*, or Neighbourhood Radio, in order to attract and retain a diverse English-speaking audience, but these initiatives had ceased by the early 1990s (J. Davies, 1994, pp. 348–49, 386).

An expanded radio market in Wales has brought about further adjustments to both services (see, for example, Williams, 1997, pp. 31–2). While it is not readily apparent from the general division of programmes shown in figure 8.2, competitive pressures have clearly been influential.[13] In the late 1990s Radio Wales began recasting itself as a service for the whole of Wales rather than the south Wales valleys, its traditional heartland. Likewise, in 1995 Radio Cymru introduced a more populist approach to its programming in order to woo a younger audience (Ellis, 2000, p. 191). While this strategy may have attracted more listeners in the 15–34 age group, it prompts questions about the station's maintenance of a differentiated public service dimension.

**Figure 8.2 Overall distribution of programme types on
BBC Radio in Wales (2002–3)**

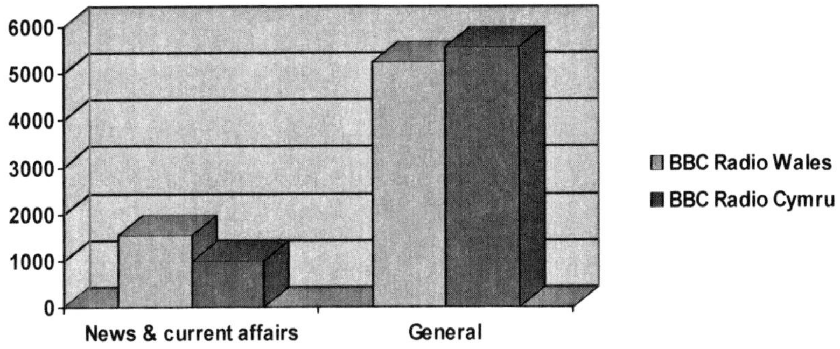

Source: adapted from BBC Wales Annual Report, 2003.

Paradoxically, the relaxation of legislation that facilitated a crop of ILR stations in Wales during the 1990s undermined the opportunity to achieve a genuinely local form of radio (see, for example, Barlow, 2003; Barlow, Mitchell and O'Malley, 2005). This is evident when examining areas such as programming, ownership and licensing. Programming has become increasingly standardized across Wales, dominated by a music-based format interspersed with advertisements, 'traffic and travel' announcements, and a UK-wide Independent Radio News service – in which Wales rarely features – supplemented by a smattering of 'local' news (Barlow, Mitchell and O'Malley, 2003; see also Hargreaves and Thomas, 2002).

Technological innovations have also helped in de-localizing the local by enabling networking between stations which results in more syndicated programming (Barnard, 2000, p. 61). As almost all syndicated programmes are sourced from outside Wales, there is less space in the schedule for local voices – in Welsh and English – whether in the form of music, DJ chatter, news or other speech-based information and cultural material. Such incursions might be likened to the English television services that flow into Wales via transmitters whose signals extend well beyond England's borders (Welsh Affairs Select Committee, 1999, para. 44). In neither the case of radio nor television services does Wales have the same facility to 'speak back'! Furthermore, with the emergence of digital broadcasting and a regulatory climate infused with market rhetoric, these inflows are set to continue.

As a result of a gradual and insidious relaxation of ownership rules, the first batch of Wales's ILR stations are now owned by companies located beyond the immediate locality, and, in all but one case, outside Wales (Ofcom Advisory Group, 2003, p. 6). Moreover, a consolidation in ILR ownership has resulted in the Wireless Group and Capital Radio dominating the most populous areas of south and south-west Wales, while GWR monopolizes the north Wales coast. Another 'distant' owner, the Guardian Media Group (GMG), operates the south Wales regional licensee, Real Radio. Although recent ILR licensees, such as Radio Pembrokeshire and Radio Carmarthenshire, are still locally owned, major radio or media companies are represented on their respective boards. The pattern in Wales is that these organizations play the role of 'stalking horses', and only move to take a majority shareholding once it becomes evident that the station in question can generate a worthwhile financial return.[14]

The gradual easing of regulation has enabled stations such as Red Dragon in Cardiff to *parade* as local – even though it has a potential audience of 887,000, provides minimal informational programming and utters barely a word in Welsh.[15] It does this, while working assiduously to maximize its locality credentials – and ratings – through carefully targeted marketing and public relations campaigns, including a quota of 'good deeds' where money is raised for local causes. Further anomalies are evident when examining the delineation of licence areas. For example, recently given city status, Newport does not have a local radio station. Moreover, its future prospects are not encouraging. Newport remains 'locked' within the broadcast reach of Red Dragon and current indications suggest that another regional licence for south Wales will take precedence over a local licence for Newport (Ofcom, 2004b, p. 4). Acknowledgement within the industry that it is regional – rather than local – licences that generate greater profit acts as a useful reminder about the centrality of economics in such decisions (Ofcom, 2004b, p. 2).[16]

Although very much in its infancy, Wales's third sector of radio has begun to demonstrate how 'social gain' might be achieved. GTFM 106.9 has introduced many new voices to the airwaves through a concerted process of training and support (Everitt, 2003, pp. 76–8). Advice provided to the minister for Culture, Sport and the Welsh Language suggests that this form of radio is 'well suited to Welsh conditions' and will assist the NAfW in expediting its plans for community regeneration (Ofcom Advisory Group, 2003, p. 33).[17] But how this sector will be funded in the longer term is unclear. Earlier suggestions that this could occur by 'top slicing' the BBC licence fee and/or allowing the use of advertising and sponsorship remain controversial (see, for example, Commercial Radio Companies Association, 2003a, p. 4; Everitt, 2003, pp. 121–9). However, to help launch this new sector the Westminster government has established a Community Radio Fund to which groups intent on establishing such stations can apply (Ofcom, 2004c, p. 21).[18]

RADIO FUTURES: WHOSE RADIO?[19]

Essentially, the decisions that ultimately shape the provision of radio in Wales are made beyond its boundaries, despite the existence of structures that purport to give the people of Wales a voice in such matters. The BCW is imagined as a bridge between the people of Wales, the BBC and its Board of Governors. Nevertheless, it attracts criticism for a number of reasons, particularly because it lacks independence and is merely advisory (Ofcom Advisory Group, 2003, p. 27; Welsh Affairs Select Committee, 1999, pp. 21–4; Williams, 1997, pp. 33–5).

Similar limitations are evident when considering commercial radio. The IBA appointed a member for Wales – to 'make the interests of Wales his [sic] special care' – and a Welsh Committee to advise the said member, who also chaired the committee (Independent Broadcasting Authority, 1977, p. 2). When the RA replaced the IBA in 1991 it operated without a member for Wales until 1999, a period during which there was a spurt of licence awards. Even when a member was appointed, no separate body – advisory or otherwise – was established in Wales to aid the authority or its Welsh representative on decisions about Welsh radio.[20] Neither has the process of devolution strengthened Wales's voice in such structures.[21] There is no place for a member for Wales on the Ofcom Board – the key decision-making body – but there is Welsh representation on a Content Board and a Consumer Panel.[22] An Advisory Committee for Wales has also been established.[23] This body is chaired by the Ofcom Director, Wales, who is a member of Ofcom's external relations team (Ofcom, 2003).[24]

Given Ofcom's mission and the make-up of its board and executive, 'regulatory capture' remains a real possibility. This is evident when examining the influence of the Commercial Radio Companies Association (CRCA). Having already made clear that it sees no reason why the NAfW should have any role in relation to radio services operating within Wales (Commercial Radio Companies Association, 1998, p. 1), the CRCA is almost boastful about its ability to shape the Communications Act 2003: '[F]rom commercial radio's point of view, a great deal has been achieved and, in every relevant area, CRCA has achieved either a relaxation of rules or a compromise on initial Government proposals to the benefit of the industry' (Commercial Radio Companies Association, 2003b, p. 1).

Non-European companies can now acquire radio stations in Wales and the relaxation of ownership rules will result in more radio mergers, a further consolidation of ownership and more cross-media ownership. It is hard to refute charges that this will diminish the already limited diversity and plurality of local radio services. Nevertheless, apologists for the industry argue that the Communications Act 2003 actually preserves (what little remains of) the 'localness' of local radio. Despite such assertions, a close reading of the legislation indicates that only a 'suitable proportion' of programmes need to be 'locally made', with Ofcom acting as judge on such matters (Ofcom, 2004d, p. 7).[25] It is, therefore, useful to remember how a cosy relationship between regulator and industry can override the public interest. For example, when asked why the ILR station he managed included no Welsh programmes, the respondent – almost with a nod and a wink – replied:

> I would suspect that our Welsh output has gone down by over 50 per cent . . . But we had a very long conversation with [person at the Radio Authority] and we said to him . . . very few people in our area speak Welsh [and] more to the point . . . I can't find anyone . . . to do the news in Welsh.[26]

Commercial imperatives also influence the availability of DAB. There are only three transmitters, or multiplexes, in Wales that broadcast the UK-wide DAB 'national' BBC and commercial radio services, one in the north-east and two serving south and south-west Wales (Ofcom Advisory Group, 2003, p. 27). Similarly, at the local or regional level, only three multiplexes exist. They broadcast to the major population centres of Swansea, Cardiff and Newport, and are owned by major industry players. Furthermore, few of the – predominantly music-based – DAB services being broadcast could be considered local or indigenous. Significantly, Radio Wales and Radio Cymru are reliant for the carriage of their DAB signal on these commercially owned multiplexes. Unless alternative technical and financial solutions are found, much of Wales will be unable to receive Welsh-originating DAB services, either from BBC Wales or commercial operators (BBC, 1999; Ofcom Advisory Group, 2003, pp. 27–8; Welsh Affairs Select Committee, 1999, para. 36).

CONCLUSION

Wales has been described as a country 'deeply penetrated by UK media' – essentially, English-produced newspapers and broadcast media – with borders more 'porous' in media terms than either Scotland or Ireland (Ofcom Advisory Group, 2003, p. 6; Talfan Davies, 1999, p. 17).[27] This resonates with Tunstall's (1983, p. 228) observation that the 'Welsh media are much less Welsh than the Scottish media are Scottish'. The penetration, or invasion, of Wales by external media has generated the idea of an 'information deficit', which is seen to have implications for an informed democracy and cultural expression (see, for example,

Welsh Affairs Select Committee, 1999, p. 46; Williams, 1997, p. 32; Wyn Jones, 1998, p. 2).

In the case of radio, the thrust of the Communications Act 2003 can only exacerbate such concerns. This is, in essence, a re-regulation of media in favour of commercial interests while purporting to favour the public interest by pro-viding more 'choice' (McChesney, 2002). Furthermore, it is worth noting that Wales has been heavily reliant on the principle of 'universal coverage' and the provision of services by publicly funded – as opposed to commercial – broad-casters for an adequate system of communications (Ofcom Advisory Group, 2003, p. 24).

Significantly, broadcasting remains a non-devolved area and the NAfW can only expect to be consulted on such matters (Department of Culture, Media and Sport, 2000).[28] When making the case for Welsh representation on the main Ofcom Board, the NAfW argued that decisions relating to communications in Wales needed to take account of the country's distinctiveness, in particular its two languages, culture, economy – particularly its relative poverty – and topo-graphy (National Assembly for Wales, 2002b).[29] Failure to respond to Welsh overtures led to the (then) Assembly minister for Culture, Sport and the Welsh Language, Jenny Randerson, reiterating her belief that Wales should be repre-sented at the highest level on Ofcom (Randerson, 2002a) and venting her frustration to the Richard Commission: 'it has proved very difficult to get the UK Government to take account of Assembly Government policy interests, and to get these reflected in the [Communications] Bill' (Randerson, 2002b, p. 7).[30]

There are many key decisions to be made about radio services in Wales. They include protecting the 'localness' of local radio, the allocation of further commercial analogue licences, the establishment of a new community radio sector, the roll-out of BBC Wales and commercial DAB services, Ofcom's intended 'privatization' of the currently publicly owned radio spectrum,[31] and judgements on radio mergers and the associated issues of consolidation and cross-media ownership. In terms of the latter, how will the Ofcom Director, Wales, and members of the Advisory Committee for Wales respond to the pro-posed merger between the GWR and Capital Radio groups?[32] The prospect of GWR stations in north Wales (Champion FM, Coast FM, MFM 103.4, Marcher Gold) and those of Capital Radio in the south (Red Dragon and Capital Gold) being operated by a single (English or American) company has implications for local production, cultural expression and democracy. What power will a Welsh *advisory* body have in influencing such decisions?[33]

Of further concern is the extent to which 'ordinary' people will be enabled input into decisions about communications matters in Wales and what weight their views will carry. In tennis parlance, Ofcom's recent barrage of consultations suggests 'advantage industry' rather than citizen.[34] Two consultations on radio, one on the future licensing of commercial stations and another on the 'localness' of local radio, allowed only a five-week response period, even though Ofcom's own guidelines recommend double that time (see Ofcom 2004b, 2004d). Even if it had intended to do so, the Advisory Committee for Wales would have been hard pressed to get a broadly based public response in such a timeframe.

Ofcom is charged with making decisions in the interests of *citizens* and consumers. However, it is neither accountable directly to the people of Wales, nor to their democratically elected representatives at the NAfW. Yet again, Wales has been allocated a marginal and predominantly advisory role in decisions about the provision of radio services within its communicative space.

ACKNOWLEDGEMENT

This article draws on work conducted for a research project (ESRC: Ref. R000223668) which ran from December 2001 to July 2003.

NOTES

[1]   Information about radio services in the UK can be found on the website of the regulatory body, Ofcom (*www.ofcom.org.uk*).

[2]   However, the NAfW failed seriously to engage with the potential of radio in its review of arts and culture in Wales (Post-16 Education and Training Committee, 2000a, 2000b, 2000c), and in its response to the UK government's plans for communications reform (National Assembly for Wales, 2002b).

[3]   The Ofcom Advisory Group was chaired by Geraint Talfan Davies and included Leighton Andrews, Delyth Evans, Arwel Ellis Owen and Professor Mike Tedd. It was established by the minister for Culture, Sport and the Welsh Language to provide advice on how Wales might respond to the UK government's plans for communications reform. Its report was submitted to Ofcom on 3 April 2003.

[4]   In this instance, 'role and scope' means exploring both the nature and potential of the services being provided while considering their stated remits. The rationale for regulating the provision of radio services continues to be based on the premise that as radio spectrum is a scarce resource access to it should come with 'public obligations' (Hooper, 2001, p. 2). Essentially, this has been interpreted as broadcasting in the public interest, which is required of public service broadcasters such as the BBC as well as commercial operators of local radio.

[5]   This is not to forget that some listeners in Wales would already have been in receipt of radio signals from Manchester and Birmingham (see J. Davies, 1994; Lucas, 1981; Scannell and Cardiff, 1991).

[6]   The BBC based its argument on technical reasons, including the lack of a suitable wavelength, the relatively low number of licences sold in Wales, and concerns about both the lack and quality of programme material likely to be available in Wales. Also, it was economic and technical considerations that determined this (and other) regional linkages, not concerns about cultural characteristics (Scannell and Cardiff, 1991, pp. 321–2).

[7]   Prior to this, the Independent Television Authority (ITA) was the regulatory body for television.

[8]   As it is a regional rather than local licensee, Real Radio, based in Radyr, is not included.

[9]   Conservative estimates suggest that 200 stations could be licensed throughout the UK over a three year period (Everitt, 2003, p. 140).

[10]   The fact that Wales was allocated only one pilot project may be related to the country's relatively low take-up of the RSL (Restricted Service Licence) category when compared to other parts of the UK.

[11]   Other groups which aspire to set up community radio services may wish to note that this 'partnership' arrangement has been problematic (Everitt, 2003, p. 120).

[12]   By way of background, Wales had earlier been deemed not sufficiently affluent to support a commercial television franchise, hence its linkage with the west of England (Curran and Seaton, 1997, p. 184; Medhurst, 1998, p. 336).

[13]   See Thomas, Jewell and Cushion (2003, p. 7) on the limited use of BBC Wales radio services as a news source during the 2003 Welsh Assembly elections.

[14]   The outcome is that stations in Wales that began operations with a community – rather than commercial – orientation have evolved by necessity into the latter. The most obvious examples are Cardiff Broadcasting Corporation (CBC) – now Red Dragon, Radio Ceredigion at Aberystwyth and Radio Maldwyn at Newtown.

[15]   The Red Dragon 24-hour schedule comprises seven segments on Sunday to Thursday (0600–1000; 1000–1300; 1300–1600; 1600–1900; 1900–2200; 2200–0100; 0100–0600). This is reduced to six on Friday and Saturday by eliminating one evening segment (2200–0100) and extending the previous one (1900–0100). With the exception of the two-hand 'Jase and Joe' *Breakfast Show*, it is generally solo DJs who anchor the same segment throughout the week. The station's target catchment area is evident in the published programme schedule, where references are made to *South Wales's Biggest Breakfast Show*, *The Great Welsh Quiz*, *South Wales Hit Music* and *Seven Days of Entertainment in South Wales*. However, its *Welsh Chart* (6–13 November 2004) appears to be a misnomer, listing the following top ten artists: i) Eminem, ii) Destiny's Child, iii) Britney Spears, iv) Christina Aguilera, v) Usher, vi) Ja Rule/R Kelly/Ashanti, vii) Eric Prydz, viii) Michael Grey, ix) Daniel Bedingfield, x) Jamelia. Readers may also wish to check out Red Dragon's sister station, Capital Gold, on the AM frequency. Here, the amount of syndicated programming is significant and references to the locality are barely evident.

[16]   See G. Davies (1991) on the allocation of an all-embracing licence for Valleys Radio in south Wales.

[17]   See National Assembly for Wales (2000, 2001) regarding plans to create a 'new' Wales.

[18]   Ofcom will oversee the application and granting process.

[19]   Peter Lewis (1978) entitled his book on the Annan Report *Whose Media?*.

[20]   Geraint Talfan Davies, a previous controller of BBC Wales, was the member for Wales on the RA Board until Ofcom assumed responsibility for radio.

21 Details of the regulatory set-up can be found on the Ofcom website (*www.ofcom.org.uk*).
22 Sue Balsom is the member for Wales on the Content Board. Appointed by Ofcom in May 2003 for a period of two years, her term has since been extended by a further year and will end in May 2006. The representative for Wales on the Consumer Panel is Simon Gibson OBE. He was appointed in February 2004 for three years by the Westminster government on the recommendation of Ofcom. The CVs of both representatives can be found on the Ofcom website (*www.ofcom.org.uk*).
23 It is not known how knowledgeable members of the Advisory Committee for Wales are about radio-related matters and how much time they will be able to devote to this medium. Prior to its demise, the RA's boast was that 'radio problems' received 'radio solutions', but that under a multi-sectoral regulatory structure, like Ofcom, radio could be relegated to a 'Friday afternoon job' (Stoller, 2001, p. 2).
24 Rhodri Williams is the Ofcom Director, Wales. Ofcom's office in Wales is located in Cardiff Bay.
25 The clause about localness appears in section 314, Communications Act 2003.
26 The respondent was interviewed in 2002 for a research project on local radio in Wales (see Acknowledgement). Interviews were granted on condition of anonymity.
27 Wales's most popular analogue radio services are BBC Radio 1 and 2, which emanate from London (see *www.rajar.co.uk*). In some parts of Wales these and other services from London are easier to access than Radio Wales and Radio Cymru.
28 This includes the appointment of Welsh representatives to key bodies such as the BBC Board of Governors and Ofcom.
29 A cogent argument for devolving broadcasting to the NAfW is provided by Osmond (1998).
30 Under the stewardship of the Rt. Hon. Lord Richard QC, the Commission on the Powers and Electoral Arrangements of the National Assembly for Wales was established in 2002 and reported in March 2004 (see *www.wales.gov.uk*).
31 The Ofcom consultation on this matter was launched on 23 November 2004 (Ofcom, 2004e; see also Reece, 2004, p. 42).
32 Plans for such a merger became public in September 2004. If this plan materializes the emergent company would become the largest radio group in the UK (Katbamna, 2004, p. 13).
33 The will of this committee is also yet to be tested. Its members are appointed by Ofcom.
34 Since coming into being in December 2003 Ofcom has initiated and finalized over ninety-seven consultations.

REFERENCES

Allan, S. and O'Malley, T. (1999). 'The media in Wales', in D. Dunkerley and A. Thompson (eds), *Wales Today*, Cardiff: University of Wales Press.
Barlow, D. M. (2003). 'Who controls local radio?', *Planet*, 158, 79–64.

Barlow, D. M., Mitchell, P. and O'Malley, T. (2003). 'Commercial radio in Wales, 1972–2003: radio and the public sphere', paper presented to Annual Conference of the Media, Cultural and Communication Studies Association, University of Sussex, 20 December.

Barlow, D. M., Mitchell, P. and O'Malley, T. (2005). *The Media in Wales: Voices of a Small Nation*, Cardiff: University of Wales Press.

Barnard, S. (2000). *Studying Radio*, London: Edward Arnold.

Baron, M. (1975). *Independent Radio: The Story of Independent Radio in the UK*, Lavenham: Terence Dalton Limited.

BBC (1999). *Memorandum submitted by BBC to Welsh Affairs Select Committee*, London: BBC Board of Governors.

BBC Wales (2003). *Annual Report*, www.bbc.co.uk/wales, last accessed 21 February 2004.

Briggs, A. (1965). *The History of Broadcasting in the United Kingdom. Vol. II. The Golden Age of Wireless*, Oxford: Oxford University Press.

Carter, M. (1998). *Independent Radio: The First 25 Years*, London: Radio Authority.

Commercial Radio Companies Association (1998). *Memorandum Submitted to Select Committee on Welsh Affairs – Second Report*, www.parliament.the-stationery-office.co.uk

Commercial Radio Companies Association (2003a). *Views on the Creation of a Third Tier of Radio 'Access Radio'*, London: CRCA.

Commercial Radio Companies Association (2003b). *The 2003 Communications Act – An Aide Memoire for CRCA members*, London: CRCA.

Crisell, A. (1997). *An Introductory History of British Broadcasting*, London, Routledge.

Curran, J. and Seaton, J. (1997). *Power without Responsibility: The Press and Broadcasting in Britain*, 5th edn, London: Routledge.

Davies, G. (1991). 'Local radio comes to rural Wales', *Planet*, 85, 109–11.

Davies, J. (1994). *Broadcasting and the BBC in Wales*, Cardiff: University of Wales Press.

Department of Culture, Media and Sport (2000). *Concordat between the Department for Culture, Media and Sport and the Cabinet of the National Assembly for Wales*, London, DCMS.

Department of Trade and Industry/Department of Culture, Media and Sport (2000). *A New Future for Communications*, London: DTI/DCMS.

Ellis, G. (2000). 'Stereophonic nation: the bilingual sounds of Cool Cymru FM', *International Journal of Cultural Studies*, 3, 2, 188–98.

Evans, G. (1944). *The Radio in Wales*, Aberystwyth: The New Wales Union.

Everitt, A. (2003). *New Voices: An Evaluation of 15 Access Radio Projects*, London: Radio Authority.

Hargreaves, I. and Thomas, J. (2002). *New News, Old News*, London: Independent Television Commission.

Hooper, R. (2001). *Regulating Communications in the Age of Convergence*, London: Radio Authority.

Independent Broadcasting Authority (1977). *Independent Broadcasting in Wales*, Cardiff: IBA.

Katbamna, M. (2004). 'The great British radio carve up', *Independent* (Media Weekly), 22 November, 12–13.

Lewis, P. M. (1978). *Whose Media? The Annan Report and After: A Citizen's Guide to Radio and Television*, London: Consumers Association.

Lewis, P. M. and Booth, J. (1989). *The Invisible Medium: Public, Commercial and Community Radio*, London: Macmillan.

Lucas, R. (1981). *The Voice of a Nation? A Concise Account of the BBC in Wales*, Llandysul: Gomer.

Mackay, H. and Powell, A. (1997). 'Wales and its media: production, consumption and regulation', *Contemporary Wales*, 9, 8–39.

McChesney, R. (2002). *Theses on Media Deregulation*, London, CPBF.

Medhurst, J. (1998). 'Mass media in 20th century Wales', in P. H. Jones (ed.), *A Nation and its Books*, Aberystwyth: NLW.

Morris, N. (1995). 'Film and broadcasting in Wales', *Books in Wales*, 1, 5–8.

National Assembly for Wales (2000). *www.betterwales.com*, Cardiff: National Assembly for Wales.

National Assembly for Wales (2001). *Strategic Statement on the Preparation of 'Plan for Wales'*, Cardiff: National Assembly for Wales.

National Assembly for Wales (2002a). *Creative Future/Cymru Greadigol: A Culture Strategy for Wales*, Cardiff: Welsh Assembly Government.

National Assembly for Wales (2002b). *Welsh Assembly Government Response to the Draft Communications Bill*, Cardiff: National Assembly for Wales.

Ofcom (2003). 'Advisory committees for the nations', press release, 12 September, London: Ofcom.

Ofcom Advisory Group (2003). *Wales and Ofcom: A Report by an Advisory Group to the Minister for Culture, Sport and the Welsh Language*, Welsh Assembly Government, Cardiff: NAfW.

Ofcom (2004a). *Licensing Community Radio: Consultation Document*, London: Ofcom.

Ofcom (2004b). *The Future Licensing of Commercial Radio*, London: Ofcom.

Ofcom (2004c). *Licensing Community Radio*, London, Ofcom.

Ofcom (2004d). *Localness on Commercial Radio Stations: An Interim Consultation Document Reviewing Localness Basics*, London, Ofcom.

Ofcom (2004e). *Spectrum Framework Review: A Consultation on Ofcom's Views as to How Radio Spectrum Should Be Managed*, London: Ofcom.

Osmond, J. (1998). 'Memorandum submitted by the Institute of Welsh Affairs', in *Broadcasting in Wales and the National Assembly*, Welsh Affairs Select Committee, London: HMSO.

Post-16 Education and Training Committee (2000a). *Policy Review: Arts and Culture in Wales – ETR 10–00*, Cardiff: National Assembly for Wales.

Post-16 Education and Training Committee (2000b). *A Culture in Common*, Cardiff: National Assembly for Wales.

Post-16 Education and Training Committee (2000c). *Meeting with Broadcasters – ETR 14–00*, Cardiff: National Assembly for Wales.

Randerson, J. (2002a). 'Call for strong Welsh voice in communications', press release, 9 July, Cardiff: National Assembly for Wales.

Randerson, J. (2002b). 'Written evidence to Richard Commission', Cardiff: National Assembly for Wales.

Reece, D. (2004). 'State to give up control over radio spectrum', *Independent* (Business), 24 November, 42.

Scannell, P. and Cardiff, D. (1991). *A Social History of British Broadcasting: Volume 1, 1922–1939*, Oxford: Blackwell.

Stoller, T. (2001). Speech to Cardiff Communications Summit, 12 June, London: Radio Authority.

Talfan Davies, G. (1999). *Not By Bread Alone: Information, Media and the National Assembly*, Cardiff, Wales Media Forum.

Thomas, J., Jewell, J. and Cushion, S. (2003). *Media Coverage of the 2003 Welsh Assembly Elections*, Cardiff: Wales Media Forum.

Tunstall, J. (1983). *The Media in Britain*, London: Constable.

Watkin, P. (1976). 'Swansea Sound: the first two years of the first commercial radio station in Wales', *Planet*, 31, 21–24.

Welsh Affairs Select Committee (1999). *Broadcasting in Wales and the National Assembly*, London: HMSO.

Williams, K. (1997). *Shadows and Substance: The Development of a Media Policy for Wales*, Llandysul: Gomer Press.

Wyn Jones, R. (1998). 'Memorandum submitted by Dr Richard Wyn Jones', in *Broadcasting in Wales and the National Assembly*, Welsh Affairs Select Committee, London: HMSO.

9. WALES, IDENTITY AND CULTURAL MODERNIZATION

William Housley

ABSTRACT

During the course of this article I explore the concept of cultural modernization and identity as it relates to Wales. Culture has become central to policy and rhetoric associated with regeneration and renewal. Through the case example of the visual arts I argue that the process of cultural modernization is characterized by two principal tensions. The article outlines some of the characteristics of these tensions and considers the possibilities of overcoming these tensions in the future. The article argues that the shape and character of cultural modernization is crucial to forging and forming cultural identity and provides the 'raw materials' for the emerging cultural dimensions of citizenship in post-devolution Wales. The article concludes by arguing that 'publics' are key to promoting a form of cultural modernization and identity that is not only regenerative but also, in the last analysis, emancipatory and inclusive.

INTRODUCTION

> The nation-state today has to respond to the twin forces of globalism and localism, while the traditional basis for national citizenship is widely reported as being eroded . . . [however] it is not that national forms of citizenship are finished but that they are being reconstituted. Our task then is to understand what cultural citizenship might mean in these contexts. (Stevenson, 2003, p. 35)

Stevenson argues that national and cultural forms of identity are not being eliminated through processes associated with globalism and localism; rather they are being 'reconstituted'. In the context of post-devolution Wales the forces of both localism and globalism are highly visible. They are visible through the process of rationalization, the relocation of manufacturing jobs to other parts of the world and through the emergence of devolved governance and institutions. Within the context of Wales, cultural and artistic practices are important resources that are being mobilized as a means of promoting a number of processes. For example, they are employed as a means of 'branding' Wales abroad in order to attract investment and regenerate 'spaces and places' within a neo-liberal aesthetic (Boltanski and Chiapello, 1999), on the one hand, and, on the other, to legitimate and promote an emerging form of post-devolved identity and citizenship. The opening of the Wales Millennium Centre in November 2004 represents a culmination of the process of utilizing culture as part of a broader strategy of regeneration. This process has also been accompanied by discussion, debate and, in some cases, rancour. Nevertheless, in terms of the arts in Wales tensions concerning venues and funding have not prevented a resurgence in the profile of culture in Wales. Indeed, in some cases this controversy has taken on a direct and explicit connection with attempts to kick-start a wider cultural renaissance within post-devolution Wales that is linked to strategies of regeneration. This move has, more often than not, provided a further space through which the contested and slippery concept of the Welsh nation can be imagined, realized, explored and represented. In terms of devolved institutions in Wales, the Culture Committee of the Welsh Assembly has recognized the importance of culture and the arts in relation to cultural policy in Wales. In a discussion paper (Welsh Assembly Government, 2000), the former cultural committee arts and cultural advisor locates the visual arts within a wider discourse of Welsh culture. The discussion paper states:

The culture of Wales is rich and deep in its diversity of expression. It is a performative culture where people are passionate to take part and enjoy others taking part – from sports to choirs to acting to brass bands to Eisteddfodau, mountaineering, films, water sports and rock concerts. It admires the skills of creativity, hard work, industry and innovation. It is hewn from the natural environment of Wales, its dramatic landscape, its education system and unique social and industrial history. Wales excels in the literary arts, in its visual culture, in its music making, its built heritage, its national institutions, its actors and its sporting achievements . . . Wales is defined by its ancient language, its modern diversity of peoples and its social compassion, but above all, by its passion for creativity. The Culture of Wales is in the process of re-shaping itself, of re-defining itself, perhaps even, of re-inventing itself for the challenging of the new century and in reaction of the new political situation in which it finds itself.

An interesting contribution to this process can be found in the context of the visual arts. I have chosen this context as a case example as it represents an area of cultural practice and organization that was not viewed as a traditional cultural strength but has recently developed and raised its profile considerably in Wales. Thus, in this article I will explore wider issues concerning the process of cultural modernization in Wales through the example of the visual arts. In the case of our chosen example of cultural practice in post-devolution Wales, it is worth beginning with Peter Lord's *Imaging the Nation* (2000). This book represents a unique move towards both the *establishment* and *recovery* of a visual narrative for Wales. With reference to the history of the visual arts in Wales and the process of the collective recovery of a national visual narrative Lord states:

> It has often been alleged that a national consciousness heavily conditioned by the needs of differentiation from a dominant neighbour is a characteristic Welsh weakness. As a result of the political and economic decline of that neighbour, a complementary growth in our own self-confidence, and a wider change in perceptions of nationality, it is the hope of many at the beginning of the twenty-first century that this essentially colonised state of mind may at last be transcended. (2000, p. 9)

For Lord, the sensible recovery of a 'Welsh' visual heritage is part of such a process. This process is also occurring during a time of significant cultural, political, social and economic change in Wales epitomized by the devolution process and attempts at the regeneration of both physical and mental landscapes. Consequently, the visual arts, as part of a wider array of cultural practices in Wales, are connected to the reinvigoration of region and 'nation'. This process has also been bolstered by Cardiff's (failed) bid for the European Capital of Culture in 2008 through which the interface between cultural concerns and economics increasingly came into focus (see the article by Kompotis in this volume). Furthermore, in 2003 Wales was represented at the Venice Biennale. This represented a profound shift in cultural representation and identity at the level of the visual arts within a high-profile international context. In one sense, representation at this high-profile international festival of the arts is significant in terms of Wales taking its rightful place at the table of modern, cultural and forward-looking nations. The representation of Wales at this event nevertheless courted some controversy. This concerned the 'Welsh credentials' of the artists chosen to represent Wales at the arts festival (*Western Mail*, 2003). A central dimension of this debate was the connection of being born in Wales, living in Wales and the production of visual artefacts. The attempt at securing the representation of Wales at a major international arts event was recontextualized in terms of a media debate where particularism, origin and notions of 'birth location' figured prominently. Despite this, the development of Wales's international arts profile has continued with the initiation of the Artes Mundi prize and visual arts festival in 2004 staged at the National Gallery and Museum. The Artes Mundi festival, as the name suggests, included artists from around the world.

Despite the process of devolution, Wales is still a constituent nation of a larger state. However, the process of devolution has relocated some features of state power into newly established quasi-legislatures and political institutions. This may be understood as an example of the increased territorialization of politics during a time when the global market extends its reach and hegemonic integrity across nations, institutions, identities and cultures. On the other hand, the devolution of political power has also provoked a reconsideration of certain ways of thinking about Wales and its place in the world. Culture is the primary means through which a transformation of ways of being and thinking can be achieved, as it deals in the stock and trade of shared understanding and meanings within a given social collective. In Wales, increased 'autonomy' has opened up a space where cultural institutions and cultural identities within a devolved space of governance have become subject to the gaze of devolved policy-makers, politicians and cultural elites. An inevitable consequence of this interest is a drive to modernize cultural institutions and generate a form of post-devolved citizenship and identity. Identity and culture are the raw materials through which the legitimating mechanism of citizenship can be formed and forged. The precise characteristics of post-devolved cultural identity and the emerging form of cultural citizenship are 'up for grabs'. In other words, cultural citizenship is open to being defined and shaped in terms of interests. One interest is that the emerging definition of citizenship should be couched in terms of the many as opposed to the few. Indeed, the struggle to define the precise characteristics of the cultural dimensions of the emerging contours of Welsh citizenship and identity is a struggle for recognition and access to resources by individuals, community groups, monopolistic elites, political groupings and other constituent members of a democratically flawed pluralism. (Where pluralism is a space in which the struggle for recognition is characterized by unequal resources, sharp differences in cultural capital and the uses/abuses of 'history' as an 'elite status' legitimating mechanism.) A central feature of this process of defining new forms of cultural citizenship and identity is the modernization of cultural institutions.[1] The process of cultural modernization can be understood as a form of democratization. Before thinking about the current characteristics of this modernization process in post-devolution Wales, it is worthwhile explaining these ideas in more detail.

CULTURAL MODERNIZATION OR DEMOCRATIZATION?

The notion of cultural modernization includes a set of processes through which cultural practice, artefacts and display move from a 'princely' to a 'public domain' (Herrero, 2002). In many respects, it has close affinity with Karl Mannheim's concept of cultural democratization and as such is bound up with what T. H. Marshall described as the cultural dimension of citizenship. Mannheim states: 'a democratising trend is our predestined fate, not only in politics, but also in intellectual and cultural life as a whole. Whether we like it or not, the trend is irreversible' (1971, p. 171).

For Mannheim, this process of democratization exhibited a potential for danger, not least the levelling effect of the democratization of culture and the dominance of mediocrity. Mannheim argued that the process of cultural democratization was characterized by three principal consequences. First, it was characterized by a belief in the power of education and the provision of cultural opportunity and excellence across all forms of social classification. Secondly, it generates a normative space, which is suspicious of experts, specialists and other monopolistic knowledge groups. Finally, the process of cultural democratization generates a form of cultural de-distantiation, namely, the blurring of the boundaries between high and low culture.

In terms of devolution in the United Kingdom, a process of cultural modernization can certainly be discerned. In some respects this is clearly a product of democratization due to its linkages with the democratic transformation at the national level afforded by the process of devolution. However, the extent to which these changes are the product of democratic forces, new cultural entrepreneurship or resurgent elites is not yet discernible. These changes have an effect both in terms of how we think of Wales as a cultural nation and how the process of modernization and democratization impacts on the emerging contours of cultural citizenship, cultural inequality and identity in Wales. However, in this article I will seek to argue that this process of cultural modernization and struggle to define cultural identity in Wales is characterized by two tensions. These tensions, which I outline in the next section of the article, are visible and manifest in a number of debates and issues prevalent in contemporary Welsh affairs: for example, debates about black Welsh identity (Williams, 1999), the establishment of a room devoted to Welsh art in the National Museum and Gallery (Housley, 2003), the need to sustain and nurture our language and who should be coaching the national rugby team.

A recent example of tensions with regard to defining cultural identity can be found in the furore concerning the possibility of holding the National Eisteddfod in Liverpool just before the initiation of its tenure as European City of Culture.

The outgoing archdruid of Wales concluded that the suggestion was absurd and asked the question 'What has Liverpool ever done for us?' on BBC Radio, adding that the 'last thing it did for us was to drown Tryweryn' (*Guardian*, 2004). This argument overlooked the fact that Liverpool has held the National Eisteddfod on a number of previous occasions in the nineteenth and early twentieth centuries. Indeed, the counter-argument is that for many people living in the north of Wales, Liverpool is the regional capital with very strong Welsh connections. The possibility of holding the Eisteddfod in the European Capital of Culture could be construed as a gift and opportunity to promote Welsh culture and language on a much bigger stage in what may be understood and experienced as a city of the Welsh if not a Welsh city. Whilst it does not represent a re-establishment of the 'Old North' it may be argued that the Welsh and Welsh language have not and never will be confined to the particular (and arbitrary) borders of Wales today. In short, the debate neatly displays the tensions concerning culture in Wales within the changing cultural geography of the United Kingdom and wider global transformations that include the transformation of old cultural pathways into new circuits of meaning. Sociologists of culture have long taken an interest in how historical colonial networks of political economy have also provided the conduits for more recent cultural innovation, remembering and the transfer of cultural practices, codes and style (Gilroy, 1987). However, it remains to be seen whether cultural agents will seize the opportunities provided through such revitalized modes of cultural capital and their potential resources and overcome the tensions inherent to the cultural modernization process.

CULTURAL MODERNIZATION IN WALES: TWO TENSIONS

How to describe these two tensions? We are familiar with their manifestation in public discourse and contemporary debates. We can recognize their expressions. One way of thinking about these tensions is as systemic (top-down) versus organic (bottom-up) generators of cultural modernization, on the one hand, and introspective versus international conceptions of culture and identity, on the other. Both these tensions and dichotomies meet at the fulcrum of the politics of recognition (Smith and Tatalovich, 2002, p. 30). The politics of recognition are of import to a small country such as Wales as this form of politics is related to cultural capital and power (as expressed through the allocation of resources) and issues concerning the remembering and forgetting of communities, peoples and struggles. Let us explore the first tension that characterizes the cultural modern-ization process as it relates to the devolved context of Wales.

Tension one: top-down versus bottom-up forms of cultural generation

Examples of top-down generators of cultural modernization would include government initiatives, private enterprise and established cultural institutions. These may find voice in non-consultative policy initiatives and the discourses of cultural elites. Organic generators would include the Butetown History and Arts Centre and other community-based cultural practice, scholarship and cultural production where, in this particular case, 'practices and products challenge prevailing images and narratives of Wales as mono-cultural and white' (Jordan, 2003). Of course, other organic generators of cultural modernization may also be involved with other forms of community work that document other 'community voices', ordinary people, the working class and other sidelined voices and experiences. These may include community art groups, local history groups, popular musicians and local artists.

Tension two: introspective versus international (outward-looking) notions of culture

The second tension refers to models of cultural practice and discourse that pertain to introspective versus international notions of culture. The notion of introspection refers to a form of cultural modernization and identity that is concerned with matters relating to national-cultural boundaries, perspectives and practices, whilst the international refers to those modes of cultural modernization that make connections with a wider world-view. In its most progressive form this international notion may correspond to a form of cosmopolitanism (Beck, 2001). In a world where the relationship between national cultures and citizenship is being decoupled (via the process of globalization and developments associated with late capitalism) cosmopolitanism represents a progressive strategy for constructing forms of citizenship that promote transnational dialogues. It represents, perhaps, the first seeds of a civic movement at the global level in response to the territorialization of politics and the globalization of the market. In other forms internationalism may be used as a by-word for the global market place and the new symbolic economy of cultural consumption. An introspective mode of cultural modernization, identity and citizenship (if it is the case that cultural identities provide the raw material of legitimacy and recognition for forging cultural citizenship) may be read as a retreat from an emerging global civic culture characterized by negotiation, ideational exchange, cooperation and synthesis. On the other hand, it may be read as a form of particularism that represents the grounds through which forms of diversity, resistance and community life may be sustained and realized in the face of global market fundamentalism.

RESOLVING THE TENSION: CULTURAL FUTURES, INCLUSIVE CITIZENSHIP AND SYNTHESIS

In the case of Wales, the tensions described above are visible in our cultural life and contemporary questions that concern Welsh identity during a period of transformation and change. For example, should there be a room designated for Welsh art (not art in Wales) in our National Museum and Gallery? Should resources be spent on an international cultural facility in Cardiff Bay? Is it possible for people born outside of Wales to represent Welsh culture and practice? Should we deal with the 'Cardiffization' of Welsh culture by insisting that Bangor is chosen as a site for a future internationally recognized national gallery? Should the Welsh National Eisteddfod be held in Liverpool again? As stated previously these questions are constituted within the tensions that criss-cross and meet at the point of the politics of recognition. Issues concerning material resources and the distribution of cultural capital underpin this form of politics. The processes, flows and arguments that stem from these tensions that are inherent to the cultural modernization process in Wales need to be both celebrated and understood (Housley, 2005). They need to be celebrated in the sense that culture in Wales, as a source of change and transformation, is on the move. They need to be understood as a means of marshalling the raw materials of cultural change and development in the course of forging a post-devolved conception of cultural citizenship. I have argued elsewhere (Housley, 2005) that the process of cultural modernization can be understood in terms of a number of general 'sequential' developments. They can be broadly conceptualized in the following terms. First, there are the processes of initiation and recovery. In the case of the visual arts in Wales these have been realized through the establishment of a number of narratives of visual culture in and for Wales: for example, the scholarly work carried out by the Centre for Advanced Celtic Studies at the University of Aberystwyth and its transfer through the Visual Culture of Wales series. The second development in the process of cultural modernization can be understood in terms of the dialectic between 'top-down' and 'bottom-up' forms of cultural practice and organization: for example, the real and perceived historical tensions between the practices, definitions and priorities for visual culture promoted by the Welsh Arts Council and cultural groups and organizations interested in promoting community art, practice, education and a particular form of national awareness (for example, the Beca Art Group founded by the late Paul Davies). The tension between cultural elites, on the one hand, and organic grass-roots cultural practice on the other is central to understanding the reorganization and re-engineering of cultural institutions in post-devolved Wales at this point in time. This leads to the third development in cultural modernization: processes associated with cultural identity composition where tensions between the 'top' and the 'bottom' are also enhanced by debates between 'introspective' and 'international' notions of culture. The cultural history of Ireland provides an interesting case example. Herrero (2002) notes that during the establishment of a modern art collection in Ireland towards the end of the nineteenth century, intellectuals were involved in a fierce debate concerning its constitution. The struggle centred on introspective arguments concerned with the need of the national collection to reflect a 'Celtic Ireland' and more international aspirations that were reflected through proposals to include artefacts from across Europe and other parts of the world. Similarly, cultural intellectuals in the immediate post-colonial experience of the West Indies were faced with a debate based around a perceived choice between Afrocentric practice and the cultural politics of international engagement. With the increasing application of post-colonial theory in relation to Wales this comparison is worthy of further consideration.

Finally, the raw products and processes identified with the cultural modernization process summarized above require resolution. The form of cultural identity(ies) adopted will be crucial in promoting or inhibiting inclusion and exclusion. The configurations of identity are crucial to the challenge of 'inclusive politics' within new devolved political frameworks (Chaney and Fevre, 2001). The emerging form(s) of cultural identity and associated public debate could represent an opportunity to overcome the tension between introspection (particular) and internationalism (universal) in the common culture and negotiate the tension between established institutions, the market and organic cultural production. By understanding these processes we will be able to meet the challenge of developing an inclusive, participatory and democratic form of cultural citizenship and development that is able to deal with the challenges of globalization, the changing character of Wales and the ancient traditions of the country and its people. Indeed, the recent development of the visual arts in Wales has been seen as a significant component of not merely regeneration and renewal but also an emergence from traditional discourses of colonization. As Adams states:

> Wales, it has been said, was England's first colony and although it is many years since it was first garrisoned, it must be observed that there is no greater garrison and no more effective coloniser than the mind itself . . . Now, emancipation from political, sexual, racial, social, religious or class repression (at most of which Wales has sometime or other excelled), and the public proclamation of that emancipation, is almost invariably conducive to art, to great art in fact, and much of what is most compelling in Welsh art today seems to stem from just such a proclamation of emancipation. (2003, p. 7)

In conclusion, the visual arts in Wales, as suggested earlier in this article and in the above quotation, need to be also understood in terms of emancipation and democratization as well as regeneration and renewal. In this article I have argued that the process of cultural modernization is characterized by tensions and fissures. However, in terms of an outcome that is consistent with interests associated with an emancipatory project it is clear that public participation will be key to the process of cultural modernization as it unfolds in post-devolution Wales. It will be key in terms of successfully negotiating the tensions inherent to the cultural modernization process in a way that defines and promotes an inclusive, outward-looking (but locally relevant), historically aware and democratic form of cultural identity and thence citizenship for Wales in the twenty-first century. Visual culture is one area through which we can appreciate and reflect on how this process unfolds within the social, political, economic and cultural landscape of our imagined community.

NOTE

1   The term modernization is used in relation to the concept of cultural modernization. The author adopts the position that late modern, late capitalist and liquid modern are more accurate societal descriptors than the terminology organized around the 'post' prefix.

REFERENCES:

Adams, H. (2003). *Imaging Wales: Contemporary Art in Context*, Bridgend: Seren Books.
Beck, U. (2001). *What is Globalisation?* Cambridge: Polity Press.
Boltanski, L. and Chiapello, E. (1999). *Le Nouvel Espirit du Capitalisme*, Paris: Gallimard.
Chaney, P. and Fevre, R. (2001). *Welsh Nationalism and the Challenge of 'Inclusive' Politics*, Cardiff School of Social Sciences, Working Paper Series, No. 2, *www.cardiff. ac.uk/socsi/publications/workingpapers*
Gilroy, P. (1987). *There Ain't No Black in the Union Jack: The Cultural Politics of Race and Nation*, London: Hutchinson.
Guardian (2004). 'Hands off our eisteddfod, bards tell Liverpool', 14 December.
Herrero, M. (2002). 'Towards a sociology of art collections', *International Sociology*, 17, 1, 57–72.
Housley, W. (2003). *Art, Wales, Discourse and Devolution*, Cardiff University School of Social Sciences, Working Paper 38.
Housley, W. (2005). 'Cultural modernization, the visual arts and identity in Wales', *The Welsh Journal of Education*.

Jordan, G. (2003). 'History, cultural democracy and regeneration', *The Bevan Foundation Review*, 2, 58–61.

Lord, P. (2000). *Imaging the Nation*, Cardiff: University of Wales Press.

Mannheim, K. (1971). *Essays on the Sociology of Culture*, London: Routledge and Kegan.

Smith, T. A. and Tatalovich, R. (2002). *Cultures at War: Moral Conflicts in Western Democracies*, Toronto: Broadview Press.

Stevenson, N. (2003). *Cultural Citizenship: Cosmopolitan Questions*, Buckingham: Open University Press.

Welsh Assembly Government (2000). *Post–16 Education and Training Committee Report*, 28 June.

Western Mail (2003). 'Wales represented at Venice Biennale', 12 June.

Williams C. (1999). 'Passports to Wales? Race, nation and identity', in R. Fevre and A. Thompson (eds), *Nation, Identity and Social Theory: Perspectives from Wales*, Cardiff: University of Wales Press.

10. MARKETING THE CITY OF CARDIFF: IS THE RED DRAGON WHITE AND MIDDLE CLASS?

Panagiotis Kompotis

ABSTRACT

This article contributes to the development of a critical analysis of place-marketing representations through an interpretation of the language used to represent, commodify and promote Cardiff. It mainly adopts a cultural studies approach to place-selling efforts that focuses more on the wider social and political meanings of place-marketing. The main purpose of the study is to investigate how city marketeers and administrators (re)imagine the city. To do this, it applies discourse analysis to the promotional material that is used for the marketing of Cardiff. The main messages and generic themes which pervade the promotional literature of the city are discussed along with the attempts of city marketeers to confront historical stereotypes of the Welsh people and character. Moreover, this article shows how the specific promotional material reflects, reproduces and justifies unequal power relations and social hierarchies. It further argues that the urban bourgeoisie uses city marketing as a means of capital accumulation and social control. The main arguments derive from a Marxist urban theory with insights drawn from the fields of culture, politics, geography and aesthetic theory. While Cardiff provides the focus for this discussion between place-marketing representations, discourse, power and society, the same analysis could be applied to representations of other post-industrial cities.

INTRODUCTION

In the last decades, deindustrialization and the extensive restructuring of the capitalist system have brought about a sea change in political, social, economic and cultural practices, structures and processes. Since the mid-1980s, Cardiff, and south-east Wales in general, an area with a rich industrial past and working-class culture, have been undergoing a massive regeneration project that has transformed them into a post-industrial service centre. In this context city marketing has emerged as one of the central tenets of urban policy-making and implementation. City administrators and marketeers now reimagine the city as a consumption centre whose physical and social attributes have become aesthetic commodities to be sold to and consumed by a number of target audiences.

This article is based on an analysis of the promotional literature used for the marketing of Cardiff and its main aim is to investigate how city administrators and marketeers (re)imagine the city. First, the article investigates the main marketing messages and generic themes that pervade the promotional material of Cardiff. Secondly, it seeks to show how urban elites use this material to reproduce and justify their hegemony and how city marketing is employed as a means of capital accumulation.

PLACE-MARKETING: MAJOR TRENDS

Reviewing the literature on place-marketing, three major trends can be identified. To begin with, some scholars (Ashworth and Voogd, 1990; Fretter, 1993; Smyth, 1994; Duffy, 1995) approach the place-marketing phenomenon from a market perspective. Their main purpose is to highlight the procedures, instruments and techniques that marketeers use or can use effectively to market places, especially cities. Although only few would dispute the theoretical and practical contribution of this kind of research to place-marketing or marketing in general, one could argue that this approach is largely technocratic, if not myopic, as it fails to connect place-marketing with wider social and cultural meanings.

On the other hand, scholars such as Booth and Boyle (1993), Holcomb (1993), Gold (1994) and Ward (1998) apply to place-selling efforts insights drawn from critical cultural studies. These writers use not only primary but also secondary discourse to analyse the language and imagery of place promotion. In their work, they examine the messages that marketing purports to convey, but at the same time they keep a critical stance when they refer to ideas about society and culture contained in the place-marketing discourse. Still, most of these studies look at cities as collections of buildings and services that are/have to be sold and consumed and not as dense social relations.

It is within cultural geography that we find the most severe academic critique of place-selling (see, for example, Harvey, 1989, 1990; Zukin, 1989, 1991;

Kearns and Philo, 1993a; Waitt, 1999). This article draws upon and contributes to an urban theory that sees the city as a spatial, economic, material and symbolic matrix of struggle over power and capital accumulation. This critical approach argues that place-marketing is inextricably bound up with the presentation and promotion of the ideology of the established power and is engineered by the bourgeois 'managers' of places to reaffirm the ideological commitments of society and imbue social consensus in an era distinguished by a sense of alienation, anomie and increasing social inequalities within cities by income, ethnic identity and life opportunities (Waitt, 1999). In other words, urban elites employ marketing techniques and resources to manipulate social, cultural and historical elements of the locality as means of capital accumulation and social control (Harvey, 1990).

In this sense, this article adopts a materialist approach without dimming, however, the autonomy of culture and politics. Indeed, many arguments in this article derive from the Marxist orthodoxy, but at the same time I try to stress the many and various forms of power that are embedded in the promotional literature and can be exercised through the resources of the city by an elite class.

This kind of materialist critique can reveal interrelations of social structure and forms of a discourse that represent, transmit and transform embedded power relations – relations that are historically mediated and socially produced. This article looks at the (modern) history of Cardiff from a class-struggle perspective – a class struggle that has its origins in the nineteenth century, when rapid industrialization resulted in the emergence of a new moneyed class of capitalists, the rise of the Welsh middle class and the creation of an immense proletariat, and continues today as deindustrialization and the rise in importance of the tertiary and quaternary services have led to the emergence in Cardiff of a new bourgeoisie and a new working class.

METHODOLOGY AND SAMPLE

The majority of case studies of which I am aware fail to reach the core of the selling-places phenomenon, which is the struggle over power and capital accumulation. In my view, this is mainly due to two reasons. First, most studies end up recycling the dominant ideology because they use an inappropriate and/or inadequate methodology (mainly interviews with city administrators and marketeers). Secondly, they fail to enrich their discussion with a deep insight drawn from the critical cultural studies.

The main methodological tool I use for the purposes of this article is discourse analysis. In general, discourse analysis is seldom used in the relevant literature.

Moreover, this is probably the first study on place-marketing that adopts a 'critical discourse analysis' approach. Critical discourse analysts take for granted the interdependence and *dialectical* relationship between language and power, meaning and social process (Fairclough, 1989; Hodge and Kress, 1993; Barker and Galasinski, 2001; Van Dijk, 2001). They use the tools of discourse analysis to study power abuse, dominance and inequality as they are expressed or reproduced by discourse and tend to take a rather materialist position indicating that they have 'an interest in a real material world independent of talk and discourse' (Wetherell, 2001, p. 392).

Given the budgetary constraints facing those involved in the marketing of Cardiff, brochures are the key tool for presenting and marketing the city to a number of target audiences. I have chosen to analyse four colour brochures that were used for the promotion of Cardiff in 2002 and 2003. Two of them (CI, 2002 and CI, 2003) are booklet-sized documents produced by Cardiff Initiative, the main organization involved in the marketing of the city. This annually produced booklet is the *only* print material whose aim is the promotion of the city and its surrounding area to the tourists who visit the city, containing articles on, for example, the city's history, heritage projects and nightlife.

At the centre of my analysis stands the promotional material that was produced for the European Capital of Culture 2008 bid. City administrators and marketeers devoted considerable marketing effort and funds to bidding for the title. What is more important, Cardiff 2008 Ltd, the organization developed to drive the project forward, worked in partnership with almost all the marketing organizations involved in the marketing of Cardiff, and Wales in general, and with a number of external consultants and advisors. First, I analyse the entry document (Cardiff 2008, 2002a – henceforth referred to as Cardiff 2008a) of the 2008 bid, which is a forty-page broadsheet brochure. This document is the most significant for my study not only because it is rich in text, but also because one of its main target audiences are the people living in Cardiff and Wales. It seems that one of the main aims of city marketeers is to sell the (new) image of Cardiff to the local people, while the achievement of popular consensus was vital to the success of the 2008 bid. It should also be pointed out that the campaign's core messages and ideas that are presented and analysed in this document were widely circulated in the local media. Secondly, I analyse a twenty-two-page tabloid-sized brochure (Cardiff 2008, 2002b – henceforth referred to as Cardiff 2008b) that was produced to promote local arts in the UK market.

The fact that the documents I analyse were targeted to different audiences is taken into consideration throughout this article. The fact that I analyse the promotional material that was produced to market Cardiff at a specific time period does not allow me to draw any conclusions about previous marketing campaigns or compare my data with the promotional material of other (British) cities. However, this sample allows me to investigate how the city marketeers (re)imagine Cardiff and whose interests this (new) image serves. That is why my first concern is to examine who the people behind the marketing of the city are and the social group(s) to which they belong.

THE RHETORIC OF CARDIFF 2008

The Cardiff 2008 bid epitomizes actions of urban entrepreneurialism. To begin with, Cardiff 2008 itself was a public-private partnership. Indeed, it was registered as a limited company. As figure 10.1 shows, only three members of the board were elected representatives: the Lord and Deputy Lord Mayor of Cardiff (both from the Labour Party) and Plaid Cymru AM Rhodri Glyn Thomas. The other nine members were mainly managers and chief executives of a number of public, private and public-private organizations. What is striking is the complete absence of multicultural and youth representation from an organization that made multiculturalism and youth culture central themes in its campaign. Cardiff 2008 acknowledges this issue (see extract 1). However, by doing so the organization manages only to pinpoint the fact that a number of ethnic and other social groups were excluded from the 'conception, planning and programming' (to use Cardiff 2008's words) of the bid. This issue will be discussed in depth later in this article:

Extract 1
There are plans to strengthen the Cardiff 2008 stakeholder group especially in the areas of tertiary education and multi-cultural and youth representation. (Cardiff 2008a, p. 18)

Cardiff 2008 cooperated with and consulted a number of marketing and management agencies. Most importantly, the organization recruited a chief executive who managed the bid together with three other appointed managers (see figure 10.1). All members of the board and management team are white, middle- and older-aged white-collar/managerial professionals belonging to the Welsh middle and upper class. No question, it is the affluent and educated urban elite that is behind the Cardiff 2008 bid and the marketing of the city in general. In the next paragraphs, I seek to build further this argument and show how the urban bourgeoisie uses city marketing to justify its power, consolidate its hegemony and silence the voices of other social groups.

Figure 10.1: Cardiff 2008 Ltd

Members of the Board
Chair: Right Honourable Lord Mayor Councillor Russell Goodway, Cardiff County Council

Vice Chair: Vincent Kane, Cardiff Initiative, Chair

Sir David Rowe-Beddoe, Welsh College of Music and Drama, Chair; *Alastair Milburn*, Western Mail and South Wales Echo, Editor; *David Davies*, Welsh Development Agency, Business Support Director; Councillor *Marion Drake*, Deputy Lord Mayor, Cardiff Council; *Rhodri Glyn Thomas* AM, National Assembly for Wales, Chair Cultural Committee; *Dr Manon Williams*, BBC Cymru Wales, Head of Public Affairs; *Peter Tyndall*, Arts Council of Wales, Chief Executive; *Jonathan Jones*, Wales Tourist Board, Chief Executive; *Gareth Davies*, Sports Council for Wales, Chair; *Dianne Bevan*, Cardiff Council, Corporate Manager.

The Bid Team

Lynne Williams, CEO
Yvette Vaughan Jones, Director of European and Community Programmes
Bet Davies, Director of Marketing
Judi Richards, Director of Programme Development

Source: Cardiff, 2008a, p. 18.

The whole bid process was carefully stage-managed. Generally, Cardiff 2008 employed a well-known management model that divides the management process into four stages: programming–organization–implementation–monitoring. The organization developed a six-year 'development strategy' which can be seen as a form of methodical, directed, sequential planning which was expected to contribute to a rational decision-making process with the overall aim being the achievement of prestated objectives. The latter are summarized at the end of the entry document. For example:

Extract 2
To support the growth of the creative industries as a means to prosperity and international connection:
• increase in number of jobs in the sector
• increase in profitability/GDP per head in the sector
• increase in exports and international joint ventures. (Cardiff 2008a, p. 38)

The 2008 bid encapsulates the very essence of urban entrepreneurialism by how it gives priority to the interests of capital (see also extract 2). Cardiff 2008 claims that its strategy will 'deliver real added value of wholly new cultural activity' and 'build the capacity of the cultural sector itself to generate income for reinvestment' (Cardiff 2008a, p. 27). One of the organization's main concerns is to identify 'the investments and returns which will connect business with the project' and offer 'an opportunity for a new kind of thinking about the way in which the business sector can benefit from, and invest in, culture' (Cardiff 2008a, p. 27). In other words, Cardiff 2008 behaves like a private real-estate developer adopting a programme that blurs the distinction between public provision for welfare goals and private production for return on investment and individual profit. This entrepreneurial approach serves the economic interests of the urban bourgeoisie by 'emphasising efficiency above equity, wealth creation above redistribution and place imaging above substance' (Waitt, 1999, p. 1064). Finally, it points to the changing patterns of capital investment and the close connection between accumulation and cultural consumption that is discussed later in this article.

Who does the talking?

In its documents, Cardiff 2008 constantly calls for debate, discussion and exchange of ideas. However, like New Labour (see Fairclough, 2000), Cardiff 2008 employs a managerial/promotional use of language that does not promote dialogue. To begin with, the Cardiff 2008 documents are made up of quite a lot of short, simple sentences which break up the message into digestible 'bites' of information, and which are set off from and related to each other in a clear and pointed way. Furthermore, both documents have a promotional layout and design. Different colours are used for every chapter, supporting information appears in different coloured 'boxes', the key objectives of every chapter are summarized in bullet points and headlines are used along with sub-headings. However, as Fairclough (2000, pp. 136–7) argues, these innocent-looking presentational devices carry a 'social and ideological ballast'; that is, they construct Cardiff 2008 as the knowledgeable teacher and the reader as the learner. Moreover, as Fairclough further notes, they are 'reader-directive' as they guide and control the way the reader sees the issues discussed in the documents while narrowing her/his options.

Furthermore, the entry document is univocal, monological and involves very little reported speech. In a document that defines actions that (will) affect the lives of all people living in Cardiff, not to say Wales, there are no reports about what citizens or groups have said/say or have written/write about all these issues.

In the entry document Cardiff 2008 is the undisputed, powerful agent. The organization chooses the issues which it wants, analyses and explains them, determines actions and steps to be followed, names things and labels people and groups. Moreover, the document is written in declarative mode; the readers are told rather than asked. The declarative statements are overwhelmingly categorical assertions; there are no uncertainties, 'maybes' or 'perhaps'. Cardiff 2008 (and by implication the urban elites) is constructed as fully knowledgeable, *authoritative* and in control. Taking all the above together, an opportunity for dialogue and debate has been missed.

On the other hand, the tabloid-sized brochure of Cardiff 2008 contains interviews with a number of people. It is interesting to see who these are. In total, fifteen people are interviewed. Nine are directors or chief executives of companies or festivals, while a further six are artists (including an architect and a furniture designer). It is, again, the discourse of the urban elites that predominates in a brochure mainly aimed to promote local arts in the UK, but does little more than give the bourgeoisie the opportunity to promote their projects, businesses and investments. In this sense, a document that seems dialogical is actually univocal. The interviewed artists belong also to the urban artistic middle class. The only person who could have articulated an alternative discourse is author and academic Charlotte Williams, who is also the only interviewee belonging to a visible ethnic minority. However, her discourse seems largely framed and her ground-breaking work on ethnic minorities and racism in Wales is not mentioned at all.

All in all, what emerges from the rhetoric of Cardiff 2008 is a centre-left version of a neo-liberal politics that bears many similarities to the New Labour discourse as analysed by Fairclough (2000). The promotional nature of the brochures discourages dialogue and excludes diverse representations and discourses. The organization treats the public as consumers rather than citizens. In its brochures, Cardiff 2008 (and by implication the urban bourgeoisie) emerges as an organization that has a special role in the planning, decision-making and control over social relations and processes of the enactment of power.

By controlling language the urban elites claim their exclusive right to meta-language that enables them to spread their representations over a wide range of social relations and present their values and norms as natural (Barthes, 2000). Needless to say, this exercise of power can only be developed on the basis of wide popular consensus or acquiescence. Control over language is again decisive. In the next section, I examine how the 'networked nation' rhetoric contributes to the achievement of this kind of consensus.

The 'networked nation' rhetoric
There are explicit references to Wales and the Welsh as a nation in the discourse of Cardiff 2008. Since nation is an 'imagined political community', as Anderson (1991) argued, people do not all necessarily 'imagine' the same community –

Cardiff 2008 tries to build the image of Wales as a 'networked nation' in its brochures:

Extract 3
As a networked nation, Wales has been at the forefront of the use of new information carriers to renew this tradition. (Cardiff 2008a, p. 7)

The above extract shows that the image of Wales as a 'networked nation' is taken for granted. The 'networked nation' concept is nowhere defined or explained. This vagueness allows Cardiff 2008 to 'iron out' any contradictions, divisions or/and antagonisms and encourages everyone in Wales to feel part of a type of 'nation' that is nothing but a bourgeois ideological construction. The image of Wales as a 'networked nation' achieves a natural state partly because it rests upon another presupposition: Europe is also imagined as a 'networked' community. Cardiff 2008 speaks of 'a networked Europe' and a 'future where Cardiff will energize the internal cultural networks of Wales and engage them in the cultural networks of Europe'. The 'networked nation' model is constructed as a given and irreversible fact. Indeed, the language of Cardiff 2008 tells us 'there is no alternative' – we have to live in a 'networked nation' and a 'networked Europe'.

Cardiff 2008 seems to have taken the 'networked nation' idea from the political discourse of New Labour (see Fairclough, 2000). The question here is: Who is behind the (re)imagining of Wales as a 'networked nation'? I believe that the answer is to be found in a publication titled *The Welsh Image* (Smith, 1998). In 1996, says the writer and MP John Smith, some Welsh agencies formed the Branding Wales group which commissioned a London consultancy

to develop ideas for a brand or image that could be *agreed* across a broad spectrum of Welsh life for projecting the country *at home* and abroad . . . the consultants stressed that Wales should aim at exploiting its distinctive sense of national identity . . . but there had to be agreement and a *sense of ownership* . . . whatever theme was chosen *must be* endorsed and supported by the Welsh nation. (1998, p. 13, my italics)

It is not a coincidence that most of the organizations comprising the Branding Wales group were members of Cardiff 2008's stakeholder group and those who invested both economically and ideologically in the bid. The development of Wales's and Cardiff's image appears to be the *exclusive* right and privilege of the bourgeoisie. However, as the above extract clearly implies, 'national' consensus is vital: the Welsh people 'must' support and endorse the development of a national image which reflects the interests of the agencies and companies that comprise the Branding Wales group. In this sense, this image is *not* an accumulation of manifold images, but a social and economic relationship that is both meditated and concealed by images.

The discourse of Cardiff 2008 is inclusive and consensual as it tries to include everyone in a coherent 'national' image that can be packaged and sold to investors and tourists. This language of consensus that represents difference as unity or identity does not only disguise and sustain unequal power relations but also legitimizes the dominant systems of cultural representation through which national identity is continually reproduced as discursive action by the bourgeois exclusive social and cultural institutions (Barker and Galasinski, 2001). The image of Wales as a 'networked nation' is transformed into a historic necessity that achieves a natural state. In this way, the bourgeoisie merges into nation which becomes the ideological device that 'allows the bourgeoisie to attract the numerical support of its numerical allies, all the intermediate, therefore "shapeless" classes' (Barthes, 2000, p. 138). On the other hand, proletarians, ethic minorities and all the other excluded groups are symbolically obliged to consume an image of a nation which is *not* theirs and negate the history of a nation which *is* theirs.

'QUALITY OF LIFE'

City marketeers try to market Cardiff as 'a vibrant and exciting city' (Cardiff 2008b, p. 13) and 'a place of exchange, a place to work, a place to play, a place to debate' (Cardiff 2008a, p. 14), two themes that clearly indicate the increasing focus on the 'quality of life' in the city. However, claims about a high 'quality of life' remain rather vague. This, of course, does not prevent city marketeers from packaging and selling it as a commodity. Let us look at a text that is titled 'Delivering Quality of Life':

Extract 4
Cardiff was the most highly rated city overall in the 1999 Healey and Baker study of the UK's best working city. It scored highly in location of offices, ease of com-muting, cleanliness, parking and shopping facilities. But for the citizens of Cardiff, quality of life is much more than this. It is about the cultural facilities and buildings made available for every individual to explore creative and cultural interests. It is also about the spaces in between – those areas where culture may be visible in the very fabric of the urban environment.
    The City already boasts an award-winning scheme of public art throughout its newly regenerated waterfront. Across the city, public squares, street furniture,

window displays, parks, gardens and streetscapes attest to the wealth of talent and expertise already brought to bear on the city. Cardiff 2008 will also work with its partners to continue the momentum of transformation in the urban fabric. We will work with the public art and design agencies to deliver enlightening and en-livening collaborative commissions in each year from 2003 to 2008. These will include temporary and ephemeral art and architecture, landscape and design, new media and performance works, the creative mapping of the city, street shows, guides, trails and tours.

   Cardiff 2008 will initiate national and international commissions, strengthening the infrastructures and creating opportunities, within which artists and designers may work to affect the very nature of our city.

   As host to the summit of the European Council in 1998, Cardiff opened the city to its artists. Cardiff Council demonstrated its capacity to seize the initiative and create a city-wide, open air gallery to welcome European Heads of State.

   Cardiff 2008 will build on this strong base and take the lead in supporting robust critical debate centred on the effect of permanent and ephemeral interventions. By creating a series of symposia, we will draw together leading artists, architects, planners and citizens to consider these and other aspects of practice across disciplines. (Cardiff 2008a, p. 35)

In the beginning of the text, Cardiff 2008 mentions Healey and Baker, a multi-national real-estate consultancy whose clients are mainly upper-class professionals, entrepreneurs and multinational operators. These are the kind of people and companies that the city marketeers try to lure in their attempt to attract new investment and 'clean' service-sector jobs. Clearly, categories of services such as those used in the survey appeal mostly to white-collar professionals. People from other social groups would probably use other criteria to define the 'best working city'. The city marketeers do appreciate the services the study praises, *but* they expand the definition to include culture and architecture. And once again Cardiff 2008 appears to speak on behalf of 'the citizens of Cardiff'.

   'Quality of life' is not defined in social and political terms, but as purely aesthetic. 'A city-wide, open air gallery', that is how the urban elites envision the city. Needless to say, this bourgeois fantasy denies any alternative definitions of 'quality of life' and obscures the social and political dimensions of the issue in a city where a large percentage of the population lives in some of the most deprived areas in Wales (Dunkerley, 1999). Moreover, change is set to be radical: the text speaks of a 'momentum of transformation'.

   In fact, Cardiff does not open 'the city to its artists' but to their patrons and to market forces, on the one hand, and to private consumption, on the other. The urban design proposed here is that of *post-modern spectacle* which combines 'temporary and ephemeral art and architecture', street shows and new media. The city is thus envisioned as a fragmented collage, a 'maniacal scrap-book filled with colourful entries' (Raban, in Harvey, 1989, p. 83). All in all, the projected image is actually one that feeds off the preferences of white-collar consumers of both high culture and trendy styles.

This image is expected to attract 'both capital and people "of the right sort", i.e. wealthy and influential' (Harvey, 1989, p. 295). At the same time, the urban elites extend and legitimize their ideological dominance by imposing their aesthetic values on the city and by transforming control over the material context of personal and social experience. Finally, all these point to the post-industrial shift in the dominant class's accumulation strategy to the production and consumption of what Bourdieu (1977) calls 'symbolic capital'. This process of capital accumulation aestheticizes both the city and *itself*, simultaneously concealing its material origins.

The univocal and monological language of Cardiff 2008 does not strike the careful reader anymore. Note that the organization seeks to 'work with the public art and design agencies' and not with citizens, community groups and ethnic minorities. However, in this case, social consensus is more than vital. I believe that this is apparent in the first paragraph where city marketeers try to achieve consensus on the definition of 'quality of life' – thus, the abstract entity 'citizens of Cardiff' is in the agent role in the third sentence. All the same, in the next paragraphs Cardiff 2008 is overwhelmingly constructed as the agent. Citizens appear again in the last paragraph at the end of a list of white-collar professionals who are to take part in the 'series of symposia' that seem to have replaced the political meetings and civic gatherings of the past. After all, the 'citizens of Cardiff' should be grateful that they are allowed to take part in these high-class 'symposia' where the bourgeoisie discuss the future of the city.

HERITAGE

A look at the relevant literature (Hewison, 1987; Gold and Ward, 1994; Ward, 1998) suggests that many contemporary cities promote local heritage assets and programming as a part of their marketing strategies. Cardiff could not be an exception. In general, heritage remains a general, undefined concept throughout the promotional literature of Cardiff, a word that seems to mean everything and at the same time nothing.

The city's promotional literature advertises a number of industrial heritage projects that are to be found in the surrounding area, such as the Rhondda Heritage

Park, the Big Pit National Mining Museum of Wales and Blaenafon, that demonstrate 'the impacts of Wales' industrial heritage on Europe past and present' (Cardiff 2008a, p. 34). Needless to say, the promotional literature also emphasizes heritage projects – mainly buildings – which are located within the boundaries of the city. The main attractions are Cardiff Castle, the 'Gothic fantasy' of Castell Coch, the Civic Centre, the National Museum and Gallery and the Museum of Welsh Life.

I should note, however, that the promotional literature of Cardiff does not overemphasize the city's heritage. Generally, Cardiff is marketed as 'a young and vibrant city' (CI, 2003, p. 33) or as 'one of Europe's youngest and most exciting cities . . . [that] has experienced a complete rejuvenation' (CI, 2003, p. 2). In this way, marketeers try to challenge negative discourses that are by no means absent today and that see south Wales as a post-industrial dump or as a decadent place stuck in its industrial past (Smith, 1998). As long as the city is being marketed as a vibrant and modern post-industrial consumption centre that 'has had to re-invent itself and re-imagine its future' (Cardiff 2008a, p. 10), any thoughtless references to the city's 'industrial heritage' would probably undermine the core messages and reinforce negative stereotypes. Nevertheless, this does not prevent city marketeers from selling former production areas as consumption sites along with restored castles and museums of any kind. In this way, as I discuss below, the urban elites who have access to the otherwise exclusive institutions of culture articulate the only acceptable meanings of past and present.

HISTORY

According to its writer, the following text seeks to tell the reader 'a little of the history of the city':

Extract 5
The area has been populated since prehistory but the real history of Cardiff starts with the Romans who arrived about AD 50. After defeating the Silures they built the first fort in Cardiff, a ten acre stronghold at a strategic point on the River Taff where the river could be forded. About AD 250 the fort was rebuilt with walls ten feet thick, backed by an earth bank and surrounded by a moat. The Romans left in the 5th century and little is known about the inhabitants of the area until the Normans arrived in the 11th century. Robert Fitzhamon, the Norman Lord of Gloucester, built his medieval castle within the boundaries of the Roman fort and a settlement grew up around it. However, this was an English town in a hostile Welsh territory and patriot Owain Glyndwr razed Cardiff in 1404.

By the Elizabethan times Cardiff was a lawless, pirate-infested port. In 1608 James I granted a Royal Charter, and by the 18th century it was a sleepy town of 1,500 people straggling around the decaying castle.

The Industrial Revolution changed everything. In the 1790s the local gentry, the Butes, built the Glamorganshire Canal to join Cardiff with Merthyr Tydfil, followed by the first Cardiff dock in 1839. Cardiff became the biggest coal-exporting port in the world. At its peak in 1913, more than 13 million tons of coal left here. Cardiff was granted city status by Edward VII and in 1955 it was proclaimed capital of Wales.

With all these influences – Roman, Norman, Industrial Revolution, Butes, Coal and Docklands – it is easy to understand why there is such a wide range of attractions that now fascinate and enthrall visitors to Europe's Youngest Capital. (CI, 2002, p. 11)

One striking feature of this text has to do with the amount of space devoted to the pre-industrial history of the city. More than half of the text deals with the Romans and the Normans, while the modern history of Cardiff is 'summarized' in one short paragraph. Why all this fuss about the Romans? I think that the writer does not only try to show that the history of the city goes back several hundred years. What (s)he does is try to link Cardiff with the Roman *myth*. For many people the Romans signify power and might. Just the fact that they built a fort in Cardiff makes the place important and allows images of an unbeatable army and a 'glorious' empire to be transferred to the city. No matter if Cardiff was an insignificant fort in a vast empire, images of heroic battles can be sold to everyone willing to consume the myth.

The writer does not try to hide something; (s)he simply distorts history by removing anything controversial and hollowing material and social meaning from historical structures. For example, on another page of the same brochure we learn that the Romans came not as conquerors but as 'visitors' in order to attend 'meetings' with the Silures:

Extract 6
Our first visitors were probably the Romans, who liked the area so much they decided to build a fort and stay far longer than the standard seven days. The Romans were also the first conference delegates to attend meetings in the area – often with the Celtic tribe known as the Silures. (CI, 2002, p. 3)

Of course, the writer does not tell us why the 'conference delegates' brought an invading army of over 40,000 with them (Howell, 2001). The promotional discourse makes everything innocent: no battles, no massacres, no plundering. Only in this way can Roman imperialism achieve a natural state and become a myth (Barthes, 2000).

Needless to say, all the above also apply to the other myths upon which Cardiff's promotional literature draws, such as those surrounding the Butes and the Industrial Revolution. Let us go back to extract 5. In the third paragraph, we learn that the Butes built the Glamorganshire Canal and the first Cardiff dock. Of course, the Butes did not build the canal and the dock by themselves. Their power and money allowed them to engage thousands of people who worked, and in some cases died, in the building of these. Workers labouring in appalling conditions for ridiculously low wages would be a context rich in meaning and political tinder (Kearns and Philo, 1993b). However, the promotional discourse of Cardiff has no space for the thousands of proletarians and, in this way, the working class is denied its space and time in the history of the city. Moreover, the discourse that is used sounds so commonsensical that, as I discuss below, it legitimizes both past and present relations of power.

The Industrial Revolution is also presented as an instant miracle, a vast source of external power that 'changed everything'. A process that was long and slow appears as if it was instantaneous, while cause and effect are collapsed together since one already implies the other. Thus, history evaporates while its subjects are denied existence. What remains is the myth of Industrial Revolution together with some glorious statistics. There is absolutely no reference to the role of the industrial working class in this 'glory' or the price they paid for it.

All in all, the promotional discourse of Cardiff removes all meaning from objects and events in terms of material context and content, thus leaving gaps which can be filled by myths that eventually replace history. As I have already suggested, these myths that rest upon common-sense assumptions help bourgeois ideology to transform continually the products of history into essential types while obscuring the ceaseless making of the world (Barthes, 2000). In this way, power relations and bourgeois norms are transformed into universal nature. This is more apparent in anachronisms like the following (see also extract 6), where marketeers try to present Cardiff as a centre of citizen-oriented and democratic (as implied by the adjective 'great') debate:

Extract 7
[City Hall and the National Museum] were part of the great debate in the early years of the 19th century, which centred on the role of cities in fulfilling the needs of their citizens. The debate continues as needs change and Cardiff now, as then, is at the forefront of new ideas. (Cardiff 2008a, p. 34)

Of course, there was no 'great debate' in the early nineteenth century (not to mention that Cardiff was not even a city at that time). At that time the Butes and the powerful landed elite were ruling over the area. Not until 1884 were the thousands of workers (only the male, of course) enfranchised. However, what the above extract does is present certain social relations and roles as natural, fixed and immutable.

CULTURE

Negative stereotypes in the English media see Wales as a 'cowed country' that 'has never made any significant contribution to any branch of knowledge, culture or entertainment' and is inhabited by 'dingy and untalented' people (Pritchard and Morgan, 2001, p. 171). No wonder that one of the main concerns of city marketeers is to confront such negative views that echo ingrained historical stereotypes of Wales and the Welsh people:

Extract 8
If you know Cardiff, you'll know we're pretty cultured, but we're about to get even better! This year, Cardiff is bidding to become European Capital of Culture in 2008. (CI, 2002, p. 8)

Extract 9
Cardiff and Wales have made major contributions to international culture, arts and sport, with artists that have graced some of the world's major galleries, singers who have taken centre stage at international venues, writers who have made an impact on world literature and sporting giants in many fields. (CI, 2002, p. 9)

As the 2008 bid indicates, culture has become the key selling point in the marketing campaign of Cardiff. In fact, Cardiff 2008 claims that Cardiff is already 'a European Capital of Culture'. Culture can help city marketeers replace negative stereotypes with images that stress rebirth, dynamism and modernity and becomes a valuable marketing tool in the promotion of Cardiff as a cosmopolitan urban centre.

Cardiff 2008 lowers the barriers between culture and business until these two merge and the former negates itself. The organization, after positioning itself as 'both a catalyst and a nexus for cultural activity in Wales' (Cardiff 2008b, p. 3), declares that it is 'determined to work with the business community to debate and devise new models for business and culture partnerships' (Cardiff 2008a, p. 19).

Indeed, the consumption of culture and the culture of consumption have become big business in an area with a rich industrial past (see extract 10). City marketeers give full priority to the interests of capital as culture becomes an investment that can offset cyclical devaluation in local industries (Zukin, 1991). As Harvey (1990) argues, the consumption of culture accelerates capital turnover time for the lifetime of consumption of images is almost instantaneous. No wonder that businesses rushed to invest in the bid (note the adverb 'immediately' in extract 11) and met to 'identify joint projects which make tangible returns for business in return for investment in the sector' (Cardiff 2008a, p. 27). All in all, the exploitation of culture for the creation of a new image for the city emphasizes the transformation of Cardiff into a product to generate *cultural* capital and hence reveals a shift in the dominant class's accumulation strategy.

Extract 10
Work undertaken by the Cardiff Council's Research Centre demonstrates that culture and tourism contributes almost £490m to a city economy of £4.9bn . . . Over recent years, the growth in this [cultural] activity has been marked. Between 1991 and 2001, activity in the sector in the city rose by 64%. In that time the proportion of city GDP accounted for by culture rose from 7.2 % to 10%. (Cardiff 2008a, p. 26)

Extract 11
Senior business leaders in Wales have spotted the potential for the project to generate significant benefit for their companies. Immediately, at the launch of the bid, these businesses have made practical sponsorship commitments of some tens of thousands of pounds to the bid itself. (Cardiff 2008a, p. 28)

The cultural capital concentrated in the hands of the bourgeoisie is translated into ideological power that allows them not only to cushion the negative effects of the painful transition from an industrial to a post-industrial society but also to generate social consensus at a time of political and economic change. In this way, cultural policy becomes what Harvey (1990) calls a 'carnival mask' that conceals social inequality, material exchanges and social struggle. The new cultural norms that result from the shift in the accumulation strategy of the urban elites enable them to facilitate and justify the exercise of 'unaccustomed forms of social control' (Zukin, 1989, p. 176).

MULTICULTURALISM

Multiculturalism and diversity are central themes in the promotional discourse of Cardiff. The usual claim made here is that Cardiff is '(one of) the oldest multicultural community (communities) in the UK'. However, such statements are not exactly the product of thorough independent research, but rather a ploy of promotional rhetoric. A tendency towards self-praise is more apparent in the following extracts:

Extract 12
Cardiff has a distinguished record of welcoming new communities and we are working closely with agencies in Wales, the UK, Europe and beyond to understand the impact of migration and, in particular, to work through culture to support asylum seekers and refugees. (Cardiff 2008a, p. 10)

Extract 13
The refugee communities in Cardiff arrive in a city which has welcomed people from all over the world throughout its history. (Cardiff 2008a, p. 12)

Cardiff 2008 draws here on the well-known self-publicized myth of Welsh tolerance and hospitality. However, the empirical evidence that does exist fails to support this widespread and culturally sustained myth (see for example, Thomas, 1993; Williams, 1999; Williams, Evans and O'Leary, 2003). In contrast to the promotional discourse and the popular orthodoxy, Cardiff does *not* have 'a distinguished record of welcoming new communities'. In fact, Cardiff and south Wales have on their record books a substantial number of violent ethnic conflicts (see, for example, Evans, 2003). Today, ethnic minorities in Cardiff overall consistently fare worse in health, education, housing, employment and other key social indicators than their counterparts in the majority population (Chaney and Williams, 2003). Williams also identifies a 'patterning of neglect, organizational inertia and a lack of knowledge and skills for addressing the needs of minority communities' (2003, p. 152).

Most importantly, discriminations are *institutionalized*. Chaney and Williams (2003) point to the lack of participation of black and ethnic minority populations in political structures in Wales, while Bradbury notes that, generally, the political parties in Wales have done 'relatively little to explicitly focus on the issue of raising black and ethnic minority political participation' (2003, p. 7).

In this context, the discourse of Cardiff 2008 protects the idea of 'there is no problem here' or a type of racial amnesia that is not productive in terms of recognizing and addressing prejudice, discrimination and inequalities. By distorting history, the urban elites first obfuscate the causes of antagonism and the facts of white hegemony in all domains of society and, secondly, construct the image of 'multi-cultural harmony' (Cardiff 2008a, p. 8) as fixed and immutable. Cultural hierarchies between different ethnic and social groups are thus legitimized, while more sharply focused concepts such as social injustice and the renegotiation of power relations are displaced. Finally, the voices of the black and ethnic communities are silenced and their political and socio-economic contributions to the city are marginalized.

CARDIFF AS A SITE OF 'SPECTACLE'

City marketeers position Cardiff as a 'capital for events' and claim that the city has 'an enviable track record in delivering world class events' (Cardiff 2008b, p. 1).

Extract 14
Where will you find a year-long calendar of major sporting, musical and cultural events against the backdrop of a vibrant, growing waterside location? Cardiff, of course – Europe's youngest capital. (CI, 2002, p. 25; CI, 2003, p. 19)

Throughout the promotional literature of Cardiff, a large number of sporting and cultural spectacles are presented and promoted. Emphasis is given to prominent events with an 'international' or 'European' character that can attract the attention of the media and investors, draw in both residents and tourists, encourage the development of local cultural industries and stimulate cultural consumption.

As Harvey (1990) notes, the capitalist trend toward acceleration in turnover time has emphasized the role of such controlled spectacles as a means of capital accumulation. In this sense, an urban area whose economy was once based on heavy industrial sectors is turned into a site of spectacle and a centre of visual consumption. City marketing, which was once mobilized to promote and sell local industries, specializes now in the acceleration of turnover time through the marketing of images. As the bourgeoisie finds new means for accumulating capital, the city is aestheticized and its physical and social attributes become commodities to be marketed and consumed, while the spectacle reveals its true nature as '*capital* accumulated to the point where it becomes image' (Debord, 1994, p. 24).

The shift in the accumulation patterns of the bourgeoisie calls for the reconstruction or 'regeneration' of the urban landscape of Cardiff that has to be 're-invented' and reimagined in order to facilitate the new forms of accumulation that emphasize consumption rather than production activities. Controlled spectacles become ideologically significant in pacifying local peoples whose places of attachment are reconstructed, not to say destroyed, to become a space of conspicuous consumption and to accommodate a spectacular architecture. In this sense, it is not a coincidence that most urban spectacles take place at Cardiff Bay, an area that was for many decades a space of disaffection and social disruption and today comprises some of the most deprived wards in Wales (Dunkerley, 1999).

In fact, those involved in the marketing of Cardiff become mediators of an ideological mechanism that aims to reproduce the social order and sell the 'status quo of symbols' to local people, especially to those who experience dislocation, deprivation and/or marginalization. In this sense, city marketing is also deployed to 'stimulate pride in achieving high profile events' (Cardiff 2008a, p. 37) and create a sense of social solidarity. This formula of social control is sometimes referred to as that of 'bread and circuses' (Harvey, 1990). It is not a coincidence that Cardiff 2008 fantasizes the city as an 'arena' – Rhodri Morgan, now Welsh first minister, once described football and rugby internationals as 'the opium of the Welsh masses' (1994, p. 18).

CONCLUSIONS

Those involved in the marketing of Cardiff have to confront a number of negative discourses which influence perceptions and representations of the city. City marketeers seek to challenge these negative views that echo historical stereotypes of the Welsh people and character and at the same time they attempt to promote the modern image of Cardiff as a 're-invented' city. Cardiff is reimagined as a vibrant and cosmopolitan urban centre, as a young and exciting European capital.

In this article, I have identified a number of themes that pervade the promotional literature of Cardiff. 'Quality of life' allows city marketeers to position Cardiff as a vibrant city that can meet the higher order needs of white-collar professionals. Former industrial areas are promoted as post-industrial consumption centres while a number of other heritage projects are marketed as attractive tourist destinations. Moreover, those involved in the marketing of Cardiff try to position the city as a young and multicultural urban centre. At the same time, culture becomes the key selling point in the marketing of Cardiff as city marketeers attempt to position the city as 'a European Capital of Culture'.

Historically, the emergence of Cardiff as an urban centre depended upon the systemic appropriation of a surplus from the Valleys and the other surrounding coal and steel areas. The appropriation of this surplus from the labour of thousands of miners, steelworkers and dockers allowed the creation of the urban bourgeoisie. However, deindustrialization brought a shift in the accumulation patterns of the urban elites, whose power and wealth depends now on the systemic appropriation of a surplus from the tertiary and quaternary service sector. This surplus is centralized as Cardiff becomes the administrative centre of Wales and the urban elites position themselves not just as 'managers' of the city but as 'managers' of the whole country (Kearns and Philo, 1993a). The above arguments derive from Marxist orthodoxy. Indeed, in many parts of this study, I adopted a Marxist perspective informed by insights drawn from the fields of culture, politics, geography and aesthetic theory to show how city marketing fits into these new accumulation patterns.

First, I argued that city marketeers serve the economic interests of the new urban bourgeoisie. As Cardiff's social and physical attributes become aesthetic commodities to be consumed, city marketeers set themselves the task of rendering them attractive to a number of target audiences. The main aim here is to enhance the appeal and interest of Cardiff to 'upmarket' tourists and secure inward investment by promoting the city's cultural and business infrastructure to companies and white-collar professionals. Moreover, the marketing of trophy buildings, cultural and heritage projects and urban spectacles promotes what Zukin (1991) calls 'symbolic consumption' that generates cultural capital and accelerates turnover time. The self-declared conversion of Cardiff to a 'quality of life' capital and the promotion of post-industrial amenity drive the value of property up and make it possible to charge high prices for housing and offices.

Secondly, I argued that city marketeers serve the political and ideological interests of the new urban bourgeoisie. To begin with, by distorting history the urban elites misrepresent power relations, justify their hegemony and deny the proletarians their pivotal role in the political and economic life of the city. By promoting Roman and Norman myths and, at the same time, stressing the modern image of post-devolution Cardiff, city marketeers leave out the industrial history of the city. This gap is either ignored or filled with the myth of the Industrial Revolution and the promotion of industrial heritage projects. In this respect, marketing discourse becomes in the hands of the bourgeoisie a powerful ideological mechanism that allows them to conceal and legitimize their hegemony by naturalizing the social order and the roles and relationships that derive from that order. At the same time, the systemic emphasis on the image of the city and the symbolic aspect of the activities and relations of production conceals the reality of economic acts, obfuscates material exchanges and perpetuates the symbolic power concentrated in the hands of the dominant class. The chairman of the European Capital of Culture 2008 jury suggested that Cardiff 2008 did not significantly include the Valleys in its bid. As I argued in this study, Cardiff 2008 did not include any of the working-class areas of south Wales in its bid. In the promotional discourse of Cardiff, there is neither proletarian culture nor proletarian art; there are no references to the contribution of the working class to the past and present of the city. However, city marketeers employ a language of consensus and inclusivity which disguises differences, divisions and deprivation extremes. In this respect, culture takes a pivotal role in engineering social consensus, while urban spectacles are deployed to create a sense of solidarity and conceal the power the urban bourgeoisie exerts both within and beyond the city.

In this article, I have sought to show how city marketeers reimagine the city and how the urban bourgeoisie employs city marketing for the purposes of economic gain and social control. Further research should consider how the excluded social and political groups and individuals imagine the city. Here, discourse analysis can be employed along with focus groups and/or an ethno-graphic approach. Moreover, comparative analysis will demonstrate if the findings of this study apply to the marketing of other (British) cities. I propose a com-parative analysis of the promotional discourse of the six British cites that were shortlisted for the 'European Capital of Culture 2008' title. As I have argued throughout this article, only a materialist approach that explores interrelations of social structure allows researchers to be engaged in a social, cultural and political critique of place-marketing.

REFERENCES

Anderson, B. (1991). *Imagined Communities*, London: Verso.
Ashworth, G. and Voogd, H. (1990). *Selling the City: Marketing Approaches in Public Sector Urban Planning*, London: Belhaven Press.
Barker, C. and Galasinski, D. (2001). *Cultural Studies and Discourse Analysis: A Dialogue on Language and Identity*, London: Sage.
Barthes, R. (2000). *Mythologies*, trans. A. Lavers, London: Vintage.
Booth, P. and Boyle, R. (1993). 'See Glasgow, see culture', in F. Bianchini and M. Parkinson (eds), *Cultural Policy and Urban Regeneration*, Manchester: Manchester University Press.
Bourdieu, P. (1977). *Outline of a Theory of Practice*, trans. R. Nice, Cambridge: Cambridge University Press.
Bradbury, J. (2003). *Black and Asian Ethnic Minorities and Political Participation in Wales*, Swansea: All Wales Ethnic Minority Association.

Cardiff 2008a. (2002a). *Cardiff: European Capital of Culture 2008*, Cardiff: Cardiff 2008 Ltd.

Cardiff 2008b. (2002b). *Cardiff: A European Capital of Culture 2008*, Cardiff: Cardiff 2008 Ltd.

Cardiff Initiative (CI) (2002). *Cardiff: Europe's Youngest Capital*, Cardiff: Cardiff Initiative Ltd.

Cardiff Initiative (CI) (2003). *Cardiff: Europe's Youngest Capital*, Cardiff: Cardiff Initiative Ltd.

Chaney, P. and Williams, C. (2003). 'Getting involved: civic and political life in Wales', in C. Williams, N. Evans and P. O'Leary (eds), *A Tolerant Nation?*, Cardiff: University of Wales Press.

Debord, G. (1994). *The Society of the Spectacle*, trans. D. Nicholson-Smith, New York: Zone Books.

Duffy, H. (1995). *Competitive Cities: Succeeding in the Global Economy*, London: E&FN Spon.

Dunkerley, D. (1999). 'Social Wales', in D. Dunkerley and A. Thompson (eds), *Wales Today*, Cardiff: University of Wales Press

Evans, N. (2003). 'Immigrants and minorities in Wales, 1840–1990: a comparative analysis', in C. Williams, N. Evans and P. O'Leary (eds), *A Tolerant Nation?*, Cardiff: University of Wales Press.

Fairclough, N. (1989). *Language and Power*, London: Longman.

Fairclough, N. (2000). *New Labour, New Language?*, London: Routledge.

Fretter, A. (1993). 'Place marketing: a local authority perspective', in G. Kearns and C. Philo (eds), *Selling Places: The City as Cultural Capital, Past and Present*, Oxford: Pergamon Press.

Gold, R. (1994). 'Locating the message: place promotion as image communication', in R. Gold and S. Ward (eds), *Place Promotion: The Use of Publicity and Marketing to Sell Towns and Regions*, New York: Wiley.

Gold, R. and Ward, S. (eds) (1994). *Place Promotion: The Use of Publicity and Marketing to Sell Towns and Regions*, New York: Wiley.

Harvey, D. (1989). *The Condition of Postmodernity*, Oxford: Basil Blackwell.

Harvey, D. (1990). 'Between space and time: reflections of the geographical imagination', *Annals of the Association of American Geographers*, 80, 3, 418–34.

Hewison, R. (1987). *The Heritage Industry: Britain in a Climate of Decline*, London: Methuen.

Hodge, R. and Kress, G. (1993). *Language as Ideology*, London: Routledge.

Holcomb, B. (1993). 'Revisioning place: de- and re-constructing the image of the industrial city', in G. Kearns and C. Philo (eds), *Selling Places: The City as Cultural Capital, Past and Present*, Oxford: Pergamon Press.

Howell, R. (2001). 'Roman Wales', in P. Morgan (ed.), *Tempus History of Wales: 9,000 B.C. – A.D. 2000*, Stroud: Tempus.

Kearns, G. and Philo, C. (eds) (1993a). *Selling Places: The City as Cultural Capital, Past and Present*, Oxford: Pergamon Press.

Kearns, G. and Philo, C. (1993b). 'Culture, history and capital: a critical introduction to the selling of places', in G. Kearns and C. Philo (eds), *Selling Places: The City as Cultural Capital, Past and Present*, Oxford: Pergamon Press.

Morgan, R. (1994). *Cardiff: Half-and-half a Capital*, Llandysul: Gomer.

Pritchard, A. and Morgan, N. (2001). 'Culture, identity and tourism representation: marketing Cymru or Wales?', *Tourism Management*, 22, 167–79.

Smith, J. (1998). *The Welsh Image*, Cardiff: Institute of Welsh Affairs.

Smyth, H. (1994). *Marketing the City: the Role of Flagship Developments in Urban Regeneration*, London: E and FN Spon.

Thomas, H. (1993). *Ethnic Minorities and the Planning System: A Case Study*, Oxford: Oxford Brookes University.

Van Dijk, T. (2001). 'Principles of critical discourse analysis', in M. Wetherell, S. Taylor and S. Yates (eds), *Discourse Theory and Practice: A Reader*, London: Sage.

Waitt, G. (1999). 'Playing games with Sydney: marketing Sydney for the 2000 Olympics', *Urban Studies*, 36, 7, 1055–77.

Ward, S. (1998). *Selling Places: The Marketing and Promotion of Town and Cities 1850–2000*, London: E & FN.

Wetherell, M. (2001). 'Debates in discourse research', in M. Wetherell, S. Taylor and S. Yates (eds), *Discourse Theory and Practice: A Reader*, London: Sage.

Williams, C. (1999). ' "Race" and racism: what's special about Wales?', in D. Dunkerley and A. Thompson (eds), *Wales Today*, Cardiff: University of Wales Press.

Williams, C. (2003). 'Social inclusion and race equality in Wales', in C. Williams, N. Evans and P. O'Leary (eds), *A Tolerant Nation?*, Cardiff: University of Wales Press.

Williams, C., Evans, N. and O'Leary, P. (eds) (2003). *A Tolerant Nation? Exploring Ethnic Diversity in Wales*, Cardiff: University of Wales Press.

Zukin, S. (1989). *Loft Living: Culture and Capital in Urban Change*, New Brunswick: Rutgers University Press.

Zukin, S. (1991). *Landscapes of Power: From Detroit to Disney World*, Berkeley: University of California Press.

11. CONSTRUCTING THE E-NATION: THE INTERNET IN WALES

Philip Mitchell

ABSTRACT

This article presents a brief overview of the development and potential of the Internet in Wales. It does so within the context of political debates about the provision of Internet access, and of the specific difficulties faced by the Welsh Assembly Government in determining financial investment and policy initiatives within the constraints of UK-wide policy-making in relation to new information and communication technologies. It begins by outlining the roll-out of Internet-related technology around Wales in recent years and summarizes the factors – economic, geographical and socio-cultural – which have placed Wales behind most of the UK with regard to many indicators of Internet usage and access (particularly domestic access), and which have also produced a set of internal imbalances. It then proceeds to evaluate the policy-makers' response to these constraints, and towards the physical expansion of the relevant infrastructure, together with further initiatives aimed at influencing citizens' attitudes towards the new technology and at fostering Internet usage by a more demographically and geographically diverse public. It concludes by evaluating the applicability to Wales of arguments in favour of a Universal Service Fund as a funding mechanism for the widening of domestic Internet access, and of such a development's potential role as part of further initiatives aimed at both extending the physical availability of Internet access and also changing public perceptions and behaviour.

INTRODUCTION

A clear post-devolutionary consensus appears to have emerged regarding the strategic importance to Wales of new information and communication technologies

(ICTs) in general and of the Internet in particular. Witness, for example, the high profile given to debates about the provision of Internet access – especially to broadband development – in the 2003 Assembly election manifestos of all the main parties.[1] This consensus is to a large extent driven by economic projections, specifically in the widespread view encapsulated in Courtney and Gibson's assessment of ICT development, that 'Wales's future prosperity depends upon its ability to exploit knowledge for commercially profitable ends' (1999, p. 3). With regard to the specific potential of the Internet, however, the case has also been made on cultural and political grounds and – more broadly – in terms of the development of Welsh identity, including amongst the diaspora.[2]

Such a consensus has in turn highlighted the need for concerted action to improve Internet access and usage in Wales. However, the development of an integrated set of relevant polices has proved consistently problematic. As with television and radio, any Wales-originated initiatives may be circumscribed by UK-wide policy-making, a problem perhaps exacerbated by the conspicuous absence within Wales of the transnational ICT firms likely to wield influence on UK-wide policy and on pan-European developments from the European Commission. The Welsh Assembly Government (WAG) has nonetheless embraced the potential of Internet-related technology with enthusiasm, as evidenced at least by its Cymru Ar-Lein and Broadband Wales initiatives. A representative view from the Welsh policy-makers is that of e-minister Andrew Davies: 'broadband links are to the twenty-first century what canals were to economic development in the nineteenth century, and motorways in the twentieth' (National Assembly for Wales, 2003a).[3] Although such thinking partakes in a wider – and arguably hyperbolic – enthusiasm for ICTs amongst politicians in the developed world (Selwyn, 2004, p. 342), nonetheless in the case of Wales a significant financial investment has indeed followed from this. By the end of 2003, for example, the National Assembly for Wales (NAfW) had committed well over £100 million to its Broadband Wales programme (NAfW, 2003b).

Against this backdrop, then, this article presents a brief overview of the Internet's development and potential in Wales by addressing two interrelated issues. First, it outlines the roll-out of Internet-related technology around Wales in recent years and summarizes the obstacles to full exploitation and access. Secondly, it considers the development of policy thinking with regard to the promotion and regulation of Internet usage. It concludes by evaluating arguments in favour of a Universal Service Fund as a funding mechanism for the wider development of domestic Internet access.[4]

GROWING PAINS: THE SLOW EXPANSION OF INTERNET ACCESS IN WALES

In undertaking its post-devolutionary initiatives for the expansion of public provision and exploitation of the Internet, Wales is starting from a notably low base. An overall, contextualizing indication of this is provided by comparative figures for the development of knowledge-based industries, as defined by the Organization for Economic Co-operation and Development. These reveal Wales to be trailing significantly behind the UK average.[5] The WAG's ambitious plans for broadband expansion are constrained by these low levels of overall economic activity (Department of Trade and Industry, 2002), by the similarly low usage by Welsh small and medium enterprises of other new information and communication technologies (Welsh Affairs Select Committee, 1999) and, not least, by problems associated with Wales's geographical makeup (Jeffs, 2002, p. 35). The Department of Trade and Industry's connectivity indicator also places Wales in a highly disadvantaged position,[6] and there is evidence, moreover, that Wales has one of the least developed regional software development sectors (Courtney and Gibson, 1999, pp. 19–20).

These difficulties have been ascribed to a variety of factors: cultural, political, technological[7] and, above all, economic – in particular, a shortage of venture capital and a resultant GDP growth which has run significantly behind the targets set by the Welsh Development Agency (WDA).[8] Some researchers have also identified shortcomings in education and training which have resulted in a lack of relevant skills (see Chaney, Hall and Dicks, 2000). Taken together, such factors have significantly compromised the competitiveness of Wales's communication networks, especially outside the main industrial areas (see Hargreaves, 1999, p. 1).

How realistic, therefore, is the policy-makers' stated goal (Gower, 2003, p. 1) of 'universal availability of high-speed Internet connections' in Wales? The core problem that the NAfW has had to address is that citizens in Wales have trailed almost all UK regions in domestic Internet access. Moreover, Wales has also shown, to some extent at least, a variety of internal imbalances and inequities, notably between suburban and remote rural areas of Wales, but also in terms of gender, age and socio-economic group. Curran and Seaton's summation of the UK-wide situation, 'the imbalance of power and resources in the offline world structure the online world' (2003, p. 260), thus has a notable resonance in Wales (see also Dutton, 1999a, p. 240, and Selwyn, 2004, p. 344).

Table 11.1, for example, highlights the fact that around the UK only Northern Ireland has had a lower domestic take-up of Internet connections than Wales. Relatedly, a set of regional disparities has also been identified within Wales (see, for example, Downing, 2002, p. 13). In particular, homes in Cardiff, the south-east and the mid-west of Wales have been seen to be in an advantageous position, in terms of both current level of access and rate of growth, in comparison with other regions, notably the more isolated rural zones and other areas of relative socio-economic deprivation. Such patterns would appear to confirm the regional biases discernible in other sectors of the media in Wales (see, for example, Bromley, 2000, p. 125). In the specific case of the Internet, any such imbalance can partly be attributed to the investment originally made by BT and NTL in their prioritizing of fixed infrastructure provision in industrialized south Wales (see Courtney and Gibson, 1999).

Table 11.1
Percentage of UK households with home access to the Internet

Region/UK county	1999/2000	2000/1	2001/2	2002/3
East of England	22	34	45	52
South-east	24	38	48	52
London	25	40	49	51
East Midlands	19	31	41	49
England	20	34	41	47
United Kingdom overall	19	32	40	46
South-west	19	37	35	44
North-west	18	32	39	43
Yorkshire and the Humber	15	29	34	42
Scotland	14	24	37	42
North-east	14	25	32	41
West Midlands	20	33	34	41
Wales	15	22	32	37
Northern Ireland	11	20	31	35

Source: Family Expenditure Survey, Office for National Statistics, 2000–3.

Nonetheless, the overall tendency discernible in figures such as those sum-marized in table 11.2 is clearly towards an overall levelling out of domestic connections around Welsh regions. With regard to generational variation, UK-wide trends are also reflected in that access is significantly higher with younger age groups. As Downing comments with regard to usage in Wales (2002, p. 9), '[a]s government services are increasingly available online it is ironic that some of the heaviest users of these services, including the 65+ age group, will be unable to access them at home by using the Internet' (see also Selwyn, Gorard and Furlong, 2005, pp. 19–20).

Table 11.2
Percentage of adults in Wales with home Internet connections, by region

Welsh region	2000	2001	2002	2003	2004
Mid/west Wales	22	25	42	44	41
Cardiff and South-east Wales	20	29	41	38	41
West/south Wales	21	29	34	33	42
North Wales	18	30	28	38	42
The Valleys	22	25	27	34	37
Total	21	28	35	37	41

Source: Tuck, 2003; Kearton, 2004.

Overall, then, there are clear indications that the Internet provides a prime illustration of Thomas, Jewell and Cushion's contention that, '[t]he Welsh media system, as it stands, is super-serving the "knowledge rich" while failing to do much to improve the situation of the "knowledge poor" ' (2004, p. 6).

TACKLING THE CONSTRAINTS: THE POLICY-MAKERS' RESPONSE

The nature of the Internet as a medium is such that several areas of media policy – for example, reducing ownership restrictions, lowering national barriers to market entry – are not directly applicable (see Dutton, 1999b, p. 293). Attention has therefore centred on, firstly, policy initiatives designed to foment the physical expansion of the relevant infrastructure (analogous to expanding or contracting the availability of the spectrum in the case of radio broadcasting policy) and, secondly, further initiatives aimed at influencing citizens' attitudes and behaviour with regard to both accessing and – to a more limited extent – exploiting the technology in question.

Within this context, a crucial factor with regard to both Welsh and UK-wide policy-making is the disparity between access from home, on the one hand, and from work or from Internet cafés, libraries and other public access points, on the other. It is perhaps especially revealing in this regard that it appears that those users who already have home access are far more likely to use the Internet outside the home (see Livingstone, 2003; Tuck 2003; Welsh Consumer Council, 2003a, 2003b). Such data would appear to call into question the confidence with which the UK government has drawn positive conclusions regarding the use of public access points and their impact on the 'digital divide' (UK Online, 2003).[9]

The UK-wide policy perspective is itself far from straightforward, however. The Labour government took a strategic decision to exclude the Internet from the scope of the Communications Act 2003, other than the act's references to 'associated facilities' and 'electronic communication networks' (Collins, 2003). In other words, the implicit overall policy approach is that the UK government sees this medium as one which can be self-regulated through an open market or through self-regulating network institutions.

Notwithstanding these constraints, the Assembly policy-makers may nonetheless have some room for manoeuvre. As Selwyn and Gorard have argued (2002, p. 196), the NAfW does have scope for forging a role for itself as local 'reconstructors' of the (Westminster-directed) National Information Infrastructure. Such a process of 'reconstruction', it would appear, has been attempted via a set of NAfW policy initiatives relevant to the Internet, channelled under policy areas which have indeed been devolved, the chief examples being industry and training; culture; education; Welsh language; economic development. The flagship of the Assembly's ICT strategy, approved by the NAfW in July 2001 and launched in November the same year, is Cymru Ar-Lein – Online for a Better Wales. Specific initiatives under this scheme have included: a full database of ICT facilities across Wales; connection of all Welsh schools to the Internet; other educational initiatives such as the establishment of the National Grid for Learning Cymru, which supports the development of the Curriculum Cymreig. Perhaps crucially, several programmes are aimed at developing and exploiting broadband provision, notably the Broadband Lifelong Learning Network, to which all public libraries in Wales will eventually be connected, and the Broadband Wales scheme, funded via the aggregating of funds already allocated to ICT development by the WAG, the WDA and via Objective One.[10] Parallel to this has been the WDA-backed broadband Wales Action Plan, launched in July 2002. Among this project's initiatives are a satellite broadband subsidy to Welsh SMEs (small- and medium-sized enterprises), awareness-raising campaigns and a 'reverse subsidy auction process to provide access to broadband where there has been market failure' (Department of Trade and Industry, 2004).[11] Similarly, the Regional Innovative Broadband Support (RIBS) project has sought EC approval for its focus on those areas of Wales which have hitherto been seen as access 'blackspots' (NAfW, 2004). There are signs, moreover, that such initiatives have seen a notable convergence of policy thinking between the Assembly and the secretary of state for trade and industry (see Department for Culture, Media and Sport, 2002, p. 1).

Such policy initiatives have met with a significant amount of praise.[12] Perhaps most notably, the Cymru Ar-Lein scheme has been enthusiastically endorsed by a

European Union-funded audit, carried out in April 2003 and designed to investigate 'whether the CAL strategy is complementing, or conflicting with, the Welsh Assembly Government's duty to deliver sustainable development' (Digital Europe, 2003, p. 2).[13] The audit commended the 'visionary approach and use of non-technical, accessible language' and suggested that the programme's attempt to harness technology for economic, social and environmental progress 'should be applauded and replicated in other regions' (Digital Europe, 2003, p. 5).

However, forthcoming policy debate in Wales is likely to focus on a number of key issues. The Welsh Consumer Council has marked out some clear policy priorities for the NAfW to take up, based on its own research which reveals that 'a staggering 55% of Welsh consumers currently make no use of the Internet at all' (Tuck, 2003, p. 17). The council calls for an explicit prioritizing of more remote rural areas and for the commissioning of further research to gain a better understanding of reasons for non-use (Jeffs, 2002, p. 106). It also makes a pointed appeal for the allocation of public funding designed to 'make broadband access available in areas where it may not be justifiable on commercial grounds alone' (Downing, 2002, p. 33).

CONCLUSION: NO PLACE LIKE HOME?

It is anticipated that a full convergence of ICTs on digital format will eventually take place, a development which is potentially of particular relevance for Wales. After all, despite its problematic position on most UK-wide indicators relating to the Internet, by 2003 Wales was actually well above the UK average in its take-up of digital television, with a presence in over 50 per cent of Welsh homes (Independent Television Commission, 2002; BBC Wales, 2003).[14] As Downing points out (2002, p. 2), '[t]his route also has the potential benefit of removing lack of computer literacy as a barrier to Internet access'.[15] Similarly, over 70 per cent of the Welsh population have mobile phones, enabling the BBC's introduction of an SMS text service for Welsh learners in March 2003.

Such developments notwithstanding, the widening of home access – rather than merely the fomenting of e-commerce – seems increasingly pivotal. From this perspective, the ideas of the Institute for Public Policy Research (IPPR), as outlined in Tambini (2000), may be relevant. Though intended for UK-wide application, they have a particular resonance for Wales, given the extent of the 'digital divide' discussed above. In dissenting from the European Commission's view, often seen as overly favourable to corporate Internet network developers and providers, the IPPR advance the counter-argument in favour of the creation of a Universal Service Fund (USF), to which all network owners would contribute and whose overarching objective would be to facilitate domestic access to the Internet, based on the idea that this USF would also expect contributions from general taxation; from an access fee (analogous to the existing television licence fee); from a national e-lottery; from the sale of advertising space on public service Internet portals.

Significantly, Wales's Ofcom Advisory Group (2003, p. 28) has pointed out that the prompt establishment of such a USF would be particularly beneficial to Wales, given that it would provide 'a source of support for network improvements, particularly in rural Wales'. The IPPR also suggests that access to sites fulfilling a definite public service remit should be earmarked for special funding initiatives or for more onerous regulatory content rules (see, for example, Tambini, 2000; Forgan and Tambini, 2001). The extent to which the BBC Wales website increasingly acts as a portal to, or directory of, other Wales-based websites would appear to bear out the usefulness of such public service resources.[16]

The USF argument also extends to the proposed creation of a department within Ofcom with responsibility for promoting universal access, and for adjudicating on Internet access rights claims. Such a move might entail a re-evaluation, on the UK government's part, not only of the general relationship between the revised regulatory system and Internet technology, but also of the precise role in these matters of the NAfW itself. In so far as the NAfW and WAG are able to develop their own priorities on these issues, however, any success will also depend on the realization that public debate surrounding Internet access may hitherto have been somewhat oversimplified. As Selwyn argues: '[the] notion of access in terms of whether technology is "available" or not obscures more subtle disparities in the *context* of ICT access . . . Any realistic notion of access to ICT must be defined from the individual's perspective' (2004, p. 347).[17] A full acknowledgement of this will also require a commitment to address the relationship between, on the one hand, the ownership of an Internet-ready PC and, on the other, the expense of signing up with a service provider – whether 'dial-up', broadband or cable – in order to begin *using* the technology, a process beset by the inherent danger of the 'commodification of access' (see Patelis, 2000, p. 91). In this context, the central issue therefore becomes the extent to which the NAfW is able to create and foster favourable circumstances – cultural just as much as infrastructural – for home access to be seen as a desirable and affordable commodity by larger and more demographically and geographically diverse sets of citizens across Wales.

NOTES

1   See Barlow, Mitchell and O'Malley (2005), pp. 159–60.
2   See, for example, Kearton (2004), Mackay and Powell (1998), Parsons (2000), Talfan Davies (1999) and Tuck (2003).
3   See also National Assembly for Wales (2004, p. 1), where the e-minister adds that 'providing broadband access is one of the Welsh Assembly Government's priorities as we transform Wales from the highly industrialized economy of the last century to a knowledge-based economy for the 21st century'.
4   Space here does not permit discussion of the representation of Wales and Welshness on the nation's websites, bulletin boards, and so on (see Barlow, Mitchell and O'Malley, 2005, pp. 173–9).
5   See Courtney and Gibson who define the Welsh economic framework as one 'weighted against high-growth, knowledge intensive activities' (1999, p. 8).
6   The DTI's connectivity figures take into account indicators such as number of websites, frequency of external e-mail use, and so on (see Department of Trade and Industry, 1999).
7   See Courtney and Gibson (1999, p. 9), who point out that in many parts of Wales these problems relate to the sheer distance between exchange and subscriber.
8   The target, set by the WDA in the 1990s, was to reach 90 per cent of the UK average by 2010 (see *www.wda.org*).
9   See Gunkel (2003) and Selwyn (2004) for discussions of a range of conceptual and methodological issues relating to the origin and use of the term 'digital divide'.
10   The scheme aims to increase the affordable availability of terrestrial broadband services in Wales by 30 per cent, bringing the services to an extra 310,000 homes and making 67,000 business lines available.
11   The WDA has also developed, in partnership with Powys local authorities, the Llwybr Pathway Initiative, aimed at providing broadband connectivity to rural areas (see Jeffs, 2002, p. 50).
12   See, for example, the views of Downing (2002, p. 32) and Selwyn and Gorard (2002, p. 46).
13   This audit was a case study by the Digital Europe project funded by the European Union under the Information Society Technology Programme.
14   Use of video conferencing is also significantly higher in Wales than in most parts of the UK, or indeed Europe (Digital Europe, 2003, p. 3).
15   See also Gower, who argues that, '[a]ccess to the Internet via the television set in front of the sofa rather than through the computer on the desk might be the way ahead in Wales' (2003, p. 1).
16   A related issue is the use of the Welsh language on the Internet. In 2003 the NAfW's Culture Committee published a self-evaluative report on its first four years. Among points it highlighted was the Assembly government's support in adopting the committee's vision of a bilingual Wales (NAfW, 2003a, p. 3).
17   Selwyn (2004, p. 352) highlights the needs for careful distinctions to be drawn between four gradations of access according to the degree of user engagement: (i) *formal/theoretical* access, (ii) *effective* access, (iii) *engagement* with ICTs, and (iv) *productive outcomes* from ICT use (see also Selwyn, Gorard and Furlong, 2005, pp. 7–8).

REFERENCES

Barlow, D., Mitchell, P. and O'Malley, T. (2005). *The Media in Wales: Voices of a Small Nation*, Cardiff: University of Wales Press.
BBC Wales (2003). *www.bbc.co.uk/wales*, last accessed 21 June 2004.
Bromley, M. (2000). 'Our market driven media', *Planet*, 139, 124–6.
Chaney, P., Hall, T. and Dicks, B. (2000). 'Inclusive governance? The case of minority and voluntary sector groups and the National Assembly for Wales', *Contemporary Wales*, 13, 98–112.
Collins, R. (2003). 'Internet governance in the UK', paper presented to the Media, Communications and Cultural Studies Association Annual Conference, University of Sussex, 19 December.
Courtney, I. and Gibson, S. (1999). *Cymru.Com: Here's How*, Cardiff: Wales Media Forum.
Curran, J. and Seaton, J. (2003). *Power Without Responsibility*, 6th edn, London: Routledge.
Department for Culture, Media and Sport (2002). *Culture, Media and Sport: Minutes of Evidence*, London: House of Commons.
Department of Trade and Industry (1999). *Regulating Communications: The Way Ahead*, London: DTI.
Department of Trade and Industry (2002). *Closing the Digital Divide: Information and Communication Technologies in Deprived Areas*, London: DTI.
Department of Trade and Industry (2004). *UK Broadband Status Report*, London: DTI.
Digital Europe (2003). *Cymru Ar-Lein and Sustainable Development: Case Study Summary*, Brussels: European Union.
Downing, J. (2002). *Net Gain? Access to and Use of the Internet in Wales*, Cardiff: Wales Consumer Council.
Dutton, W. H. (1999a). 'Social and economic constraints on the consumption of ICTs', in W. H. Dutton (ed.), *Society on the Line: Information Politics in the Digital Age*, Oxford: Oxford University Press.
Dutton, W. H. (1999b). 'Regulating the provision and production of ICTs', in W. H. Dutton (ed.), *Society on the Line: Information Politics in the Digital Age*, Oxford: Oxford University Press.
Forgan, L. and Tambini, D. (2001). *Content*, London: IPPR.
Gower, J. (2003). 'Internet in Wales', *www.bbc.co.uk/wales*
Gunkel, D. (2003). 'Second thoughts: toward a critique of the digital divide', *New Media and Society*, 5, 4, 499–522.
Hargreaves, I. (1999). 'Introduction', in G. Talfan Davies, *Not By Bread Alone: Information, Media and the National Assembly*, Cardiff: Wales Media Forum.
Independent Television Commission (2002). *Memorandum to the Culture Committee of the National Assembly of Wales on the Communications Bill*, Cardiff: National Assembly for Wales.
Jeffs, M. (2002). *Rural Isolation: Consumer Access to Goods and Services*, Cardiff: Welsh Consumer Council.
Kearton, L. (2004). *Internet Inequality in Wales: Update 2004*, Cardiff: Welsh Consumer Council.
Livingstone, T. (2003), 'Can't surf, won't surf', *Western Mail*, 25 March.

Mackay, H. and Powell, A. (1998). 'Connecting Wales: the Internet and national identity', in B. D. Loader (ed.), *Cyberspace Divide: Equality, Agency and Policy in the Information Society*, London: Routledge.

National Assembly for Wales (NAfW) (2003a). *Cymru Ar-Lein, www.cymruarlein.wales. gov.uk*

National Assembly for Wales (NAfW) (2003b). 'Objective One steps in to support innovative broadband projects', press release, (*www.cymruarlein.wales.gov.uk*).

National Assembly for Wales (NAfW) (2004). 'Christmas campaign to encourage more people to sign up to broadband', press release, 22 December, Cardiff: NAfW.

Ofcom Advisory Group (2003). *Wales and Ofcom: A Report by an Advisory Group to the Minister for Culture, Sport and the Welsh Language*, Welsh Assembly Government, Cardiff: NAfW.

Office for National Statistics (2000). *Family Expenditure Survey*, London: HMSO.

Office for National Statistics (2001). *Family Expenditure Survey*, London: HMSO.

Office for National Statistics (2002). *Family Expenditure Survey*, London: HMSO.

Office for National Statistics (2003). *Family Expenditure Survey*, London: HMSO.

Parsons, W. (2000). 'From Beulah Land to Cyber-Cymru', *Contemporary Wales*, 1–26.

Patelis, K. (2000). 'The political economy of the Internet', in J. Curran (ed.), *Media Organisations in Society*, London: Arnold.

Selwyn, N. (2004). 'Reconsidering political and popular understandings of the digital divide', *New Media and Society*, 6, 3, 341–62.

Selwyn, N. and Gorard, S. (2002). *The Information Age: Technology, Learning and Exclusion in Wales*, Cardiff: University of Wales Press.

Selwyn, N., Gorard, S. and Furlong, J. (2005). 'Whose Internet is it anyway? Exploring adults' (non)use of the Internet in everyday life', *European Journal of Communication*, 20, 1, 5–26.

Talfan Davies, G. (1999). *Not By Bread Alone: Information, Media and the National Assembly*, Cardiff: Wales Media Forum.

Tambini, D. (2000). *Universal Internet Access: A Realistic View*, London: Institute for Public Policy Research.

Thomas, J., Jewell, J. and Cushion, S. (2004). *Media Coverage of the 2003 Welsh Assembly Elections*, Cardiff: Wales Media Forum.

Tuck, R. (2003). *Internet Inequality in Wales*, Cardiff: Welsh Consumer Council.

UK Online (2003). *Annual Report*, London: HMSO.

Welsh Affairs Select Committee (1999). *Broadcasting in Wales and the National Assembly*, London: HMSO.

Welsh Consumer Council (2003a). 'New research identifies high levels of Internet resistance in Wales', press release, Cardiff: Welsh Consumer Council.

Welsh Consumer Council (2003b). 'Widespread Internet resistance in Wales', press release, Cardiff: Welsh Consumer Council.

12. THE NEWSPAPER PRESS IN WALES

Tom O'Malley

ABSTRACT

The newspaper press in Wales has been understood as having played a key role in shaping the cultural and political identity of the country. There is, however, insufficient empirical work to sustain many of the generalizations that have been made about the press in Wales. There has been some notable work on press history and structure in Wales, but this needs to be built on. This article therefore outlines the structure of the contemporary press in Wales. It examines the nature of assertions about the Welsh press by surveying aspects of the content of the press and critical issues such as the 'information gap', and the influence of the press on politics, national identity and the Welsh language. In all of these cases the empirical foundations of these assertions are criticized. It argues that we do not know enough about how the press operates in contemporary Welsh society nor about the ways in which it has been implicated in social transformation in Wales. It calls for a more sustained programme of research into the newspaper press so as to place it in proper relation to the wide range of factors with which it has interacted in Welsh society.

INTRODUCTION

There is still a tendency amongst Welsh intellectuals and political activists to attribute great influence to the press. The 19th century myth of the newspaper as a "great engine of thought" is still firmly entrenched amongst political and intellectual elites in Wales. (Williams, 1994, p. 252)

The newspaper press in Wales has its origins in the eighteenth century. Since then, like the newspaper press in the UK, the press in Wales has been understood to have played a key role in shaping the cultural and political identity of the country (Jones, 1993, 1996, 2000a). As will be argued here, Kevin Williams's point holds good for the early part of the twenty-first century, even though there is insufficient historical and sociological evidence to sustain such an strong model of influence.

It is notable that the most authoritative single-volume study of the sociology of Wales had no substantial literature on which to draw in relation to the press and broadcasting and as such they do not play a major role in the book (Day, 2002). The pioneering work of Jones (1993, 1998, 2000a, 2000b) and Mackay and Powell (1997) still needs to be built on if we are to grasp more fully the historical and sociological relationship between the newspaper and society in Wales. This article therefore outlines the structure of the contemporary press in Wales, and then, through a survey of aspects of content and some of the critical frameworks used to interpret the role of the press in Welsh society, argues the case for a more sustained programme of research into the role of the newspaper in Welsh society.

STRUCTURE

Trends in the ownership and linguistic make-up of the Welsh press were established in the twentieth century and remain well established (Jones, 1993; Mackay and Powell, 1997; Allan and O'Malley, 1999). The expansion in the economy and population of Wales in the nineteenth century fuelled a massive growth in newspapers. During the nineteenth century over one hundred Welsh-language titles were launched. The climax of this growth was reached in the 1880s, when one hundred new titles were launched, most of which were in English (Jones, 2000b, pp. 1–5). The intense competition in the industry contributed, as in the rest of the UK (Curran and Seaton, 2003), to a dramatic contraction in the numbers of titles. In 1914 there were 119 English-language and 20 Welsh-language titles produced in Wales; by 1960 this had dropped to 101 English- and 8 Welsh-language titles (Jones, 1993, p. 209).

By 2003 there were approximately seventy titles produced on a weekly, bi-weekly, morning or evening basis, thirty of which were freesheets (Newspaper Society, 2003; see also, Barlow, Mitchell and O'Malley, 2005). From 1973 onwards a number of highly local, small-circulation Welsh-language publications started to appear, the *papurau bro*; sixty-eight of these were launched between 1973 and 2001, of which eleven closed in that time (National Library of Wales, 2001). In addition, by 2004 plans for an all-Wales Welsh-language daily, *Y Byd* were well developed (N. Thomas, 2003/4; *Y Byd*, 2004).

With the exception of the *papurau bro* the trends in ownership in the Welsh press have mirrored those in the UK. By the mid-twentieth century a pattern of concentration of ownership was well established in Wales (Jones, 1993; Mackay and Powell, 1997; Curran and Seaton, 2003). In 2003 two UK-wide companies dominated the top five owners of Welsh papers (see table 12.1). Trinity Mirror not only owned the UK tabloid, the *Mirror*, but its dominance in Wales was evident in its ownership of the *Western Mail*, the *Daily Post* and a clutch of other important papers (see table 12.2). With the stabilization of concentration of ownership in the twentieth century went a secular decline in the circulations of paid-for newspapers, offset only by the rise in the weekly freesheet market. Table 12.3 illustrates the shifts in circulations between 1966 and 2002.

Table 12.1
Ownership of the Welsh press* by circulation at December 2002

Company	% of circulation
Trinity Mirror plc	41.67
Northcliffe Newspapers	17.81
North Wales Newspapers	16.74
Newsquest	15.1
Tindle Newspapers	8.68
Total	100.00

* Paid mornings, evenings, weeklies and bi-weeklies, plus freesheets.
Source: figures based on Newspaper Society, 2003.

Table 12.2
Titles owned by Trinity Mirror plc in 2002

Weeklies	Dailies	Free
Caernarfon Herald (series)	*Liverpool Daily Post*	*Bangor Mail*
Chester Chronicle	*South Wales Echo*	*Barry Post*
Cynon Valley Leader	*Western Mail*	*Bridgend Post*
Glamorgan Gazette		*Buy and Sell Flintshire*
Gwent Gazette		*Buy and Sell S. Cheshire and*
Holyhead Mail (series)		*N. Shropshire*
Merthyr Express		*Buy and Sell* Wrexham edition
Neath and Port Talbot Guardian		*Chester Mail*
North Wales Weekly News		*The Post* – Cardiff
Pontypridd Observer (series)		*Vale Advertiser* (series)
Wales on Sunday		*Visitor* (series)
Whitchurch Herald		*Wrexham Mail*
		Yr Herald

Source: Newspaper Society, 2003.

Table 12.3
Circulations of local papers in Wales, 1966–2002

Year	Morning	Evening	Weekly/bi-weekly	Free	Total
1966	103,000	285,000	679,000		1,067,000
1986	97,000	229,000	526,000	1,119,000	1,971,000
2002	160,164	180,050	494,714	1,068,231	1,903,159

Source: Newspaper Society, 2003; Press Council (various). (The categories used to define a Welsh newspaper in these two sources vary slightly, but do not make a substantial difference to the overall picture.)

By 2002 the circulation of Welsh-language paid-for papers was minimal; *Y Cymro*'s was 4,126 and *Yr Herald*'s was 1,832 (Newspaper Society, 2003). Set against this has been the continued publication of *papurau bro*, which individually have tiny circulations averaging 1,292, but which cumulatively have been estimated as having a circulation of 70,000 per month (Huws, 1996, pp. 84–5). In 1999 most *papurau bro* were eligible for up to £1,000 per year from the Welsh Language Board and an additional grant of £350 from the Arts Council of Wales (Hughes, 1998).

As Jones (1993) and Mackay and Powell (1997) have pointed out, the local press in Wales has been faced with direct competition from English-language titles produced from England since the nineteenth century. Thomas, Jewell and Cushion (2003, pp. 9, 35, 37) report that in 2002, 85 per cent of daily morning newspapers purchased in Wales came from the UK, outside of Wales. The *Western Mail* and the *Daily Post* made up just 13 per cent of the daily morning sales. The *Sun* reached 19.6 per cent of all Welsh homes, with an estimated circulation of 473,000 for its Monday–Friday edition. This was followed by the *Mirror* at 16.8 per cent and the *Daily Mail* at 11.7 per cent. The *News of the World* reached almost 20 per cent of all Welsh households.

Finally, there has never been an all-Wales national daily. All the papers produced in Wales, including the *Western Mail* and the *Daily Post*, have local or sub-national circulations (Barlow, Mitchell and O'Malley, 2005). In 2002, the *Western Mail* had a circulation of 46,732, but it existed alongside a strong sub-regional evening sector, exemplified by papers like the *South Wales Echo* (61,757) and a robust local weekly market occupied by papers like the *Carmarthen Journal* (21,846) (Newspaper Society, 2003). Therefore, although the London-based titles had a UK-wide readership, local (evening and weekly) publications continued to survive by meeting the needs of local communities in ways that other media (radio and TV) had not yet fully rivalled. For example, an Independent Television Commission survey published in 2002 found that 'television and local newspapers run neck and neck' as sources for local news in the UK, with '45 per cent naming television as their main source and 39 per cent newspapers' (Hargreaves and Thomas, 2002, p. 64). In addition, these publications provide a vehicle for local advertising of a more targeted nature than can be provided by TV or radio, an ability to tap into local advertising markets (Future Foundation, 2000).

So in Wales most daily newspapers are UK-wide publications. The two daily Welsh publications are sub-national papers without a large Wales-wide readership. The bulk of the newspapers are locally focused and are owned by UK-based companies, a localism that is also reflected in the development of the *papurau bro*. This situation is the result of trends that were established by the 1920s and which accelerated after 1945 (Jones, 1993; Mackay and Powell, 1997).

CONTENT

There is little historical or sociological work on the content of newspapers in Wales. It is therefore very difficult to generalize about long-term trends or contemporary characteristics. It is, however, possible to distil some key dimensions of content from the literature.

As in the UK (Curran and Seaton, 2003), advertising became the bedrock on which the economic health of the Welsh press rested by the early twentieth century. The amount of advertising in the *Western Mail* rose from ten to sixty columns between 1889 and 1914 (Cayford, 1992, appendix 5). It continues to be a mainstay of the press in Wales, but we know little about its nature, how it has changed over time and how it relates to local circuits of knowledge formation and economic and cultural exchange.

We know more about aspects of the political content of the press, but not enough. Newspapers shift their political foci over time. During the 1926 General Strike, 'the *Western Mail*, which was vicious in its condemnation of the strikers, appeared on every one of the "Nine Days" of the strike' (Davies, 1994, p. 554). This vehemently anti-trade union stance had disappeared from its pages by the end of the century, yet we lack any studies that map this historically or contemporaneously. In 1979 it was 'beyond doubt that the "collective" editorial line of the English language press was overwhelmingly opposed to the Assembly. Only the *Western Mail* held out in favour' (Osmond, 1983, p. 161). By the time of the 1997 referendum, 'the Welsh press was in contrast with the situation in 1979, highly supportive of the case for an Assembly. Many of the leading papers editorially declared themselves in favour of a "Yes" vote. Those that did not remained neutral' (Williams, 2000, p. 97).

These insights and other work carried out on content during periods of heightened political controversy (cf. Thomas, Jewell and Cushion, 2003) need to be built on to provide maps of the shifting political and cultural content of newspapers over time, and studies of specific issues of concern to contemporary sociology in Wales.

Equally, the extent to which the representation of Wales in the dominant UK daily morning press has changed over time and has related to shifting political and social affairs *within both* Wales and the United Kingdom would bear more study. There is a well-argued view, for instance, that Neil Kinnock was depicted in the UK-wide papers during his leadership of the Labour Party (1983–92) as a representative of a south Wales working-class community alien to most voters, and that this 'linked up with and related to more fundamental explanations for his and Labour's defeat in 1992' (Thomas, 1997, p. 108). This echoes another view that there is a problem in the way Wales is depicted, or more commonly under-reported in the UK press as a whole (Nurse, 2001; Thomas, Jewell and Cushion, 2003). Again, these insights need developing. To what extent is the UK-based press guilty of perpetuating stereotypes of 'Welshness' across time and in particular instances? Even if it is shown so to do, what techniques can be used to determine the relationship between these representations and other factors in shaping Welsh political and cultural life?

A similar set of problems exist around the reliance by the UK press and the Welsh press on official sources (Speers, 2001; Thomas, Jewell and Cushion, 2003). What is the extent of this reliance and to what extent does this reliance distort or misrepresent the news agenda in Wales? Equally, the issue of the depoliticization of the press in Wales, noted by Kevin Williams (1994, p. 251), relates to much wider and more controversial issues about the extent to which the UK press as a whole has become more entertainment driven and less focused on political news (Street, 2001). Some (Curran and Seaton, 2003) view this critically, while others (McNair, 2000) are more sanguine, seeing the more populist treatment of politics by the media in terms of scandal and personalities as a positive development, communicating political issues to people otherwise not interested in mainstream politics. With few exceptions (for example, Thomas, Jewell and Cushion, 2003) this kind of issue remains underexplored in studies of the Welsh press.

CRITICAL ISSUES

While we know about the changing structure of the press in Wales, we know less about its content and how that content is involved in shaping the lives of people in the country. Aled Jones has argued that it is very difficult to specify the social influence of the newspaper press in nineteenth-century Wales (1998, p. 219). There is less work on the twentieth-century Welsh press. We do not know enough about the decline of the press in Wales as a major source of information relative to radio, television and the Internet. Equally, we do not know enough about how the press has related to these other institutions nor about what have been the social consequences of these shifting roles. Yet these gaps have not prevented the emergence of a commentary that implies we know more about the relationship of the press to society than the available evidence reveals.

The lack of a national daily press in Wales has, it has been argued, contributed to an 'information gap' in Wales: 'It is not just facts that we are missing, nor merely an understanding. It is rather that we do not have sufficient competing understandings of our circumstances' (Talfan Davies, 1999, p. 17). Thomas, Jewell and Cushion have produced evidence that suggests that on political issues the media system in Wales 'is super-serving the "knowledge rich" while failing to do much to improve the situation of the knowledge poor' (2003, p. 16). Nonetheless, the question of what is precisely meant by an information or a knowledge gap, or how these compare to similar 'gaps' amongst the populations of England and Scotland, and in particular to the role of the newspaper, has not received detailed academic attention in the Welsh context.

This echoes another theme in writing about the press in Wales; that is, its assumed influence on behaviour and attitudes. Writing in 1983 Jones and Wilford argued that the 'cumulative effect' of the 'hostility or indifference to Welsh devolution' of the London dailies, 'compounded by their role as general vehicles of political acculturation, should not be ignored' (1983, p. 228). More recently, Wyn Jones, Trystan and Taylor, have asserted that the 'limited' audience for 'Wales-based mass print media . . . has major implications for the future legitimacy of the National Assembly' (2000, p. 173). In neither case was any evidence cited for these media-centric assertions. The writers cannot be blamed, however, for seeking to make sense of the role of the press in a context where they have so little research on which to draw. The point has been well made by Thomas, Jewell and Cushion in relation to the thesis that the Welsh press has depoliticized over time. Referring to the issue of the prominence of campaign coverage in Welsh newspapers during the 2002 elections for the National Assembly, they point to the fact that the 'absence of any longer-term data about campaign prominence makes it difficult to tell whether this offers any signs of depoliticization of press content' (2003, p. 42).

Two other related issues have been prevalent in commentary about the Welsh press; these are the issues of national identity and the survival of the Welsh language. The historian of the nineteenth-century Welsh press has argued that it 'enabled new forms of national identity to gain currency' (Jones, 2000a, p. 310) and that it aided 'the construction of national identities' in 'complex but durable form' (Jones, 1998, pp. 218–19). Even those critics of the way a language-based, rural model of national identity came to influence Welsh politics in the 1960s and 1970s attribute an important role in this process to the press. Dai Smith has argued that:

> The production of Wales that was proceeding apace in the Cymricising suburbs of Cardiff, in academic and journalistic circles, on the subsidised pages of a Welsh-language press and on the airwaves, had no real need to take account of those who did not fit into the picture. (1999, p. 47)

The question of the formation, sustenance and nature of national identity and nationalism has been a subject of ongoing debate in history and sociology (for example, Anderson, 1983; Adamson, 1991; A. Smith, 1991; Gellner, 1998; O'Leary, 2002). Within this the role of print has remained controversial. Although much of the press produced in Wales since the nineteenth century discussed 'Welshness', it did so in the context of other competing models of 'Welshness' in newspapers (Jones, 1993; O'Malley, Allan and Thompson, 1997). Equally, a great deal of the printed news in circulation in Wales during the twentieth century originated in England and must have played some role in shaping understandings of Welsh identity. In addition, there were other social processes which were factors in shaping contemporary and historical understandings of Wales of industrial change, rural depopulation and in-migration (see Davies, 1994; Day, 2002). We still do not know enough about the relationships between these various factors, either today or through much of the twentieth century, in shaping ideas of Welsh identity.

The question of national identity can be brought into sharper focus by con-sidering the relationship between the Welsh language and the newspaper press. As Balsom has argued:

> To a general sigh of relief the long awaited Welsh language statistics from the 2001 Census found that the number of Welsh speakers has increased, reversing nearly a century of decline. The new Census found 576,000 Welsh speakers aged 3 and over, that is 21 per cent overall and a two per-cent increase on the equivalent number in 1991. (2003, p. 33)

The causes of linguistic change are complex. Gwynfor Evans has articulated the widely held view that the decline in Welsh speakers in the twentieth century was associated with 'the English education system provided in schools, English television, the English press and many other anglicising factors' (2001, p. 164). The precise role of the press in this process has not, however, been demonstrated. This argument emerged again in the most authoritative study to date of language and the 2001 census. Aitchison and Carter (2004) see the media as one of four key factors governing language reproduction. The family, education and community are the primary agencies of reproduction, 'with the media being a further agency'. In Wales, however, 'it would appear that in the case of Welsh the family has become a much less certain agency than once it was, whilst the conflict within the community, arbitrated by the media, will determine the course of education, a prime basis of contemporary reproduction' (2004, p. 27). Drawing on a model of the media that views it as an agenda-setting agency, they argue that 'anecdotally at least, it is possible to maintain that the language was made into an issue put continually before the public'. This was done by the emerging 'Welsh-speaking bourgeisie' who 'played a significant role in the decision-making echelons of the media and was consistently able to insert the language into the agenda of matters of public importance, and furthermore to keep it there'. Plausible as this hypothesis is, it suffers from the absence of relevant data. The authors consider that the collection of the kind of data needed to test their hypothesis, that is, content analysis of the press and broadcasting over time, is 'hardly feasible'. (2004, p. 18). Yet such a study of the press would be feasible, given time and resources, especially as most of the newspapers are accessible to scholars and the techniques involved have been used for many years in history and the social sciences (Berridge, 1986; Deacon et al., 1999, pp. 114–31).

The claims being made for the influence of the press in this argument are very strong. Yet surely they need to be set more precisely in the context of other factors driving public attitudes towards, and political action in relation to, the Welsh language after 1945? These would include, at least, demographics, industrial change, pressure group politics, party politics, Westminster politics and government spending. In the post-war period, when the spread of anglicizing media (radio, TV, and, after 1990, satellite) has been so strong in Wales, is it plausible to attribute to the press such a significant role in the maintenance of language? Again, the speculation about the link between the media, and the press, and language survival is a very interesting one, but it will remain a speculation until we have more research.

PUTTING THE PRESS ON THE RESEARCH AGENDA

The evidence surveyed in this article points in three directions. First, there needs to be more empirical work on the history and contemporary structure and sociology of the press in Wales. We simply do not know enough about how the press operates in Welsh society. For example, it is very difficult to compile simple historical data about trends in the circulation of the Welsh press because UK newspapers do not publish publicly available figures on their Welsh circulation. We cannot begin to chart properly the position of the press relative to the emerging world of the Internet and digital TV in Wales until there is public access to a range of industry data about circulation and numbers of websites, their content, function and use by the population. At the very least, we need a central accessible hub for the collection and dissemination of data on the press in Wales.

Secondly, the press is clearly implicated in social transformation in Welsh society. Yet we do not know enough about its relationships with society in Wales to make generalization about the links between the press and questions such as voting behaviour, depoliticization, national identity and linguistic change. It is not surprising that writers in areas that touch on the press in Wales resort to intuition and informed assertion, when they have so few studies on which to draw for answers to their questions.

Finally, the relationship between the press and Welsh society is likely to prove complex as we move towards a better understanding of its position within wider patterns of cultural and political change. We need to take the press's role more seriously and systematically in historical and sociological research in Wales, and in so doing place it in its proper relation to the range of factors with which it interacted, and continues to interact, in the shaping of Welsh society.

REFERENCES

Adamson, D. (1991). *Class, Ideology and the Nation: A Theory of Welsh Nationalism*, Cardiff: University of Wales Press.

Aitchison, J. and Carter, H. (2004). *Spreading the Word: The Welsh Language 2001*, Talybont: Y Lolfa.

Allan, S. and O'Malley, T. (1999). 'The media in Wales', in D. Dunkerley and A. Thompson (eds), *Wales Today*, Cardiff: University of Wales Press.

Anderson, B. (1983). *Imagined Communities: Reflections on the Origins and Spread of Nationalism*, London: Verso.

Balsom, D. (2003). 'Ticking the box', *Agenda*, Cardiff: Institute of Welsh Affairs, Spring, 33–4.

Barlow, D., Mitchell, P. and O'Malley, T. (2005). *The Media in Wales: Voices of a Small Nation*, Cardiff: University of Wales Press.

Berridge, V. (1986). 'Content analysis and historical research on newspapers', in M. Harris and A. Lee (eds), *The Press in English Society from the Seventeenth to the Nineteenth Centuries*, London and Toronto: Associated University Presses.

Cayford, J. (1992). 'The *Western Mail* 1869–1914: the politics and management of a provincial newspaper', unpublished Ph.D. thesis, University of Wales.

Curran, J. and Seaton, J. (2003). *Power without Responsibility: The Press, Broadcasting and New Media in Britain*, 6th edn, London: Routledge.

Davies, J. (1994). *A History of Wales*, London: Penguin.

Day, G. (2002). *Making Sense of Wales. A Sociological Perspective*, Cardiff: University of Wales Press.

Deacon, D., Pickering, M., Golding, P. and Murdock, G. (eds) (1999). *Researching Communications*, London: Arnold.

Evans, G. (2001). *For the Sake of Wales*, Cardiff: Welsh Academic Press.

Future Foundation (2000). *Renaissance of Regional Nations*, London: Newspaper Society.

Gellner, E. (1998). *Nationalism*, London: Phoenix.

Hargreaves, I. and Thomas, J. (2002). *New News, Old News*, London: Independent Television Commission.

Hughes, G. (1998). 'Keeping it in the community: the *papurau bro* in Wales', unpublished MA thesis, University of Leicester.

Huws, G. (1996). 'The success of the local: Wales', *Mercator Media Forum*, 2, 84–93.

Jones, A. (1993). *Press, Politics and Society: A History of Journalism in Wales*, Cardiff: University of Wales Press.

Jones, A. (1996). *Powers of the Press: Newspapers, Power and the Public in Nineteenth-Century England*, Aldershot: Scolar Press.

Jones, A. (1998). 'The newspaper press in Wales 1804–1945', in P. H. Jones and E. A. Rees (eds), *A Nation and its Books: A History of the Book in Wales*, Aberystwyth: National Library of Wales.

Jones, A. (2000a). 'The nineteenth-century media and Welsh identity', in L. Brake, B. Bell and D. Finkelstein (eds), *Nineteenth-Century Media and the Construction of Identities*, Basingstoke: Palgrave.

Jones, A. (2000b). 'The Welsh newspaper press', in H. T. Edwards (ed.), *A Guide to Welsh Literature c.1800–1900* Vol. V, Cardiff: University of Wales Press.

Jones, J. B. and Wilford, R. (1983). 'Implications: two salient issues', in D. Foulkes, J. B. Jones and R. A. Wilford (eds), *The Welsh Veto: The Wales Act and the Referendum*, Cardiff: University of Wales Press.

Mackay, H. and Powell, A. (1997). 'Wales and its media: production, consumption and regulation', *Contemporary Wales*, 9, 8–39.

McNair, B. (2000). *Journalism and Democracy: An Evaluation of the Political Public Sphere*, London: Routledge.

National Library of Wales (2001). *Rhestr o Bapurau Bro Gorffenaf 2001*, Aberystwyth: National Library of Wales, online catalogue.

Newspaper Society (2003). *www.newspapersoc.org.uk*, accessed 11 August 2003.

Nurse, K. (2001). 'Taffy was a Welshman . . .', *New Welsh Review*, 54, 36–8.

O'Leary, B. (2002). 'In praise of empires past', *New Left Review*, 2nd series, 18, 106–30.

O'Malley, T., Allan, S. and Thompson, A. (1997). 'Tokens of antiquity: the newspaper press and the shaping of national identity in Wales, 1870–1900', in M. Harris and T. O'Malley (eds), *Studies in Newspaper and Periodical History 1995 Annual*, Westport, Connecticut and London: Greenwood Press, pp. 127–52.

Osmond, J. (1983). 'The referendum and the English language press', in D. Foulkes, J. B. Jones and R. A. Wilford (eds), *The Welsh Veto: The Wales Act and the Referendum*, Cardiff: University of Wales Press.

Press Council (various dates). *The Press and the People*, London: Press Council.

Smith, A. (1991). 'The nation: invented, imagined, reconstructed?', *Millennium: Journal of International Studies*, 20, 3, 353–68.

Smith, D. (1999). *Wales: A Question For History*, Bridgend: Seren.

Speers, T. (2001). *Welcome or Over Reaction? Refugees and Asylum Seekers in the Welsh Media*, Cardiff: Wales Media Forum.

Street, J. (2001). *Mass Media, Politics and Democracy*, London: Palgrave.

Talfan Davies, G. (1999). *Not By Bread Alone: Information, Media and the National Assembly*, Cardiff: Wales Media Forum.

Thomas, J. (1997). '"Taffy was a Welshman, Taffy was a thief": anti-Welshness, the press and Neil Kinnock', *Llafur*, 7, 2, 95–108.

Thomas, J., Jewell, J. and Cushion, S. (2003). *Media Coverage of the 2003 Welsh Assembly Elections*, Cardiff: Wales Media Forum.

Thomas, N. (2003/4). '*Y Byd*: papur dyddiol cenadlaethol', *Agenda*, Cardiff: Institute of Welsh Affairs, 62–4.

Williams, K. (1994). 'Are we being served? The press, broadcasting and a Welsh parliament', in J. Osmond (ed.), *A Parliament For Wales*, Llandysul: Gomer.

Williams, K. (2000). 'No dreads, only some doubts: the press and the referendum campaign', in J. B. Jones, and D. Balsom (eds), *The Road to the National Assembly for Wales*, Cardiff: University of Wales Press.

Wyn Jones, R., Trystan, D. and Taylor, B. (2000). 'Voting patterns in the referendum', in J. B. Jones and D. Balsom (eds), *The Road to the National Assembly for Wales*, Cardiff: University of Wales Press.

Y Byd (2004). Website, *www.ybyd.com/english.shtml*, accessed on 30 November 2004.

13. AN UNCERTAIN ERA: WELSH TELEVISION, BROADCASTING POLICY AND THE NATIONAL ASSEMBLY IN A MULTIMEDIA WORLD

Kevin Williams

ABSTRACT

Welsh television is changing. New technology, changing forms of regulation, a new political environment, profound social and cultural transformation and changed economic circumstances are creating a new broadcasting environment. This environment poses both opportunities and dangers. There is the potential for growth. The new political order created by the devolution of some political power to Wales in the form of the National Assembly is an incentive for more home-produced media. However, this opportunity comes about in conditions which can be seen as actively working against such efforts. It is possible to argue that the evolving social, political and economic circumstances threaten the very continuation of distinct Welsh media. Whether you accept this assessment or not the new environment does pose a challenge to policy-makers and in particular the National Assembly. This article outlines the recent changes in the ecology of Welsh television and the reaction of Welsh broadcasters. The policy implications of these changes and the responses to them are explored as well as the ways in which policy-makers in Wales and the United Kingdom have engaged with these developments. It examines the debates and enquiries into the state of broadcasting in Wales as well as the relationship between Cardiff and London over broadcasting matters. What is apparent from this examination is that there is considerable confusion, uncertainty and insecurity over the future of Welsh broadcasting. There is little direct public engagement with this debate. Given the political, economic and cultural importance of broadcasting to Wales this state of affairs, it is argued, presents a clear and present danger to Welsh society.

INTRODUCTION

Broadcasting plays a more crucial role in Wales than it does in other parts of the United Kingdom, being 'disproportionately important . . . in helping to shape a sense of national community' (Andrews, 2004a, p. 4). Welsh television and radio are concerned with more than informing and entertaining people. They play a significant role in shaping public understanding of what is and what it means to be Welsh. Not only do they enable Welsh people to present themselves to the outside world, thereby challenging the limited stereotypes that appear in the UK media and beyond, but they are vital ingredients in the building of a sense of collective identity. Welsh broadcasters emphasize their cultural mission. The comments of one former senior HTV executive are typical: 'Welsh broadcasting's *raison d'être* is the reinforcement of our identity; to present the Welsh to the Welsh and to be proud, in so far as it is justifiable, of who we are' (quoted in K. Williams, 1997). The importance of broadcasting in the formation of Welsh identity is accentuated by the underdevelopment of an indigenous national press in Wales. It is not surprising that John Davies (1994) in his official history of the BBC and broadcasting in Wales claims that post-war Wales is a 'cultural artefact produced by broadcasting'.

The self-conscious articulation and pursuit of this cultural mission poses problems. There is the challenge of trying to find the right images to represent the nation. The sharp social, geographic, linguistic and political divisions in Wales present formidable obstacles. The highly fragmented nature of Welsh identity inevitably means that media representations of Welshness are contested (see, for example, Ryan, 1986; K. Williams, 1997). In the face of these obstacles many in Welsh television have fallen back on older romantic notions of Welshness, refusing to embrace the new images of who we are as a society and a people. There is also a 'burden of representation' placed on Welsh broadcasters which can get in the way of making good programmes or good art or good enter-tainment (Blandford and Upton, 1996). The cultural mission can impede the writer, artist, entertainer or programme-maker in his or her efforts to produce popular, accessible and engaging material. The intervention of a mission to build a nation, support a language or develop national consciousness does not always sit comfortably with making entertaining programmes and providing information.

One consequence of broadcasting's cultural mission is that Welsh politicians have to respond to the concept of the nation as given shape by Welsh television and radio. Since 1999 members of the National Assembly, and in particular the Welsh Assembly Government (WAG), have found it difficult to adjust to the central part played by television in shaping the national agenda and people's understanding of Wales and Welshness. TV news in Wales has always had a greater political content than that in the English regions. One estimate places the proportion of BBC Wales's news output as high as 30 per cent (Talfan Davies, 1999, p. 36). The nature and quality of this output is increasingly criticized by politicians. The first first minister, Alun Michael, called on broadcasters to 'report constructively' and provide 'mature discussion', believing that failure to do so would 'be letting Wales down'. Michael promoted the notion of 'Team Wales' and took umbrage at critical coverage. His successor, Rhodri Morgan, has been more outspoken, accusing the Welsh broadcast media of being 'undoubtedly hostile' to devolution with their 'flip, glib, quick cynical' judgements (see K. Williams, 2003). Such comments reflect the disproportionate importance of television in Welsh life. For all their limitations television and radio are the primary actors in giving Wales concrete form. They are the only major actors who regularly report and represent an all-Wales perspective. They are the main channels of communication for the National Assembly to 'get its message across' to the people of Wales. They provide the most significant forum for discussion and debate about issues affecting the whole of Wales.

Broadcasting is not only politically significant in Wales. It was estimated that in 1998 the arts and cultural industries in Wales accounted for 23,000 full-time equivalent jobs and £1.1 billion of turnover, of which the media sector (film, broadcasting and multimedia) contributed almost £350 million in turnover and 3,000 jobs (Welsh Affairs Committee, 1999, p. xix). BBC Wales alone contributed over £100 million to the Welsh economy in 2002–03 (Morgan, 2004) while the organization employed 1,300 people and supported another 1,000 indirect jobs (Hill, 2003). The importance of the 'creative industries' is acknowledged by the Assembly in its cultural strategy for Wales, *Creative Future: Cymru Greadigol*, launched in 2002, which emphasizes the central role of broadcasting, film and new media in the economic, social and cultural renewal of Wales (Barlow, Mitchell and O'Malley, 2005). Broadcasting also strongly influences matters such as language, education, the arts and culture over which the Assembly has devolved power.

Broadcasting is not part of the devolution settlement but it is becoming apparent that the Assembly cannot ignore what is happening to broadcasting. This is reinforced by regulatory changes at the UK national and European levels which demand some form of input or response from the Assembly. The concordat agreed with the Department of Culture, Media and Sport (DCMS) in June 2000 stipulates that the secretary of state will consult the Assembly on 'broadcasting matters of special relevance to Wales' as well as on specific broadcasting appointments. In March 2004, DCMS announced a review into the performance of S4C as part of an appraisal of broadcasting in the United Kingdom. Last year consultations over the renewal of the BBC's Royal Charter in 2006 were launched. There are several reasons why the Assembly should become more involved in broadcasting and many are urging it to do so. A Welsh Affairs Committee report into broadcasting and the National Assembly in 1999 gave 'constant encouragement . . . to the National Assembly to take a strong interest in broadcasting policy' (Andrews, 2004a). The pressure on the Assembly to play a greater role in broadcasting policy comes at a time when fundamental change is taking place.

CHANGE

The unprecedented changes in Welsh broadcasting are usually seen as driven by technological advances. Cable, satellite and now digital television are seen as radically changing the broadcasting landscape in Wales. They are responsible for the emergence of multi-channel television. The mountainous geography of the country poses barriers for the provision of access to broadcasting and com- munications services. As a result the penetration of multi-channel television has been greater in Wales than the rest of the UK. In December 2003, it is estimated that 61 per cent of Welsh homes had access to multi-channel television compared to 48 per cent of the UK as a whole (S4C, 2004a, p. 25). In such households the terrestrial channels compete with a variety of other channels which has led to a decline in their share of the audience. Between 1996 and 2002 BBC1's share of viewing across the UK fell from 32.5 per cent to 26.2 per cent while ITV's fell from 35.1 per cent to 24.1 per cent. UK government policy is to switch off analogue television as soon as possible, with 2010 the preferred date. Switch-off will pose more than technical problems for broadcasters in Wales. It has profound implications for the future provision of Welsh programmes in both of the nation's languages.

New technology has been accompanied by a considerable restructuring of the regulatory mechanisms overseeing broadcasting in Wales and the UK. The variety of bodies that have shaped British broadcasting have been merged into a single, new super-regulator, the Office of Communication (Ofcom). Its arrival in 2003 coincided with the loosening of the public service commitments of broadcasters. BBC Wales, HTV (now ITV Wales) and S4C are all products of public service broadcasting. Public service is based on the view that radio and television are too important politically and culturally to be left to the market. Broadcasting should not simply seek to make profits but should also inform, educate and entertain its audiences. Obligations to contribute to the cultural and political life of the UK were enforced by regulatory bodies such as the Independent Television Commission (ITC), Radio Authority and Broadcasting Standards Council (BSC). Amongst other commitments public service regulation ensured that broadcasters had a duty to represent the regions and nations of the UK. Despite all their faults and limitations, these arrangements assisted the broadcast media to give expression to Welsh culture in both languages. They also ensured the provision of public finance and subsidy in the case of S4C and BBC Wales to guarantee this can be carried out.

These arrangements have been eroded since the 1980s. The dismantling of public service commitments began with Mrs Thatcher. The shift to 'light-touch regulation' enabled unregulated broadcasters such as BSkyB to become part of the ecology of British broadcasting. Unlike terrestrial companies, BSkyB has never been required to adhere to such obligations. The 1990 Broadcasting Act paved the way for the development of a single ITV company. Set up in 1955, ITV was a network of regional broadcasters, including a franchise for Wales and the West. ITV was in part established as an antidote to the highly centralized nature of the BBC in the immediate post-war period. Two decades of 'light-touch' regulation have resulted in ITV's regional companies becoming one large plc. Only STV, Border and UTV remain separate. New Labour's new regulatory arrangements further reduce the obligations on broadcasters. New Labour considers broadcasting as primarily part of industrial policy. It is one of the 'creative industries' to be exploited for economic benefit and profit rather than a vital and essential part of cultural and political life. This represents a reversal in the party's attitude to broadcasting (Freedman, 2003). Crudely put, New Labour has become the party of media concentration, media millionaires and media markets. After years of opposing private media monopolies, the Labour Party accepts the need for the existence of media monopolies and encourages the growth of large media corporations, hence the support for the loosening of the cross-media ownership restrictions. According to the 1998 *Regulating Communications* Green Paper: '[s]ome concentration of ownership has been regarded as inevitable and possibly desirable, since it confers advantage in terms of global competitiveness' (quoted in Freedman, 2003, p. 176). New Labour has created and embraced media millionaires, the courting of Rupert Murdoch being the most obvious sign of New Labour's cosy relationship with big business. MAI's Lord Hollick, BBC's Greg Dyke and Granada's Gerry Robinson had close relations with the party. Ofcom is headed by a former Blair advisor and a former managing director of the highly unsuccessful and hugely debt-ridden cable company NTL. Finally, New Labour emphasizes the market as the key mechanism to ensure quality, diversity and fairness in broadcasting. While lip service is paid to public service broadcasting and the BBC, New Labour's vision is to 'make the UK home to the most dynamic and competitive communications and media market in the world' (DTI/DCMS, 2000, p. 10).

The 2003 Communications Act, as Tom O'Malley has pointed out, makes explicit New Labour's commitment to making broadcasting more competitive. Tessa Jowell, secretary of state for Culture, Media and Sport, announced the publication of the draft bill in May 2002, stating that: 'For too long the UK's media have been over-regulated and over-protected from competition . . . The draft Bill we published today will liberalise the market, so removing unnecessary regulatory burdens and cutting red tape.' The new regulatory body, Ofcom, represents a departure from traditional broadcasting regulators who defined their role in terms of both cultural and economic objectives. Ofcom's philosophy poses a challenge to Welsh broadcasting, threatening the structures that have traditionally provided broadcasters in Wales with the capacity and ability to represent Wales and Welsh life. What has been the response from Wales to change in the broadcast media and broadcasting regulation?

WELSH AFFAIRS COMMITTEE REPORT, 1999

The first consideration of broadcasting in a post-devolution world came in 1999 when the Welsh Affairs Committee conducted an enquiry into 'Broadcasting in Wales and the National Assembly'. This enquiry took evidence from all the major actors in Welsh broadcasting and issued a report which considered a range of possibilities regarding its future development, concentrating on the implications of the Assembly for broadcasting in Wales and the problem of television reception (Welsh Affairs Committee, 1999). The latter issue was connected to the 'information deficit' in Wales. The committee was told that nearly 400,000 people in Wales did not watch Welsh television, preferring or having to look at services from England. This situation, together with 87 per cent of people buying morning newspapers not produced in Wales, was seen as a major reason for the low turn-out at the 1997 referendum. The committee considered the situation as a 'very serious matter' and one 'not being adequately addressed by the broadcasters' (1999, p. xix). The committee was critical of 'a certain resistance in the industry' to provide full information about the areas affected by reception problems and strongly recommended that the Assembly 'maintain pressure on the broadcasters to tackle both the continuing problems of reception of Welsh television in many parts of Wales and the failure of Welsh television to attract a large number of Welsh viewers' (1999, pp. xvii and xix).

The matter of accountability figured most prominently in the committee's recommendations and conclusions. The committee had been convinced of the need for 'better accountability' in Welsh broadcasting. It expressed concern at the lack of provision for regular review of S4C's performance and deemed its mechanisms for ensuring accountability 'weak'. It was critical of BBC Wales accountability arrangements and recommended that the national governor for Wales should not chair the Broadcasting Council for Wales (BCW), which in the long run should be radically reformed and separated from BBC management. This would, the committee argued, allow the BCW to oversee S4C as well as the BBC, thereby helping 'to reinforce the need for co-operation between the two organizations and to ensure that public money is used to better effect'. The committee took the view that appointments to broadcasting bodies such as the BCW and the S4C Board should be made directly by the Assembly or at least require its approval. Direct appointment, it argued, would 'underline the account-ability of these appointees to the people of Wales' and 'enhance the inde-pendence of the bodies involved'. It rejected the government's view that such power would carry the 'risk of unbalancing' the BBC's independence. The committee stopped short of recommending that responsibility for S4C be transferred directly from DCMS to the National Assembly. It did not accept that the channel would become a 'political football' in the midst of the competing demands for funding from other sectors, but did concur with the view that any devolution of broadcasting should be done 'gradually'. The report strongly hoped that the 'Assembly will take a close interest in broadcasting matters' and identified specific areas in which it should do so. The committee charged the Assembly to 'ensure that HTV keeps to its commitments' to 'develop and extend its service to Wales' and to 'keep closely in touch with the continuing negotiations on the date of the "analogue switch-off" in order to ensure that the interests of the Welsh viewers are safeguarded'.

The Assembly's first foray into broadcasting came in response to the committee's report. The plenary debate was an open-ended discussion highlighting a mish-mash of concerns about broadcasting (NAfW, 1999). The first minister, Alun Michael, laid out the Assembly's 'responsibilities' in broadcasting matters. It would be consulted on appointments to broadcasting bodies and broadcasting matters of particular relevance to Wales, including proposals for future primary legislation. This was the basis for the concordat agreed with DCMS in 2000. Matters regarded as of relevance to Wales are defined as those relating 'solely or principally to S4C, the Channel 3 franchisee for Wales and the West or the BBC in Wales', that 'impact solely or principally on viewers and listeners in Wales, or the broadcasting industry in Wales' and that 'relate materially to the Welsh language, or to the distinctive culture of Wales' (DCMS/CNafW, 2000). Public service broadcasters and regulators would present their annual reports to the Assembly, and the Government of Wales Act 1998 allows the Assembly 'to consider any matter which affects Wales', which includes broadcasting and the media. The Assembly is also responsible for regulating the broadcasting of its own proceedings through the Assembly Broadcasting Company. What was interesting about this debate was the limited engagement with the Select Committee's call for the Assembly to play a more significant role in Welsh broadcasting.

What was equally apparent was the initial timidity of the Assembly's response. This could be explained by Alun Michael. As secretary of state for Wales he had appeared before the committee on the government's behalf to give evidence. As Wales's man in Westminster he was sceptical of any moves to increase the Assembly's involvement in broadcasting. Caution determined his approach. However, the Assembly's Post-16 Education and Training Committee, whose responsibilities included cultural matters, did make a contribution. As part of a review of the arts and culture in Wales, the committee took evidence from broadcasting organizations in early 2000. They were asked about their contribution to the culture of Wales (Post-16 Education and Training Committee, 2000). In June 2000, the committee, responding to the resolution passed by the Assembly following its debate on the Select Affairs Committee report, took evidence 'to gain an understanding of key issues in broadcasting', 'to identify issues of significance to Wales' and to ascertain possible areas on which the Assembly could be asked to make representations to the UK government (Post-16 Education and Training Committee, 2000; Andrews, 2004a). The committee was due to publish its findings in the autumn of that year. Nothing happened as the committee was disbanded in the wake of the Labour–Liberal partnership agreement.

The new political arrangements in the National Assembly saw the appointment of a minister of Culture, Sport and the Welsh Language and the setting up of a Culture Committee whose terms of reference included media and broadcasting. The minister and committee were more proactive than their predecessors. This was partly due to the committee's responsibility for the development of a cultural strategy for Wales. More significant was the part the committee played in the deliberations over the establishment of Ofcom. The committee held hearings on the Ofcom legislation, the evidence from which was fed into the Assembly Cabinet's response. This legislation played a crucial role in increasing the National Assembly's involvement in broadcasting policy.

OFCOM AND WALES

The UK's new regulatory mechanisms were shaped by three key pieces of legislation: the 1998 Green Paper, *Regulating Communications – Approaching Convergence in the Information Age* (DTI, 1998), the 2000 White Paper, *A New Future for Communications*, December 2000 (DTI/DCMS, 2000) and the 2002 draft Communications Bill. The publication of each of these documents provided the opportunity for interested parties in Wales to contribute to the debate about the future shape of broadcasting policy. *Regulating Communications* laid out the basic principles of government policy, emphasizing the 'promotion and protection of the consumer interest as the overriding objective of regulation' (para 3.48). The document conceived viewers purely as consumers, ignoring the role of broadcasting in the promotion of citizenship (Freedman, 2003, p. 173). Technological change, the Green Paper argued, made redundant traditional forms of regulation. Regulation should be reduced to a minimum and focus on economic and market realities. The idea of having one regulator to oversee all the broadcasting and telecommunications sectors was proposed. The Green Paper represented a radical rethinking of UK broadcasting policy and elicited seventy-nine responses, of which only three came from organizations with a clear Welsh connection: the Catholic Bishops Conference of England and Wales, the Welsh Advisory Committee on Telecommunications and S4C (Barlow, Mitchell and O'Malley, 2005).

The 2000 White Paper put flesh on the proposal for a new mechanism of regulation. Ofcom would replace all the existing regulators apart from the BBC and S4C. The commitment to the viewer and listener as a consumer was now matched by a degree of commitment to 'ensuring that citizens' interests are properly respected'. However, the main thrust of the White Paper was to ensure that Ofcom would play a key role in 'creating a dynamic market' which is 'fundamental to securing choice, quality of service and value for consumers' (para 2). The protection and promotion of competitiveness was seen as critical but, to show that the new body was responsive to consumer concerns and views about service delivery, a new consumer panel would be established to advise the regulator (para 7.1). *A New Future for Communications* saw public service broadcasting having a future in the new digital era but it proposed a new structure of regulation with commercial broadcasters subject to less prescriptive regulation. Ofcom's relationship with Wales was discussed only in a broad and vague way. The new regulator would have to maintain links and consult with relevant Assembly committees and the Assembly Cabinet' (para 8.7). The White Paper also stated it should be organized to take into account 'the interests of the different parts of the UK' (para 8.6). However, unlike the regulatory bodies it replaced Ofcom had no Welsh representation on its main board.

The White Paper brought forth more reaction from Wales than its predecessor. The National Assembly Cabinet, after deliberation, drafted a response which focused on three areas: the availability of digital, the content of programmes and the structure of the new regulatory body and its relationship with Wales (Andrews, 2001, 2004a; Barlow, Mitchell and O'Malley, 2005). The Assembly Cabinet's concerns were: first, everyone in Wales should have access to digital communications services; secondly, public service obligations should remain, in particular the maintenance of national services for Wales; and, thirdly, Wales should have a representative on the Ofcom board appointed by the Assembly. The minister for Culture suggested 'changes to the structure of the new regulator' which included 'a Member for Wales on its board, a Welsh representative on the Consumer Panel and a Welsh Advisory Committee' as well as arguing for a statutory requirement for the new body 'to link and consult with devolved administrations' (NAfW, 2001).

The Cabinet's response was resoundingly endorsed by Assembly members. Support came from all the political parties in the Assembly. Amendments were accepted from the Welsh Conservatives asserting and reaffirming the importance of S4C, and from Plaid Cymru recognizing the importance of the creative industries in Wales and acknowledging their contribution to the Welsh economy. The only point of contention in the plenary debate was Plaid's amendment calling for a communications users' council in Wales to supplement Ofcom's work. Owen John Thomas, in proposing this amendment, drew attention to the historical marginalization of Wales's distinct broadcasting problems. A users' council, he argued, would guarantee the peculiarities of Welsh broadcasting as well as ensuring the views of the Welsh audience would not be ignored by the new regulatory arrangements. This was not endorsed by the Assembly. Rejecting the amendment the minister stated that there was no need to add yet another layer to what had already been proposed by the Assembly to hear the voice of Welsh users and consumers.

The publication of the draft Communications Bill in May 2002 saw some softening in the government's position. Representation for Wales on Ofcom's main board was not accepted, but the government agreed on the specific representation of Welsh interests on the Content Board and Consumer Panel 'as far as was practicable'. The latter's role concerns issues of quality and standards in broadcasting while the former focuses on consumer concerns in matters of communication excluding content issues. Ofcom's structure was to dominate what passed for public debate on the proposed legislation in Wales. Many interested parties expressed their support for greater Welsh representation on the new body. The general feeling was that Ofcom was not directly accountable to Wales. Media organizations, trade unions and pressure groups as well as AMs and MPs expressed their concern that the proposed legislation did not go beyond expressions of good intent towards the nations and regions. The Welsh Assembly Government (WAG, 2002) was unequivocal on the matter of accountability. It demanded Welsh representation on Ofcom's main board as well as guarantees for specific representation on the Consumer Panel and Content Board. A statutory duty on the National Assembly to appoint the Welsh members on the Content Board and Consumer Panel was requested. In addition, WAG asked for the setting up of a Wales Communications Council 'to consider all the functions of Ofcom in Wales'. Ofcom should also be required to consider all representations on broadcasting from the Assembly and commitments to hold regular meetings in Wales, produce Wales-specific research and establish an office in Wales should be written into the legislation.

Intense lobbying produced some movement from the government. Reporting back, the minister stated that Ofcom's main board would not be increased to accommodate a representative from Wales but the Content Board and Consumer Panel would incorporate such representation (Andrews, 2004a). In addition, a Memorandum of Understanding was to be drawn up between Ofcom and the Assembly on the appointments. Following Ofcom's birth a Welsh representative was appointed to the Content Board and to the Consumer Panel. These appointments were made by the secretary of state for Wales in consultation with the Assembly but a memorandum is still today not agreed. Most significantly Ofcom was required to establish an advisory committee to ensure Wales has its say on a range of broadcasting, telecommunications and wireless communications matters as well as an input into shaping regulatory policy. The setting up of Ofcom's Advisory Committee for Wales as well as representation on the Content Board and the Consumer Panel was a success for the Assembly.

These appointments do not resolve the issue of accountability in Welsh broadcasting. The composition of the Advisory Committee was confirmed in March 2004. Ofcom's Welsh director says that the committee's membership represents a cross-section of the Welsh public (Ofcom, 2004a). The committee is comprised of a political consultant, a consultant radio telecommunications engineer, a former chairman of the ITC's Viewers Consultative Committee, the Disability Rights Commissioner for Wales, an e-professor at Cardiff Business School, a former director of personnel, the director of the WDA's digital media programme, an educational consultant who has worked for the BBC and S4C and a deputy head teacher. This is hardly representative of the Welsh public. The future of broadcasting in Wales, like its past, will be decided without a direct input from the Welsh public. This need not be so. Elsewhere in Europe public service broadcasting has found ways to involve the public directly. For example, in Austria licence-fee payers are allowed to elect one third of the members of the Audience Council which advises on programming issues (Trappel, 2004).

THE LOBBYING EFFORT

The debate around the establishment of Ofcom emphasized one aspect, the issue of Welsh representation. The minister of culture, Jenny Randerson, believed the Assembly had made progress by ensuring Wales had its voice heard in the new regulatory mechanisms and by establishing good working relations with Ofcom (Andrews, 2004a). It is also possible to claim that the Assembly's lobbying efforts helped to contribute to a shift, at least on paper, in the balance of interests between citizens and consumers. The Act, which became law in July 2003, confirmed that Ofcom's principal duty was to 'further the interests of citizens' *and* 'to further consumer interests in relevant markets where appropriate by promoting competition'. The chairman and chief executive of the new body were not happy with this decision (Barnett, 2002) and it remains to be seen how the concept of the 'citizen-consumer' will be interpreted in practice.

The Assembly's involvement in the Ofcom debate was not without its difficulties. Randerson, in her evidence to the Richard Commission, referred to the difficulties she encountered in getting the UK government 'to take account of Assembly Government policy interests, and to get these reflected in the Bill' (Randerson, 2002, p. 7). She told Richard she had to 'lobby hard'. She had regular meetings with DCMS and Welsh Office ministers, although no Westminster minister attended the Culture Committee (Andrews, 2004a). While Welsh MPs were made aware of the Assembly's concerns, it was members of the House of Lords who were most active in taking up these concerns in the passage of the Communications Bill through Parliament. Cross-bench members, such as Baroness Finlay whose amendment led to the government accepting the need for the establishment of National Advisory Committees, were particularly effective (Andrews, 2004a). There was also no public consultation by the Assembly on the proposed legislation. This was not necessarily the result of any failure on the Assembly's behalf but reflected the narrow time frame within which the legislation passed through Parliament. Public debate on the draft legislation was negligible. The crucial development was that the National Assembly established its right to have an input into broadcasting matters.

RENEWING ITS COMMITMENT? THE FUTURE OF THE BBC IN WALES

The BBC is going through one of the most turbulent periods in its history. The Hutton report was the culmination of sustained tensions between the BBC and New Labour. Blair's antipathy towards the corporation stems from several factors: the traditional distrust the Labour Party has of the BBC; New Labour's obsession with news management and spin control; and its ideological commitment to marketization and deregulation. The appointment of two New Labour supporters, Greg Dyke and Gavyn Davies, can be seen as part of an agenda to modernize 'Auntie'. However, the day-to-day pressures of setting the news agenda and the high political costs of the war against terrorism and the Iraq conflict strained relations between Dyke's and Davies's BBC and the government. Alastair Campbell's sustained attacks on the corporation reached their crescendo over Andrew Gilligan's report on the *Today* programme which set into motion a series of events which resulted in the death of Dr David Kelly. The Hutton inquiry into who was to blame unequivocally and, for most commentators, unfairly plumped for the BBC. Dyke's and Davies's resignations came in the midst of the renewal of the BBC's Royal Charter.

The importance of the BBC in Welsh life cannot be overestimated. The corporation has played a central role in Welsh political and intellectual life since the creation of the Welsh region of the BBC in the 1930s (Davies, 1994). The influence of BBC Cymru/Wales stems as much from its broad range of cultural and community activities as it does from its programme output. As a patron of the arts, a supporter and promoter of sports and sporting events, a major contributor to the economy, a key player in the maintenance of the Welsh language and the primary reporter of politics, there are few areas of Welsh public life the BBC does not reach (Jones, 2004). Most people in Wales identify BBC Wales as their main source of information (D. Williams, 2003; Andrews, 2004a). However, the growth of BBC Cymru/Wales has taken place in a context in which policy is controlled by London, described as a process of 'co-option by the centre of critical voices in the periphery' (Barlow, Mitchell and O'Malley, 2005). Proposals for more autonomous broadcasting structures for Wales, such as a Welsh Broad-casting Corporation put forward by Plaid Cymru in 1944 and more recently reiterated by the party in a policy paper *Broadcasting and Communications* (see Pritchard, 2003), have been rejected. The BBC in economic and cultural terms is a 'profoundly London-centric organisation' highlighted by the statistics that today 80 per cent of its budget is spent in London and 63 per cent of its employees are based in London (Morgan, 2004).

The reorientation of UK broadcasting policy towards the market and devolution have led to a gradual realignment of the relationship between the centre and periphery in British broadcasting. In Wales this can be seen in the 'nationalization' of broadcasting. Since the 1970s there has been an expansion of Welsh television and radio. A new television channel, increased Welsh representation on regulatory bodies, the growth of Welsh broadcasting output in both languages and the small increase of Welsh material on network television are all indications of this. BBC Wales has made a major contribution to this development, launching Radio Cymru and Radio Wales as well as contributing 520 hours free every year to S4C. One recent step forward was the launch of BBC 2W in 2001. A digital service, this channel is dedicated to serving English-speaking Wales. Increased financial support in the form of the 'devolution dividend' has assisted this process.

This process is now under threat. Following a review, Ofcom foresees major changes in public service broadcasting in the UK (Ofcom, 2004b). The BBC's own proposals, outlined in *Building Public Value: Renewing the BBC for a Digital World*, envisage a major restructuring of its operation (BBC, 2004a). Perhaps the most crucial relates to the governance of the corporation which proposes a new relationship between the BBC governors and management. The aim is to make the governors more independent of BBC management and enable them to scrutinize more effectively what the broadcasters do. A new public-value test underpins the process of scrutiny, applying criteria such as reach, quality, impact and value for money to the performance of the BBC. The role of the governors will be strengthened and a number of means will be developed to make them more responsive to the public and their concerns. One such means will be to enhance the ability of the BBC's Broadcasting, Regional and Local Advisory Councils to commission their own research.

In Wales these developments will see changes in the role of the national governor and the BCW. There appears to be support for the recommendation of the Welsh Affairs Committee report in 1999 that the BCW should be radically reformed and separated from BBC management. Little attention has been paid to the composition of the BCW. Supposed to represent the views of the Welsh public, the BCW is 'unrepresentative of the audience' and 'representative only of the professional middle class' (Andrews, 2004b). Maintaining the present composition would seem an inappropriate means to represent the views of the people of Wales in the post-devolution world. Rather than reform the body some AMs advocate the BCW's abolition, proposing instead that the National Assembly is the 'best forum for determining a Welsh input into communication issues' and to ascertain the views of the Welsh public on broadcasting matters (Andrews, 2004b).

The BBC aims to make the organization 'less London centric' (BBC, 2004b, p. 108). To facilitate this, it is considering plans to increase network expenditure outside London, to encourage network production across the UK, to transfer some commissioning power outside the M25 and to devolve administrative and support operation out of London which is an increasingly expensive area for such activities. Specific targets are attached to this wish list. By the end of the next charter period 50 per cent of the BBC's public service staff will be based outside London, there will be an increase of 35 per cent in the amount spent on programming outside London and a fifth of commissioning decisions will be made outside of London. Whether these targets will be achieved depends on internal mechanisms. Recent changes in BBC management raise some doubts about who is going to guarantee that these targets are met.

Under Greg Dyke the BBC controllers in the nation-regions did not have a place on the BBC's Executive Committee, where all the major decisions about the running of the corporation are made. But they did have a representative, the director of nations and regions, based in London, who was a member of the committee. In recent years this person negotiated how much of the BBC's licence fee is spent in Wales and the other nations and regions. The Executive Committee is responsible to the Board of Governors on which sit the national governors for Wales, Scotland and Northern Ireland. Not perhaps the most satisfactory arrangements for the input of the views of the nations and regions but one at least where their interests were directly represented at the top table. These arrangements have been one of the casualties post-Hutton. New Director-General Mark Thompson has reduced the size of the Executive Committee, removing the nations and regions director. BBC Wales no longer has a direct line of communication into the BBC's main decision-making forum. This decision runs counter to sentiment in Wales, which since devolution supports greater representation for Wales. The Welsh Affairs Committee summed up the view of many in Wales when it agreed that there was far too much control of BBC Wales from London and recommended that the controller of BBC Wales be given 'greater status' within the BBC, and that more decision-making and budgetary control be devolved to Cardiff.

WAG's response to the BBC charter review process is to reaffirm its faith in 'what the BBC does and what it stands for' and welcome the increased investment the BBC has made in Wales since devolution (Pugh, 2004a). The thrust of the minister of Culture's comments resonate with the 1999 Welsh Affairs Committee report which stressed the need to guarantee the accessibility of the BBC's services to all the people in Wales in the post-analogue world. The problems of reception in Wales are again stressed as well as the need to increase BBC Wales's contribution to the network. WAG's emphasis on the BBC's 'overall remit to service the UK as a whole' corresponds with the BBC's stated desire to become less London-centric. However, the minister is not convinced that the promised dispersal of staff and production out of London will benefit Wales (Pugh, 2004b). Other responses to the charter review include support for the extension of licence-fee concessions and independent mechanisms to assess complaints of bias against the BBC. WAG does not believe the governors should be the 'sole judge' of impartiality and accuracy. Finally, there is a plea for a 'stronger link between the BBC and the people of Wales' and a 'clearer role' for the Assembly in relation not only to the BBC but to broadcasting in Wales. In relation to the latter, the minister, in response to Ofcom's public service review, expressed concerns about the future of S4C and ITV Wales.

WHITHER S4C?

The digital world poses a 'challenge' to S4C which is becoming more acute as the date for switching off analogue comes nearer. S4C launched its digital service in 1999. Today it has two digital channels. S4C1 operates twelve hours per day, seven days a week, including simultaneous transmission of the analogue service. This channel will be the Welsh-language channel for Wales when analogue is switched off. S4C2 is a joint operation with BBC Wales and provides coverage of National Assembly proceedings in both languages. The future of this channel is not clear. In addition, S4C leases several more channels through the company SDN in which it holds a substantial interest. To maintain a distinct identity, deliver a comprehensive service and produce programmes of high quality in the proliferation of channels in a multi-channel age, S4C faces several problems. The most pressing is how to make enough programmes to fill additional airtime. At present S4C is sustained by Channel 4 programmes and ten hours of free programming from BBC Wales each week. The 'sustaining service' of Channel 4 disappears in the digital world. The present funding formula is insufficient to enable S4C to meet the shortfall. Already S4C spends almost £10 million per annum to support the digital service (*Herald*, 2002; *Western Mail*, 2002a). In 2002 S4C appealed to the DCMS for additional funds without which Chief Executive Huw Jones warned the channel's 'ability not only to continue to deliver digital services but to deliver sponsorship, training' would be damaged (*Broadcast*, 2002). Unlike other broadcasters in the UK, S4C has not received any increase in financial support to develop and deliver digital services (S4C, 2004a, p. 33). Seeking additional subsidy is politically sensitive. S4C's subsidy has risen by about 20 per cent since 1997; it received £86 million from DCMS in 2004

(DCMS, 2004, p. 9). The level of subsidy has brought forth regular criticisms from sections of Welsh society (see *Swansea Evening Post*, 2001a, 2001b). For long-term critics such as Labour MP Llew Smith, the subsidy would be 'better spent tackling poverty in [the] valleys . . .' (*Welsh Mirror*, 2002). In such circumstances it was not a surprise that the request was turned down.

Justifying additional spending at a time when the number of people watching the channel is declining is a further problem. The channel's twentieth anniversary coincided with what was described as an 'alarming slide in popularity' (*Herald*, 2002). Between 1996 and 2004 the channel's share of the Welsh-speaking audience viewing at peak time has fallen from around 20 per cent to just above 10 per cent (DCMS, 2004, p. 12). Weekly reach to all viewers in all hours has dropped by one third. Young viewers are put off: 'we are proud our parents struggled to set up S4C – but we can't bring ourselves to watch it' (*Western Mail*, 2002b). Flagship programmes such as the long-running soap opera *Pobol Y Cwm* have seen a significant fall in their audience. By 2002, S4C's share of all viewing was only 5.2 per cent. Dwindling audiences are experienced by all terrestrial channels but for a channel with a small viewing public it is a serious matter. Increasing digital penetration is making the situation worse as S4C has to face greater competition from the wide variety of other channels and non-Welsh speakers have little incentive to tune in as S4C Digidol has no English programmes.

Without an injection of additional funds S4C has targeted the BBC as a way to solve its digital problem. S4C asks that the 'nature and scale of the BBC's contribution to the S4C service, and consequently to Welsh language television, should be re-defined . . .' (S4C, 2004b, pp. 5–6). What this means in practice is that the BBC should contribute more than the present ten hours per week of free programming. S4C believes the BBC's charter should be amended to stipulate that the BBC has a 'duty to contribute to programmes for broadcast alongside those produced under S4C's programme strategy' in order to 'ensure that the BBC's programming contribution is led by the need to contribute to the delivery of that strategy' (S4C, 2004b, p. 7). In other words, S4C wants more control over what kinds of programmes are made for them by the BBC. The DCMS's review into S4C came to the same conclusion (DCMS, 2004). The BBC's response remains to be seen but it is clear that relations between Wales's two public service broadcasters will become increasingly important in the future development of Welsh broadcasting. Rivalry has characterized the relationship in recent years. S4C's decision to bid for the rights to Welsh rugby in 1999, to which it already had free access from BBC Wales, was seen as an example of unnecessary competition which operated against the public interest (Welsh Affairs Committee, 1999, xii, pp. 14–15). Closer ties on programme provision raise the question as to whether there should be a more fundamental restructuring of the management and running of Welsh-language television.

ITV WALES – BROADCASTING IN THE GRAVEYARD?

As BBC Wales and S4C wrestle with the problems of cooperating in a world without analogue, ITV in Wales is contemplating the winding up of the distinct regional service it has provided to Wales since the mid-1950s. Much has happened since 1999 when the Welsh Affairs Committee charged the Assembly with ensuring that HTV would continue its commitment to Wales. HTV executives pledged to increase their output and make it 'a better reflection of the Welsh culture' in response to devolution and, in particular, to double their drama from ten to twenty hours per year from 1999 (Welsh Affairs Committee, 1999, p. 11). The committee welcomed these promises but appeared sceptical as to the company's ability to deliver. This scepticism was well founded. Since 1999 commercial broadcasting in Wales has been diminished. HTV Wales and the West is no more, swallowed up by a much larger company. Maintaining a separate identity for Wales within the dual franchise was always an issue. In 2000 HTV was taken over by Carlton, resulting in the abandonment of the commitment to increase drama output and a consequent reduction of jobs (Equity, 2002). In 2003 the Carlton and Granada merger saw HTV Wales and the West became a small component of a much bigger concern. HTV's on-screen identity had already disappeared to be replaced by the ITV logo.

The restructuring of ITV has been at the expense of the regional character of the network. In spite of an extra £3 million and the drawing up of a 'new charter for the nations and regions' in 2002, the new ITV has increasingly marginalized local programming and commitments to the nations and regions of the United Kingdom. On screen there has been a standardization of regional programming. This is most noticeable in news output, with ITV regional news programmes adopting a similar format. The number of hours of regional programming has fallen – in 2002 ITV1 reduced local output by 12 per cent (BBC, 2004a, p. 77). Besides news and major sporting events most of ITV's local programming in Wales is broadcast outside of prime time, shunted to late-night or afternoon slots. In July 2004 concerns were expressed by staff from ITV Wales that there would be a 25 per cent cut in programmes made in Wales in the next year, with some of ITV Wales's flagship programmes such as the current affairs show *Wales This Week* at risk (*Western Mail*, 2004a). Such claims are rejected by the company although staff were worried enough to meet with Ofcom to discuss their fears.

Staff concerns are shared by others. The House of Commons Culture, Media and Sport Select Committee report, *Broadcasting in Transition* (2004), backed the view that ITV regional news should be produced locally and criticized the speed and way in which ITV had proceeded with the downgrading of regional production facilities. It stated that the 'protection and maintenance of regional commitments by Channel 3 licensees' would be the first 'major test of Ofcom'. ITV's commitments to Wales, according to a leading figure in Welsh television, can be guaranteed only by a robust regulator (*Western Mail*, 2004b).

Ofcom has not passed its first major test and has proven itself far from robust in the defence of regional television. It has recently reduced ITV's obligations to make programmes specifically for the English regions, halving the amount to a mere ninety minutes a week. Armed with research findings that go against the welter of data over the years that local programming is popular with audiences, Ofcom is presiding over a radical restructuring of local broadcasting and the nature of public service. Many broadcasters and, less understandably, commentators seem to have been publicly cowed by the aggressive stance of the new body. Ofcom can be seen as trying to determine rather than regulate broadcasting. The chairman of the Media Select Committee, Gerald Kaufman, is worried about 'the way in which Ofcom is extending its remit' and its desire to 'remodel broadcasting' (*Broadcast*, 2004). A 'Big Brother' organization unrepresentative of the public, committed to promoting the market and failing to defend fully the needs and wants of local communities has major implications for the future of broadcasting in Wales.

CONCLUSION

There are many reasons for the National Assembly to become more involved in broadcasting policy. Since 1999, whether it has wanted to or not, the Assembly has slowly become more involved. In particular its lobbying around the legislation to set up new regulatory arrangements ensured that a Welsh voice, albeit a weak one, would be heard inside Ofcom. However, in the new broadcasting world that is being built there is a demand from, amongst others, WAG for the Assembly to play an increased role in broadcasting matters. There are strong arguments for this especially in the area of accountability. There is a question over the Assembly's ability and capacity to do this. Some of the contributions to Assembly debates on broadcasting have not indicated a high degree of maturity and knowledge. In particular, the degree of hostility vented against S4C by some AMs must raise concerns about its well-being. The recent spats between BBC Wales and WAG over the reporting of the Assembly do not show an awareness of the long-term importance of broadcasting to national and public life in Wales. Above all, there is the failure of the Assembly since 1999 to adopt an effective communication policy. But if broadcasting in Wales is to survive and thrive it is essential that there is concerted, informed and vocal political and public pressure to ensure that BBC, ITV and S4C maintain their commitments to Wales. Welsh broadcasting is too valuable to be left in the hands of Ofcom, an organization whose actions indicate an indifference to broadcasting in the periphery.

REFERENCES

Andrews, L. (2001). 'Fears over regional isolation', *Western Mail*, October 17.
Andrews, L. (2004a). 'Finding its voice – the National Assembly for Wales and Broadcasting Policy 1999–2003', paper presented to Communications in Wales after the Communications Act conference held at the University of Aberystwyth, 29 March.
Andrews, L. (2004b). BBC Charter Review: a response to the consultation document from Leighton Andrews AM, *www.bbccharterreview.org.uk*
Barlow, D., Mitchell, P. and O'Malley, T. (2005). *The Media in Wales: Voices of a Small Nation*, Cardiff: University of Wales Press.
Barnett, S. (2002). 'Caught between Alastair and the deep Tory blue sea', *Observer*, 13 July.
Blandford, S. and Upton, J. (1996). 'Courting the network', *Planet*, 117, June/July, 70–6.
BBC (2004a). *Building Public Value: Renewing the BBC for a Digital World*, London: BBC.
BBC (2004b). *Review of the BBC's Royal Charter: the BBC's Response to the DCMS Consultation*, London: BBC.
Broadcast (2002). 'S4C appeals for cash injection', 8 March.
Broadcast (2004). 'Ofcom's blue sky thinking', 8 October.
Davies, J. (1994). *Broadcasting and the BBC in Wales*, Cardiff: University of Wales Press.
Department of Culture, Media and Sport (DCMS) (2004). *S4C: An Independent Review*, London: DCMS.
Department of Culture, Media and Sport (DCMS) and Cabinet of the National Assembly for Wales (CNAfW) (2000). 'Concordat between the Department for Culture, Sport and Media and the Cabinet of the National Assembly for Wales', June 2000, *www.wales.gov.uk/kepubconcord/content/concordats/dcms_e.htm*
Department of Trade and Industry (DTI)/Department of Culture, Media and Sport (DCMS) (2000). *A New Future for Communications*, London: DTI / DCMS.
Department of Trade and Industry (DTI) (1998). *Regulating Communications: Approaching Convergence in the Information Age*, London: HMSO.
Equity (2002). *Submission to the National Assembly Culture Committee on the Communications Bill*, Cardiff: National Assembly for Wales.
Freedman, D. (2003). *Television Policies of the Labour Party 1951–2001*, London: Frank Cass.

Herald (2002). 'TV awards fail to keep S4C viewers', 11 July.
Hill, S. (2003). *The Welsh Connection: The Economic Impact of BBC Wales*, Glamorgan Business School: University of Glamorgan.
House of Commons, Culture, Media and Sport Committee (2004). *Broadcasting in Transition*, Third Report 2003–4, London: HMSO.
Jones, M. (2004). Foreword to *Defining a Nation: Wales and the BBC*, Cardiff: BBC Wales.
Morgan, K. (2004). 'London v The Rest: the polycentric challenge cup', in *Defining a Nation: Wales and the BBC*, Cardiff: BBC Wales.
National Assembly for Wales (NAfW) (1999). 'Broadcasting in Wales'. Plenary Record, 16 November, Cardiff: NAfW.
National Assembly for Wales (NAfW) (2001). 'Assembly Debates Communications in Wales', press release, 8 February. Cardiff: NAfW.
Ofcom (2004a). 'Ofcom appoints members of Advisory Committee for Wales', press release, 27 February, London: Ofcom.
Ofcom (2004b). Ofcom *Review of Public Service Television Broadcasting*, London: Ofcom.
Post-16 Education and Training Committee (2000). Minutes of 10 May, 2000 ETR 10–00 (min).
Pritchard, G. (2003). *Broadcasting and Communications Policy for Wales 2003–2007*, *www.plaidcymru.org.polbroadcastingdisc.html*
Pugh, A. (2004a). Response to Review of BBC's Royal Charter, 25 May, *www.bbccharterreview.org.uk*
Pugh, A. (2004b). 'Remote control', *Western Mail*, 12 August.
Randerson, J. (2002). Written evidence to the Richard Commission, Cardiff: National Assembly for Wales.
Ryan, M. (1986). 'Blocking the channels: TV and film in Wales', in T. Curtis (ed.), *Wales: the Imagined Nation*, Bridgend: Poetry of Wales Press.
S4C (2004a). *S4C Review: A Welsh Language Television Service fit for the 21st Century?*, Cardiff: S4C.
S4C (2004b). *S4C Response to the Review of the BBC's Royal Charter*, Cardiff: S4C, March.
Swansea Evening Post (2001a). 'S4C costs £214k a day', 5 July.
Swansea Evening Post (2001b). 'Welsh channel hits back over cost flak', 9 July.
Talfan Davies, G. (1999). *Not By Bread Alone: Information, Media and the National Assembly*, Cardiff: Centre for Journalism Studies.
Trappel, J. (2004). 'Austria', in M. Kelly, G. Mazzoleni and D. McQuail (eds), *The Media in Europe*, London: Sage.
Welsh Affairs Committee (1999). *Broadcasting in Wales and the National Assembly*, London: HMSO.
Welsh Assembly Government (WAG) (2002). 'Response to the draft communications Bill', *www.wales.gov.uk/subculture/content/resp-comms-e.htm*
Welsh Mirror (2002). 'Axe struggling S4C, MP urges', 3 July.
Western Mail (2002a). 'S4C must learn to switch on the viewers again', 3 August.
Western Mail (2002b). 'S4C refused extra cash to meet rising costs of digital service', 4 October.
Western Mail (2004a). 'Worried TV staff meet the man from Ofcom', 20 July.
Western Mail (2004b). 'Watchdog "must make sure Wales doesn't lose out under single ITV"' 17 October.

Williams, D. (2003). 'Stirring up apathy', in *Agenda: The Journal of the Institute of Welsh Affairs*, Winter.

Williams, K. (1997). *Shadows and Substance: The Development of a Media Policy for Wales*, Llandysul: Gomer Press.

Williams, K. (2003). 'An uneasy relationship: the National Assembly and the press and media', in J. Barry Jones and J. Osmond (eds), *Building a Civic Culture*, Cardiff: Institute of Welsh Affairs.

14. IDENTIFYING NEED: DEVOLVED SPENDING IN WALES, SCOTLAND AND NORTHERN IRELAND

R. Ross Mackay

ABSTRACT

The implicit assumption of the Barnett Formula is that expenditure levels in Wales, Scotland and Northern Ireland should move ever closer to those in England. This implicit assumption ignores differences in prosperity and differences in need. Relative needs vary from country to country. The measures used in this article suggest that relative devolved spending is already too low in Wales. Moreover, more realistic measures of relative need would be important in moderating the Barnett squeeze on Northern Ireland and Scotland. With devolved spending in Wales, Scotland and Northern Ireland determined by relative need, there would be rough consistency across eleven of the twelve UK regions. Expenditure on London's public services would remain well above London's level of need (as measured by relative poverty, or relative income). The growing imbalance within the UK economy has contributed to the exceptionally high cost of the capital's public services.

INTRODUCTION: LET NEED BE THE GUIDE

It is a long-established principle that all areas of the UK are entitled to the same level of public services and that *expenditure on them should be allocated according to relative need*. (Treasury, 1979, p. 4, author's italics)

In its report on the Barnett Formula, the Treasury Committee agreed with Treasury officials that . . . all governments would subscribe to the fact that spending should broadly reflect needs. (Edmonds, 2001, p. 17)

This article concentrates on devolved spending in Wales, Scotland and Northern Ireland. It takes its central theme from the Treasury's continued acceptance of relative need as the correct guide to public spending in the four countries of the United Kingdom (see introductory quotations above). The existing financial settlement embraces the Barnett Formula and accepts an arbitrary target: convergence on English spending levels. That arbitrary target ignores differences in need and will (in the fullness of time) notably reduce relative spending in the devolved territories. As this article illustrates, the approaches and measures that have been suggested do not point to the desirability of convergence on English spending levels. In building from principle, we take relative need as the guide to devolved spending.

The Barnett Formula is a divergence-reducing mechanism. Given the Barnett Formula, there are two elements in deciding the annual block grant (for Wales, Scotland and Northern Ireland). First, there is an inherited expenditure bias (pre the rigorous application of Barnett), with devolved spending per head higher in Northern Ireland, Scotland and Wales than in England. Secondly, year-by-year changes in devolved spending are divided equally in line with population. With inherited spending frozen, expenditure per head in Northern Ireland, Scotland and Wales will, over time, move closer and closer to (without ever quite reaching) English levels. The pace of convergence will depend on the rate of growth of relevant public spending. Inflation, as well as real expenditure increases, will reduce divergence.

As a rough-and-ready guide, given a 5 per cent annual compound growth in UK block spending, the increments (allocated according to population) would be equal in importance to inherited levels in roughly fourteen years. With 8 per cent annual compound growth, the increments would equal the inherited levels within nine years.[1] A week may be a long time in politics, but nine years is a brief introduction to a financial settlement that decides relative spending in Wales, Scotland, Northern Ireland and England. In any one year the Barnett squeeze is gentle. But considered over a number of years the effect would be ruthless and substantial. It would ensure that the Welsh, the Northern Irish and the Scots all lose. Spending on medicine, education and law and order would be confined. Standards of public goods would be difficult to maintain and jobs would be lost.

Devolved spending is central to this article. But devolved spending connects to wider themes that explore the relationship between regions. These include fiscal transfer between regions, growing regional imbalance within the UK economy, non-market forces, automatic stabilizers and national unity. These wider themes connect to arguments introduced by Myrdal (1957) and Hirschman (1958). Myrdal and Hirschman argue that non-market forces may be the key to understanding any reduction in regional inequality. The non-market forces that contain regional divergence emerge naturally, almost inevitably within advanced nation-states: they may be just as 'automatic' as market forces. They are a response to weaknesses of capitalism; they address problems the market cannot reach. Regional tax and regional public expenditure are sensitive to regional income levels: they adjust to shifts in relative prosperity. Compensation systems (transfers from rich to poor regions) are both a product of national solidarity and a source of national identity (see Myrdal, 1957; Hirschman, 1958; Mackay, 1993, 1994, 2001a).

Public spending is above tax in Scotland, Wales and Northern Ireland. This 'subsidy' is seen as unfair to the English taxpayer. Public spending is above tax in seven of the twelve UK regions, including four out of nine English regions (see Mackay, 2001a). Public expenditure above tax is the standard pattern in the poorer parts of a free market economy such as the United States of America and also in the poorer parts of more collective economies such as Sweden and Norway. The nation is a civil society. People have rights and obligations of citizenship. Within the welfare state, the well-being of each citizen is weighted on a broadly equal basis. Equal treatment of equal citizens is an Enlightenment ideal. Everybody is important: the key to valuable lives is that each citizen be given the opportunity to develop potential. Transfer flows from the attempt to ensure that payment of tax at the same rate in prosperous and less prosperous parts of the nation-state result in comparable levels of service.

Wales, Scotland and Northern Ireland remain part of a wider community. Within the nation there are common bonds and obligations that link people who will never meet. Transfers are political: they keep the Kingdom United. They are also economic. The forms of competition that emerge in practice are completely different from the economists' competitive ideal. Actions and conditions that promote growth move the economy away from perfect competition. Growth depends on innovation. Innovations destroy, even as they create and creation and destruction are geographically separate. Growth is, by its very nature, unbalanced and uneven (Schumpeter, 1943). It is more like a series of explosions than gentle, incessant transformation. The destructive side of creative destruction is real and it hurts. It removes resources and possibilities that supported families and communities. The dislocations, upheavals and losses that flow from competition are not accidental by-products, they are part and parcel of capitalist reality. Fortunately, within the nation-state, we do not have to rely exclusively on yet more intense competition and even greater mobility to save us from trouble.

Transfer is consistent with federal systems that grant substantially more power to states (or regions) than has been devolved to Scotland, Wales or Northern Ireland. The important distinction between federal states and unitary states is that transfers are likely to be clear, explicit and recognized in the former, but they are often a source of surprise in unitary states. The UK remains a unitary state. No sub-national tier of government has (as yet) constitutional status. It is unlike other unitary states. It does not have a uniform system of government below national level. Asymmetrical devolution ensures that the UK is also a union state. The Welsh and Scottish nations and the Northern Irish have special status within the framework of government. Special status includes responsibility for devolved (or block-grant) expenditure. With devolution, the financial settlement between England, Wales, Scotland and Northern Ireland becomes a means of transferring money between governments, not a system internal to one government (Heald, 1998, p.76). A financial settlement between governments should be open and explicit; it should build from principle and be acceptable to all parts of the United Kingdom.

The key claim of this article is that the Barnett squeeze is not inevitable. The Treasury accepts that need is the fair and correct guide for devolved spending. The Barnett Formula is in place only because there is no accepted compromise on how to measure relative country need. Convergence on England would (in the fullness of time) notably reduce relative spending in Wales, Scotland and Northern Ireland. The second section of this article looks at devolved spending in the twelve regions and four countries of the United Kingdom: it also explores regional imbalance. The third section considers different approaches to measuring country need: it recommends a poverty-based measure. The fourth section concludes.

DEVOLVED SPENDING

The Committee was disappointed that no Government studies had been made in relation to . . . [how] the Barnett Formula . . . relates to needs . . . it is important that there should be maximum possible agreement . . . in all parts of the UK. (Treasury Committee, 1997, p.12)

The UK is a union state. There is a formal reservation of specific powers to the Scottish Parliament and the Welsh and Northern Ireland Assemblies. Block-grant expenditure funds those powers. Devolution is designed to add to citizen choice. The Scottish Parliament and the Assemblies can select the spending patterns that are relevant to their populations. Special status creates the need for clear, specific guidelines on relative spending levels.

The published data do not allow us to calculate block-grant expenditure precisely, but they do permit estimates that are reasonably close. In this article

devolved spending is regional identifiable spending, less expenditure on social
security and agriculture.[2] Devolved spending is not the responsibility of regional
tiers of government within England, but it is possible to identify devolved
spending levels in the nine English regions. In the UK, devolved spending is less
than half of total public spending. In the UK, and also in Scotland, Wales and
Northern Ireland, health, education and law and order dominate devolved
spending. These three account for 8 out of every 10 pounds of devolved spending
in the UK. Health is the major component of devolved spending – 4 out of every
10 pounds – with education the second most important – 2.5 out of every 10
pounds. When considering need, it is important to remember that health, education
and law and order dominate devolved spending.

Figure 14.1 Variable labour markets
work income – by region 2001

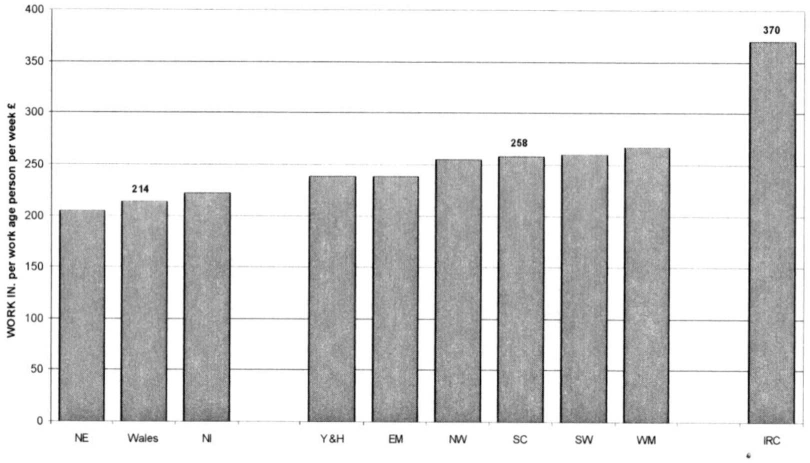

Source: Employment and Self Employment Data from *Regional Trends* and *Labour Market Trends*.

Employee earnings data from NOMIS.

Self employed earnings from Inland Revenue.

Needs connect to low opportunity, low incomes and to concentrations of poverty. Low incomes and poverty contribute to ill health, to educationaldisadvantage, to antisocial behaviour, including crime and drug abuse. Low incomes and poverty add to the pressures on the welfare state. Figure 14.1 shows work income per person of working age in different regions of the United Kingdom. Work income combines income from employment and self-employment: it includes part-time work. The regions separate into three groups. The low-income group is the North East, Wales and Northern Ireland. The high-income territory is the Inner Region Core (IRC) and accounts for three of the nine English regions (London, South East, East) and over one-third of the UK population. The Inner Region Core comprises the capital city and its extensive commuting zone and has substantially higher levels of work income than all other parts of the United Kingdom. The middle-income group includes Scotland. The differences in regional work income are substantial and they have expanded notably in the last quarter of the twentieth century (see Mackay, 2003).

Regional differences in claimant count unemployment are slight, but regional differences in employment and in levels of work are substantial. In the low-opportunity regions, a high proportion of the potential workforce is inactive. Discouraged workers and disguised unemployment are the key to understanding the considerable differences in productive employment within the United Kingdom.[3] In the nine regions outside the IRC, work income per person of working age was only 67 per cent of the IRC level in 2001. Capital, employment, income and people (particularly the well qualified) have been drawn to the most prosperous and high-cost part of the UK. Welsh work income per person of working age is only 58 per cent of the Inner Region Core level and 83 per cent of the Scottish level.[4] Low work incomes in Wales, Northern Ireland and the North East are a product of too few jobs and low earnings in work.[5] The key to a well-functioning labour market is that jobs should be available.[6]

In looking for an overall pattern to devolved spending, one might expect that the lower the level of prosperity, the higher the level of devolved spending. Given such a pattern, the state would be using a common fund (the national exchequer) to support citizens in regions that have the least successful labour markets.[7] Given such a pattern, the state would compensate for some of the disadvantages that follow from a weak economic base. Given such a pattern, the social wage would be raised in relatively poor regions. A pattern of devolved spending that favoured low-income regions would recognize that those who live by their labour are at particular risk when their capacity to earn is removed or notably reduced in a process of structural decline.

Figure 14.2 allows regional per capita devolved spending to be checked against per capita Gross Value Added (GVA) in each of the twelve UK regions. Gross Value Added is a broader measure of income than work income (it includes profit and rent, as well as work income). It is close to the measure used by the European Union in deciding eligibility for Objective One status. It is the form of measure most often employed when comparing regional living standards within and across countries. For nine regions, relative prosperity (Gross Value Added) is a rough guide to devolved spending levels. If we accept that relative income is a guide to relative need, the pattern in those nine regions is consistent with the Treasury belief that 'spending should broadly reflect needs' (see introductory quotations).[8]

**Figure 14.2 Devolved expenditure prosperity
related – three clear exceptions**

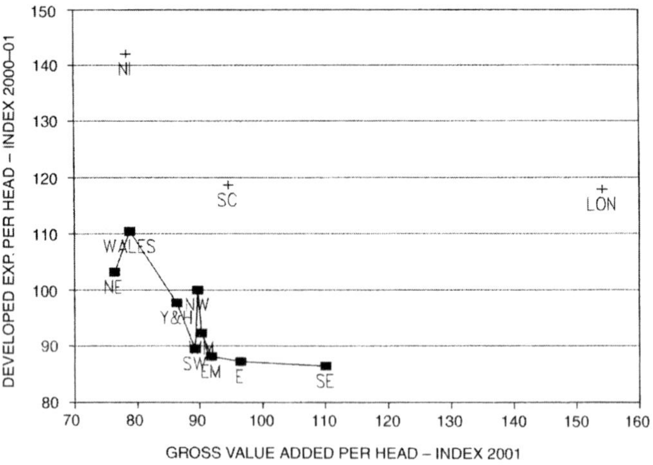

Source: Treasury 2002 and *Economic Trends.*

There are three clear exceptions to the rough consistency between relative regional income and relative devolved spending. In Northern Ireland, Scotland and London devolved spending is far higher than their prosperity levels would indicate. Scotland has higher levels of devolved spending than seven regions that have lower living standards. London is by a considerable margin the most prosperous region within the United Kingdom, but devolved spending in London is comfortably above the levels in all other English regions and 18 per cent higher than the United Kingdom average. The differences in devolved spending are substantial. In 2000–1, devolved spending per head was £1,600 higher (64 per cent) in Northern Ireland than in south-east England. In the same financial year, devolved spending per head was £859 higher (34 per cent) in London than in the east Midlands.

The high levels of public expenditure in London are the product of the capital's high cost of living. London is 'jaw-droppingly expensive' (Lonely Planet, 2003, p. 92). That horrendous expense applies to public goods and services, as well as those provided by the market. High levels of public expenditure in London do not provide public services that are the envy of the rest of the country. The concentration of political power is central to the production of regional inequality within the UK. The centralization of political and economic power is a problem. Indeed, the substantial cost of the capital's public services is both a burden on the rest of the country and an excellent guide to the economic and social advantages that would flow from decentralization (Mackay, 2003). Capitalist evolution is not and cannot be smooth. Creative destruction is the driving force of the capitalist economy. Creation and destruction are geographically divorced. The new destroys the old, but it does not grow out of the old. The UK regional problem is that creation has promoted the most prosperous, most congested, most expensive parts of the UK and settled on locations where development is a problem and is frequently opposed (see Mackay, 1993). Destruction has concentrated on less prosperous parts of the UK, leaving gaps in communities and voids in the economy which individuals and families struggle to bridge. Without a strong regional policy, there is always a danger that markets will concentrate wealth and opportunity on the already prosperous parts of the nation.[9] The uneven development within the United Kingdom is a problem. It produces inflationary tendencies in some parts of the economy, while resources remain underdeveloped and undiscovered in others (see Treasury, 2001, p. 29). A regional policy that favours all regions is inadequate to the growing disparities within the UK. Differentiating between regions is in the national interest. It would even add to the well-being of those who live and work in the most prosperous but also the most pressured and congested parts of the UK.

Figure 14.3 Devolved spending by country and prosperity

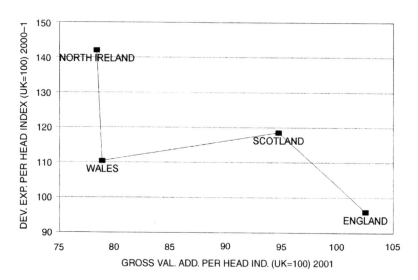

Source: Treasury 2002 and *Economic Trends.*

Figure 14.3 shows Gross Value Added per head and devolved spending per head in the four countries of the United Kingdom. There are two reasons for this diagram. First, English devolved spending is more accurately measured than devolved spending in the individual English regions (Treasury, 2002; Nuffield College, 2003). Secondly, the diagram allows direct comparison of Wales, Scotland, Northern Ireland and England. Wales is a less prosperous country than Scotland, with GVA per head only 83 per cent of the Scottish level, but devolved spending is 7 per cent lower. High levels of devolved spending in Scotland flow from the strength of the Scottish Office, the influence of Scottish secretaries of state and from the delicate union between Scotland and England. Scotland's favoured treatment, McCormick and Alexander (1997, p. 159) claim, 'reflects, or simply buys off, Scotland's legitimate aspirations for genuine democratic control of its own affairs' (for greater detail, see Mackay and Williams, forthcoming; McLean and McMillan, 2003). In Northern Ireland, devolved spending per head is 29 per cent above the Welsh level, even though the two countries now have similar standards of living. The 'troubles' are relevant to high public spending in Northern Ireland.

MEASURING NEED

The Barnett Formula has 'become a mechanism for transferring money *between tiers of government*, not a mechanism *internal to one government*'. (Heald, 1998, p. 76, emphasis in original).

Dividing public money between governments requires a system that is transparent and reasonably acceptable to all. Within England, relative need is an important guide to spending levels in different parts of England. Let us take three relevant examples:

1. A recent policy announcement suggested that it might be desirable to encourage young adults aged 17–18 to remain in school. This could involve cash incentives and these would be means tested.
2. Standardized Mortality Ratios are used to represent and identify regional differentials in need for medical services. The higher the mortality rate, the higher the regional expenditure on health services.[10]
3. The Acheson Inquiry into inequality in health concluded 'those with low levels of educational achievement have poor adult health. . . . Logic and Equity argue that children in need should receive increased resources for their education' (Acheson, 1998, pp. 37–8). The inquiry recommended that the Revenue Support Grant Formula should be more generously weighted to reflect need and socio-economic advantage. Education is critical to health and the report argued for a health policy designed to 'favour the less well off', so reducing health inequalities.

The key point (there are many other relevant examples) is that needs (usually connected to low incomes and poverty) are used to guide relative spending and changes to relative spending within England. But needs and changes in needs are not reflected in the Barnett approach. The implicit assumption of the Barnett Formula is that expenditure levels in Wales, Scotland and Northern Ireland should move ever closer to those in England. This implicit assumption ignores differences in prosperity and differences in need.

Resource allocations are a sensitive political issue. Decisions have to be made on the basis of imperfect knowledge. The Treasury Needs Assessment Study (Treasury, 1979) of the late 1970s was undertaken because of the then expected devolution to Scotland and Wales and the desire to find a more defensible basis for divisions of public expenditure. The study proved unequal to the challenge. The study constructed an overall measure of relative country need from six measures of programme need (health, education, housing, other environmental services, roads and transport, law and order). The overall indicators of relative per capita need for 1976–7 (the amount required to provide the same range and level of services in each country) were: England, 100; Wales, 109; Scotland, 116; Northern Ireland, 131.

The figures are of historic interest, but the Needs Assessment Report is an important guide to Treasury thinking. We may learn from this failure to identify relative country need. There are four clear indications of failure. First, the study has never been repeated. Secondly, it has had no influence on relative expenditure in the four countries. Thirdly, the Barnett Formula rather than relative need became the *apparent* guide to change in relative expenditure levels. Fourthly, the Barnett Formula remains in place even though it has been more honoured in the breach than in the observance. The Treasury Needs Assessment Report admitted, 'there is no "right" answer, either overall or *a fortiori for the individual programmes*' (Treasury, 1979, p. 3, author's italics). A 'right' answer will remain beyond reach. The Treasury study failed because it did not provide an acceptable compromise. The report emphasized the importance of objective indicators. Again and again it accepted past expenditure relatives as objective measures of relative country need. This is a curiously circular approach and we now know (as many knew at the time of the Treasury study) that relative expenditure levels were a product of an insider system that provided Scotland, in particular, with strong bargaining power. An approach to relative country need that builds from detail and from individual programmes could be more successful in the future, but the first attempt provides warning signals.

The inability to discover an approximately 'right' answer led to the unsatisfactory Barnett Formula. The formula is a puzzle. It was intended to be temporary; it has lasted for more than twenty years. It was designed to produce convergence; the reality is divergence. If used rigorously from now on (and that appears to be the intention), it will bring expenditure levels in Wales, Northern Ireland and Scotland below the levels implied by relative need. The inappropriate nature of the formula ensured that it was often ignored and consistently by-passed. To the surprise of many, the formula has been embedded in the post-1997 devolution settlement. If Barnett is applied strictly, devolved expenditure in Wales, Northern Ireland and Scotland will converge on English levels, even though Wales and Northern Ireland are notably poorer than England.

The Treasury study hints that measuring overall need directly might be easier than building from separate indicators for each detailed programme. In considering general measures of need, we have to go back to first principles. Need is the true guide to country-by-country devolved spending. The needle of need has no practical impact without a measure of need. In the UK, eight out of every ten pounds of devolved spending is on education, health and law and order. The relative need for these and other public services will change over time. The measure of need should be sensitive to change in economic circumstance.

Needs are likely to be greater in locations with low levels of income and high levels of poverty. Low incomes and particularly poverty connect to a range of ill-health conditions and to premature death. Low incomes and particularly poverty create educational disadvantage. Low incomes and particularly poverty add to crime and crime concentrates on poorer communities. Low incomes and poverty link to antisocial behaviour and drug abuse. Low incomes and poverty add to the pressure on public services and they contribute to social exclusion. In going back to first principles, we can perhaps accept that: first, need is the true guide to country-by-country devolved spending; secondly, the need to which we refer is some measure of command over goods and services.

Within England, Scotland, Wales and Northern Ireland it is possible to allow for differences in need and changes in relative need. The Barnett Formula is population based and takes no account of shifts in productive capacity. It does not allow for the turmoil and dislocation that are natural to capitalism. McLean and McMillan use inverse Gross Domestic Product (GDP) (or inverse Gross Value Added) as their measure of relative country need. GDP (or GVA) is not the only possible measure of relative income, but GDP (or GVA) per capita is perhaps the most widely used single measure of relative prosperity. Bell and Christie prefer a poverty-based approach and Mackay and Williams follow their example. The particular poverty measure used by both sets of authors takes country social security expenditure as the guide to relative country need. 'High levels of social security payments tend to be linked with high levels of unemployment, inactivity, dependency and low levels of income' (Bell and Christie, 2001, p. 142). Dependency levels identify those unable to rely on the market more consistently and accurately than other approaches. Moreover, the rates and regulations for social security are identical in all parts of the United Kingdom.

The case for a poverty-based measure is strengthened if one accepts the basic theme of Rawls's *A Theory of Justice* (1971). A just society, Rawls claims, would have particular regard for the welfare of the most disadvantaged and vulnerable. The poor have limited choice; their needs are greater. Social and economic inequalities are to some extent inevitable, but they should be so arranged that they are to the greatest benefit of the least advantaged. Inequalities that add to the well-being of the least advantaged are acceptable; inequalities that are stronger and lie deeper are a problem. The Rawls approach places particular emphasis on those in poverty. It is they who are often divorced from society. Poverty removes the social basis for self-respect and for respect between citizens. Poverty makes it difficult to maintain and improve human capital. Poverty ensures that many, including the children of the poor, fail to realize their potential. Moreover, it is concentrations of the seriously disadvantaged that are a particular challenge to public policy. On these grounds, a poverty-based measure (such as share of social security expenditure) is preferred to an average income measure.[11]

Agreement on an acceptable compromise is more important than a search for perfection. Table 14.1 below (using recent figures for social security expenditure and GVA) indicates the implications of substituting either a poverty or an income measure of need for the Barnett Formula. With a strict application of the Barnett Formula, devolved spending per head in Wales, Northern Ireland and Scotland would move towards English levels (table 14.1, column 2). Taking dependency (social security) levels as a measure of relative need (column 3) suggests that devolved expenditure per head should be roughly one-fifth higher in Wales and Northern Ireland than in England and more than one-tenth higher in Scotland than in England. Taking inverse GVA as the guide (column 4), devolved expenditure per head in Wales and Northern Ireland should be about 27 per cent higher than in England and devolved expenditure in Scotland should be 6 per cent higher than in England. In Wales, taking income or poverty as the guide to changes in devolved spending would raise public spending per head relative to England. *According to both approaches to identifying relative need, devolved expenditure in Wales is already too low.* In Northern Ireland and Scotland, public expenditure would continue to be squeezed, but more gently. Scotland would benefit if a poverty (dependency) rather than an income (GVA) measure were used: both Wales and Northern Ireland would be better served by an income approach. The convergence targets would adjust year by year with change in relative position. The sums involved are substantial. They are far more impressive than the levels of additional expenditure that could be realized by the use of the Tartan Tax (or its hypothetical equivalents in Wales and Northern Ireland). For example, and taking recent expenditure levels as a rough guide, the strict application of the Barnett Formula would (in the fullness of time) reduce devolved spending in Wales by almost 15 per cent and would mean a reduction of over £400 per head in Welsh devolved spending. The substitution of a dependency-based approach for the Barnett Formula could (over time) raise devolved spending in Wales by close to 19 per cent. Taking 2000–1 expenditure figures as a guide, this would imply an extra £500 per year, per capita devolved spending in Wales.[12]

Table 14.1
Devolved spending – different forms of convergence avoiding the Barnett squeeze

	Actual spending levels per head*	Convergence targets		
		Barnett Formula	Dependency level**	Inverse GVA***
England	100	100	100	100
Northern Ireland	148	100	123	128
Scotland	124	100	113	106
Wales	115	100	119	127

* calculation based on financial year 2000–1
** calculation based on 2000–1
*** calculation based on 2001
Source: Regional Trends, Treasury 2002, Economic Trends.

Poverty and low incomes have inter-generation effects. Four-fifths of devolved expenditure goes on health, education and law and order. But response to the problems that develop from poverty need not rely entirely on conventional expenditure on medicine, schools and policing. The impact of medical care is *not* one of the major contributors to improvements in health and lifespan: social influences are more significant (see Wilkinson, 1995, p. 37; Acheson, 1998). Much of medical care is restorative, it deals with the consequences of ill health. Early life interventions, including child development programmes, may be more effective in improving health. In education, as in health, the importance of habits and lifestyle established early is critical. In their statistical study of violent crime, Fajnzylber, Lederman and Loayza (2002) emphasize that crime waves are difficult to contain and control once they have built momentum. There are strong imitation effects. For health, education and crime the general emphasis of the concerned literature is on broad social initiatives that are inter-sectoral and connect to improving opportunity. A key theme is that early intervention and quick reaction is more effective than delayed response. Once decline has become all too visible to the general public, it may be too late.

With devolved spending in Wales, Scotland and Northern Ireland determined by need, there would be a consistent pattern across eleven of the twelve UK regions. Expenditure on London's public services would remain high. The substantial burden of London's public services is an introduction to the broader argument for more balanced regional development.

CONCLUSION

The test [assessing relative need] involves judgments of great complexity and *political sensitivity*. (White Paper that foreshadowed the Treasury Study of Relative Need, Treasury, 1979, p. 3, author's italics)

Nation-state responses (often unrecognized) are important in adding to individual security and in reducing regional inequality. Closure and exit (mobility) are not the only responses to the problems that flow from unsuccessful competition (Hirschman, 1970).[13] Regional inequalities are contained 'by policy interferences . . . of the nation state', Myrdal (1957, p. 63) emphasizes; solidarity and created harmony are narrowly confined within national boundaries.[14] Hirschman's argument is that non-market forces have effect even when there is no overall plan, or conscious recognition of their power. When the market fails to achieve reasonable balance, society will recognize the gap: state policies and social institutions will emerge in an attempt to bridge it. We become nationalists through genuine, objective, practical necessity and non-market forces are an important part of the sense of belonging that holds a created community (a political union) together.

'People in equal positions should be treated equally' is the Musgrave (1959, p. 160) guide to tax and spending within the nation. Equal treatment develops from the basic liberal principles of equality before the law and equal concern for all citizens. Each citizen has the right to potential dignity and to potential self-realization. Equal treatment of equal people implies transfers from richer to poorer parts of the nation-state. Automatic stabilizers and transfers from richer to poorer regions draw strength from social security and progressive taxation. However, if devolved expenditure is also to contribute to this process, then some attempt must be made to distribute devolved expenditure according to relative need.

A union state remains a nation-state. Transfer between governments is more sensitive than transfers organized within one government. Relative need is accepted by the Treasury as the true guide to devolved spending in Wales, Scotland and Northern Ireland. The Needs Assessment Study of the late 1970s proved unsuccessful, but it was informed by two realities. Relative per capita needs vary from country to country and they change over time. The inability to measure relative need led to the Barnett Formula. This involved a crude political judgment. Judged in relation to England, expenditure in Scotland, Northern Ireland and Wales was too high. Convergence on English expenditure was imperfect, but it was at least in the right direction. The correct assumption of the Barnett approach was that relative change should be gradual rather than abrupt.

For complex reasons, the Barnett Formula was often ignored and bypassed in the 1980s and 1990s. Devolved spending levels in Scotland, Wales and Northern Ireland rose relative to England. The present intention is to apply the Barnett Formula strictly. If this is done, the embrace will confine devolved spending in Wales, Scotland and Northern Ireland. The year-by-year constraint will be moderate, but over time the squeeze will be uncomfortable.

Relative needs vary from country to country. The measures used in this article suggest that relative devolved spending is *already too low in Wales*. Moreover, more realistic measures of relative need would be important in moderating the Barnett squeeze on Northern Ireland and Scotland. The nation-state is a collective enterprise. National identity and national solidarity depend on an appeal to all parts of the United Kingdom. The financial settlement involves an agreement between countries. Such an agreement has to be open, above board and acceptable to all nations within the United Kingdom.

Poverty and low income add to the problems faced by medical services, education and law and order. A true measure of relative need should be sensitive to downturn or expansion in the economies of Wales, Northern Ireland and Scotland. With such a measure, devolved expenditure would become one of the stabilizers that keep the Kingdom United. Convergence on English spending levels would depend on improvement in the Welsh, Scottish and Northern Ireland economies.

ACKNOWLEDGEMENTS

My thanks to the Board of Celtic Studies, University of Wales. Their support was important. My thanks also to anonymous referees and to the editors of *Contemporary Wales*. Their advice improved this article.

NOTES

[1] The increase in UK block spending in the financial year 2000–1 was about 8.3 per cent (Treasury, 2002).

[2] Regional identifiable spending is expenditure on behalf of the citizens of a region. It does not include expenditure on national public goods. This article is primarily concerned with government expenditure for a region. Public expenditure for a region is not public expenditure in a region. The uneven distribution of expenditure on national public goods contributes to regional imbalance. Much of the expenditure on national public goods (defence, overseas aid, national broadcasting, central administration) is concentrated on London and its surrounding regions. Political centralization

contributes to economic centralization. 'Some might see [defence expenditure] as a hidden form of regional policy' (Gripaois, 2002, p. 688) that consistently favours the South West, London and the South East.

3   We know that the claimant count is unreliable, indeed increasingly misleading. What is perhaps insufficiently clear is that unreliability of the claimant count (and the better but still imperfect Labour Force Survey measure of unemployment) follows consistent, if perverse, rules. For males of working age, the regional record shows that the higher the level of male non-work, the lower the proportion of non-work that is captured by unemployment. The greater the degree of individual labour market disadvantage (age, health, location, lack of qualifications), the more likely it is that the person without work will be inactive rather than classified as unemployed. The general rule is the lower the level of opportunity, the less appropriate is unemployment as a measure of labour-market slack. In difficult labour markets discouraged workers withdraw from the labour market because they believe that work is out of reach. Low levels of opportunity add to measured sickness, with large numbers on sickness benefit and classified as unfit for work (see Beatty, Fothergill and MacMillan 2000; Mackay, 1999; Anyadike-Jones, 2004). Explanations of high and persistent unemployment place some emphasis on hysteresis. Recovery, following a loss of effective demand, will not necessarily return unemployment to its original level. The worker, at first merely unemployed, becomes, in time, unemployable. The worker, once accepted as sick, is difficult to restore to the labour market. Labour-market shocks alter the way we view ourselves and also how potential employers view us.

4   The Keynesian emphasis is that the level of effective demand is the key to high employment. In the context of the UK, a rightly distributed demand is also important.

5   If regional work levels are low for males, they are also low for females (the correlation coefficient is 0.959). In regions with low levels of work, earnings are low for males and females. The correlation between regional male and female employment pay is 0.978. Differences in regional levels of effective demand are the key to regional differences in opportunity and pay.

6   The Adam Smith emphasis is that our labour is our 'most sacred and inviolable' property and the foundation of all other property (Smith, 1776, p. 123). Our labour is our most important resource. The potential to work is more widely and democratically distributed than other sources of income. Important to our understanding of economic and social change in the last quarter of the twentieth century is the strong and sustained shift away from full employment (see Dow, 1998). Also crucial was the substitution of a price standard (exclusive emphasis on low inflation and sound money) for a labour standard (full employment and a high level of effective demand). Work provides income and gives substance to life. Full employment reduces inequality (see Reder, 1995; Galbraith, 1998; Mackay, 2001b), adds to social mobility, improves the fiscal balance (by adding to tax and reducing social security – see Keynes, 1929; Galbraith, 1998) and provides the opportunity to pursue an effective regional policy (see Keynes, 1937; Mackay, 2003).

7   Labour-market flexibility can add to insecurity. Bauman (2001, p. 22) draws a contrast between labour markets with lasting implicit contracts, its 'capital and workers united for richer and poorer in health *and sickness*', and the present emphasis on job mobility, short-term contracts, rolling contracts or no contracts. Trust and

obligation fail to emerge in labour markets that celebrate uncertainty and insecurity. In labour markets with weak ties, poor health and extra years add notably to risk of job loss.

8   The third section of this article develops two measures of relative country need. An income-based measure (GDP or GVA per head) and a poverty-based measure (social security spending per head). In the nine non-exception regions, the correlation coefficient between regional GVA (income) and regional devolved spending is –0.81. In the same nine regions, the correlation coefficient between social security spending per head and devolved spending is 0.91. For these nine regions, relative need is a good, if rough, guide to public spending.

9   As early as 1940 the Barlow Commission drew attention to the problems presented by the 'excessive growth . . . of London and the Home Counties'. The commission linked excessive growth in the South East to the unemployment problem in the less prosperous areas and argued that unbalanced growth was contrary 'to the wellbeing of the population of London' (Barlow Commission, 1940, p. 84).

10   Standardized Mortality Ratios are higher in regions of low income and particularly in areas with concentrations of poverty.

11   The Rawls emphasis is given practical support by the social determinants of health literature. Poverty and ill health are intimately connected. The poor are sick more often, they stay sick longer and they die younger. Poverty not only hurts, it kills. In high-income countries, it is relative income not absolute income that is the key to health quality and to lifespan (see Wilkinson, 1996, and Marmot and Wilkinson, 1999). The Black Report (DHSS, 1980) identified substantial north–south health inequalities connected to inequalities in material goods. The north–south health divide intensified in the 1980s and 1990s (see Welsh Office, 1998).

12   The comparable figure for Scotland is £300 per head and for Northern Ireland over £600 per head.

13   Migration (exit) may be difficult and contrary to purpose. The difficulty and expense of migration has encouraged exit without migration. Large numbers work in London and its zone of influence without moving house. They commute, often for a week or longer, often from considerable distance (see Green, 2004). In a tight island economy, migration may have undesirable effects: the need is to correct existing inefficiencies and imbalances, not to compound them by the movement of resources out of regions that are already relatively poor.

14   'The Nation-State . . . was the only "success story" of community in modern times, or, rather, the sole entity which made the bid to a community status with any degree of conviction and effect' (Bauman, 2000, p. 173). The nation-state and the welfare state lose some of their power when capital is less homespun and with easier movement of goods, ideas, people and finance. They remain important. Moreover, there are underlying tensions that warn against pure market solutions. In flexible, insecure labour markets, with weak ties between employers and employees, there are problems in relying on the market for pension provision, or even for reasonable security in the working-age years. In an individualistic age, the ability of the individual, the family or the community to look after its own is paradoxically, but intimately, connected to collective provision: to our willingness to accept responsibility for others.

REFERENCES

Acheson, R. (1998). *Independent Inquiry into Inequalities in Health Care*, London: The Stationery Office.

Anyadike-Jones, M. (2004). 'The real north–south divide? Gradients in UK male non-employment', *Regional Studies*, 38, 1, 85–95.

Barlow Commission (1940). *Report of the Royal Commission on the Distribution of the Industrial Population*, Cmnd 6153, HMSO, reprinted 1960.

Bauman, Z. (2000). *Liquid Modernity*, Cambridge: Polity Press.

Bauman, Z. (2001). *The Individualized Society*, Cambridge: Polity Press.

Beatty, C., Fothergill, S. and Macmillan, R. (2000). 'A theory of employment, unemployment and sickness', *Regional Studies*, 34, 7, 617–30.

Bell, D. and Christie, A. (2001). 'Finance – the Barnett Formula: nobody's child?', in A. Trench (ed), *The State of the Nations 2001*, Thorverton: Inprint Academic,.

DHSS (Department of Health and Social Security) (1980). *Inequalities in Health: Report of a Working Group* (Black Report), London: HMSO.

Dow, J. C. R. (1998). *Major Recessions*, London: Oxford University Press.

Edmonds, T. (2001). 'The Barnett Formula', Economic Policy and Statistics Section, Research Paper 01/08, London: House of Commons Library.

Fajnzylber, P., Lederman, D. and Loayza, N. (2002). 'Inequality and violent crime', *Journal of Law and Economics*, XLV, 1, 1–40.

Galbraith, J. K. (1998). *Created Unequal: The Crisis in American Pay*, New York: The Free Press.

Green, A. E. (2004). 'Is relocation redundant? Observations on the changing nature and impacts of employment – related geographical mobility in the UK', *Regional Studies*, 38, 6, 629–41.

Gripaois, P. (2002). 'Regional spending: a comment on Mackay', *Regional Studies*, 36, 6, 685–9.

Heald, D. (1998). 'Fiscal opportunities', in *Hard Choices, Political Autonomy and Priority Setting in Public Expenditure*, Northern Ireland Economic Council (Occasional Paper 10), pp. 71–88.

Hirschman, A. O. (1958). *The Strategy of Economic Development*, New Haven: Yale University Press.

Hirschman, A. O. (1970). *Exit, Voice and Loyalty*, Cambridge, Mass: Harvard University Press.

Keynes, J. M. (1929) [1973]. 'Can Lloyd George do it?', in *The Collected Writings of John Maynard Keynes*, vol. 9, Cambridge: Cambridge University Press.

Keynes, J. M. (1937) [1973]. 'How to avoid a slump, *The Times* 12th–14th January', in *The Collected Writings of John Maynard Keynes*, vol. 21, Cambridge: Cambridge University Press.

Lonely Planet (2003). *Lonely Planet – Britain*, 5th edn, London: Lonely Planet Publishers.

Mackay, R. R. (1993). 'A Europe of the regions: a role for nonmarket forces?', *Regional Studies*, 27, 5, 419–31.

Mackay, R. R. (1994). 'Automatic stabilisers, European Union and national unity', *Cambridge Journal of Economics*, 18, 571–85.

Mackay, R. R. (1999). 'Work and nonwork: a more difficult labour market', *Environment and Planning A*, 31, 1919–34.

Mackay, R. R. (2001a). 'Regional taxing and spending: the search for balance', *Regional Studies* 35, 6, 563–75.

Mackay, R. R. (2001b). 'Opportunity and inequality', *International Journal of Human Development*, 1, 1, 17–41.

Mackay, R. R. (2003). 'Twenty-five years of regional development', *Regional Studies*, 37, 3, 303–17.

Mackay, R. R. and Williams J. (forthcoming). 'Thinking about need: public spending on the regions', *Regional Studies*.

Marmot, M. and Wilkinson, R. G. (1999). *Social Determinants of Health*, Oxford: Oxford University Press.

McCormick, J. and Alexander, W. (1997). 'Scotland, towards devolution', in M. Guibernau and J. Rex (eds), *The Ethnicity Reader*, Cambridge: Polity Press.

McLean, I. and McMillan, A. (2003). 'The distribution of public expenditure across the UK regions', *Fiscal Studies*, 24, 1, 45–71.

Musgrave, R. A. (1959). *The Theory of Public Finance*, New York: McGraw-Hill.

Myrdal, G. (1957). *Economic Theory and Under-Developed Regions*, London: Duckworth.

Nuffield College (2003). *Identifying the Flow of Domestic and European Expenditure in to the English Regions*, London: Office of the Deputy Prime Minister.

Rawls, J. A. (1971). *A Theory of Justice*, Cambridge, Mass.: Harvard University Press.

Reder, M. W. (1995). 'The theory of occupation wage differentials', *American Economic Review*, 45, 838–52.

Regional Trends (various years). London: HMSO.

Schumpeter, J. A. (1943). *Capitalism, Socialism and Democracy*, London: Unwin University Books.

Smith, A. (1776) [1904]. *The Wealth of Nations*, ed. E. Cannan, London: Methuen.

Treasury (1979). *Needs Assessment Study – Report of an Interdepartmental Study, coordinated by HM Treasury on the Relative Public Expenditure Needs in England, Scotland, Wales and Northern Ireland*, London: HM Treasury.

Treasury (2001). *Productivity in the UK: 3 The Regional Dimension*, London: HM Treasury.

Treasury (2002). *Public Expenditure, Statistical Analyses, 2002–03*, Cm.5401, London: HM Treasury.

Treasury Committee (1997). *The Barnett Formula*, HC 341, 1997/98, London: HMSO.

Welsh Office (1998). *Better Health, Better Wales*, Cm.3922, London: HMSO.

Wilkinson, R. G. (1995). 'The relationship between health and income equality among families', in R. Bayley, A. Condy and C. Roberts (eds) *Families, Work, Poverty and Resources*, London: Family Policy Studies Centre.

Wilkinson, R. G. (1996). *Unhealthy Societies: The Afflictions of Inequality*, London: Routledge.

15. INTELLECTUAL PROPERTY IN THE WELSH PRODUCTION SECTOR

Nigel J. Moore and Lynn Mainwaring

ABSTRACT

Intellectual property (IP) rights are the successful outcomes of innovative and entrepreneurial activity. In this article, we exploit a substantial and uniquely constructed database to analyse patenting and trademarking among Welsh production firms, by mapping creative outputs according to firm size, sector of activity, ownership (Welsh versus non-Welsh) and location. For Wales, as a whole, production firms are relatively active in the appropriation of knowledge assets: the proportion of firms attempting to acquire IP is high. However, the number of IP registrations per firm (both patents and trademarks) is low, the number of single-registration firms is high (suggesting a failure to develop economies of IP clustering) and, in the case of patents, the attrition rate between publications and currently live patents is also high. The implication is that recent policy initiatives to stimulate technological awareness are insufficient to ensure effective technological appropriation. The distribution of holdings within Wales is uneven and does not necessarily accord with expectations. Former coalfield unitary authorities score highly on patenting, while rural areas in the north and west do well in trademarking – suggesting that cultural distinctiveness is a public asset that can successfully be exploited to private advantage.

INTRODUCTION

Intellectual property (IP) rights – patents, trademarks, designs and copyrights – are the successful outcomes of innovative and entrepreneurial activity. Although a great deal is known about some aspects of IP (especially patents) at the level of large national economies, very little work has been done in respect of regional or smaller national economies. In this article, we analyse patenting and trade-marking among Welsh production firms, making use of a substantial and uniquely constructed database containing information on the IP assets of 2,049 companies. Smaller datasets (each of 700 firms) have also been constructed for three other 'regions' of the British Isles: the Republic of Ireland, Scotland and the west of England. We report fully on the cross-regional comparisons of IP performance elsewhere (Moore and Mainwaring, 2004; Mainwaring and Moore, 2004). In this article we focus on the extent and pattern of Welsh IP holdings by mapping creative outputs according to firm size, sector of activity, ownership (Welsh versus non-Welsh) and location. However, summary references to regional comparisons are included in order to put the Welsh figures into context. The data presently exist for only one year (2002) so that a proper time-series analysis is not possible (though some inferences may be made from the history of patent holdings of firms in the database).

Intellectual property rights are means by which inventors, creators and designers attempt to appropriate an income stream from their efforts. Of the various rights, patents have been the main object of scrutiny by economists. By maintaining, in principle, a protected monopoly on a new product or process for a fixed period (normally twenty years), patents provide an incentive to invention and innovation. Since patenting is an output of a creative process, the intensity of patenting activity may be used as a proxy for technological dynamism in a firm, industry or economy. Trademarks, which have received less attention, do not have the same dynamic-efficiency justification as patents. Their main benefits are in informing consumer choice by providing reputational signals. Thus the volume of trademark holdings is best thought of as indicating a degree of market power. Even so, trademarking intensity – the flow of new trademarks – may reasonably be regarded as a measure of creative and entrepreneurial activity. Registered designs are not considered in this article. The number of registrations is very small compared to the other two instruments and we have little faith in the robustness of inferences drawn from them.

The next section of the article gives a fuller description of the two IP instruments together with a brief survey of the existing empirical literature and the data currently available for Wales. That is followed by a discussion of the findings drawn from our data for Wales as a whole and then an examination of the distribution of IP holdings according to Welsh unitary authority. The final section summarizes the findings and draws out their policy implications.

THE NATURE AND CHARACTERISTICS OF PATENTS AND TRADEMARKS

IP procedures[1]

In the UK an invention is eligible for patent protection if it is 'novel', 'involves an inventive step' and 'is capable of industrial application' (Patents Act 1977). Patent protection begins once an application is filed. The patent application is normally published eighteen months after the date of filing and will be granted if the patent examiner is satisfied that it complies with the criteria of eligibility. An application may be withdrawn prior to publication, or it may be rejected after publication, by the examiner. The patents will be registered at the stated address of the holder and will normally expire after twenty years from the filing (or 'priority') date. For British patents, patentees pay an initial examination fee but no further fee for the first five years of protection. Thereafter, there are annual renewal fees rising in steps from £50 to £400. Similar fee structures apply in other jurisdictions. There may well come a point in the lifetime of a patent where the estimated marginal value to the holder no longer exceeds the renewal fee and the patent is allowed to lapse. Evidence (for example Shankerman and Pakes, 1986) suggests that few patents are pursued to their full term and this is corroborated by our findings.

Firms have a choice of jurisdictions and geographical coverage for their patents. They can take out patents in individual countries (paying appropriate fees each time);[2] they can get protection in designated European states via the European Patent Office (EPO); or they can get global coverage via the Patent Cooperation Treaty. The appropriate choice is clearly a matter of balancing fee costs against the benefits of enhanced coverage, and will depend largely on which markets are targeted, whether as exporters, direct investors or licensors. It seems probable that patentees will nearly always seek protection in the home market even if they forego wider coverage.

UK trademarks may be registered on signs that are 'capable of being represented graphically' and 'capable of distinguishing goods and services of one business from those of another' (Trademarks Act 1994). Following payment of the initial fee, trademarks persist indefinitely subject to ten-yearly renewal fees. Firms register separate trademarks in each territorial jurisdiction within which they seek protection (including the European Union). Again, it seems likely that trademarks will, at a minimum, be used to protect the home market.

Existing empirical evidence

For British large- and medium-size firms over the period 1986–95, Greenhalgh, Longland and Bosworth (2000) report declining levels of patenting in the UK and rising levels in the USA and Europe. Taken together, the overall level of patenting has fallen. We are not aware of equivalent time-series findings for small- and medium-size firms in the UK. The distribution of patenting activity by production sector has been thoroughly explored; see, for example, Levin et al. (1987) and Mansfield (1986) for the USA; Malerba and Orsenigo (1990) for Italy. Patenting seems to be the favoured means of IP protection in pharmaceuticals and other chemicals and to a lesser extent in electronics. Other sectors which are subject to rapid technological advance rely more on trade secrets, quick lead times and learning-curve effects for appropriation. For the UK, Greenhalgh, Longland and Bosworth (2000) detect a recent decline in patenting in high-technology areas, especially chemicals. In contrast to patents, these same authors find a rising trend in trademarking among British medium/large-size firms, in both the UK and the USA.

Patent studies that specifically include Wales as a separate entity are scarce – and possibly unique to Santangelo (2002). She reported regional patent performance in high-technology sectors for three European countries, including Britain. Of five performance categories, Wales and Scotland made up the fourth, ahead of the North and Yorkshire and Humberside and one category below South-west England (one of our comparator regions).

IP acquisition is a measure of technological and creative dynamism which usefully complements indexes based on R and D expenditure. The latter are restricted by the fact that R and D is an input rather than output of the creative process and that an understanding of what constitutes R and D (that is, how much is 'R' and how much 'D') varies from firm to firm. Patent publications are a better indicator of general outputs and granted and active patents superior indicators of commercial value. On the other hand, the value attached to individual patents and trademarks may vary hugely, a matter of concern in cross-regional comparisons where statistical samples are small.

If IP acquisition is a measure of creative outputs then we might reasonably expect this to be reflected in productivity, profitability or, more generally, value added. These gains ought to be detectable at the level of the firm, the industry and the economy. (The industry and economy gains may be more than the sum of firm gains because of positive externalities, that is, spillover effects.) Care, however, is needed in interpreting 'IP acquisition'. According to Greenhalgh and Longland (2002), to gain any benefit firms have to increase the intensity of IP relative to other factors; hence the title of their paper: 'Running to stand still?'. Their regression results for a sample of large British firms show that:

> Adding just one extra patent per firm and one trade mark per year would increase value added permanently by a quarter of one per cent. Raising all firms' IP levels by one standard deviation would raise real value added by 6 per cent for UK patents and trade marks, whilst for EPO patents and UK trade marks this would raise it by 8 per cent. (2002, p. 15)

These gains may be dissipated through hiring additional non-production labour. Greenhalgh, Longland and Bosworth (2001) show that this workforce expansion effect is most pronounced among high-technology firms.

The Greenhalgh and Longland findings are broadly consistent with Nelson and Wolff's (1997) industry-level study of technological appropriation in the USA. They conclude that the *level* of appropriability affects the *level* of the industry's knowledge stock but not its *rate of growth*. Thus appropriation needs to grow continuously if it is to have a positive impact on the rate of advance. Numerous studies have been undertaken at a country level. Fagerberg (1988), for example, finds a positive relationship between patenting (measured as the ratio of external patent applications to exports) and GDP per capita, and a positive relationship between the growth of external patenting and the growth of GDP per capita. Gould and Gruben (1996) detect a positive relationship between growth rates and the institutional strength of a country's patenting regime – the more so for more open economies.

These findings are generally consistent with the literature on national and regional innovation systems (Freeman, 1987, and, for an application to Wales, Rees and Morgan, 1991). They are also consistent with the more recent literature on the 'learning economy' (Lundvall and Johnson, 1994, and, again, for Wales, Morgan, 1997). They suggest, in short, that the capacity of a regional economy to compete and, in the case of Wales, to converge towards its best-practice neighbours, depends on its ability to put in place institutional structures that promote learning and innovation (Fagerberg, Verspagen and Caniels, 1997; Mainwaring, 1995). But they say something else. Innovation and creativity may be wasted if the assets they generate are not fully appropriated. The importance of intellectual *property* is that it gives some assurance that the value added from innovation feeds through to indigenous incomes.

UK Patent Office regional data

Data is available on a UK regional basis for three years, 2000–2, for annual patent applications and patent grants, and for four years, 1999–2002 for trademark applications and trademark registrations.[3] These are flows rather than stocks (in contrast to our data) and, in that respect, give a better picture of the temporal changes in innovative and creative capacity. But, even for that purpose, they are limited by the short period of availability, making it difficult to ascertain long-run trends. Unlike the data on the IP Wales database, which is confined to production firms, the Patent Office statistics refer to all applicants with a regional address whatever economic sector they belong to. It is not possible from the published information to determine the characteristics of the property holders. The IP Wales data measure the cumulated holdings of IP and thus give a picture of the intellectual 'wealth' of firms, rather than current additions to that wealth.

Table 15.1 shows the number of patent applications and grants for Wales, Scotland and South-west England. (The applications may or may not subsequently have been published.) For the UK as a whole, roughly two-thirds of applications fail to reach the publication stage. Applying that factor to Wales would suggest that around 250 applications each year would reach publication. (The IP Wales database records 43 publications for 2000, which, very roughly, would amount to 18 per cent of those implied by the statistics of table 15.4.) Since patent grants follow applications with a lag of about two years, the 2002 figures for grants should be compared to the 2000 figures for applications to get a rough idea of the eventual success rate. For Wales and South-west England, it appears that about a fifth of applications finally succeed; for Scotland, it is about one seventh. However, very little should be read into what is effectively a single observation.

Table 15.1
Patent applications and patent grants by UK region, 2000–2002

	Wales		Scotland		South-west England	
	Applications	Granted	Applications	Granted	Applications	Granted
2000	703	70	1198	141	1686	267
			(688)	(81)	(991)	(157)
2001	782	88	1120	107	1683	262
			(643)	(61)	(990)	(154)
2002	793	130	1165	163	1666	327
			(669)	(94)	(980)	(192)

Note: Figures in parentheses for Scotland and South-west England have been scaled by 2001 population relative to Wales.

In addition to the absolute numbers of applications and grants, the columns for Scotland and south-west England also report (in parentheses) *scaled* figures obtained by multiplying the absolute figure by the ratio of Welsh to local-region population (for 2001). On that basis it can be seen that Wales has performed reasonably well compared to Scotland, but rather poorly compared to south-west England. Both measures also show strong Welsh growth, but one should be wary of investing confidence in growth rates given the short time span and potential volatility of the data.

One interesting finding noted in Moore and Mainwaring (2004) is that the UK regional rankings of patent applications and grants (corrected for size of region) are inversely correlated with the ranking of regional business R and D expenditure reported in *Regional Trends*. It turns out that the ratio of grants to R and D is higher in Wales than any region other than London, whose grant performance would anyway be inflated by the concentration there of firm headquarters. It is highly likely that official R and D figures are not capturing the informal R and D that may be being undertaken by smaller Welsh firms. But our comparative analysis also gives grounds for thinking that the typical Welsh patent is of lower commercial value than patents in our comparator regions.

The trademarks comparison is altogether less flattering to Wales (table 15.2). On a population-adjusted basis, Welsh filings and registrations are about two-thirds of those in Scotland and fewer than half those of south-west England. One might be tempted to ascribe these performance variations to differences in economic structure. However, much the same picture emerges from our analysis of trademark stocks in the production sector (Mainwaring and Moore, 2004).

Table 15.2
Trademark applications filed and registered by UK region, 1999–2002

	Wales		Scotland		South-west England	
	Applications	Granted	Applications	Granted	Applications	Granted
1999	370	286	1056	787	1432	942
			(605)	(451)	(842)	(554)
2000	539	329	1174	889	1613	1221
			(673)	(509)	(948)	(718)
2001	397	301	1044	772	1501	1396
			(598)	(442)	(883)	(821)
2002	444	321	1164	891	1688	1307
			(667)	(511)	(993)	(769)

Note: Figures in parentheses for Scotland and South-west England have been scaled by 2001 population relative to Wales.

ANALYSIS OF IP WALES DATA

The data presented below relate to production firms listed on the Kompass CDs, dated June 2003, for the UK and for the Republic of Ireland. 'Production' is defined broadly to include manufacturing, extraction and food and timber processing. Information is provided on company location (by unitary authority in the case of Wales), annual sales, employment, industry sector and the nature of the parent/division relationship. All 2,049 firms located at Welsh addresses were extracted and 700 each from Scotland, Ireland and south-west England.

Once the firms were extracted, a patent and trademark search was undertaken. This determined whether the firms have IP registered at their Welsh addresses or, in the case of divisions of non-Welsh companies, whether IP is registered at addresses outside of Wales. For IP held at Welsh addresses, the exact number of registrations was recorded. In the case of patents, the records distinguish between patent applications published (together with the year of publication), applications not granted, patents granted but lapsed (together with the year of lapsing) and current live patents. For parent companies holding IP outside of Wales, only the country of registration was recorded. It was neither practicable nor sensible to attempt the same level of detail as home-region registrations. A company based in Tokyo, say, may have literally thousands of registrations, very few of which have any relevance to a specific branch plant.

Patenting activity and success

Our data allow us to distinguish between comparative levels of patenting activity, via the numbers of published patent applications, and patenting success, via the numbers of patents granted and the commercial lifespan of granted patents. The key conclusion to emerge is that Welsh firms are relatively 'patent-active' but relatively less successful in commercialising their efforts.

From 1983 to 2001, 147 firms from our Welsh sample (that is, 7.17 per cent) were patent-active, publishing between them a total of 478 applications. (This compares with 6.43 per cent for Scotland, 5.86 for South-west England and 4.14 per cent for Ireland. These figures almost certainly underestimate the actual number of regional patent applications over the period, in the production sector, because some patent publishers from the early part of the period may no longer be in business.) Of the Welsh firms, 76 – over half – published only one application. The proportion of single-publication firms is higher in Wales than in the other regions. This must be regarded as a negative feature of Welsh patenting performance given that patents tend to have greater value as part of a patent portfolio or 'cluster'.

For each publication there are three possibilities. It may be that the patent was not granted because of a challenge by another patent holder or because the applicant withdrew. It may be that the application succeeded but the patent holder stopped paying renewal fees, in which case it is considered as lapsed. Or it may be that the application is still being processed (but in the post-publication stage), or has been granted but is not yet subject to renewal fees, or is having the renewal fees paid. In these cases we describe the patent as 'live'. The distribution of live patents according to firm size is reported in tables 15.3 and 15.4.

Table 15.3
Production firms with patent applications (between 1983 and 2001) and currently live patents registered at a Welsh address, by annual sales for 2002

Firm sales in £ millions	Number and % with a patent application published			Number and % with a current live patent			Sample size
(Missing)	(8)			(4)			(245)
0.02–0.5	8	1.67		2	0.04		480
0.5–1	15	5.98		10	3.98		251
1–2	15	5.17		9	3.10		290
2–5	36	11.96		24	7.97		301
5–10	17	10.49		8	4.94		162
10–20	19	15.83		12	10.00		120
20–50	20	18.35		·17	15.60		109
50–75	1	4.00		1	4.00		25
75–125	4	14.81	11.59	4	14.81	10.14	27
125–250	3	17.66		2	11.76		17
250–500	1	7.7		0	0		13
500–1000	0	0	4.55	0	0	0	6
1000+	0	0		0	0		3
Total	147	7.17		93	4.54		2049

Note: Figures in italics are percentage of the sample size in each size category.

Focusing initially on the totals, it can be seen that only 93 firms currently have a live patent registered at a Welsh address. This amounts to 63 per cent of the 147 patent-active firms – a lower percentage than for the other regions studied. (However, these 93 firms amount to 4.54 per cent of the full Welsh sample, a higher figure than for Scotland and Ireland.). Each figure in italics in tables 15.3 and 15.4 reports the corresponding absolute number as a percentage of the number of sampled firms in the relevant firm-size category. This gives some limited insight into the distribution of the intensity of patenting activity and possession according to firm size. Inferences are, however, compromised by the fact that many firms and, more especially, larger firms do not register their patents at regional addresses. For those that do, it is clear (and perhaps not surprising) that the intensity of activity is weakest amongst the very smallest firms. Firms with annual sales of £20–50 million have the greatest intensity and a very low rate of attrition between applications and live patents. Much the same qualitative picture emerges when employment is used as the measure of firm size, with firms employing 251–500 having the strongest record of publication and possession. (There is, in fact, a very strong correlation between the two firm-size measures.)

Table 15.4
Production firms with patent applications (between 1983 and 2001) and currently live patents registered at a Welsh address, by on-site employment for 2002

Employees on site	Number and % with a patent application published		Number and % with a current live patent		Sample size
(Missing)	(6)		(5)		(91)
1–10	12	*1.93*	6	*1.00*	623
11–20	15	*4.45*	10	*3.00*	337
21–50	28	*6.31*	18	*4.05*	444
51–100	27	*11.30*	17	*7.11*	239
101–250	31	*15.74*	18	*9.14*	197
251–500	22	*29.33*	15	*20.00*	75
501–1000	3	*15.80*	3	*15.80*	20
1000+	3	*13.04*	1	*4.35*	23
Total	147	*7.17*	93	*4.54*	2049

Note: Figures in italics are percentage of the sample size in each size category.

Of the 478 applications published in Wales between 1983 and 2001, 97 failed, a further 93 were granted but have subsequently lapsed and 288 remain alive. Most of the patents that lapse do so within seven years of filing. The time-weighted mean lapse date (of lapsed patents) is, to the nearest decimal point, 7.7 years.

Patenting activity is highly concentrated, with seven Kompass sectors (out of 89) accounting for over half of patenting firms. (Note that a firm may be allocated to more than one code, as therefore will be its patents, so this may involve a degree of double-counting.) The relevant sectors are: plastic products; metal constructions for building; metal-ware; electrical equipment; measuring and optical equipment; transport and transport equipment; and engines and machines. The patenting distribution corresponds to some extent to the distribution of firm numbers but with notable exceptions. Forging and metalworking, for example, is well represented in terms of firm numbers but has only three patent publications.[4] Pharmaceuticals has fewer firms than metals but eight publications.

It is probable that Wales suffers from its inherited industrial structure and the relative absence of truly high-technology sectors such as biotechnology and pharmaceuticals.

One of the problems of interpreting our data has been the tendency of multi-regional firms to register IP holdings at addresses outside of Wales. Tables 15.5 and 15.6 report the percentage of firms with a parent company based outside of Wales and the percentage with patent applications published at their headquarters address. Unsurprisingly, the latter percentages are small for small firms. More surprisingly, they tend to fall again at the top end of the size range, at least as measured by sales.[5] On average (for Wales), 16 per cent of multi-regional firms registered their patent publications elsewhere. (This includes well-known companies like the steel-maker Corus which appears to register all its UK inventions at its London address, and multinationals like Sony and Panasonic which register their patents at their Japanese headquarters.) Against this, we estimate that around 15 per cent of patents held at Welsh addresses were invented outside of Wales. This tendency to extra-regional registration creates an obvious problem for the interpretation of the statistics but it also highlights issues of policy.

Table 15.5
Percentage of firms with a parent company based outside Wales and percentage with patent applications published at their parent company address, by annual sales for 2002

Firm sales in £ millions	% with non-Welsh parent	% with patent held at parent address
(Missing)	(48.57)	(25.31)
0.02–0.5	4.58	0.42
0.5–1	15.94	3.98
1–2	22.41	6.21
2–5	39.20	13.95
5–10	57.41	31.15
10–20	64.17	35.00
20–50	81.65	43.12
50–75	84.00	52.00
75–125	81.48	70.37
125–250	100	58.82
250–500	76.92	61.54
500–1000	100	50.00
1000+	33.33	33.33
Total	34.01	16.01

Table 15.6
Percentage of firms with a parent company based outside Wales and percentage with patent applications published at their parent company address, by on-site employment for 2002

Employees on site	% with non-Welsh parent	% with patent held at parent address
(Missing)	(45.05)	(19.78)
1–10	14.29	3.85
11–20	21.36	7.42
21–50	33.33	11.49
51–100	53.56	29.71
101–250	64.47	38.58
251–500	76.00	52.00
501–1000	85.00	40.00
1000+	78.26	52.17
Total	34.01	16.01

Of course, many large multinational companies often confine serious research activity to locations in their home economies. Some devolve minor developmental activity (typically local adaptation) to their Welsh branch plants but some do undertake both basic research and development in those plants (Phelps et al., 2003). To the extent that patenting is intended as a measure of regional *innovative capacity*, it will clearly underestimate the performance of peripheral economies heavily dependent on multinational firms, that is, economies like Wales; and it will overestimate performance in metropolitan economies like London and the south-east of England. The effect is less serious to the extent that extra-regional registrations are more or less offset by patent 'imports'. Where patents are used as a measure of regional *technology availability*, the failing may be more serious since we have no way of knowing what patents registered at a Tokyo head office are relevant to a branch plant in Wales. More pointedly, we have no way of knowing how much that branch plant pays for that knowledge via internal transfer prices. That is to say, Welsh plants could be paying inflated transfer prices for technology developed in those very same plants. (This point is elaborated in Moore and Mainwaring, 2004.)

Trademark activity and success
Once trademarks are registered the cost of maintaining them is very low so that the failed-lapsed-live distinctions that applied to patents are not particularly significant. This section, therefore, focuses directly on the numbers of live trademarks. As with other forms of IP, trademarks may be registered within Wales or at a parent firm's non-Welsh address. Home-registered trademarks are

more likely to reflect entrepreneurial and creative capacities located within Wales. External registrations imply IP assets that are potentially available to Welsh firms but not necessarily at zero cost. These assets may be paid for at prices that may deviate, one way or the other, from arm's length prices. We begin by considering trademarks held within the region.

Tables 15.7 and 15.8 report the distribution of trademark-active firms by firm size (measured by sales and on-site employees, respectively). There were 334 firms – 16.30 per cent of the sample – which held trademarks on a Welsh address. For the other regions, the sample proportions are: 21.29 per cent for Scotland; 16.71 per cent for south-west England; and 16.14 per cent for Ireland. Although the proportion of firms active in trademarking is similar across regions, the intensity of the activity (as with patents) is much lower in Wales. Relative to the full sample, the number of trademarks per firm is 0.79, compared to 1.42 for Scotland, 2.20 for South-west England and 1.63 for Ireland.

Table 15.7
Production firms with active trademarks (TMs) held on Welsh addresses and on parent company addresses, as a percentage of each annual sales category

Firm sales in £ millions	% of firms with TMs held at Welsh addresses	% of firms with TMs held at parent addresses
(Missing)	(13.47)	(40.82)
0.02–0.5	4.38	0.83
0.5–1	11.55	7.17
1–2	13.79	9.31
2–5	19.60	15.61
5–10	32.72	26.54
10–20	28.33	31.67
20–50	35.78	33.94
50–75	20.00	60.00
75–125	25.93	55.56
125–250	41.18	58.82
250–500	38.44	61.54
500–1000	0	66.67
1000+	66.66	33.33
Total	16.30	17.91
Total number	334	

In the case of trademarks, it is possible to represent the industrial distribution of activity either by official trademark category or by Kompass code. The advantages of using trademark categories are that they are designed specifically for the purpose of classifying trademarks and, anyway, are clearer and more explicit than the Kompass codes.[6] In terms of trademark categories, then, the strongest showings for all four regions are in: metals; scientific instruments; and scientific and technological services. It is difficult to pick out special strengths in Wales. For Scotland and Ireland, extensive trademarking in food products suggests that firms there are determined to exploit their cultural heritage in order to add maximum value to their agricultural outputs.

Table 15.8
Production firms with active trademarks (TMs) held on Welsh addresses and on parent company addresses, as a percentage of each employment category

Employees on site	% of firms with TMs held at Welsh addresses	% of firms with TMs held at parent addresses
(Missing)	(12.09)	(40.66)
1–10	6.74	7.54
11–20	10.39	10.98
21–50	17.34	16.22
51–100	21.76	29.29
101–250	33.50	28.93
251–500	46.67	36.00
501–1000	35.00	40.00
1000+	39.13	52.17
Total	16.30	17.91
Total number	334	

Tables 15.7 and 15.8 also report the percentage of each size-class of firms holding trademarks at their parent's external address. For example, 60 per cent of sampled firms with sales of £50–70 million had trademarks registered externally. The distribution of trademarks across categories is probably related to the sectoral distribution of multi-regional firms. Thus, in addition to the categories noted above, which were prominent among internal registrations, there are strong showings in: machines and machine tools; lighting and heating apparatus; paper and pulp; rubber and extruded plastics; building materials; furniture; and construction.

The distribution of IP activity within Wales
The Kompass entries allow us to locate each Welsh firm by unitary authority (UA). Table 15.9 reports the spatial distribution of all the firms in the sample, using population as a comparator, and records their IP performance. Not surprisingly, rural areas such as Anglesey, Gwynedd, Ceredigion and the Vale of Glamorgan are under-represented in terms of firms, while the major urban centres in east Wales, Cardiff, Newport and Wrexham are over-represented. The table also shows the percentage of the firms in each UA that do not have a Welsh home address.

Table 15.9
IP performance of Welsh production firms, by unitary authority

Unitary authority (UA)	Sample firms		Population (persons)	Firms based outside Wales	Patent applications		Live patents		Registered trademarks		Registered trademarks and/or live patents	
	No. of firms	Firms as a % of sample	Population as a % of Welsh total	Firms as a % in UA	No. of firms	Firms as a % in UA	No. of firms	Firms as a % in UA	No. of firms	Firms as a % in UA	No. of firms	Firms as a % in UA
Anglesey	15	0.73	2.21	53.33	1	6.67	1	6.67	2	13.33	2	13.33
Blaenau Gwent	56	2.73	2.45	48.22	1	1.79	1	1.79	4	7.14	5	8.93
Bridgend	106	5.17	4.49	36.45	11	10.38	8	7.55	19	17.92	21	19.81
Caerphilly	107	5.22	5.79	37.97	7	6.54	6	5.61	21	19.63	22	20.56
Cardiff	319	15.57	11.03	33.96	18	5.64	9	2.82	50	15.67	52	16.30
Carmarthenshire	92	4.49	5.75	28.26	8	8.70	5	5.43	14	15.22	15	16.30
Ceredigion	30	1.46	2.45	10.00	1	3.33	1	3.33	6	20	7	23.33
Conwy	43	2.10	3.81	30.23	3	6.98	2	4.65	5	11.63	6	13.95
Denbighshire	52	2.54	3.10	30.77	8	15.38	5	9.61	7	13.46	9	17.31
Flintshire	123	6.00	5.01	30.4	10	8.13	5	4.06	22	17.87	23	18.70
Gwynedd	41	2.00	3.95	34.14	3	7.32	0	0	10	24.39	10	24.39
Merthyr Tydfil	37	1.81	1.91	32.43	3	8.11	2	5.26	11	29.73	11	29.73
Monmouthshire	68	3.32	2.96	29.41	3	4.41	3	4.41	7	10.29	10	14.71
Neath Port Talbot	94	4.59	4.70	30.85	4	4.26	3	3.19	9	9.57	10	10.64
Newport	148	7.22	4.70	34.67	7	4.73	5	3.38	22	14.86	23	15.54
Pembrokeshire	58	2.83	3.88	27.59	1	1.72	1	1.72	11	18.97	10	17.24
Powys	105	5.12	4.29	28.57	13	12.38	6	5.77	15	14.29	18	17.14
Rhondda Cynon Taff	135	6.59	8.21	51.47	14	10.37	9	6.67	24	17.78	27	20.00
Swansea	158	7.71	7.83	27.68	11	6.96	5	3.16	29	18.35	31	19.62
Torfaen	86	4.20	3.06	32.18	14	16.28	11	12.79	16	18.60	20	23.25
Vale of Glamorgan	49	2.39	4.12	24.00	3	6.12	2	4.08	7	14.29	7	14.29
Wrexham	127	6.20	4.26	38.28	3	2.36	3	2.36	23	18.11	24	18.90
Total	2049	100	100	34.01	147	7.17	93	4.54	334	16.30	363	17.72

Patent activity is measured according to whether firms have published patent applications, on the one hand, and current live patents, on the other. Under each heading, the active firms in each UA are reported as an absolute number and as a percentage of all the sample firms in the UA. Comparing this percentage with the corresponding figure for Wales as a whole tells us whether firms in the UA are performing above or below the Welsh average. Given the small number of firms in each UA, these figures should be regarded as no more than suggestive. Notwithstanding this caveat, some interesting – and perhaps surprising – findings are thrown up by table 15.9.

The most surprising is that those areas of production concentration noted above, Cardiff, Newport and Wrexham, have very low levels of intensity for both publications and currently live patents. Easily the most dynamic UA in terms of patenting is Torfaen (significant at the 5 per cent level), followed by Denbighshire, Bridgend and Rhondda Cynon Taff. Powys does well on publications and Swansea on live patents. It may be that these peculiarities are related to the nature of industrial location policy in recent decades, with newer (and possibly more dynamic) firms being found greenfield sites outside of the urban UA boundaries. The very poor showing of Blaenau Gwent, and to a lesser extent Neath Port Talbot, might conform to prior expectations but is a little surprising given that the other 'Valleys' UAs have performed above average. However, before we place too much weight on this observation, we should recall the earlier concerns about the external registrations of firms active in Wales. In particular, it was noted that Corus does not register patents at Welsh addresses. That means that any formal and informal R and D activity that had taken place at Port Talbot and Ebbw Vale, leading to patented outcomes, would not show up here. With the ending of formal R and D activities at Port Talbot and the complete closure of the Ebbw Vale plant, this consideration holds little comfort for the future. Among the rural UAs, it is, as might be expected, the more peripheral – Gwynedd, Pembrokeshire and Ceridigion – that underperform. (Anglesey has the smallest number of production firms and its apparently high live-patent performance should definitely be treated with caution.)

Succeeding columns repeat the exercise for Welsh-registered trademarks and for trademarks and live patents combined. For trademarks, the most remarkable finding is that almost twice as many firms in Merthyr Tydfil are trademark active compared to firms in Wales as a whole. Notable performances are also returned by Gwynedd, Ceredigion and Pembrokeshire, in a reversal of their showing for patents. Yet other rural areas to the east have poor trademarking intensity. This is possibly a reflection of the importance of heritage and cultural factors in the marketing of rural products. In this respect, the northern and western areas appear to be emulating Scottish and Irish practice. The weakest performances, as with patents, are Blaenau Gwent (significant at 5 per cent) and Neath Port Talbot, again running counter to the Valleys as a whole.

The live-patent and trademark statistics are combined to give a more inclusive picture of IP activity. In view of what has already been said, the weakest UAs hold no surprises. If there are findings that run counter to expectations, they are the generally strong returns for most of the Valleys UAs and the somewhat muted performances of the south-east urban centres, Cardiff and Newport, and the more prosperous eastern rural areas, Monmouthshire, the Vale of Glamorgan, Powys and Denbighshire.

SUMMARY AND CONCLUSIONS

Over the last few years, much has been made of the need to recreate Wales as a learning economy. Extensive public policy initiatives, such as the Regional Technology Plan (Morgan, 1997) have been instituted to underpin the concept. Such policies help promote R and D and learning inputs. IP holdings (especially patents) give us a measure (albeit imperfect) of learning outputs and, importantly, the extent to which those outputs have been appropriated. The measure is more fallible the smaller the economy because registration addresses do not necessarily represent the locus of creative activity. They are still, probably, the best measure we have.

For Wales, as a whole, the picture that emerges is that production firms are relatively aware of and active in the appropriation of knowledge assets. In other words, the proportion of firms engaged in the process of trying to acquire IP is high. But there are less encouraging findings: the number of IP registrations per firm (both patents and trademarks) is low (thus countering the high activity rate); the number of single-registration firms is high (suggesting a failure to develop economies of IP clustering); and, in the case of patents, the attrition rate between publications and currently live patents is also high. Clearly, policy initiatives to stimulate technological awareness and engagement are insufficient to ensure effective technological appropriation. A major objective of IP Wales (via its 'commercial' remit) has been to help small- and medium-sized enterprises make more profitable use of legal IP instruments.

The spatial distribution of holdings within Wales is uneven and does not necessarily accord with expectations. Some Objective One areas perform very well: former coalfield unitary authorities score highly on patenting, while rural areas in the north and west do well in trademarking. This latter finding, consistent with our observations for Scotland and Ireland, suggests that cultural distinctiveness is a public asset that can successfully be exploited to private advantage. Yet

Wales as a whole is lagging behind in this respect. It is likely that Scotland and Ireland have a more developed global identity. This merely underlines the potential tangible benefits from the public promotion of Wales's cultural heritage in the wider world.

ACKNOWLEDGEMENTS

We thank our colleagues Andrew Beale, David Blackaby, Mark Clement and Iwan Davies for comments on earlier drafts, Jeff Watson of the UK Patent Office for help in obtaining and interpreting data, and a referee for a number of helpful suggestions. The research has been supported by the European Regional Development Fund and the Welsh Development Agency. Needless to say, we take full responsibility for the contents of this article.

NOTES

[1] For further details of the legal criteria and procedures governing IP, see Beale and George, 2001.

[2] As a matter of official terminology, patents with UK coverage are described as 'British' (GB), whereas trademarks are identified as 'UK'.

[3] The Irish Patent Office publishes similar data but the particularities of the way in which it is compiled renders it unsuitable for comparative purposes.

[4] In the case of two sectors, metal constructions for buildings and measuring and optical equipment, activity is significantly greater (at the 5 per cent level) than implied by a random distribution. In the case of forging and metalworking it is significantly lower.

[5] A referee has suggested that this may be because of the need, among very large firms, to manage coordination via decentralization.

[6] The Kompass categories do have the advantage of allowing a comparison with the industrial distribution. This shows that five sectors, food and tobacco, drinks, furniture, electrical equipment and research testing, have significantly positive levels of trademarking. Forging and metalworking (as with patents) is significantly negative.

REFERENCES

Beale, A. and George, A. (2001). 'IP Wales report: a web-based project', *Wales Law Journal*, 1, 423–53.

Fagerberg, J. (1988). 'Why growth rates differ', in G. Dosi, C. Freeman, R. Nelson, G. Silverberg and L. Soete (eds), *Technical Change and Economic Theory*, London: Frances Pinter.

Fagerberg, J., Verspagen, B. and Caniels, M. (1997). 'Technology, growth and unemployment across European regions', *Regional Studies*, 31, 457–66.

Freeman, C. (1987). *Technology Policy and Economic Performance*, London: Frances Pinter.

Gould, D. M. and Gruben, W. C. (1996). 'The role of intellectual property rights in economic growth', *Journal of Development Economics*, 48, 323–50.

Greenhalgh, C. and Longland, M. (2002). 'Running to Stand Still? Intellectual property and value added in innovating firms', *mimeo*, Oxford: Intellectual Property Research Centre.

Greenhalgh, C., Longland, M. and Bosworth, D. (2000). 'Protecting intellectual property: British, European and American patents and trademarks of selected UK companies 1986–95', *Discussion Paper* 53, London: Centre for Economic Performance, LSE.

Greenhalgh, C., Longland, M. and Bosworth, D. (2001). 'Technological activity and employment in a panel of UK firms', *Scottish Journal of Political Economy*, 48, 260–82.

Levin, R. C., Klevorick, A., Nelson, R. R. and Winter, S. G. (1987). 'Appropriating the returns from industrial research and development', *Brookings Papers on Economic Activity*, 3, 783–820.

Lundvall, B.-A. and Johnson, B. (1994). 'The learning economy', *Journal of Industrial Studies*, 1, 23–42.

Mainwaring, L. (1995). 'Catching up and falling behind: south-east Asia and Wales', *Contemporary Wales*, 8, 9–28.

Mainwaring, L. and Moore, N. J. (2004). 'Trademark holdings of production firms in Britain and Ireland', *IP Wales*, Swansea: University of Wales Swansea.

Malerba, F. and Orsenigo, L. (1990). 'Technological regimes and patterns of innovation: a theoretical and empirical investigation of the Italian case', in A. Heertje and M. Perlman (eds), *Evolving Technology and Market Structure: Studies in Schumpeterian Economics*, Ann Arbor: University of Michigan Press.

Mansfield, E. (1986). 'Patents and innovation: an empirical study', *Management Science*, 32, 173–81.

Moore, N. J. and Mainwaring, L. (2004). 'Patent holdings of production firms: a cross-region analysis', *IP Wales*, Swansea: University of Wales Swansea.

Morgan, K. (1997). 'The learning region: institutions, innovation and regional renewal', *Regional Studies*, 31, 491–503.

Nelson, R. R. and Wolff, E. N. (1997). 'Factors behind cross-country differences in technical progress', *Structural Change and Economic Dynamics*, 8, 205–20.

Phelps, N. A., MacKinnon, D., Stone, I. and Braidford, P. (2003). 'Embedding the multinationals? Institutions and the development of overseas manufacturing affiliates in Wales and north east England', *Regional Studies*, 37, 549–78.

Rees, G. and Morgan, K. (1991). 'Industrial restructuring, innovation systems and the regional state: south Wales in the 1990s', in G. Day and G. Rees, (eds) *Regions, Nations and European Integration*, Cardiff: University of Wales Press.

Santangelo, G. D. (2002). 'The regional geography of corporate patenting in information and communications technology (ICT): domestic and foreign dimensions', *Regional Studies*, 36, 515–29.

Shankerman, M. and Pakes, A. (1986). 'Employment and technological innovation: evidence from UK manufacturing firms', *Journal of Labour Economics*, 15, 255–84.

16. THE WELSH ECONOMY: A STATISTICAL PROFILE

David Brooksbank

INTRODUCTION

This article is the annual statistical profile of the Welsh economy that mirrors the established format common to volumes nine to sixteen of *Contemporary Wales*. The discussion in the main text covers seven topics, namely: output, income and expenditure; employment; unemployment; earnings; house prices; and regional competitiveness. Once again this year there have been a few changes to the way in which the Office for National Statistics (ONS) has compiled the data for the regions, as well as some more substantial changes to the New Earnings Survey and these have has resulted in changes to some of the tables reproduced below. Where changes have occurred, the accompanying commentary describes the effect on the information. The tables are based on information made available prior to November 2004 and, as noted in previous surveys, compilation and production lags with respect to certain official statistics mean that 'latest' figures occasionally 'lag' by two or three years.

The review has been completed at a time when Wales has just 'celebrated' the award of £1 billion under the current round of EU structural funding and is looking to the future in terms of business support provision when such funding will not be so readily available. The announcement by the first minister, Rhodri Morgan, that the major quangos (Welsh Development Agency, ELWa and the Wales Tourist Board) will all be merged into the Assembly Government from April 2006 has sent a shockwave through the business support community and many commentators are now questioning what the longer-term impact of that decision will be on the Welsh economy. The information summarized in the tables below illustrates the profound nature of the economic development challenges that still lie ahead and it will be interesting to observe how, if at all, the economic development policies and programmes change under that new structure to address them. Appropriate data is available at a unitary authority

(UA) level and where comparisons are made with other UK regions, this review uses government office regions.

OUTPUT, INCOME AND EXPENDITURE

Gross Domestic Product (GDP) is an important indicator of the economic activity of a region and is the generally accepted means of comparing both national and regional performance. In recent years ONS has moved to calculate Gross Value Added (GVA) as its indicator of income and table 16.1 gives details of the GVA per head at basic prices for the government office regions of the UK in 2002. These are the latest figures available for the review and GVA per head in Wales was estimated to be £12,010, compared to an average GVA per head for the UK of £15,300. In 2002 Wales continued to slip further behind other regions with only 78.8 per cent of the UK average, a fall of 1.7 percentage points from the 1999 figure reported in last year's review.

In 2002, the south east had the highest growth at 4.7 per cent. Annual growth was lowest in the north east at 1.4 per cent. GVA per head in London (£20,000) was 31 per cent higher than the UK average of £15,300. In Northern Ireland it was 21 per cent lower and in the north east it was 23 per cent lower. The estimates for 2002 saw GVA per head rise above £11,000 in every region of the UK.

Individual consumption expenditure measures expenditure by households and non-profit-making institutions serving households resident in a region. There are no estimates of individual expenditure below the regional level (that is, below government office regions – NUTS level 1)[1] and hence it is now not possible to repeat the split by unitary authority or former council area in Wales.

The data available for household disposable income per head and individual consumption expenditure per head have not changed since the last review was written. ONS was unable to confirm the date for release of updated figures and so a time lag of five years now exists on these figures. Consideration will be given to their usefulness if the situation remains unchanged next year, but they are reported again in this review for completeness and consistency. Therefore, table 16.1 shows that in 1999 Wales had household disposable income per head of £9,113, with only the north east and Northern Ireland having a lower level. This represents a gap of 9.6 percentage points from the UK average. Whilst London and the south east skew most series of economic data, it is still evident that Wales falls behind comparable regions elsewhere in the UK.

Table 16.1
Regional accounts

	GVA per head at basic prices 2002		Household disposable income per head 1999		Individual consumption expenditure per head 1999	
	£	% of UK	£	% of UK	£	% of UK
London	20000	130.9	12036	119.4	12250	124.2
South east	18400	120.5	11249	111.6	11392	115.5
East	16800	110.0	11255	111.7	10077	102.2
South west	13900	91.4	9825	97.5	9600	97.3
West Midlands	13800	90.1	9195	91.2	9262	93.9
East Midlands	14000	91.8	9346	92.7	9057	91.8
Yorkshire and the Humber	13200	86.4	9305	92.3	8907	90.3
North west	13800	90.1	9375	93.0	9321	94.5
North east	11800	77.0	8353	82.9	8003	81.1
England	15600	102.5	10237	101.6	10057	102.0
Scotland	14400	94.6	9558	94.8	9459	95.9
Northern Ireland	12000	79.2	8659	85.9	8281	83.9
Wales	12010	78.8	9113	90.4	8206	83.2
United Kingdom	15300	100	10088	100	9864	100

Note 1: Gross Value Added (GVA).
Note 2: The differences between the old Standard Statistical Regions (SSRs) and the Government Office Regions (GORs) are that East Anglia SSR is combined with Essex, Hertfordshire and Bedfordshire to create the new Eastern GOR; London is a separate GOR; and Cumbria transfers from the old North SSR to the new North West GOR with the remainder of the North SSR becoming the North East GOR.
Note 3: Based on the European System of Accounts 1995 (ESA95).
Source: Office for National Statistics.

The index of production and construction for Wales is shown in table 16.2. Updated figures are reported to the second quarter of 2004 and show reasonably buoyant trading conditions to that date for the UK. The first two quarters of 2004 saw a small decline in the production industries sector and an even sharper decline in mining and quarrying. Output in mining and quarrying continued to fall in the UK, but the fall was slightly greater in Wales.

Within the manufacturing sector the largest falls were in the textile products categories, whilst the substantial positive growth seen in the transport equipment group in the UK was not mirrored in Wales. The decision by Marks and Spencer to source a larger proportion of its clothing products abroad and the closure of Baird's factories have had a significant impact on the textile sector in Wales over the past three years, especially in mid and west Wales. The re-based figures reflect this with a fall. Construction showed very positive growth of 17.7 per cent in the 2004 figures compared to a 6.3 per cent rise in the UK as a whole.

Table 16.2
Index of production and construction for Wales,[1,2,3,r] seasonally adjusted:[2] 2001 = 100

1992 Standard industrial classification			2001 Weights per thousand	Annual indices		Quarterly indices					Percentage change over latest 4 quarters on	
Section	Sub-section	Description		2002	2003	2003 Qtr 2	2003 Qtr 3	2003 Qtr 4	2004 Qtr 1	2004 Qtr 2	WALES	UK[3]
C–F		Production and construction	1000	101.5	102.2	101.1	101.2	105.4	104.3	107.4	3.0	1.6
C–E		Production industries	815	100.3	98.1	97.3	95.9	100.5	97.4	100.6	-0.8	0.4
C		Mining and quarrying	16	103.4	100.0	98.2	100.0	98.5	93.7	93.5	-6.9	-6.5
D		Manufacturing	723	98.6	97.2	96.7	96.0	98.4	96.1	97.9	-1.2	1.3
	DA	Food products, beverages and tobacco	78	110	113	108	109	116	113	119	1.6	0.2
	DB–DC	Textiles, textile products, leather and leather products	17	85	78	77	79	80	78	72	-3.7	-3.6
	DE	Pulp, paper and paper products; printing and publishing	62	105	101	94	104	112	82	78	-5.9	-1.5
	DF	Coke and refined petroleum products	26	105	95	103	75	101	111	117	-2.0	-2.5
	DG	Chemicals, chemical products and man-made fibres	70	103	96	97	94	92	100	100	-4.1	3.9
	DI	Other non-metallic mineral products	25	100	104	105	107	106	111	105	6.7	5.0
	DJ	Basic metals and fabricated metal products	118	88	76	76	73	75	78	81	-6.2	-0.5
	DK	Machinery and equipment not elsewhere classified	44	97	99	99	103	99	99	104	5.4	4.3
	DL	Electrical and optical equipment	112	89	92	91	92	90	92	93	0.4	-0.4
	DM	Transport equipment	76	105	113	114	114	109	101	108	-3.8	5.9
	DD, DH, DN	Other manufacturing (inc. rubber, plastic and wood)	94	102	105	105	103	109	107	106	2.6	n/a
E		Electricity, gas and water supply	77	115.7	106.4	103.7	94.0	120.6	110.3	127.3	4.4	2.2
F		Construction	185	106.9	120.2	117.6	124.5	127.5	134.7	137.4	17.7	6.3

[1] Revisions to the series are normally made each quarter to take account both of more recent information and improved seasonal factors.

[2] All series are seasonally adjusted unless otherwise stated in the notes for editors.

[3] UK production figures as published by ONS National Statistics on 29 September 2004. The series DD, DH, DN is not published separately for the UK.

[r] All data has been revised since previous publication.

Table 16.3
Identifiable general government expenditure: 2001–2002

	£ per head					Index (United Kingdom identifiable expenditure = 100)			
	England	Scotland	Wales	Northern Ireland	United Kingdom	England	Scotland	Wales	Northern Ireland
Agriculture, fisheries, food and forestry	76	345	185	398	114	67	302	162	348
Trade, industry, energy and employment	125	210	194	287	141	89	149	138	204
Roads and transport	195	224	177	146	195	100	115	91	75
Housing	62	165	86	102	73	85	226	117	140
Other environmental services	176	368	302	177	199	89	185	152	89
Law, order and protective services	379	438	368	701	393	97	112	94	178
Education	816	986	891	1048	841	97	117	106	125
Culture, media and sport	93	35	94	42	86	107	40	109	48
Health and personal social services	1224	1512	1355	1374	1260	97	120	108	109
Social security	1809	2007	2112	2204	1853	107	40	109	48
Miscellaneous[a]	50	35	111	138	54				
Total	5005	6324	5874	6616	5207	96	121	113	127

[a] Expenditure includes the costs of central administration of the offices of the secretaries of state of the territorial departments.
Source: HM Treasury.

The buoyant commercial property market in the major cities appears to have fuelled this rise and building programmes in Cardiff, Newport and Swansea continue apace.

Table 16.3 indicates that identifiable government expenditure per head was 14 per cent higher than in England for the financial year 2001–2. Once again the figure of £5,874 was the lowest of the three Celtic regions. The activities that grew most over the past year, relative to the average UK expenditure per head, were agriculture, fisheries, food and forestry and culture, media and sport. Unlike the previous year, the figures for departmental spending fell below that for England in the areas of roads and transport and law, order and protective services.

EMPLOYMENT

Comparative information about the workforce in Great Britain is given in tables 16.4 and 16.5. Table 16.4 shows the seasonally adjusted figures for employees in employment, giving data for government office regions, whilst table 16.5 illustrates the sectoral breakdown by industry for Wales and Great Britain. Table 16.4 is based on the most up-to-date Labour Force Survey (LFS) data available. These figures are felt, by ONS, to reflect better the actual number of employees and are published quarterly after the completion of each new wave of the LFS. This new data also includes the rate of employment that can be used to build comparative information over the next few years. A particularly important aspect of the National Economic Development Strategy for Wales is the creation of new and the safeguarding of existing jobs and targets for these will require close monitoring.

Table 16.4 shows that the numbers of employees in Great Britain increased over the past year by 0.3 per cent and, as unemployment has fallen nationally, many government office regions have seen a modest increase in employees. The LFS estimate of employment in Wales was 1,097 thousand in the March–June 2004 period, compared to 1,080 thousand in the same period a year earlier. Examining changes in employment by gender over the last year shows that male employment fell slightly by 0.1 per cent nationally whilst in Wales it rose by 0.7 per cent, equivalent to some 4,000 employees. Female employment rose by 1 per cent nationally, whereas female employment in Wales rose by 2.4 per cent.

Looking in more detail at the causes of these changes, table 16.5 shows that again Wales bucks the national trend in terms of the proportions of new jobs that are part time. Whilst Great Britain shows an increase in male part-time jobs of

0.3 per cent and a rise in female part-time jobs of 1.4 per cent, Wales shows a rise of 3.9 per cent for males and a rise of 2.4 per cent in the number of part-time jobs for females. This suggests that the pattern identified in previous reviews, when the question was raised as to the ability of Wales to secure full-time jobs as the major component of employment growth, has returned. Job creation rates for 2004 in Wales are slightly higher than the national average and the growth is accounted for by part-time employment. In 2004, female employment exceeded male in Wales and the rate of growth in female employment was higher than that for males. This is broadly the same as the picture on a national scale, although for Great Britain male employment was essentially static between 2003 and 2004 whereas for females it increased. Some commentators continue to express the view that many of the new full-time jobs created in Wales have been in areas where job security and pay rates are low (such as assembly line and call-centre type jobs).

This argument is not well supported by the figures for particular sectors presented in table 16.5. Again, despite the reported strength of parts of the manufacturing sector in Wales, this sector saw a fall of 2.2 per cent in 2004, equivalent to 4,000 jobs. Wholesale, retail, trade and repairs saw a rise of 0.6 per cent, or just 1,000 jobs. The overall position for employment was the net gain of some 17,000 jobs accounted for primarily by rises in public sector employment. Indeed, areas where Wales saw positive growth rates were education (2.8 per cent), public administration (2.4 per cent) and community, social and personal activities (8.5 per cent).

The argument between academics and industrialists alike over the impact and role of foreign direct investment (FDI) in Wales has continued apace over the past few years. Fewer new arrivals, together with high-profile closures in favour of cheap labour abroad, have also intensified the debate about the relative value of sterling against the Euro. The closure of plants with moves to eastern Europe has inevitably been blamed on the strong pound and the difficulty of competing in the export market. Table 16.6, which is unchanged from last year, illustrates the continuing importance of the foreign-owned plants to the Welsh economy. With some 320 plants, employing 68,000 people directly, they make up approximately 5 per cent of the employed workforce in Wales. It is still the case that many more jobs rely on their presence as part of the supply chain that now supports them. Employment in Wales is concentrated, therefore, in small firms, with current figures from the National On-line Manpower Information Service (NOMIS) estimating that 58 per cent of employees work in firms with fewer than 100 workers. The geographical distribution remains concentrated along the northern corridor created by the A55 and the southern corridor created by the M4. Bridgend now accounts for 8.8 per cent of foreign-owned manufacturing jobs,

with Rhondda Cynon Taff having 7.6 per cent, Caerphilly 7.1 per cent and
Wrexham 9.3 per cent. Newport has continued to attract new FDI and has risen to
9.0 per cent from 8.9 per cent.

Table 16.4
Employment: Wales, Great Britain and regions, thousands, seasonally adjusted

	March 2003–June 2003			March 2004–June 2004		
	Male	Female	Total	Male	Female	Total
London	2073	1852	3924	2115	1863	3979
South east	1846	1799	3646	1841	1803	3644
East	1135	1118	2253	1134	1124	2258
South west	1037	1036	2073	1038	1052	2091
West Midlands	1188	1129	2317	1166	1145	2311
East Midlands	889	863	1752	874	872	1745
Yorkshire and the Humber	1065	1056	2121	1067	1068	2135
North west	1494	1467	2961	1489	1489	2978
North east	506	498	1004	498	504	1002
Scotland	1093	1140	2233	1096	1145	2241
Wales	534	546	1080	538	559	1097
Great Britain	12861	12504	25365	12856	12624	25450

Note 1: Government Office Regions as described for table 16.1.
Source: Labour Market Trends.

As the earlier commentary stressed, economic regeneration over the next few
years will have to prioritize activities that lead to job creation. Indeed, as part of
the National Economic Development Strategy (A Winning Wales), the Welsh
Assembly Government set ambitious targets for new jobs which are not clearly
categorized by 'value added' to the economy. At a time when the UK economy
as a whole is close to or at full employment, it is the type of job that is important
because GDP will not be raised if the jobs created are low level. Just as previous
reviews have highlighted the rapid nature of global change (which has been
blamed for the failure of some high-profile inward investment projects), commentators are now becoming increasingly worried about the methods proposed
to create the required new jobs to achieve these targets. Essentially the debate
now centres on the correct recipe for economic regeneration. Should policies and
financial effort be directed to support the creation of higher-level, well-paid jobs
based on higher value-added production/R and D/skills, which will take a long
time to achieve, but will raise long-term living standards in Wales? Alternatively,
with political pressure to deliver new jobs quickly for a wide cross-section of
society, should support be given to the new breed of inward investors and
projects which create jobs rapidly? Whilst the final decisions inevitably become

clouded by political considerations, Wales has had a number of high-profile successes in the new 'call centre' market, with major new operations in Merthyr Tydfil and Swansea creating many hundreds of new jobs.

Table 16.5
Employee jobs (thousands) in Great Britain and Wales, by industry (SIC92),
June 2003 and June 2004

	Great Britain			Wales		
	June 2003	June 2004	% change	June 2003	June 2004	% change
Agriculture, hunting, forestry and fishing (A, B)	213	212	–	13	12	-8
Mining and quarrying (C)	61	57	-7	2	2	–
Manufacturing (D)	3362	3273	-3	184	180	-2
Electricity, gas and water supply (E)	130	129	–	9	9	–
Construction (F)	1151	1210	5	49	50	2
Wholesale, retail, trade and repairs (G)	4404	4426	1	176	177	1
Hotels and restaurants (H)	1740	1756	1	72	76	6
Transport, storage and communication (I)	1547	1520	-2	49	48	-2
Financial intermediation (J)	1084	1066	-2	21	22	5
Real estate, renting and business activities (K)	3898	3916	1	98	101	3
Public administration and defence: compulsory social security (L)	1428	1454	2	84	86	2
Education (M)	2189	2238	2	108	111	3
Health and social work (N)	2776	2842	2	153	156	2
Other community, social and personal activities (O–Q)	1343	1357	1	59	64	9
Service industries (G–Q)	20409	20575	1	821	841	2
Total male	12819	12827	–	533	536	1
Male part time	1956	1961	–	77	80	4
Total female	12515	12629	1	546	559	2
Female part time	6068	6155	1	274	282	3
Total	25334	25456	1	1078	1095	2

Note: Not seasonally adjusted.
Source: Labour Market Trends.

Table 16.6
Employment in overseas-owned manufacturing plants in Wales, by unitary authority, 2001

	Plants	Employees (thousands)	Percentage of total employees
Blaenau Gwent	22	3.0	4.4
Bridgend	15	6.0	8.8
Caerphilly	32	4.8	7.1
Cardiff	17	3.2	4.7
Carmarthenshire	15	3.2	4.7
Ceredigion	*	0.3	0.4
Conwy and Denbighshire	*	1.9	2.8
Flintshire	35	5.9	8.7
Gwynedd	7	1.2	1.8
Isle of Anglesey	6	1.0	1.5
Merthyr Tydfil	8	1.3	1.9
Monmouthshire	*	1.3	1.9
Newport	17	6.1	9.0
Neath and Port Talbot	14	4.6	6.8
Pembrokeshire	*	1.0	1.5
Powys	8	0.8	1.2
Rhondda Cynon Taff	39	5.2	7.6
Swansea	12	2.9	4.3
Torfaen	14	3.4	5.0
Vale of Glamorgan	12	4.6	6.8
Wrexham	36	6.3	9.3
Wales	320	68	100

* Figures suppressed to avoid disclosure.
Source: Welsh Register of Manufacturing Employment.

UNEMPLOYMENT

Unlike many of its European neighbours, high unemployment has become less of a problem for the UK in recent years. Table 16.7 displays regional unemployment rates in the UK over the last decade. Unemployment was generally fairly low at the end of the 1980s, but rose sharply during the recession of the early 1990s. Since 1994, official unemployment rates have fallen steadily, reaching their lowest levels since 1980 in 2003, at 3.0 per cent. This pattern has been replicated by all of the UK government office regions, with the exception of London which saw a very small rise. Unemployment in 2003 fell in Wales to 3.4 per cent (3.6 per cent in 2001), still being 0.4 percentage points above that for the UK average, but the gap between Wales and the rest of the UK does appear to be closing. Looking at the change in unemployment rates for other regions, Northern Ireland,

Scotland and the north east continue to have higher rates than Wales. London and the West Midlands also have higher rates than Wales and saw small rises in unemployment.

Table 16.8 shows unemployment for the government office regions in the UK in terms of the claimant count. The table shows the number of jobseekers claiming benefits, broken down by government office region. The count of jobseeker's allowance claimants is mostly derived from the Benefits Agency computer records. However, for various reasons (for example, when a claimant's National Insurance number is not known) a few claims have to be dealt with manually by local offices and these claimants are not then analysed by age and duration. Table 16.8 illustrates claimant count unemployment for the government office regions in the UK in March 2003 and March 2004 (that is, the number of jobseekers claiming benefits, broken down by government office region). All regions witnessed a fall in the number of claimants in the period. This applied in most cases to both males and females, providing further evidence that the economy is continuing to perform well. In Wales the stock of claimants fell by 9 per cent, compared to a fall of 6.1 per cent for the UK as a whole. This may be the tentative first sign that Wales has begun to buck the trend of being amongst the lowest-performing regions in the UK. Statistics such as these have been grasped quickly by the Welsh Assembly Government and are certainly worthy of following up over time as this review develops over the period of structural funding. Wales appears to have set itself extremely ambitious development targets for the next decade and yet the economic evidence from the data has been that those targets are actually accelerating away every year. Some economists have started to argue that this is the legacy or consequence of the lack of investment in the infrastructure required to support higher-level functions in Wales. This year for the first time in a decade there is some evidence that the economy may not be moving away from the rest of the UK as badly as had been predicted.

Table 16.9 provides information about the age of claimants combined with the duration of spells of unemployment by government office region. The past year has seen a fall in the numbers of 'unemployed for more than one year' category in every government office region. In September 2004 in Wales the percentage of total unemployed who had been out of work for more than one year was 15.5, an increase of 0.9 percentage points over the previous year. Long-term unemployment continues to be a difficult and stubborn problem across the UK. When combined with the issue of high economic inactivity rates in Wales, the correct or most appropriate mix of policies to address the problem becomes even more difficult to identify.

Table 16.7
Annual average unemployment rates, Wales, United Kingdom and regions, (claimant count)
males and females combined, seasonally adjusted, 1994–2003

	1994	1995	1996	1997	1998	1999	2000	2001	2002	2003
South east	7.3	5.9	5.0	3.4	2.7	2.4	1.8	1.6	1.7	1.7
East	8.1	6.5	5.9	4.1	3.3	3.0	2.3	2.1	2.2	2.2
London	10.7	9.4	8.5	6.4	5.3	4.8	3.7	3.3	3.6	3.7
South west	8.1	6.8	6.1	4.3	3.5	3.1	2.3	2.1	2.0	1.9
West Midlands	9.9	8.1	7.2	5.5	4.7	4.6	4.1	3.7	3.5	3.5
East Midlands	8.7	7.4	6.7	4.9	4.0	3.8	3.4	3.2	2.9	2.9
Yorkshire and the Humber	9.6	8.5	7.8	6.3	5.5	5.1	4.3	4.0	3.7	3.4
North west	8.7	8.5	7.7	6.0	5.3	4.9	4.2	3.7	3.6	3.3
North east	12.4	11.2	10.2	8.4	7.5	7.2	6.3	5.5	5.0	4.6
Scotland	9.3	7.9	7.6	6.4	5.7	5.4	4.6	4.2	4.1	3.9
Northern Ireland	12.6	11.2	10.7	8.2	7.4	6.5	5.4	5.0	4.6	4.3
Wales	9.3	8.4	8.0	6.4	5.6	5.2	4.5	3.9	3.6	3.4
United Kingdom	9.3	8.0	7.2	5.5	4.7	4.3	3.6	3.2	3.1	3.0

Note 1: Government Office Regions as described for table 16.1.
Note 2: Rates for 2003 reflect revision for the census 2001 population changes and latest revisions to the mid-year population data.
Source: Labour Market Trends.

Table 16.8
Unemployment: Wales, United Kingdom and regions. Claimants, thousands,
not seasonally adjusted, March 2003 and March 2004

	March 2004			March 2003		
	Male	Female	Total	Male	Female	Total
South east	58.0	20.5	78.5	59.4	20.4	79.8
East	43.8	17.0	60.8	45.6	16.9	62.5
London	121.3	47.0	168.4	125.4	48.6	174.0
South west	34.9	13.0	47.9	39.0	14.2	53.2
West Midlands	72.0	23.3	95.2	95.9	23.5	99.4
East Midlands	42.9	15.7	58.6	46.4	16.2	62.6
Yorkshire and the Humber	62.3	19.2	81.6	69.6	21.4	90.9
North west	83.8	25.7	109.5	94.1	27.0	121.1
North east	39.7	11.3	51.0	45.4	12.5	57.9
Scotland	79.5	24.0	103.5	82.5	24.6	107.2
Northern Ireland	25.1	7.3	32.4	26.9	7.7	34.6
Wales	33.9	10.8	44.6	37.6	11.4	49.0
United Kingdom	697.2	234.8	932.0	747.9	244.4	992.3

Note: Government Office Regions as described for table 16.1.
Source: Labour Market Trends.

It is not only at the national level where unemployment rates have converged over the last decade, as a similar process has been occurring in Wales, as shown in table 16.10, which reports unemployment rates by unitary authority (UA). The rates range from 1.5 per cent in Monmouthshire and Wrexham to 3.7 per cent in Blaenau Gwent. Most areas experienced a fall in the overall rate of unemployment between September 2003 and September 2004, despite some job losses following closures in a number of areas. These falls are general and not restricted to either urban or rural areas. Looking at the larger towns and cities, Cardiff's rate of unemployment fell from 3.0 per cent to 2.4 per cent, Swansea's fell from 3.0 per cent to 2.5 per cent, Newport's fell again from 3.5 per cent to 2.6 per cent and Wrexham's fell from 2.2 per cent to 1.5 per cent. In the rural areas, for example, Ceredigion's rate fell from 1.9 per cent to 1.4 per cent and Gwynedd's fell from 3.4 per cent to 2.3 per cent. Male unemployment continues to be a major problem. Table 16.10 shows that in Blaenau Gwent this remains at the high level of 8.7 per cent, with a similar rate of 8.7 per cent on the Isle of Anglesey. Female unemployment rates remain much lower, with no UA having a rate above 4.8 per cent (Blaenau Gwent).

Table 16.9
Male unemployment by duration and age: Wales, United Kingdom and regions, September 2004

	Unemployed for over 52 and up to 104 weeks	Unemployed for over 104 weeks	Per cent claiming over 1 year
South east	5393	2227	15.7
East	3925	1686	14.9
London	16567	7974	21.6
South west	2549	1153	13.3
West Midlands	7526	4264	18.6
East Midlands	4204	2073	17.7
Yorkshire and the Humber	5084	2314	14.2
North west	7416	3783	15.7
North east	3229	1848	15.5
Scotland	7731	3502	17.0
Northern Ireland	4249	2059	27.9
Wales	2777	1625	15.5
United Kingdom	70650	34508	17.5

Note: Government Office Regions as described for table 16.1.
Source: Labour Market Trends.

UA unemployment is the lowest level for which unemployment rates are given because unemployment rates for travel-to-work areas (TTWAs) are not reported in this section due to the recent debate over the legitimacy of these statistics. The TTWA unemployment rate is defined as the claimant unemployment rate in the area divided by the sum of the employees within the area plus the resident unemployed. Therefore, the unemployment rate in areas with a large number of in-commuters will be underestimated, for example, in urban centres, whereas the unemployment rate will be overestimated in those areas where there is out-commuting, for example, in rural areas. UA unemployment rates are also open to the same argument of self-containment but its effect will be reduced because of the greater geographical size of UAs.

Table 16.10
Unemployment by unitary authority and Wales, unadjusted, workforce base, September 2004

	Male		Female		All	
	Number	Rate	Number	Rate	Number	Rate
Blaenau Gwent	1147	8.7	381	4.8	1528	3.7
Bridgend	1121	4.2	435	1.2	1556	2.0
Caerphilly	2001	5.9	682	2.5	2683	2.6
Cardiff	3582	3.8	1102	1.0	4684	2.4
Carmarthenshire	1385	5.6	534	1.7	1919	1.9
Ceredigion	493	2.9	191	1.5	684	1.4
Conwy	893	5.2	276	1.2	1169	1.9
Denbighshire	775	3.5	249	1.0	1024	1.9
Flintshire	1049	2.9	416	1.2	1465	1.6
Gwynedd	1212	6.2	385	2.0	1597	2.3
Isle of Anglesey	989	8.7	350	2.9	1338	3.4
Merthyr Tydfil	799	7.9	247	2.7	1046	3.1
Monmouthshire	512	2.9	229	1.1	741	1.5
Neath and Port Talbot	1486	5.1	500	2.4	1986	2.5
Newport	1623	4.6	529	1.1	2152	2.6
Pembrokeshire	1262	7.0	398	1.7	1660	2.5
Powys	790	2.1	373	1.4	1163	1.6
Rhondda Cynon Taff	2200	4.9	860	2.3	3060	2.2
Swansea	2551	5.2	842	1.4	3393	2.5
Torfaen	777	4.9	294	1.5	1072	2.0
Vale of Glamorgan	1120	4.9	386	1.5	1506	2.1
Wrexham	879	3.6	336	0.7	1215	1.5
Wales	28646	3.9	9995	1.1	38641	2.2

Note: Rates are calculated as wholly unemployed claimants as a percentage of the working-age population of the area.
Source: NOMIS.

EARNINGS

The decline of Welsh earnings relative to the British average over the past twenty years has been extremely well documented. Indeed, it is the low level of earnings which contributes directly to low GDP and hence the need for European Structural Fund help. Once again, according to the 2003 *New Earnings Survey* (NES03), Wales still lags behind every other region of Great Britain in terms of earnings, apart from north-east England. Table 16.11 provides a broad earnings picture of the main subgroups of full-time employees in the regions of Britain in 2003. The average weekly wage is £414.5 for Welsh employees, who earn £12.40 more than their counterparts in north-east England. Employees in Wales saw average earnings growth of 3.7 per cent in the twelve months to April 2003, compared to a national increase of 2.3 per cent, so the gap may be starting to narrow. However, Welsh employees continue to earn far less than 90 per cent of the British average of £475.8 a week. Again, here is evidence that some economic development targets are going to prove more difficult than others to achieve.

The earnings performance of Welsh females has been relatively better than that of the males in recent years and this was again marginally the case in 2003. As a region, Wales is no longer the worst-performing area, having crept ahead of north-east England for the first time in five years. Welsh female earnings continue to be only one place ahead of their male counterparts with figures showing a ranking of ninth out of the eleven GB regions. The annual earnings increases for 2002–3 were 3.6 per cent and 3.5 per cent respectively for Welsh males and females, compared with 2.2 per cent and 3.3 per cent for Britain as a whole. Unfortunately, in 2003, the NES stopped producing data that identifies the split between manual and non-manual workers and so there is no further comparative data to report in this review.

Given the lower average earnings in Wales, one would expect Welsh employees to be more heavily concentrated at the bottom of the earnings distribution than the other regions. This is confirmed by table 16.12, which reports the percentage of employees earning less than specified lower earnings thresholds. These were set at £250 for males and £180 a week for females in 2003. Welsh males again ranked tenth out of the eleven regions and Welsh females fared slightly better as the East Midlands and the north east had a greater percentage of their workers earning less than £180 per week.

Table 16.13 illustrates the wide variation of earnings within Wales. Data is presented for all unitary authorities where sample sizes were sufficient in the *NES03* to allow for publication. Simple observation of the figures shows the marked difference in average weekly earnings that exists between even neighbouring unitary authorities and the skewed distribution of income within authority areas is further highlighted by the 90/10 earnings differential. Earnings data were available for 14 out of the 22 UAs in 2003, with Blaenau Gwent, Ceredigion, Denbighshire, Isle of Anglesey, Merthyr Tydfil, Monmouthshire, Pembrokeshire and the Vale of Glamorgan unable to meet the sampling criteria of the *NES*. In 2003, Cardiff had the highest average earnings of the UAs reported of £455 per week, although this again fell short of the Great Britain average of £476. Table 16.14 also shows that Swansea remains below the Welsh average with earnings of £385. Gwynedd has the lowest reported weekly earnings of the 14 UAs with a figure of £360.20 a week.

The 90/10 earnings differential, which is expressed as the earnings figure which the top 10 per cent of workers earn more than, divided by the respective figure for the bottom 10 per cent, stayed constant in 2003 at 3.14. This simple measure suggests that earnings inequality stayed the same and therefore did not improve in 2003. Looking at the county-based data, earning inequality worsened in Blaenau Gwent, Flintshire, Newport, Rhondda Cynon Taff, Swansea, Torfaen and Wrexham. In the remaining authority areas the inequality was reduced slightly.

A major drawback of the *NES* data published in the tables is that they exclude part-time workers altogether and miss out many of those with low wages because they only cover full-time workers who earn in excess of the lower earnings limit. The tables and the survey itself also ignore the self-employed on the grounds that earnings data from this group is highly unreliable. Unfortunately, the problem of 'missing data' is important for Wales, where the proportion of part-time employees is higher and wages are lower than the national averages. The true position in Wales is therefore likely to be worse than that shown. Analysis has revealed that the part-time workforce remains overwhelmingly female and is continuing to grow. Some 45 per cent of all women workers in Great Britain work part time (less than thirty hours) compared with 10 per cent of male workers. The female part-time workforce has increased by 28 per cent over the last ten years while the female workforce as a whole grew by 22 per cent. However, a growing number of men now work part time. In ten years the male part-time workforce has grown 138 per cent. Also, whilst the majority of people working part time do so out of choice, the proportion who do so involuntarily because they cannot find full-time work has risen by 50 per cent in the last ten years, from 8 per cent to 12 per cent. This growth is likely to be accounted for by the large number of unemployed men aged 50–60, who may prefer to work part time rather than not to work at all. Part-time work is concentrated in three occupations – clerical work, personal and protective services and sales – together these employ six in ten part-timers. Part-time workers earn just 70 per cent of the average hourly earnings of full-timers and just 5 per cent of part-timers are in managerial jobs compared with 15 per cent of employees as a whole, but twice as many male part-timers make the managerial grade compared with women part-timers.

Table 16.11
Average gross weekly earnings: Wales, Great Britain and regions, £s. All industries and services. Full-time employees on adult rates, April 2003

	Males	Females	All employees
London	716.5	516.5	636.9
South east	560.9	415.7	505.6
East	528.5	382.7	475.9
South west	485.1	364.7	440.6
West Midlands	477.1	367.7	435.8
East Midlands	467.3	357.4	428.7
Yorkshire and the Humber	463.8	360.4	425.5
North west	483.1	367.9	437.6
North east	437.8	347.3	402.1
Scotland	483.7	372.4	436.8
Wales	448.3	357.3	414.5
Great Britain	525.0	396.0	475.8

Note: In 2003 the NES stopped the production of statistics splitting manual and non-manual employees.
Source: New Earnings Survey, 2003.

Table 16.12
Distribution of gross weekly earnings: Wales, Great Britain and regions, £s. All industries and services. Full-time employees on adult rates, April 2003. Percentage with weekly earnings less than £250

	All males	All females
London	6.7	11.1
South east	8.7	18.4
East	9.5	24.3
South west	12.2	27.5
West Midlands	11.0	28.5
East Midlands	11.9	31.6
Yorkshire and the Humber	12.1	28.9
North west	13.1	27.9
North east	16.5	31.6
Scotland	13.2	26.1
Wales	15.2	30.8
Great Britain	11.1	24.1

Source: New Earnings Survey, 2003.

Table 16.13
Average gross weekly earnings, £s, and the 90/10 differential, Wales and unitary authorities.
All industries and services, full-time employees on adult rates, April 2003

	All employees	90/10 differential
Blaenau Gwent	–	–
Bridgend	428.0	3.12
Caerphilly	388.9	3.24
Cardiff	455.3	3.22
Carmarthenshire	379.2	2.95
Ceredigion	–	–
Conwy	385.4	3.03
Denbighshire	–	–
Flintshire	445.8	2.86
Gwynedd	360.2	3.46
Isle of Anglesey	–	–
Merthyr Tydfil	–	–
Monmouthshire	–	–
Neath and Port Talbot	447.3	3.09
Newport	421.9	2.99
Pembrokeshire	–	–
Powys	401.7	3.02
Rhondda Cynon Taff	396.1	3.45
Swansea	385.3	2.98
Torfaen	407.6	2.84
Vale of Glamorgan	–	–
Wrexham	388.7	3.05
Wales	414.5	3.14

Notes: – denotes not available as sample requirements were not met.
Source: New Earnings Survey, 2003.

There is little empirical research evidence conducted to date that has adequately, or indeed accurately, determined the impact of the minimum wage on workers in Wales. The types of industries most affected are likely to fall in the hospitality and business services areas, as well as care services. Anecdotal evidence suggests that the relatively low level of minimum wage has had little impact on employment levels, but that employers are taking advantage of the ability to offer a minimum wage for a wider, larger number of certain types of employee. One consequence, if this is true, is that earnings will rise only by the amount of any statutory increase in the minimum wage and thus closing the gap with other regions becomes even more difficult if large numbers of workers are effectively taken out of the equation.

HOUSE PRICES

In 2003 there was a continuation of the dramatic increases in house prices seen across the UK. The property boom has seen prices rise by 20.5 percent during the year, according to the *HBOS House Price Index*. The steady rise in prices has been fuelled by the low cost of borrowing and has emanated in waves from London and the south east. At the regional level, prices have risen in every area, with record rises in Wales, the north and the north west, where the shortage of properties for sale has created a market where buyers queue to view and the phenomenon of gazumping has returned. In the south east, the rate of rise has slowed and in some cases reversed very slightly. However, the ripple effect has by no means come to a stop in the regions. Despite five small increases in interest rates over the past year, there appears to be no immediate sign that the housing market is going to collapse or that we will return to the days of negative equity last seen in the recession of the early 1990s.

Table 16.15 gives seasonally adjusted regional house price data for the UK regions in the third quarter of 2004. The largest rise has been in Wales itself, where the cost of an average semi-detached house has risen to £142,388, an annual rise of 37.5 per cent. Outside London, the north saw a rise of 36.8 per cent, with an average house now costing £129,632. Far more modest rises have been evident in the south east (10.9 per cent).

According to the HBOS Bank, the average homebuyer in Wales now spends just over 22 per cent of their gross annual income on mortgage payments compared to a peak of 33 per cent in 1990. Equally, most of the housing activity has been based on the urban areas, especially Cardiff, Newport and parts of Swansea, where there are now reported shortages of property coming onto the market. Property 'hotspots' continue in the Cardiff area as demand continues to outstrip supply. The housing market has remained flat in some of the Valleys and parts of West Glamorgan, observations that seem to mirror local economic conditions. As yet the HBOS Index does not provide information on a UA basis; instead data is available for some former counties which allow for comparison at a sub-regional level.

Demand for property in fashionable areas such as Cardiff and Newport has pushed up the costs of housing, especially for first-time buyers who are now finding it even harder to find properties within their reach. The difficulties faced by first-time buyers in Wales are, of course, widespread. However, the major regional differences in house price inflation that have accompanied this boom also make it very difficult for workers of all levels who own properties to relocate out of Wales (and make relocation to Wales from outside relatively inexpensive). Whether this is good or bad for the economy is open to debate.

The figures for county variations in table 16.14 continue to show evidence of a north–south and east–west divide in Wales. The HBOS Bank figures show that along the M4 corridor in south Wales average prices for a semi-detached property are £160,672 in Cardiff, £130,706 in Newport and £131,153 in Swansea. In Wrexham in the north, the same property would cost £146,846.

Table 16.14
Average house prices, third quarter 2004, United Kingdom, regions and former Welsh counties

Regions of the UK	£	Annual % change	Welsh counties and cities	£
South east	219,153	10.9	South Glamorgan	161,815
East Anglia	164,043	17.4	Gwent	133,033
South west	184,869	17.1	Clwyd	141,914
West Midlands	158,802	19.6	Mid Glamorgan	113,639
East Midlands	146,346	21.4	West Glamorgan	121,404
Yorkshire and Humberside	119,098	26.6	Dyfed	141,549
North west	124,908	30.5	Gwynedd	134,854
North	129,632	36.8	Cardiff	160,672
Scotland	99,904	22.4	Newport	130,706
Northern Ireland	106,445	21.0	Swansea	131,153
Wales	142,388	37.5	Wrexham	146,846
United Kingdom	161,746	20.5		

Notes: Counties figures are average semi-detached prices.
Source: HBOS House Price Index.

COMPETITIVENESS

This final section of the review considers the most recent data from the Department of Trade and Industry's (DTI) Regional Competitiveness Indicators (September 2002). In this year's review there are data series from 1999 through to September 2003 which summarize the variables considered by the DTI to be most important in making regional comparisons of this sort. These are gross domestic product (measured as explained earlier by GVA) per head, household disposable income per head, total income support claimants and manufacturing investment by foreign- and UK-owned companies.

GVA and household disposable income measure different aspects of a region's income. The former gives an indication of the size of the local economy – regardless of where the income from that economy accrues – and the latter gives an indication of the income residents within regions have to spend on goods and services.

GVA per head is here repeated in index form from table 16.1. It is measured as the income of those working in a region including commuters (workplace basis) and these data are used in international comparisons at sub-national level because they are readily available internationally. Wales has the third lowest GVA per head figure (some 78.8 per cent of the UK average), after Northern Ireland and the north east, of all regions in the UK in 2002. The 'Winning Wales' targets are for this gap to narrow to only 10 percentage points. Such a change means that Wales must grow on average by approximately 1 per cent per annum more rapidly than the average for the rest of the UK. Such a growth rate, which to date has not been achieved by Wales, is one that this review must track carefully over the coming years.

Household disposable income is here again defined according to the European System of Accounts 1995 (ESA95). The figures are again unchanged from last year's review and are for 1999. They show that Wales had a level of 90.4 per cent of the UK average, above that for Northern Ireland and the north east. As the section above on earnings discussed, income levels in Wales continue to lag behind other UK regions and the reduction of unemployment over the last year appears to have been achieved without a consequent increase in relative earnings.

The number of income support claimants is a measure of social deprivation in a region. The indicator used shows the number of income support claimants as a proportion of the population aged over sixteen. Since the introduction of the job seekers' allowance the figures for the unemployed are no longer included in the income support claimant figures. This has resulted in the figures being between 3–6 percentage points lower than those published earlier in the series. In August 2003, Wales had 10.2 per cent of the population claiming income support, compared to the UK average of 8.8 per cent.

Manufacturing investment and output by foreign-owned companies is a measure of the attractiveness of a region to foreign investors and the importance of foreign investment to the manufacturing base of a region. Table 16.15 shows the same figures as were presented in last year's review. In 2001 just over £16 billion was invested in the UK, a third of which was from foreign-owned companies. Investment is measured by net capital expenditure. Individual yearly data should be treated with caution as large one-off investment decisions by companies can make significant differences to total investment figures in a particular region. This indicator covers only manufacturing; a comparison with the service sector is not possible due to lack of data.

Table 16.15
Regional competitiveness indicators

Region	GVA per head (UK=100) 2002	Household disposable income per head (UK=100) 1999	Total income support claimants (proportion of population over 16) % August 2003	Manufacturing investment by foreign- and UK-owned companies (£ million) 2001	
				Foreign	UK
London	130.9	119.4	9.8	229	686
South east	120.5	111.6	5.7	724	1101
East	110.0	111.7	6.4	429	1009
South west	91.4	97.5	6.9	633	860
West Midlands	90.1	91.2	9.3	856	933
East Midlands	91.8	92.7	7.7	344	942
Yorkshire and the Humber	86.4	92.3	9.3	437	976
North west	90.1	93.0	10.8	453	1592
North east	77.0	82.9	11.6	636	548
England	102.5	101.6	8.4	4740	8646
Scotland	94.6	94.8	10.6	502	957
Northern Ireland	79.2	85.9	13.9	161	281
Wales	78.8	90.4	10.2	361	500
United Kingdom	100	100	8.8	5774	10384

Source: Regional Competitiveness Indicators (DTI).

OVERVIEW

The economic make-up of the Welsh economy continues to change over time. In the last thirty years it has ceased to rely on heavy manufacturing and extractive industries and has developed capacity in areas of new technology. However, many of the new industries have not been in the high value-added sector and so Wales has a major problem in developing its GDP using means available to other regions of the UK. Much of this change has been forced on it through economic necessity and the policies that were pursued to reduce unemployment and regenerate industry were kept in place for many years. These policies generally involved large-scale inward investment and the building of related supply chains. The emphasis has now swung quite dramatically towards the promotion of indigenous businesses and in the space of five years a whole raft of business support programmes and funding opportunities have sprung up to support enterprise and entrepreneurship. Now in its second term, the Labour-led National Assembly has a whole series of ambitious strategies and policies aimed at developing the economy. The Winning Wales overall strategy is complemented by an Entrepreneurship Action Plan for Wales, an Innovation Action Plan and an unprecedented move to amalgamate all centrally funded business support from the WDA and ELWa into the Welsh Assembly Government from April 2006. Whether being civil servants will enable the employees of these support services to deliver better outcomes for the economy, only time will tell.

NOTE

[1] NUTS (Nomenclature des Unites Territoriales Statistiques) was established by the Statistical Office of the European Union (EUROSTAT) to provide a uniform breakdown of territorial units for the production of regional statistics. NUTS is a five-level hierarchical system with Wales being NUTS1 and the two sub-regional units of West Wales and the Valleys and East Wales being NUTS2).

REFERENCES

Regional Competitiveness Indicators (2002). *Department of Trade and Industry*, September edn, London: DTI.
Department of Trade and Industry (2002). *Regional Competitiveness Indicators*, September edn, London: DTI.

17. BOOK REVIEWS

Molly Scott Cato, *The Pit and the Pendulum: A Co-operative Future for Work in the Welsh Valleys*, Cardiff: University of Wales Press, 2003. Pp. xx, 274. £17.99.

It has been a long-lived and oft-repeated refrain that 'something must be done' to regenerate the economic fortunes of the south Wales Valleys. Yet, after decades of various kinds of targeted policy programme, the area still faces scandalously high levels of socio-economic deprivation. This book represents an important and timely contribution to the continuing question of 'what is to be done' in the Valleys. In particular, it bravely sets out fresh analysis and radical thinking which seeks to identify solutions that will not repeat the tired, worn-out formulas that have already been tried and failed. Taking the most impoverished Valleys local authority district, Rhondda Cynon Taff (RCT), as its focus, the book presents both original research and a useful summary of available statistics. Here is an up-to-date profile of the area's economic and labour market characteristics, representing a valuable contribution to the literature on this under-researched locality. This shows how policies of job creation in the Valleys both prior to and since devolution, mainly focused on attracting foreign inward investment (though now increasingly controversial), have had only very limited success in reducing the area's high unemployment rates. Against this, Scott Cato argues for 'a realization of the need for us, the people of Wales, to revitalize our own economy' (p. 89).

The book's real strength, however, is its scope. In investigating local workers' values and attitudes, the author manages to produce a more penetrating representation of the complexity of RCT's situation than one based on economic information alone. For example, chapter 5 is given over to a discussion of the negative impacts of industrial closure and unemployment on communities and individuals, and there is also valuable analysis of the values and beliefs of local people when it comes to attitudes to various forms of work. Scott Cato points out that in the recent talk amongst policy-makers of the need for 'embedding' – that is, for inward-investing companies to 'integrate' into the locality – there is a persistent tendency to define the locality in purely economic terms (such as skill levels and the local supply chain), and to ignore the realities of its established cultural and social relations. The solutions the author proposes lie in cooperative or 'associative' models of job creation that will better fit, it is argued, with the culture of the local inhabitants. Hers is a project located within that politically committed but often sidelined genre of academic work which insists on recognition of the human and political implications of policy and research. It does so by arguing that policy-makers must recognize the link between their interventions and the needs and desires of the people they are supposed to serve. The author concludes: 'It is our money that is spent on creating jobs, good or bad, and it is therefore our right, and the right of people in RCT, to have jobs that we choose, not those that are chosen to suit the profit-drive of global corporations' (p. 142).

At the core of the original research reported on in the book lies a study of the attitudes of a sample of RCT workers towards different kinds of work. The occupations studied were divided into the private, public and cooperative sectors (with the latter represented by workers at Tower Colliery). In particular, the author examined the relationship between respondents' assessments of their own job satisfaction and their perception of the 'social value' and earnings value of different jobs. The results suggest that the Tower workers score most highly in terms of both job satisfaction and satisfaction with earnings (its manual workers earn more than the high-skilled workers at a local engineering company). Although the high levels of occupational gender segregation in the sectors surveyed made direct comparison difficult, the data obtained suggests that those employed in the private sector have a lower level of job satisfaction and lower pay levels than those in the public or cooperative sectors. The survey also suggests that the kind of jobs seen as socially valuable by RCT workers in all sectors are those in the traditionally working-class, craft-based, practical or caring occupations – such as nursing, rubbish collection and plumbing. Less valued are the more 'elite' occupations of company executive and surveyor. More importantly, in terms of job creation, all sectors valued most highly the creation of jobs with a 'living wage' and good security – considerations which, as Scott Cato notes, have not been influential in driving Wales's long-established foreign inward-investment strategy. As she shows, most jobs created by inward investment offer poor wages and low levels of job security.

The survey insights are supplemented by a small number of qualitative interviews, which add considerably to the richness of the data and the fullness of the picture the author is able to paint (though her choice of interviewees appears rather arbitrary). This data offer support for previous studies (for example,

Thomas, 1988; Rees and Thomas, 1994) which have identified in Valleys ex-industrial workers a marked absence of entrepreneurial 'spirit' or readiness to start up in business. This reflects, according to the author's research, a lack of motivation in local people's employment choices for becoming 'rich or powerful'. Instead, those interviewed valued job security and a wage that would support 'living' rather than just 'survival'. In addition, they valued camaraderie and personal autonomy in work routines, and disliked what they perceived as the 'robotic' monitoring of workers in factory employment. This was reflected in the high number of ex-miners employed elsewhere who said they would return to mining 'tomorrow' – if such jobs were still available.

The author's solutions are for economic policies based on local self-reliance and 'associative entrepreneurship'. Such a policy, she contends, should take advantage of Wales's four most valuable and underused resources: its people, its land, its coal and its water. It should promote the development of 'co-operative businesses that prioritize making a living above making a profit and that involve their workers in workplace decisions or are even wholly owned by their workers'. These, she contends, 'would be a far better "fit" with the local culture than the individualist entrepreneurial model propagated by government agencies' (p. 227). Specifically, she advocates the active stimulation of third-sector and non-competitive business start-ups supported by radical policy changes. These include adoption of a citizen's income (a basic allowance given to everyone, over and above their earnings, designed to enable people to escape the benefits trap) together with increased use of credit unions, community banking and even government-supported local currencies. Though these solutions may seem far-fetched to those inured to the market-led consensus of most mainstream policy-making, there is no doubt that radical solutions are needed for RCT (and indeed for other impoverished areas of Wales and the UK). The ones Scott Cato proposes are based on detailed, in-depth and convincing analysis of the area's specific problems.

Although the analysis of values and attitudes was one of the book's real strengths, I was less sure about the conclusions drawn from it regarding local 'identity'. If I have a criticism of the author's approach, it is the frequent equations drawn between the employment policies advocated and the 'culture' imputed to local people. Although careful both to acknowledge the dangers of myth-ologizing community attributes as well as generalizing from small-scale data-sets, Scott Cato appears confident in making quite sweeping assertions (evidenced in claims such as 'Welsh people are more concerned with quality of life than with profit', p. 206). In making her case for economic self-reliance, in other words, she seeks justification in the essential qualities of 'the people of Wales' –

assuming in the process a cultural unity which is surely more imagined than real. Although differently expressed, the same kind of uneasy equation between economic success and cultural identity also underpins much of Wales's failed policy approaches of recent times, as Scott Cato herself identifies (as in the widely prevalent assumption that Valleys people have low expectations and are unable to help themselves). It would have been more convincing, perhaps, to make the same arguments by asserting what is in local people's *interests*, rather than in claims about what reflects their authentic 'identity'. The other reservation I have is based on the widespread view that in the light of today's globalized economic relations and free-trade agreements, there is little that can be done by localities to instigate locally derived economic policies. I would have liked to see more analysis of how such barriers might be overcome – though perhaps this topic is best reserved for the author's next book.

Bella Dicks
Cardiff School of Social Sciences

REFERENCES

Thomas, M. (1988). 'Colliery closure, entrepreneurship and industrial change', *Coalfield Communities Campaign Working Paper*, 15.
Rees, G. and Thomas, M. (1994). 'Inward investment, labour market adjustment and skills development: recent experience in south Wales', *Local Economy*, 9, 48–61.

Peter Garrett, Nikolas Coupland and Angie Williams, *Investigating Language Attitudes: Social Meanings of Dialect, Ethnicity and Performance*, Cardiff: University of Wales Press, 2003. Pp. x, 251. £45.00.

In Wales the expression 'After all, English is "the" language' is commonly heard. What is meant is the kind of discussion of English as the 'hypercentral' language of the world (De Swaan, 2001), or as a language whose influence in the world has no historical precedent (Crystal, 1997). However, even the most powerful head of state in the world can 'read bedtime stories' and be 'a wonderful dad' according to Jenna and Barbara Bush (Republican Party Convention, Manhattan, NY, 9 January 2004). Likewise 'the' language, as Peter Garrett, Nikolas Coupland and Angie Williams make plain can give expression to localized meanings and is spoken and listened to as a resource for the construction of identities by members of local communities in Wales. The book is also an exploration of methods of investigating social meanings of particular varieties of English, so it has importance for anywhere in the world where English is very much a local language, on its own or alongside others.

Many of the findings of the book have importance beyond the realm of linguistics. In many social science studies in Wales, the 'three-Wales model' (Balsom, 1985), based on analysis of voting patterns, has been a valuable guide. It remained so for interpreting results of the referendum on political devolution held in 1997, as the authors acknowledge (pp. 75–6). But, as far as varieties of English are concerned, there are more than three zones. There may be much in common between inhabitants of south-east Wales and north-east Wales, and their voting patterns justify the label 'British Wales'. But English speakers in south-east Wales seem to consider their variety of English as somehow 'more Welsh' than the north-eastern varieties, as the fifth chapter of the book explains. Again, on the basis of much social research it is possible to consider 'Y Fro Gymraeg' or the western parts of both north and south as a single zone. But they need to be carefully distinguished when varieties of English are considered. None of this would be so clear without the painstaking comparison of results from different methodologies for studying attitudes to language which form the bulk of the text. The book is written at postgraduate researcher level. The reliance on statistical applications, such as multidimensional scaling, might deter potential readers with anxieties about quantitative research techniques, but formal procedures have been interwoven with interpretations of the incidence of key terms extracted from open-ended interviews gauging reactions to recorded samples of speech.

The research participants were teachers and adolescents accessed at schools representing six well-scattered geographical regions in Wales. The early chapters review previous research on attitudes to varieties of different languages. Contrived linguistic materials were used in procedures followed by many previous researchers. So the authors seem to have felt the need to build a case for their preference for elicited narratives or 'stories that young people your age tell' as materials for obtaining reactions to accent and dialect. Although elicited, the examples of stories recorded for use in the study (pp. 100–5) read like authentic texts. Many readers unfamiliar with the background literature might well fail to appreciate how useful a contribution to methodology is provided by this book. It is also important that more than one recording for each area was used. Without several examples for each area, it would not have been possible to discover how people can be influenced by affective reactions to accent and dialect, rather than linguistic features alone.

Much was revealed about identity construction by getting people to identify dialects which they felt the recordings exemplified. Many people in Wales without linguistic training show considerable awareness of linguistic variables, such as the pronunciation of the long /a/ in 'Cardiff'. They also pick up on conversational tags not used where they live, such as the 'aye' which commonly ends informal utterances in the Bangor (Gwynedd) area. But that does not mean that 'folk' linguistics is as focused on forms of expression as formal linguistics. Because a combination of methodologies was used, the authors demonstrate that factors such as the likeability of a speaker influence judgements in folk linguistics. This is not just because younger people may have limited contact with different dialects. When answering 'Where is the speaker from?' there were high levels of agreement for some of the recordings that the speaker came from the respondents' own area. This was in spite of the presence of features in the speech which were reliable indicators (on the basis of majority judgements) of belonging to a different area. As the authors emphasize, '[the respondents] did not merely recognize or fail to recognize speakers as belonging to specific communities' (p. 200). It was possible to link the likeability of the speaker to 'claiming' or appropriating to the in-group – a social psychological process concerned with group cohesiveness. Thinking someone belongs to where the listener comes from (a 'claiming process', pp. 207–8) is to do with social (though not necessarily personal) attraction and group cohesiveness. The suggestion accords with informal observations of the reviewer during a study of language groups in south-east Wales (Bellin et al., 1999). Social attractiveness of an individual to adolescents in south-east Wales can be indicated by the description of the person as 'safe' to members of an in-group. In the valleys the term 'pukka' can also be heard. Being 'claimed', as Garrett and his colleagues describe the process, shows how members of a community construct their social and sociolinguistic knowledge and 'use it creatively to reflect and refine their group priorities and memberships' (p. 209). The research described in the book is very much a contribution to the study of social group cohesiveness as well as attitudes to language.

It is difficult to evaluate the 'ambiguous findings concerning standard English' (pp. 143–7). The final conclusion (p. 217) is that Welsh adolescents and even 'to some extent' teachers regard received pronunciation, or a 'regionless variety', as indexical of or 'the voice of' success. However, the suggestion that it is very much not 'our voice' might be true of communities in the south of England where the variety of English known as 'estuary English' could be usurping the prestige of Received Pronunciation (Coggle, 1993). Contributions to debates concerning local varieties of English out of Wales would benefit from the combining of research methods, which Peter Garrett and colleagues consider to be the achievement of the book. The 'differentiated set of techniques and perspectives' which they followed contrasts with following 'a discrete, banded and even dogmatic methodology' to study language attitudes. The pay-off is a substantial contribution to studying the sense of place in Wales and social group cohesiveness rather than a limited vision of the relative status and social attractiveness of accents and dialects.

Wynford Bellin
Cardiff School of Social Sciences

REFERENCES

Balsom, D. (1985). 'The three-Wales model', in J. Osmond (ed.), *The National Question Again: Welsh Political Identity in the 1980s*, Llandysul: Gomer.
Bellin, W., Farrell, S., Higgs, G. and White, S. (1999). 'The social context of bilingual Welsh medium education in south east Wales', *Journal of Sociolinguistics*, 3, 2, 173–93.
Coggle, P. (1993). *Do You Speak Estuary?*, London: Bloomsbury.
Crystal, D. (1997). *English as a Global Language*, Cambridge: Cambridge University Press.
De Swaan, A. (2001). *Words of the World: The Global Language System*, London: Polity.

CONTEMPORARY WALES
GUIDELINES FOR CONTRIBUTORS
OF ARTICLES

General policy:
Contemporary Wales is an annual review of economic and social developments and trends in Wales. It provides an authoritative analysis drawing upon the most up-to-date research, and represents the only comprehensive source of analysis across the range of economic and social research about Wales. It is a Board of Celtic Studies journal published once a year, and contains articles selected for their quality and significance to contemporary society in Wales. Submissions are refereed and are accepted for publication on the assumption that they have not been previously published and are not currently being submitted to any other journal. The normal maximum length for articles is about 5,000 words. An abstract of up to 200 words is required.

Preparation of typescripts:
If possible, please e-mail papers as Word attachments to one of the editors:
Paul Chaney (*chaneyp@cardiff.ac.uk*)
Elin Royles (*ear@aber.ac.uk*)
Andrew Thompson (*athompso@glam.ac.uk*)

If e-mail is not possible, please post 3 copies on single-sided A4 to:

either Paul Chaney
Cardiff School of Social Sciences
The Glamorgan Building
King Edward VII Avenue
Cardiff
CF10 3WT

or Elin Royles
Department of International Politics
University of Wales
Aberystwyth
Ceredigion
SY23 3DA

or Andrew Thompson
School of Humanities and Social Sciences
University of Glamorgan
Pontypridd
CF37 1DL

The editors can provide further guidance as to the form and style in which contributions should be submitted, but the following gives a brief guide for potential contributors. Additional general information is available on the UWP website, *www.wales.ac.uk/press* under the heading 'Guidelines for presentation of texts for publication'.

Articles submitted should be typed using double spacing with wide margins, unjustified on the right. Pages should be numbered throughout consecutively.

Preparation of typescripts on disk:
Once a paper has been accepted for publication, it should be sent to the editor in disk form, provided that a hard copy/printout of the full up-to-date text has also been submitted. Authors should retain a back-up copy of both disk and printout of their papers. PC disks using Word are preferred, but other softwares may be acceptable.

Notes and references

Notes and references should be supplied at the end of the article, also in double spacing. Notes should be numbered consecutively. References should be in alphabetical order of author (see below for style).

Tables, maps and diagrams

These will eventually appear within the printed page but should be provided on separate pages in the typescript and their position indicated by a marginal note in the text. Tables and figures should be provided in separate Excel/Tiff files, not embedded in Word. Some other kinds of software may be acceptable – please contact UWP for further information. All figures, diagrams, maps, charts, etc. must be saved in **black only**, not full colour, and should be saved at 1200 pixels per inch.

Diagrams and maps may be submitted in best possible condition on paper if the contributor is unable to supply a disk version. References in the text to illustrative material should take the form 'Table 1' etc. for tables and 'Figure 1' etc. for other illustrations including maps, not 'in the following diagram' since there is no guarantee that pagination will allow this precise positioning. The tables and figures will eventually be labelled 'Table 1.1', 'Figure 2.1', etc. according to the number of the chapter in which they appear.

Style of text:

Quotations within running text should be in single quote marks (double for quotes within quotes). Quotations of more than forty-five words should be indented without quotation marks and with a line space before and after.

Underline or type in italic any words which are to appear in italic. In English-language articles, single words or short phrases in any language other than English should be in italic, but longer quotations in another language should be in roman within single quotation marks.

Dates should be expressed as 1 January 1999; the 1990s; the twentieth century (but 'a twentieth-century record'); 1988–9; 1914–18 (not 1914–8). Numbers up to ninety-nine should be spelt out in full except in a list of statistics or in percentages (e.g. 25 per cent).

Use -ize endings when given as an alternative to -ise, for example, realize, privatize, organize; but note analyse, franchise, advertise.

Capitalization should be kept to a minimum in the text; for titles, initial capitals should be used only when attached to a personal name (thus 'President Clinton', but 'the president of the United States').

Journal style is that 'south' in 'south Wales' should take lower case (also 'north', 'east', 'west' Wales/England, etc.), since this is not a specific political, administrative or geographical region. South America or South Africa would take upper case since the term refers to the name of a continent or political entity respectively. When referring to a specific area for economic assessment, e.g. the South West of England, upper case may be used for clarity.

References
References in the text should be given in the Harvard system in the following format: (Dower, 1977), (Welsh Office, 1986), (White and Higgs, 1997), (Gripaios et al., 1995a).

The form of references listed under the heading 'References' at the end of the text should be as follows:

Ambrose, P. (1974). *The Quiet Revolution*, London: Chatto & Windus.
Buller, H. and Hoggart, K. (1994b). 'The social integration of British home owners into French rural communities', *Journal of Rural Studies*, 10, 2, 197–210.
Dower, M. (1977). 'Planning aspects of second homes', in J. T. Coppock (ed.), *Second Homes: Curse or Blessing?*, Oxford: Pergamon Press, pp. 17–45.

Note the use of lower case for all initial letters except the first in an article or unpublished thesis title, and capitals for initial letters of all significant words in book and journal titles.

Publications by the same author in the same year should be differentiated by means of a, b, or c, etc. after the year of publication, both in the text reference and in the list of references.

Proofs and complimentary copies:
Checking of proofs will be done by editors, with contributors expected to reply promptly to queries. Upon publication, contributors will receive one complimentary copy of the issue of the journal in which their article appears.